D1203362

# The Treasure of Auchinleck

JAMES BOSWELL (1740–1795)
From the portrait by Reynolds.

# THE
# TREASURE
# OF
# AUCHINLECK

*The Story of the Boswell Papers*

BY

David Buchanan

*HEINEMANN: LONDON*

William Heinemann Ltd
15 Queen Street, Mayfair, London W1X 8BE

LONDON  MELBOURNE  TORONTO
JOHANNESBURG  AUCKLAND

First published in Great Britain 1975

ISBN 434 09410 2

*For Mary Hyde*

*and in memory of Donald F. Hyde*

# Contents

# List of Illustrations
# with Acknowledgments and Credits

*In addition to the specific acknowledgments below, special thanks are due to the following for their help and kindness in tracing and supplying pictures: the Librarian of Carlisle Public Libraries; the Secretary of Durham University; Mr. George Burnet; Sir Arthur Boswell Eliott of Stobs; Mr. W. H. Haslam; Mrs. Donald F. Hyde; Mr. J. T. Isham; Mr. H. W. Liebert; the late seventh Lord Talbot de Malahide; Joyce, Lady Talbot de Malahide; Mr. Ronald Mansbridge; Mrs. Kirstie Milford; Lord Milligan; Professor F. A. Pottle; Mrs. Peter Somervell; Lady Stevenson; and the Boswell Office at Yale University.*

# Preface

INCLUDED IN MY OFFICE MAIL one morning in October 1961 was an air-mail letter from America. I looked at the envelope curiously because it was addressed to my father, who had been dead for more than four years. The sender was Donald F. Hyde, whose name was familiar to me as the American lawyer and close friend of the late Colonel R. H. Isham.

I knew that my father had acted for many years as Isham's lawyer in Scotland in support of his fight to reassemble the scattered papers of James Boswell. In the postwar years, my father and Hyde had collaborated in looking after Isham's interests on both sides of the Atlantic. Hyde now wrote that he and his wife planned to visit Edinburgh shortly, and they wanted to see my father to discuss a proposed history of the Boswell papers. They thought that his legal records, dating back to 1936, should provide much useful information.

At that time, I knew little or nothing of the Boswell papers or Isham's epic battle in trying to salvage them. My father, although deeply involved, never discussed his professional responsibilities with his family. I replied to Hyde's letter, explaining that my father was dead and that I was now a partner in the same law firm. I promised to search our archives and to produce what material I could find for his inspection when he came to Edinburgh.

I did not realize then what I had undertaken. I soon discovered that all our prewar records had been cleared out and dumped in a subterranean storage room deep below a large Edinburgh department store. Nobody had been there for years. Even the store manager seemed to have forgotten that he had a room full of our papers. With an assistant to show me the way, I descended successive flights of stairs until, far from the light of day, I came to the storeroom. It was crammed with files and loose papers in considerable confusion, all covered with a thick layer of sticky black dust. We set to work going through everything systematically. Four hours later we emerged, begrimed but triumphant, with enough material on the Boswell papers to fill a large trunk. Shoppers stared at us as we staggered across the main sales floor, laden with files. Several journeys were needed to bring everything up to street level.

By the time that Mr. and Mrs. Hyde arrived, the material was stacked ready for their inspection in our conference room. They spent two days examining the piles and acknowledged defeat. Clearly many months of work were needed to make anything of such a prodigious mass of material. Hyde asked me to undertake the task, and I accepted, for I had already become ensnared by the fascination of the Boswell story.

My original brief was not to write a book, but merely to undertake research. As time went by, however, the scope of this research expanded so greatly that a detailed history of the Boswell papers became the logical end-product. My quest for materials and information has taken me to Ireland, all over Scotland and England, and four times to America. More than a decade has been needed to finish my task, but during these years the demands of a busy legal practice have severely limited the amount of time that could be devoted to authorship.

The completion of this book is due above all to the unfailing support and encouragement I have received from Donald and Mary Hyde. It was Donald who ignited the spark of my interest and helped me with my initial research in every possible way. His sudden death in 1966 was a numbing shock. I doubt if I should have had the heart to carry on but for Mary Hyde's continuing support and her quiet determination that I must persevere. She has done so much for me that I find it difficult to express my gratitude adequately.

I must also make special mention of my great debt to Professor F. A. Pottle. In 1951, he published a 42-page history of the Boswell papers as an introduction to the deluxe printing of Boswell's *London Journal* (1762–63). He subsequently revised and expanded this history with a view to its inclusion in the forthcoming catalogue of the Boswell papers at Yale. Hyde, as a member of the Advisory Committee, read the new version and requested that its publication be delayed because he felt that the first extended history of the Boswell papers should contain a much fuller account of Isham's role. That was the situation in 1961 when I was asked to begin the research which has resulted in this book. The Yale Editorial Committee, after reading my typescript, decided that it was inappropriate in scale and content for inclusion with their catalogue, but they supported its publication as an independent work.

Pottle's new version of the history has yet to appear, but he has nevertheless made his text available to me and has permitted me to use his own unpublished material with complete freedom. Without this advantage, I should hardly have known how to acquire the necessary framework of knowledge for my own work. More than this, both he and Mrs. Pottle, whose knowledge of the Boswell papers is second to none, have dealt with numerous scholarly enquiries and have provided me with very detailed notes and corrections on my entire text. They have saved me from committing many blunders, and I am deeply grateful to them both for their unselfish generosity.

I have received help and kindness from many others, and I should like to express my particular thanks to the following: to Heyward and Jonathan Isham for hospitality to me in America, for allowing me to inspect and use their father's papers, and for helpful information about their father; to Lady Talbot de Malahide for hospitality in Ireland and for allowing me to inspect and use her files relating to the Boswell papers; to Mrs. Peter Somervell for hospitality at Fettercairn and for allowing me free access to her papers and library; to Delight Ansley for her expertise in preparing the index at the end of this book; and to Robert F. Metzdorf and Gabriel Austin for reading and revising my drafts, for valuable help with my research, and for many other kindnesses.

Besides those whose names I have already mentioned, I am also indebted to the following who have contributed in various ways towards this book: the late C. Colleer Abbott, James H. Van Alen, G. Campbell Becket, Alan Bell, the Boswell Office at Yale, Frank Brady, Freda M. Buchanan, G. M. Byres, James L. Clifford, D. M. Davin, Sir Arthur Boswell Eliott, Mrs. Persifor Frazer, W. H. Haslam, Frederick W. Hilles, Gordon P. Hoyle, Susan B. W. Laing, Herman W. Liebert, Lord Milligan, the late Sir John Murray, G. Campbell Paton, William L. Payne, L. F. Powell, the late Sir Sydney C. Roberts, Robert Shackleton, and the late seventh Lord Talbot de Malahide.

Finally, I am grateful for permissions to quote from various materials published and unpublished granted by: The Clarendon Press, C. C. Abbott's literary trustees, Yale University Library, the Bodleian Library, the Hyde Collection, the Signet Library, the Australian National University Press, and the Georgia Historical Society.

# Short Titles and Abbreviations

Books of Council and Session: the principal register of deeds in Scotland. Except in the case of a few early deeds, the original document is retained at Register House in Edinburgh for preservation. The register is open to public inspection, and official extracts (nowadays photocopies) of any registered deed can be obtained. Boswell's original holograph will is preserved at Register House.

*Boswelliana: Boswelliana. The Commonplace Book of James Boswell,* ed. Rev. Charles Rogers, 1874.

*Correspondence, etc., re Life: The Correspondence and Other Papers of James Boswell Relating to the Making of The Life of Johnson,* ed. Marshall Waingrow, 1969.

Davin letter: a long letter from D. M. Davin to the author dated 8 November 1962 expanding and explaining the information contained in "Davin Memo" (q.v.).

Davin Memo: "Fettercairn Papers," a memorandum of events covering the period 1930–1936, prepared in 1962 by D. M. Davin, then Assistant Secretary of the Clarendon Press, and taken from the files of the Press. The memorandum relates to the dealings of the Press with Lord Clinton and Professor Abbott over the Boswell papers found at Fettercairn House.

*Fettercairn Catalogue: A Catalogue of Papers Relating to Boswell, Johnson & Sir William Forbes Found at Fettercairn House, a Residence of The Rt. Hon. Lord Clinton 1930–31,* by Claude Colleer Abbott, Oxford, at the Clarendon Press, 1936.

Fettercairn Papers: a large collection of papers from Fettercairn House, Kincardineshire, the property of Mrs. Peter Somervell, now on deposit with the National Library of Scotland. This collection comprises those papers in the *Fettercairn Catalogue* (q.v.) which formed part of Sir William Forbes's rather than JB's archives; also other items not in the catalogue of Boswellian or Johnsonian interest, and a mass of Forbes family papers, including

Sir William Forbes's materials for his Life of Beattie. For further details of this deposit, see below p. 125 n. 28.

*Footsteps: Footsteps of Dr. Johnson (Scotland),* by George Birkbeck Hill, 1890.

Hyde Collection: the collection of books and manuscripts, etc., at Four Oaks Farm, Somerville, New Jersey, the property of Mrs. Donald F. Hyde.

Hyde's legal papers: papers and correspondence formerly held by the late Donald F. Hyde, as attorney of Lt.-Col. R. H. Isham.

IFP: Isham family papers, being correspondence and other personal papers of Lt.-Col. R. H. Isham, now in the custody of his son Jonathan Isham at New Canaan, Connecticut.

ILP: Isham legal papers, mostly related to the lawsuit over ownership of the papers found at Fettercairn House. These papers, or copies of them, are located in the archives of Isham's Scottish solicitors (Steedman Ramage & Co., W.S., Edinburgh) or in IFP (q.v.) or, most frequently, in both.

JB: James Boswell, the Biographer.

*JB Letters: Letters of James Boswell,* ed. C. B. Tinker, 2 vols., 1924.

*Life: Boswell's Life of Johnson, Together with Boswell's Journal of a Tour to the Hebrides and Johnson's Diary of a Journey into North Wales,* ed. G. B. Hill, rev. L. F. Powell, 6 vols., 1934–50; vols. V and VI, 2nd ed., 1964.

*Literary Career: The Literary Career of James Boswell, Esq.,* by F. A. Pottle, 1929; reprinted 1966.

*Malahide Catalogue: The Private Papers of James Boswell from Malahide Castle in the Collection of Lt.-Colonel Ralph Heyward Isham,* a catalogue by Frederick A. Pottle and Marion S. Pottle, 1931.

*Malahide Index: Index to The Private Papers of James Boswell from Malahide Castle in the Collection of Lt.-Colonel Ralph Heyward Isham,* compiled by Frederick A. Pottle with the assistance of Joseph Foladare, John P. Kirby, and others, 1937.

Private edition: *The Private Papers of James Boswell from Malahide Castle in the Collection of Lt.-Colonel Ralph Heyward Isham,* ed. Geoffrey Scott and F. A. Pottle, 18 vols., 1928–34.

Register of Sasines: the register of deeds in Scotland affecting land. Unlike the Books of Council and Session (q.v.) the original deeds are not retained at Register House in Edinburgh, only copies. The register is public.

SJ: Dr. Samuel Johnson.

*SJ Letters: The Letters of Samuel Johnson, with Mrs. Thrale's Genuine Letters to Him,* ed. R. W. Chapman, 3 vols., 1952.

Spingarn Letter: a long letter dated 24 April 1942 from Joyce, Lady Talbot de Malahide, to A. B. Spingarn, a New York attorney whom she instructed to look after her interests in connection with the Boswell papers. A copy of this letter is in TFP (q.v.).

S.R. & Co.'s Business Ledger: a series of ledger volumes in the archives of Steedman Ramage & Co., W.S., Edinburgh, containing *inter alia* a detailed summary of all correspondence, meetings, telephone calls, and other actings by them on behalf of Lt.-Col. R. H. Isham.

S.R. & Co.'s papers: correspondence and other papers in the archives of Steedman Ramage & Co., W.S., Edinburgh.

TFP: Talbot family papers, being correspondence and other papers in the possession of Joyce, Lady Talbot de Malahide.

TLP: Talbot legal papers, being legal correspondence and other papers in the possession of Joyce, Lady Talbot de Malahide, or her solicitors, David Shaw & Co., Ayr.

*Tour: Boswell's Journal of a Tour to the Hebrides with Samuel Johnson.* Unless otherwise stated, references are to the text printed in the Hill/Powell edition of the *Life.* (See above under *Life.*)

# The Treasure of Auchinleck

JAMES BOSWELL, "THE JOURNALIST"
From *Picturesque Beauties of Boswell,* a set of twenty engravings by Thomas
Rowlandson after original sketches by Samuel Collings.

# I

# The Legend of Destruction

IN September 1762, a month before his twenty-second birthday, James Boswell set out on a jaunt through Ayrshire, Galloway, and the border counties of England and Scotland. He made it the occasion to begin a journal which he headed "Journal of my Jaunt, Harvest 1762."[1] This was the first of a series of journals which, by the time of his death some thirty-three years later, filled more than 8,000 manuscript pages.[2] These journals are one of the great achievements of English Literature. Their extraordinary length demonstrates Boswell's passion for recording. "I should live no more than I can record," he wrote, "as one should not have more corn growing than one can get in. There is a waste of good if it be not preserved."[3] The journals, some of them fully written and some only in note form, furnished essential material for three best-selling books: the *Account of Corsica* (1768), the *Tour to the Hebrides* (1785), and the *Life of Johnson* (1791). But they are much more than a mere reservoir of information for other works. They contain one of the most detailed and revealing self-portraits ever written; and at the same time they animate a cast of characters of outstanding interest and diversity against a background of the eighteenth-century scene in London, Scotland, the Continent of Europe, and elsewhere. Boswell's special genius was for dramatic

[1]The journal runs from 14 September to 14 November 1762. The manuscript extends to 195 pages and is published in private edition, I, pp. 55–138.

[2]The 8,000 pages include journal notes, memoranda, etc., as well as fully written journals. JB had made earlier attempts at journalizing, as, for example, when he accompanied his father on the Northern Circuit in 1758 and 1761, but the great series of journals begins with the Harvest Jaunt in 1762.

[3]Private edition, XI, p. 150.

reporting and it was in his journals that this genius found its truest expression.

In bulk, the journals were only a relatively small part of a much larger mass of private papers which Boswell accumulated during his lifetime. His correspondence was immense. He preserved most of the letters he received and kept copies of many of those he sent. On his own admission, he had "no uncommon desire for the company of men distinguished for talents and literature,"[4] and he deliberately sought letters from celebrated contemporaries to add to his "archives at Auchinleck."[5] His attitude was that such letters "would be a treasure for the next generation."[6] He had a true collector's concern for condition. To John Wilkes he wrote: "I have two favours to beg of you; one that your letters may be signed John Wilkes; another, that they may be sealed in such a manner that I may not tear a word in opening them."[7] His friendship with Johnson and his membership of "The Club"[8] enabled him to include among his correspondents some of the most remarkable men of his age: Johnson himself, Burke, Garrick, Goldsmith, Malone, Reynolds, and many others. Where no acquaintance existed, he had no inhibitions about establishing one. Horace Walpole once complained: "Boswell, is a strange being, and, . . . has a rage for knowing anybody that ever was talked of. He forced himself upon me in spite of my teeth and my doors."[9] He certainly did not hesitate to make himself known to Rousseau and Voltaire during his

---

[4]"Memoirs of James Boswell, Esq." printed in *European Magazine*, vol. XIX (1791). Reprinted in *Literary Career*, pp. xxix–xliv.

[5]In his advertisement for the second edition of the *Life* (1793), JB writes: "I have been regaled with spontaneous praise of my work by many and various persons eminent for their rank, learning, talents and accomplishments; much of which praise I have under their hands to be reposited in my archives at Auchinleck." For examples of JB's specific requests for letters, see his letters to Lord Chatham (8 April 1767), Goldsmith (29 March 1773), and Wilkes (26 May 1775, 14 February 1783, 26 March 1783, and 25 June 1791). He also mentions in his letter to Mrs. David Garrick (16 April 1781) that he has a good many "gay and freindly letters" of her late husband "which he fondly preserves as brilliant gems in his literary cabinet." All letters mentioned are printed in *JB Letters*.

[6]From JB's letter to Sir David Dalrymple, 2 August 1763, referring to the possibility of his obtaining and preserving letters from Wilkes (*JB Letters*, p. 41).

[7]Letter, JB to Wilkes [August 1765] (*JB Letters*, p. 84).

[8]The literary club founded in 1764 by Sir Joshua Reynolds, Dr. Johnson, and others, to which JB was elected in 1773. It boasted a remarkable membership of distinguished men, as to which see *Life*, I, pp. 477–81, and V, p. 109, n. 5.

[9]Letter, Horace Walpole to Gray, 18 February 1768. See *The Correspondence of Horace Walpole*, ed. W. S. Lewis, G. L. Lam, and C. H. Bennett, 1948, vol. 14, p. 170.

Continental tour in 1764.[10] No sooner was the young man of twenty-four on speaking terms with two of Europe's most famous authors, than he set about soliciting letters from them. His parting request to Voltaire was: "May I write in English, and you'll answer?";[11] and to Rousseau, he wrote a few days after his visit: "Voulez-vous donc m'écrire aussi souvent que vos occupations, vos souffrances, et vos chagrins vous permettront?"[12]

Boswell also corresponded intimately and at length with certain close friends, notably with the Reverend W. J. Temple whom he had first met in the class of Greek at Edinburgh University.[13] He continued this correspondence throughout most of his life in a series of letters which are remarkable for what have been described as "the most outspoken and unblushing confessions ever made in English Literature."[14] Temple wrote shortly after Boswell's death: "Our letters were frequent & written with unreserved confidence. Hardly a thought arose in our minds that we did not communicate."[15] This correspondence stands in importance next only to the journals as a source of biographical information.

For Boswell, acquaintance usually involved correspondence and he had, as his friend Malone remarked, "as numerous & respectable a Circle of acquaintance, as almost any private Gentleman . . . could boast of."[16] It is not surprising that by the time of his death his collected correspondence ran to several thousand individual items.[17]

The remainder of Boswell's archives consisted chiefly of literary

[10]See *Boswell on the Grand Tour: Germany and Switzerland 1764* (in the Yale Edition of the Private Papers of James Boswell), p. 191 *et seq.* (Heinemann Edition).

[11]Ibid., p. 296.

[12]Letter, JB to Rousseau (in French), 31 December 1764 (*JB Letters*, p. 66).

[13]In 1756–1757. JB's letters to Temple were first published in 1857 (issued December 1856), by Richard Bentley, London. They were republished in 1908 in an edition by Thomas Seccombe and were also printed in *JB Letters*. Other intimate correspondents of JB's were Sir David Dalrymple (Lord Hailes) and John Johnston of Grange. (See *The Correspondence of James Boswell and John Johnston of Grange*, the first Research Volume in the Yale Edition of the Private Papers of James Boswell.)

[14]Lewis Bettany so described them. See *Diaries of William Johnston Temple* (ed. Bettany), Oxford, at the Clarendon Press, 1929, p. lxvii. The letters run from 1758 to 1795, a few days before JB's death.

[15]Letter, Temple to Sir William Forbes, 27 April 1796 (Fettercairn Papers).

[16]Letter, Sir William Forbes to Edmond Malone, 30 June 1796 (Hyde Collection).

[17]See *JB Letters, Malahide Catalogue,* and *Fettercairn Catalogue.* Many additional letters not printed or catalogued in these works will be included in the forthcoming catalogue of Boswell papers at Yale. See also volumes 1 and 2 of the Yale Research Edition of Boswell's Correspondence.

manuscripts and related materials accumulated during a lifetime of prolific authorship.[18] The largest and most important group was his material for writing the *Life of Johnson,* including the original manuscript of that work. His prime source was, of course, his own journals and the letters from Johnson to himself; but, over a period of more than twenty-five years, he gathered together a mass of additional material including many letters from Johnson to various correspondents, and notes, memoranda, anecdotes, and the like.[19] Besides these materials, he preserved numerous papers relating to his other works, published and unpublished, and to various projects which he planned but never completed.[20] He also interested himself in the literary activities of his friends and, whenever he could, procured from them manuscripts of interest to add to his "store of treasure" at Auchinleck.[21]

Such then was the huge miscellany of papers contained in Boswell's archives at his death. Essentially, it was made up of his journals, correspondence, and literary materials. There was also a residue which did not fall within any of these categories—for example, papers relating to family affairs, the conduct of his legal practice, and the management of Auchinleck estate. Considered as a whole, the archives represent one of the most fascinating and varied collections of eighteenth-century papers ever formed. They are certainly one of the largest. For editors, scholars, biographers, and historians, they offer almost limitless scope for productive research. But their most exciting promise has lain in their potential for direct publication, especially as, with the passage of years, it has become possible to contemplate publication of what Boswell himself would have considered unpublishable.

Boswell's contemporaries can have had little doubt as to the general content of his archives. The celebrated caricaturist, Thomas Rowlandson, depicted him clutching his journal and carrying a large bundle of papers marked "Materials for the Life of Saml. Johnson L.L.D."[22]

[18]As to JB's publications, see *Literary Career.*

[19]Full details of this material and the manner of its acquisition are contained in Marshall Waingrow's *The Correspondence and Other Papers of James Boswell Relating to the Making of the Life of Johnson,* 1969, the second volume in the Yale Research Edition of Boswell's Correspondence, elsewhere cited in this book as *"Correspondence, etc., re Life".*

[20]A life of Lord Kames, for example.

[21]These included original manuscripts of SJ and Reynolds.

[22]Thomas Rowlandson (1756–1827). In 1786, he published his "Picturesque Beauties of Boswell after original Sketches by Samuel Collings." This set of 20 prints was mostly based on incidents from the *Tour* which had appeared the year before. Number 2 of the set ("The Journalist") is the one described and reproduced in the illustration facing p. 1.

His habit of journalizing was well known to friends and public alike. In the *Tour*, he told his readers that his text was, with minor adaptations, "the *very Journal which Dr. Johnson read.*"[23] In his advertisements for the *Life*, he mentioned his "large Store of Materials," collected over a period of more than twenty years and including a great number of letters from Johnson and several original pieces by Johnson.[24] When the *Life* was published in 1791, his readers found further references to the journals.[25] They must have realized that much of the book was taken from journal material and that Boswell had by no means exaggerated the importance of his Johnsonian collection.

One would have expected the family home of Auchinleck to become increasingly the focus of attention by scholars and collectors in the years following Boswell's death. It was clear that the archives should contain the journals, the materials for the *Life*, and presumably also other literary materials and correspondence. There was every incentive to enquire, but in more than a century only one outsider is known to have approached Auchinleck in specific quest of the archives, and that approach was abortive.[26] The main deterrent, no doubt, was a widely held belief that Boswell's papers had perished.

BOSWELL DIED in his house at 47 Great Portland Street, London, on 19 May 1795, survived by five children: Veronica, Euphemia, Alexander, James, and Elizabeth.[27]

The transmission of his papers was governed by his will, made ten years previously.[28] To Alexander, his elder son and heir to the entailed estate of Auchinleck, he bequeathed "greek and latin Books, as also all Manuscripts of whatever kind lying in the House of Auchinleck." To his friends Sir William Forbes, the Reverend William Temple, and Edmond Malone, he left: "all my Manuscripts of my own composition and all my letters from various persons to be published for the

[23]*Life*, V, p. 78, n. 5.
[24]See *Literary Career*, p. 163.
[25]See, for example, *Life*, II, pp. 3–4, and III, pp. 209 and 415.
[26]The outsider was J. W. Croker (see below pp. 22–25 and 207–09). We have definite knowledge of two other approaches by outsiders to Auchinleck before 1900, but each was for a limited purpose which did not extend to enquiries about the main bulk of JB's archives (see below pp. 13 and 31).
[27]Veronica (born 15 March 1773), Euphemia (born 20 May 1774), Alexander (born 9 October 1775), James (born 15 September 1778), and Elizabeth (born 15 June 1780).
[28]On 28 May 1785.

benefit of my younger children as they shall decide that is to say they are to have a discretionary power to publish more or less. . . ." By "younger children" Boswell seems to have meant all his children except Alexander, although Veronica and Euphemia were both in fact older than Alexander.

A few months later, he added a codicil entrusting to Malone the care of his "Collection of papers and letters and memorandums for writing the Life of Dr. Johnson" and expressing the wish that Malone would not divulge anything from his journals "which ought to be concealed."[29] He certainly never contemplated publication of his journals without expurgation. On 30 July 1779, he had written: "Were my Journal to be discovered and made publick in my own lifetime, how shocking would it be to me! And after my death, would it not hurt my children?"[30] His policy of complete frankness about himself and others gave him good reason to ask Malone to be discreet.

Both the will and the codicil were registered after Boswell's death,[31] and were freely available for public examination at the Register House in Edinburgh. They showed that he was particularly concerned about the care of his archives and the proper exploitation of their publication value. There was no reason to suppose that Forbes, Temple, and Malone would not carry out their trust. Malone, in fact, let it be known to his friends that he took charge of the papers in the London house immediately after Boswell's death. Farington records in his diary for 19 May 1795: "Poor Boswell died this day. . . . Boswells papers are put into Mr. Malones possession.—No preparations for a regular work appear.—quantities of parts of newspapers are tied up together probably intended for some purpose He had schemed."[32]

Malone had collaborated with Boswell on the first two editions of the *Life* and was wholly responsible for the third, fourth, fifth, and sixth editions. Until his death in 1812, he dominated Boswellian scholarship. As one of the literary executors and a friend of the family, he would be presumed to have had access to any papers of interest to him. He would also be expected to have known if any of the papers

[29]Codicil dated 22 December 1785.

[30]Private edition, XIII, p. 275.

[31]The will and codicil were registered in the Books of Council and Session (Durie) at Edinburgh on 7 August 1795. Boswell left other testamentary writings which did not affect the transmission of his papers. The original will, entirely in Boswell's hand, is still preserved at the Register House in Edinburgh.

[32]*The Farington Diary*, by Joseph Farington, R. A. (ed. James Greig), New York, 1923, 3rd ed., vol. I, p. 95.

had been destroyed. There was no reason to doubt him, therefore, when he wrote in a footnote in the fifth edition of the *Life* that he had been unable to verify the text of a letter from Johnson, "the original letter being burned in a mass of papers in Scotland."[33] This footnote was the *only* direct evidence of the burning of any papers. Coming from Malone, it seemed reliable, especially as it reappeared in the sixth edition.[34] It is doubtful, however, whether it received much attention. Later editors do not refer to it when speaking of the destruction of the papers and, even if it is accepted at its face value, it does not say what papers were burned or whether any survived.[35]

Of Boswell's five children, the only ones to marry were Alexander and Elizabeth. His eldest daughter, Veronica, survived him by just a few months.[36] Euphemia, his second daughter, was eccentric and improvident. She embarrassed her family by accusing them of neglect and by publicly advertising for charity and sending begging letters to distinguished persons.[37] Alexander, exasperated by her behaviour, wrote to Sir William Forbes: ". . . Her conduct . . . has been extravagant in the extreme, in absurd dress in particular, & I am convinced also that were her income five times what you propose it could not suffice. . . . Every sixpence more than is barely sufficient is giving her the facilities of indulging in unsuitable folly."[38] She lived for a time in London and had notions of supporting herself by writing operas, one of which she claimed had been considered for production at Drury Lane. She died in 1837 at the age of 63.[39]

Elizabeth, the youngest member of the family, married her second cousin, William Boswell,[40] who practised as an advocate at the Scottish Bar and became Sheriff of Lanarkshire. She died in 1814,[41] survived

[33]Fifth edition (1807), III, p. 391, n. 4.

[34]Sixth edition (1811), III, p. 393, n. 4.

[35]Croker, whose edition of the *Life* appeared in 1831, certainly read the footnote, for he accepted Malone's conjectural emendation of "affecting" for "asserting," but he disregarded the important statement that the letter was "burned in a mass of papers in Scotland" (IV, p. 227). Croker began work on his edition with a belief that the journals had survived. (See below p. 22.)

[36]She died on 26 September 1795 (*Gentleman's Magazine*, 1795, II, p. 880).

[37]See *Boswelliana*, pp. 195–96.

[38]Letter, Alexander Boswell to Sir William Forbes, undated (Fettercairn Papers).

[39]On 7 September 1837 (*Gentleman's Magazine*, 1837, II, p. 434). In *Boswelliana*, Rogers tells us that in her will, Euphemia expressed the wish (not complied with) to be buried in Westminster Abbey near Dr. Johnson. It would be interesting to know where Rogers saw the will. Recent attempts to trace it were unsuccessful. (See below p. 170.)

[40]Son of Robert Boswell, W. S., JB's cousin. "W. S." signifies that Robert Boswell was a Writer to the Signet. The Society of Writers to H. M. Signet was, and still is, an ancient and respected Scottish legal society. See *The Society of Writers to His Majesty's Signet, etc.*, Edinburgh, 1936.

[41]*Scots Magazine*, lxxvi (1814), p. 159.

by her husband and four children.[42] The match was strongly opposed
by Alexander, who avoided all communication with his sister or her
family after the marriage except on essential business matters.[43] This
attitude seems to have persisted even after Elizabeth's death; for, as
late as 1825, we find Alexander's widow writing: "The marriage was
so much against the inclinations of her family we had very little communication with them [i.e. Elizabeth's children] & I feel a reluctance
in applying to them if it can be avoided."[44]

Boswell had a special affection for his younger son, James. "My
second son is an extraordinary boy," he wrote to Temple. "He is much
of his father. (Vanity of vanities!)."[45] Others noted young James's re-
semblance to his father. Malone remarked: "He grows every day very
like his father, but will not have his vivacity or wit; on the other hand,
he will be more studious and more steady."[46] And Croker described
him as "very convivial; and in other respects like his father, though
altogether on a smaller scale."[47] By all accounts, he was a most likeable
person who inherited not only his father's love of good company,
but also his literary bent. He was educated at Westminster School
and Brasenose College, Oxford, later becoming a Fellow of this College.
He settled in London and became a close friend and protégé of Malone
who was "extremely kind & like a father"[48] to him. Later, Malone
paid him the compliment of appointing him his literary executor. He
collaborated with Malone on the latter's great edition of Shakespeare,
which he completed after Malone's death. He was also sufficiently
interested in his father's work to help Malone in his editing of the
*Life*. Several of his notes appear in the third edition and he added
some new notes to the sixth edition, as well as reading over and correcting the entire text.[49] He died suddenly on 24 February 1822 at the
age of forty-three, never having married. He seems to have inspired
affection in all who knew him. Sir Walter Scott is said to have been

[42]See below for genealogy, p. 354.

[43]This is clear from a mass of family correspondence in the Fettercairn Papers.

[44]Draft letter, Lady Boswell to Mr. William Murray, 8 July 1825, about family affairs (at Yale).

[45]Letter, JB to Temple, 28 November 1789 (*JB Letters*, pp. 384–85).

[46]Letter, Malone to Sir William Forbes, 25 April 1796 (Fettercairn Papers).

[47]Croker's edition of the *Life* (1831), IV, p. 233, n. 4.

[48]So wrote Alexander in a letter to Sir William Forbes, 25 June 1796 (Fettercairn Papers).

[49]See Malone's Advertisement to the sixth edition of the *Life* in which he pays tribute to the
work of James Boswell junior. L. F. Powell suggests that the "O" in the "J. B.—O." with which
James signed his notes to the third edition must indicate Oxford as James was a student of
Brasenose College at the time.

AUCHINLECK HOUSE

BOSWELL'S EBONY CABINET
Now at Malahide Castle.

"warmly attached" to him,[50] and Alexander described him as "a Brother who has never injured me & who has ever been my steady friend & to think on whom has ever thrown a gleam of sunshine on my mind."[51]

Alexander, as Boswell's elder son, was heir to the entailed estate of Auchinleck. Some of his letters survive which show that he was deeply attached to his father and proud of his literary achievements. On 19 April 1799, he wrote to Sir William Forbes: "A few days ago, I read the Life of Doctor Johnson which I know not if I ever read with care before. . . . I cannot but wonder at my Fathers talent for recording which he had in an eminent degree."[52] Another letter, dated 21 March 1809, recovered recently, proves his concern for his father's Johnsonian materials.[53] Even as a schoolboy at Eton, he composed Latin verses in his father's honour to commemorate the publication of the *Life*.[54] Boswell wrote to his son to say that the verses were to him "truly wonderful." He suggested they should be revised and improved so that they might be deposited in his ebony cabinet.[55]

This ebony cabinet has acquired an extraordinary mystique for Boswellians. It is widely believed that Boswell kept his papers in it and that they remained there after his death. Popular accounts of the history of the Boswell papers have made a feature of this;[56] and even a scholar such as Geoffrey Scott referred to "the cabinet in which he [i.e. Boswell] preserved his most valued papers, diaries, correspondence, and literary materials."[57] Boswell does mention putting certain papers in the cabinet—the Latin verses from Alexander, for example, and letters from Wilkes and Garrick.[58] But although he may have kept a few precious items in the cabinet, it was not the general repository of his archives. At his death, its most important contents were a collection of coins and medals. In a legal document of 1803,

[50]J. G. Lockhart: *Memoirs of the Life of Sir Walter Scott, Bart.* (1837–38), V, p. 179.

[51]Letter, Alexander Boswell to Sir William Forbes, undated (Fettercairn Papers).

[52]Letter in Fettercairn Papers.

[53]See below p. 201, n. 89.

[54]*Malahide Catalogue*, No. 323.

[55]Letter, JB to Alexander, 14 March 1791. This letter was printed in private edition, XVIII, p. 290, by courtesy of Alwin J. Scheuer, who purchased it at Sotheby's, 1 June 1932 (Lot 265). As to this sale, see below pp. 102–04.

[56]See for example "The Secret of the Ebony Cabinet" from *The Scholar Adventurers* (1950), by Richard D. Altick.

[57]From a letter to *The Times*, London, published 17 September 1927.

[58]See letter, JB to Wilkes, 26 May 1775 (*JB Letters*, pp. 226–27), and letter, JB to Mrs. Garrick, 16 April 1781 (*JB Letters*, p. 311).

the coins and medals were referred to as "an Appendage to the Ebony Cabinet, being always kept in it";[59] and in a letter of 4 November 1805 to his law agent, Alexander described in some detail "the whole contents of the Ebony Cabinet in which the collection of Coins & Medals were deposited."[60] Other contents were said to include a few rose diamonds and some "toilets of lace work."[61] In December 1805, Alexander purchased (amongst other things) the whole contents of the ebony cabinet from the "younger children" who had succeeded to them under their father's will. The legal document giving effect to this purchase refers to these contents as "consisting of a seal ring, miniature pictures of our father James Boswell Esqre. and of Miss Cuningham and sundry curiosities natural and artificial."[62] It is also probable that at some time the cabinet housed the dressing plate of Veronica Van Sommelsdyck, a family heirloom which Boswell sought in his will to entail along with the cabinet itself.[63] The interest in the ebony cabinet seems to have arisen because Boswell tried by his will to ensure that it would always remain in his family, and because it was used by later generations as a convenient place in which to store some of the papers.

Shortly after his father's death, Alexander travelled to Germany to study at Leipzig.[64] On his return, he was content to settle down as Laird of Auchinleck. He interested himself in public affairs and was elected Member of Parliament for the constituency of Plympton Erle, which he represented from 1816 to 1821.[65] In 1821, he received a baronetcy. He was also an antiquarian and a poet of distinction (a much better one than his father). He ran a private printing press[66] and published a number of rare historical works as well as compositions of his own and of his father. He was a member of the Roxburghe Club and friendly with Sir Walter Scott and his circle. He knew many

[59]"Answers and Claim for Alexander Boswell Esq. of Auchinleck to the Memorial and Claim of his Brother and Sisters," dated 15 February 1803 (copy in ILP).

[60]Letter, Alexander Boswell to Harry Davidson, 4 November 1805 (copy in ILP).

[61]Ibid.

[62]"Assignation of Moveables and Discharge by Elizabeth Boswell and Others to Alexander Boswell," dated 21 and 31 December 1805 (copy in ILP).

[63]"Observations for the Younger Children on Notes by the Arbiter," dated 26 October 1803 (copy in ILP).

[64]An amusing account of Alexander's spell in Germany is contained in a series of long letters to Sir William Forbes (Fettercairn Papers). Alexander arrived in Leipzig in September 1795. In April 1796 he moved to Dresden, and a month later he was in Berlin. He does not seem to have spent much time studying. By June 1796, he was back in London.

[65]G. P. Judd: *Members of Parliament 1734–1832*, 1955.

[66]The Auchinleck Press.

of his father's Johnsonian friends. Lockhart says of him that he "had all his father *Bozzy's* cleverness, good humour, and joviality, without one touch of his meaner qualities,—wrote *Jenny dang the Weaver*, and some other popular songs,[67] which he sang capitally—and was moreover a thorough bibliomaniac."[68]

Sir Walter Scott, however, presents a different picture. He says: "Sir Alexander was a proud man and, like his grandfather, thought that his father had lowered himself by his deferential suit and service to Johnson. I have observed he disliked any allusion to the book or to Johnson himself, and I have heard that Johnson's fine picture by Sir Joshua was sent up-stairs out of the sitting apartments at Auchinleck."[69] Scott's characterization is probably unjust, but it influenced later writers such as G. Birkbeck Hill, who spoke of Alexander's illiberal feelings about Johnson, and Wildred Partington, who wrote that the family papers "were held like State secrets because the son, Sir Alexander, thought his father had lowered himself by his association with Johnson."[70]

Alexander deserves to be vindicated. Mention has already been made of his letters expressing respect for Johnson and pride in his father's book. Far from holding the family papers like "state secrets," he was prepared to accede to a reasonable request for access by at least one outsider. The request came from A. F. Tytler, who, in 1808, was planning a second edition of his *Memoirs of Lord Kames*.[71] Tytler had learnt from Forbes of the materials assembled by Boswell for a life of Lord Kames and he wrote to Alexander requesting permission to inspect these.[72] He explained that he had already obtained the consent of the literary executors. Permission must have been granted because when the second edition of Tytler's book appeared in 1814

[67]Another of his well-known songs is "Jenny's Bawbee."

[68]J. G. Lockhart: *Life of Scott* (1837–38), IV, p. 159.

[69]Letter from Scott to J. W. Croker printed in *The Correspondence and Diaries of the late Right Honourable John Wilson Croker, LL.D., F.R.S., Secretary to the Admiralty From 1809 to 1832*, 1885, ed. Louis J. Jennings, II, p. 32.

[70]See G. B. Hill: *Footsteps of Dr. Johnson (Scotland)* (1890), pp. 283–84, and *The Private Letter-Books of Sir Walter Scott*, ed. Wilfred Partington, London, 1930, p. 193 n. More recently certain scholars have rejected Scott's views. See R. W. Chapman: "Boswell's Archives," an essay published in vol. XVII of *Essays and Studies* (of 1931). See also F. A. Pottle: "The History of the Boswell Papers" from the de luxe edition of the *London Journal* (London, 1951) at p. xviii: "I do not believe that such a man later turned snobbish, reverted to the traditional stiff-necked pride of Auchinleck, and grew ashamed of his father's deference to Johnson."

[71]The first edition had appeared in 1807.

[72]Letter, A. F. Tytler to Alexander Boswell, 27 June 1808 (at Yale).

it contained several quotations from "Mr. Boswell's MSS."[73]—an indication to the public, one would have thought, that even if Malone's report of a burning were correct, at least some of the papers had survived and could be seen by a responsible scholar.

Scott's other charge, based on hearsay, was that Alexander had Johnson's portrait removed from the sitting apartments at Auchinleck. Christopher Morley, in his preface to the American trade edition of the *London Journal,* went further by stating that, according to Scott, the portrait was removed to the attic, face to the wall. The facts of the matter, such as we know them, are these. Johnson's portrait and several other pictures had already been taken from Auchinleck to London before Boswell died. Under his father's will, Alexander succeeded only to the pictures actually at Auchinleck. The other pictures went to the younger children, and any which Alexander wanted he had to buy. On 21 October 1795, he wrote to Sir William Forbes: "As to the Pictures there is one in particular of my Father which I would not part with on any account. It is a 50 guinea head which Sir Joshua Reynolds gave in a present to my Father. That & indeed all the Pictures in London he meant to have sent to Auchinleck but I cannot fulfill that intention as the prices are such as I cannot afford to give such as 100 for Dr. Johnson & 80 for a Landscape of Rubens."[74] Forbes wrote to Malone that he could not think of Alexander "depriving himself of Dr. Johnson's portrait, which never ought to go out of his family."[75] The portrait certainly went to Auchinleck, for Alexander complained to his brother James that it was difficult to hang there because of its size.[76] His difficulties in this respect may even have given rise to Scott's accusation. The picture probably remained at Auchinleck until after Alexander's death in 1822. In 1825, his widow sent it to Sotheby's for inclusion in the sale of the library of young James.[77] She regretted doing so, for it fetched only £76.13/–, much

---

[73]*Memoirs of Lord Kames,* 2nd ed., Edinburgh, 1814, pp. 14, 19, 61, 65, and 82. JB's materials on Lord Kames, now at Yale, run to 81 folio and quarto pages. It is not clear whether Tytler saw all of these, but his extracts correspond to pp. 4, 10, 11–12, 21, 23–24, and 49–50 of the manuscript. It is possible he never saw pp. 51–81 as there is a natural division in the manuscript at this point—a shift from folio to quarto sheets.

[74]Letter in Fettercairn Papers.

[75]Letter, Sir William Forbes to Malone, 30 June 1796 (Hyde Collection).

[76]Letter, Alexander to James, 2 June 1810 (at Yale).

[77]*Bibliotheca Boswelliana. A Catalogue of the entire Library of the late James Boswell, Esq. . . . which will be sold by auction, by Mr. Sotheby . . . on Tuesday, May 24, 1825 ff.* (Annotated copies at Yale and in the Hyde Collection.) Johnson's portrait was lot 3293 and was sold for £76.13/- to John Graves, a hop merchant of Southwark. It is now in the National Portrait Gallery, London.

less than she had hoped for. "With regard to Dr. Johnson's picture," she wrote, "it certainly went for its real value. At the same time had I known it was to bring so trifling a sum I would not have sent it up; but some foolish people here talked of its bringing £1,000 or *at least* £500 & I therefore thought it an excellent opportunity of realizing such a sum which it was my intention to send to the Executry fund."[78]

Alexander, like his father, was an ardent Tory and given to publishing anonymous attacks against his political opponents. In 1821,[79] a series of outrageous articles directed against James Stuart of Dunearn appeared in the Edinburgh *Beacon*. When this paper ceased publication, the attacks continued in a Glasgow periodical, the *Sentinel*. Stuart, who was described amongst other things as a "bully," a "coward," and a "dastard," was determined to discover the identity of the author. In February 1822, Sir Alexander received news of the sudden death of his brother James and went to London to see about his affairs. During his absence, Stuart made contact with William Borthwick, a former proprietor of the *Sentinel,* then in jail for debt. Stuart promised not to press suit against Borthwick for the libels he had published as editor, if he would procure the manuscripts which would reveal the author of the lampoons. On his release from jail, Borthwick obtained entry to the office in Nelson Street, Glasgow, occupied by Robert Alexander, then editor and proprietor of the *Sentinel,* and stole several manuscripts by Sir Alexander. These included the *Whig Song* in which Stuart, an Edinburgh lawyer, was referred to thus:

> Ilk body's a limb o' the Law man,
> Tacks, bonds, precognitions,
> Bills, wills and petitions
> And aught but a trigger some draw, man.[80]

[78]Draft letter, Lady Boswell to Mr. William Murray, 8 July 1825 (at Yale). The passage quoted is deleted in the draft. The wish to make a substantial payment to the executry fund of young James was presumably because he was thought to have died insolvent and his affairs were in the hands of his creditors (as to which see below, p. 19). She also had in mind, no doubt, that if young James's debts could be paid in full, any surplus would be paid over to Sir Alexander's estate, as Sir Alexander was James's sole heir.

[79]The narrative which follows is based on information from *The Trial of James Stuart, Esq. Younger of Dunearn, before the High Court of Justiciary, at Edinburgh, on Monday, June 10, 1822. Taken in Short Hand. With an Appendix of Documents,* 2nd ed., Edinburgh, 1822.

[80]The verse implied that Stuart would draw legal documents but not a trigger. "Ilk body" — that same person (i.e., Stuart); "A limb o' the Law"—a reference to Stuart's profession; "Tacks, bonds, precognitions, Bills, wills and petitions" — all types of legal documents.

The repeated accusations of cowardice were too much for Stuart, and when Sir Alexander returned from burying his brother, he found a challenge waiting for him. The duel, originally planned for France,[81] took place on 26 March 1822 on the farm of Balbarton, near Auchtertool, Fife. Sir Alexander, realizing perhaps that he had been at fault in making such vicious attacks on Stuart, fired into the air. Stuart also discharged his pistol without taking aim and "was never more thunderstruck than when on the smoke clearing he saw his adversary sinking gently down."[82] By a cruel stroke of luck, the ball had hit Sir Alexander in the neck and he died from his wound the next day.

On returning to Edinburgh, Stuart went to the chambers of Mr. James Gibson, W.S. There, covering his face with his hands, he burst into tears, saying he had taken no aim. He wished to God he had done so, for if he had, he was certain he would have missed. He added that he had never fired a pistol on foot in his life before.[83] Stuart fled to France, but afterwards returned to Edinburgh to face trial on a charge of murder. Stuart's counsel, the great Jeffrey, quoted Boswell's and Johnson's approval of the practice of duelling from the *Life*. After the judge had finished his summing up, the jury consulted for a few moments without retiring, and then returned a unanimous verdict of "not guilty."

Sir Alexander was survived by his wife, Grace Cuming, and three children, James, Janet Theresa, and Margaret Amelia. During his lifetime he had lived in considerable style. When Farington called on Euphemia in 1801, she remarked that Alexander's income was greatly beyond that of his father and he had his carriage and four, his hounds, and his racehorses.[84] At his death, however, he was hopelessly insolvent.[85] The entailed estate was not affected by the debts, but none of his children dared enter into succession to the remaining estate for fear of becoming personally liable to the creditors. It was many years before Sir Alexander's tangled affairs were finally sorted out.

[81]A letter from Sir Alexander to his friend Robert Maconochie dated 24 March 1822 is preserved in the Signet Library, Edinburgh. Sir Alexander asks Maconochie to be his second and suggests the duel might take place at Calais. This letter is fully quoted on page 15 of the Appendix to *The Trial of James Stuart Esq.*, cited above.

[82]So Stuart told Lord Cockburn. See Lord Cockburn's *Memorials*, Edinburgh, 1856, p. 395.

[83]Evidence of James Gibson at the trial. See *The Trial of James Stuart Esq.*, pp. 103–104. See also Lord Cockburn's *Memorials*, p. 394: "Stuart, an awkward lumbering rider, had never fired a pistol but once or twice from the back of a horse in a troop of yeomanry."

[84]*The Farington Diary* (cited above p. 6, n. 32), I, p. 325.

[85]See below p. 204.

SIR ALEXANDER BOSWELL (1775–1822)
Boswell's elder son.
From the portrait by Raeburn.

SIR JAMES BOSWELL (1806–1857)
Sir James is shown with his racehorse Constantine (ridden by Halloway), a
winner at the Ayr meeting, 1839. From the portrait by J. F. Herring.

JANET THERESA BOSWELL,
afterwards LADY ELIOTT (d.
1836). From a portrait now destroyed (artist unknown).

MARGARET AMELIA BOS-
WELL, afterwards MRS. VASSALL
(d. 1890). With her husband, Maj.-
General Vassall.

Meanwhile, in London, the affairs of James Boswell junior also ended up in the hands of his creditors. He too had died in debt and it was left to William How, one of the creditors, to take out letters of administration.[86] In 1825, James's "entire library" was auctioned and the printed sale catalogue lists a number of items which must have come from his father's archives.[87] There was an important group

[86]Letters of Administration in favour of William How dated 18 November 1824, embodying a copy of James's will by which he left his whole estate to Alexander, subject to payment of his debts (photocopy in author's possession). The sale of the library realized £2,045 (the total shown in annotated copies of the catalogue at Yale and in the Hyde Collection). This left a balance due to Alexander's estate, but How died without completing the administration. It was taken over on 23 April 1834 by Mrs. Jane Douglas Boswell who was then also administering Alexander's estate (indicated in above photocopy). On 15 July 1835 a balance of £547 was paid over to Alexander's estate (excerpt from "Account Auchinleck Estate Personal," a book produced by Mr. J. D. Boswell, quoted in Pursuer's Print of Documents, etc., *in causa* Montgomerie v. Boswell—ILP). See below p. 206, n. 109.

[87]See catalogue referred to above p. 14, n. 77. Manuscripts were sold on Friday 3 June 1825, the tenth day of the sale. Apart from the uncatalogued bundles auctioned at the end of the sale, the contents of which are uncertain (see below p. 22, n. 95), the following Boswellian and Johnsonian items were sold:

*Lot*

3118 Chronological List of the Johnson Club by Malone; Elegy on the Death of Sir Joshua Reynolds; and various papers of extracts, notes on Shakespeare, etc., by Malone and others, a bundle—sold to Thorpe for £1.11.6d.

3151 Manuscript notes by SJ to part of Lord Hailes' Annals of Scotland with four letters from Lord Hailes to JB—sold to Thorpe for £14–.

3152 Original MS. of the Plan of SJ's Dictionary, addressed to Lord Chesterfield—in the hand of an amanuensis but with copious corrections by SJ and signed by him—sold to Thorpe for £8.15/–.

3153 A Short Scheme for Compiling a New Dictionary of the English Language—entirely in SJ's handwriting—sold to Thorpe for £17.6.6d.

3154 The Life of Nicholas Rowe by SJ. Original MS. in his own hand—sold to Thorpe for £3.15/–.

3155 The Life of Pope—Original MS. in SJ's own hand—sold to Thorpe for £16.5.6d.

3158 Included a letter from E. Hector to Boswell accompanied by the original MS. of the Verses by SJ to a Lady who gathered a sprig of Myrtle—sold to Smedley for £2.

3160 SJ's Journal of his Tour in France—Original MS.—sold to Thorpe for £10.10/–.

3162 A pocket book of SJ with miscellaneous contents—sold to Thorpe for £1.3/–.

3163 SJ's diary, Easter 1766—sold to Valentyne for £11.–.6d.

3164 SJ's diary, 1781 and 1783—sold to Thorpe for £5.

3165 Repertorium—a small book of miscellaneous contents by SJ—sold to Thorpe for £3.3/–.

3166 Book of Prayers by SJ—sold to Upcott for £9.9/–.

of Johnsonian manuscripts, letters, and annotated proof sheets; also
the materials for Boswell's proposed dictionary of the Scottish language,
the manuscript of *Boswelliana* (a "Collection of Anecdotes, Bon Mots,
Repartees, &c., &c."), and another lot described as "Johnsoniana—a
Selection of Scraps from periodical Papers—2. Proof Sheets of the
first Edition of Boswell's Life of Johnson . . . and a parcel of loose
Papers, Letters and Memoranda, relating to the Life of Johnson."
This last lot was purchased for £9 by William Pickering, the well-known
publisher and bookseller.[88] A year later, Pickering published a new
edition of the *Life* in the Oxford English Classics series, edited by
F. P. Walesby.[89] In the preface the editor states: "We have also before
us a mass of original papers, purchased at the Boswell sale." This
edition contains little evidence that the "mass of original papers" was
put to much use, though it is possible to cite a few instances.[90]
J. W. Croker, whose edition of the *Life* appeared in 1831, also refers
to material purchased at the Boswell sale:

> Mr. J. L. Anderdon[91] favoured the editor with the inspection
> of a portfolio bought at the sale of the library of Mr. James Boswell,
> junior, which contained some of the original letters, memoranda,
> and note books, which had been used as materials for the *Life*.

3167 SJ's letter of thanks to the Vice-Chancellor of Oxford for the degree of M.A.—sold to
     Pickering for £7.

3168 Two letters from SJ to Malone and one from Byng to Malone—sold to Thorpe for
     £3.15/–.

3169 Three letters from SJ to Sir Joshua Reynolds and the original draft of SJ's letter to the
     Lord Chancellor *re* the augmentation of his pension—sold to Thorpe for £6.6/–.

3170 A large bundle of proof sheets of SJ's *Lives of the Poets* corrected in his own hand—sold
     to Upcott for £3.13.6d.

3171 *Johnsoniana*—a selection of scraps from periodical papers; proof sheets of the first edition
     of the *Life*, corrected in JB's hand; and a parcel of loose papers, letters, and memoranda,
     relating to the *Life*—sold to Pickering for £9.

3172 A Dictionary of the Scottish Language in MS. by JB—sold to Thorpe for 16/–.

3173 Boswelliana: "A Collection of Anecdotes, Bon Mots, Repartees, &c., &c.," by JB
     sold to Thorpe for £18.

3293 Reynolds' Portrait of SJ—sold to Graves for £76.13/–.

[88]William Pickering (1796–1854). In 1825 his shop was at 57 Chancery Lane, London.
[89]Published in 4 volumes by William Pickering, London, and Talboys and Wheeler, Oxford.
[90]See, for example, footnotes on pp. 55 and 144 of vol. I.
[91]John Lavicount Anderdon (1792–1874). A collector and man of letters.

Their chief value, now, is to show that as far as we may judge from this specimen, the printed book is a faithful transcript from the original notes, except only as to the suppression of names. Mr. Anderdon's portfolio also contains Johnson's original draft of the *Prospectus* of the Dictionary, and a fair copy of it (written by an amanuensis, but signed, *in form,* by Johnson), addressed to Lord Chesterfield, on which his lordship appears to have made a few critical notes.[92]

It is possible that Mr. Anderdon's portfolio contained at least some of the items included in the lot originally purchased by Pickering; but it also contained material from another lot, for the *Plan* of the Dictionary was listed separately.

William Upcott, who purchased lots 3166 and 3170 (the Book of *Prayers* and proof sheets of the *Lives of the Poets),* wrote shortly after the sale to his friend J. T. Smith:[93]

The last day's sale of the late James Boswell's Books and Manuscripts took place yesterday at Sotheby's—and every article of interest produced great prices. Indeed the *Johnsonian* MSS. together with the various Letters of Burke, Warton, Dryden, Percy, Kemble, Steevens, Farmer, Windham, Tyrwhitt, Blackstone, Gibbon, and other eminent literary Characters—brought large sums. I was fortunate to obtain a lot of original proof-sheets of Johnson's Lives of the Poets, corrected by his own hand, with numerous additions by himself. As a specimen of these sheets would be a valuable acquisition to a *Johnsonian Collector,* I have much satisfaction in presenting to Mrs. Smith a fragment of his Life of Cowley with the Doctor's Manuscript revisions for her interesting Illustrated Copy of Boswell's Life of that great Biographer and Moralist.

It is impossible to be certain what papers from Boswell's archives were dispersed in the 1825 sale. At least nine uncatalogued bundles were auctioned at the end of the sale and they probably included the large manuscript collection of verses by Boswell bequeathed by

[92]Preface to Croker's edition (1831), pp. xix–xx.
[93]Letter Wm. Upcott to J. T. Smith, 4 June 1825 (Hyde Collection). J. T. Smith (1766–1833) was a topographical draughtsman and antiquary and Keeper of Prints in the British Museum. He collected signatures.

Francis Douce to the Bodleian Library.[94] What else they may have contained is anyone's guess.[95] What is certain is that some of the papers which were in the library of James junior at his death found their way back to Auchinleck. These included not only some of James's own personal papers, but also papers of Malone which James had inherited under Malone's will. The most likely explanation is that when Sir Alexander came to London to bury his brother, he went through the library and removed any papers which he considered to be private or of family interest.

The next outsider to approach Auchinleck in quest of Boswell manuscripts was J. W. Croker,[96] whose edition of the *Life* was published by John Murray in 1831. Croker's great achievement lay in tracking down and printing a mass of important new material, including about one hundred unpublished letters of Johnson.[97] His reference to Mr. Anderdon's portfolio made it widely known that part at least of Boswell's archives had survived. His first thoughts, however, were of Auchinleck and the treasures which it might contain. Sir Walter Scott had told him: "I do not think there is anything to be had at Auchinleck,"[98] but Croker was unconvinced. He wrote to Isaac D'Israeli: "What can have become of Boswell's *original* Diary? It would be invaluable, and cannot, I think, have been destroyed";[99] and in a letter to Sir Walter: "I cannot but think that Boswell's *original Diary* must be in

[94]Bodl. Douce MS. CXCIII. F. A. Pottle has suggested (*James Boswell, The Earlier Years,* New York, 1966, p. 476) that the MSS. were included in the sale, and recent research by Professor Paul J. Korshin, of the University of Pennsylvania, supports this. A book auction catalogue, identified only as N.R.E. 26, March 2, 1826, in the British Museum, noted by Korshin, lists as item 319 "Boswell Papers: a large quantity of MSS. in the handwriting of James Boswell, and his son James, and other literati, consisting chiefly of Original Poetry, Epigrams, Songs, etc., etc., Behn £1/2/–."

[95]It is tempting to attribute the provenance of any unexplained Boswellian manuscripts which made their appearance about this time to the sale of 1825, but such attributions must be conjectural. The 9 letters from Boswell to Malone which came into the collection of William Upcott and were printed in Croker's second edition of the *Life* (X, p. 209) may have been purchased at the sale, but if Upcott was the original purchaser, he does not mention them in his letter to J. T. Smith cited above p. 21, n. 93.

[96]Tytler preceded him in 1808 (see above p. 13), but whereas Tytler was interested only in materials about Lord Kames, Croker was after the journals and the materials for the *Life.*

[97]In his third edition of the *Life,* Croker printed for the first time Boswell's *Errata and Observations on the Tour to the Hebrides.* These were remarks which Boswell sent to Johnson in 1775 immediately after publication of the latter's *Journey to the Western Islands of Scotland.* Croker made a transcript of the text from the MS. in the Anderdon Collection. The MS. is now in the Hyde Collection.

[98]roker's *Correspondence and Diaries,* cited above p. 13, n. 69. Letter from Scott to Croker, 30 January 1829.

[99]Ibid. Letter from Croker to D'Israeli, 25 April 1829.

existence somewhere. It clearly was not what was printed from. I suspect (indeed Boswell says so somewhere) that there are masses of manuscripts at Auchinleck. Who are the young Laird's guardians? or, how could we have inquiry made? It would be a pity that for want of taking a little trouble such a prize as the original journal would be, should escape me".[100]

The young Laird was Sir James Boswell, only fifteen years old when he inherited the estate in 1822. Croker wrote to him in December 1829, but got no reply. He told Scott: "I wrote a month ago to *Sir James Boswell, Bart., Auchinleck, Mauchline, N.B.* asking, very civilly I hope, after his grandfather's papers; and I stated my acquaintance with his father and his uncle. I have had no answer. Now, *pray,* find out from somebody in Ayrshire whether the young Baronet is at home, or where he may be. I need not add that if you could, thro' any channell, get at him or his Mamma, and find whether the Journals are at Auchinleck you would confer a great favour on me and on the literary world."[101] Scott had no success. He wrote to Sir James and, like Croker, received no reply.[102] He called on Sir James and found him not at home; and when Sir James returned the call, it was Scott's turn to be out. Scott is said to have enlisted the help of a gentleman residing in Edinburgh having "extraordinary influence" with the Boswell family. The identity of this gentleman remains a mystery, but "all his importunities and influence" were apparently unavailing.[103] Scott also consulted his fellow advocate, William Boswell, who had married Boswell's daughter, Elizabeth.[104] William Boswell provided Croker with a genealogy and probably other information, but it is unlikely that he tried to intercede directly with the family at Auchinleck. Relations with them had been strained ever since his marriage and he was hardly the right person to obtain favours.

[100]Ibid. Letter from Croker to Scott, 28 August 1829.

[101]Letter, dated 16 January 1830, printed in *The Private Letter-Books of Sir Walter Scott*, 1930, p. 193.

[102]Letter, Scott to Croker, undated, present ownership unknown. Sold as Lot 301, Cat. 144, sale at the Walpole Galleries, 10 East 49th St., New York, 5 March 1920. According to the catalogue description, Scott states that as Sir James Boswell was at Callender House, he wrote to him but received no reply.

[103]Letter, William Mackenzie to I. K. Tefft of Georgia, 1 February 1844 (in the collection of the Georgia Historical Society). See below pp. 206–08 where the implications of this letter are more fully considered.

[104]William Boswell's name is mentioned at least twice in the Scott-Croker correspondence at Yale. One letter (undated) reads, "I enclose the genealogy which will be I hope useful. I got it from William Boswell, Advocate, and a near relation of James Bozzy whose daughter he married."

Scott could do no more and Croker had to accept defeat. In the preface to his edition of the *Life,* he wrote:

> Of course, his first inquiries were directed towards the original
> manuscript of Mr. Boswell's Journal, which would no doubt have
> enabled him to fill up all the blanks and clear away much of
> the obscurity that exist[s] in the printed *Life.* It was to be hoped
> that the *archives of Auchinleck,* which Mr. Boswell frequently and
> pompously mentions, would contain the original materials of these
> works, which he himself, as well as the world at large, considered
> as his best claims to distinction. And the editor thought that he
> was only fulfilling the duties of courtesy in requesting from Mr.
> Boswell's representative any information which he might be dis-
> posed to afford on the subject. To that request the editor has
> never received any answer: though the same inquiry was after-
> wards, on his behalf, repeated by Sir Walter Scott, whose influence
> might have been expected to have produced a more satisfactory
> result.[105]

In a footnote Croker explained:

> Sir Walter Scott and Sir James Boswell, to whom, as the grandson
> of Mr. Boswell, the inquiries were addressed, unfortunately missed
> one another in mutual calls; but the editor has heard from another
> quarter that the original journals do not exist at Auchinleck:
> perhaps to this fact the silence of Sir James Boswell may be
> attributed . . . it appears from a memorandum book in Mr. Ander-
> don's possession, that Mr. Boswell's materials were in a variety
> of forms; and it is feared that they have been irretrievably dis-
> persed.[106]

Croker certainly read Malone's footnote about the "burning,"[107] but he does not refer to it specifically, and it did not prevent him from believing that there might be important material at Auchinleck. He does not disclose the source of his subsequent information that there were no journals at Auchinleck, nor how he came to believe that the papers had been "irretrievably dispersed." His informant may have been William Boswell, who, being estranged from Sir Alexander's

[105]Preface, pp. xvi–xvii.
[106]Ibid., p. xvii.
[107]See above p. 7, n. 35.

family, could have been mistaken about what papers remained at Auchinleck.[108]

As evidence of the destruction of the papers, Croker's remarks were inconclusive, the only certain facts being that he wrote to Sir James and, despite Scott's intercession, received no reply. Whatever may be made of Sir James's silence,[109] Croker's preface established the belief in the loss of the papers and, so far as we know, for at least forty years no outsider thought it worth while to approach Auchinleck again.

Sir James is described by G. Birkbeck Hill as a man of great natural ability who, had he chosen, might have become distinguished.[110] He was a sportsman rather than a scholar, and there is little to suggest that he cared much about his grandfather's literary activities. Yet Hill says he shared his father's illiberal feelings about Johnson and relates how Miss Macleod of Macleod one day made Sir James very angry by suggesting that he name one of his race-horses "Boswell's Johnsoniana."[111] Sir James's reaction to this rather silly suggestion is understandable, and there is no real evidence that his feelings towards Johnson were illiberal, any more than were those of Sir Alexander. Hill is probably nearer the mark when he suggests that Sir James felt a strong sense of grievance against his grandfather for agreeing to limit the entail of Auchinleck estate to male succession.[112] Sir James had two daughters, but no son, and if the entail had been followed at his death, Auchinleck would have passed from his immediate family to the descendants of the Biographer's uncle, Dr. John Boswell.[113]

In 1830, Sir James married his cousin, Jessie Jane Cuninghame, and two daughters were born of this marriage: Julia Grace Jessie Jane, who married Mr. George Mounsey, a solicitor in Carlisle and at one time mayor of that city; and Emily Harriet, who married the Honourable Richard Wogan Talbot, eldest son of the fourth Lord Talbot de Malahide, of Malahide Castle, near Dublin. Sir James was determined that Auchinleck should remain in his family after his death, and sought a means of breaking the fetters of the entail. The deed was carefully examined and his sharp-eyed lawyers spotted a flaw:

[108]William Boswell may himself have been misled by his father, Robert Boswell, W. S., JB's cousin and man of law. See below pp. 28–29.

[109]The implications of Sir James's silence are considered more fully below, pp. 208–09.

[110]G. B. Hill: *Footsteps of Dr. Johnson (Scotland)*, 1890, p. 284.

[111]Idem.

[112]Idem.

[113]See below p. 26, n. 115.

a single word, but a vital one, had been written over an erasure. This was enough to enable Sir James to have the entail set aside by the Court of Session in 1852,[114] despite the opposition of Thomas Alexander Boswell of Crawley Grange, who would otherwise have succeeded.[115] Auchinleck thus became Sir James's to dispose of as he wished.

During Sir James's lifetime occurred one of the most extraordinary episodes in the whole history of literary discovery.[116] About the year 1840,[117] a certain Major Stone, in the service of the Honourable East India Company, made a purchase in a shop in Boulogne which he received wrapped in a fragment of a letter bearing the signature of James Boswell. He asked the shopkeeper, Madame Noël, where she had obtained it and was told that it had come from an itinerant hawker of waste-paper who visited Boulogne every few months. Major Stone was able to buy from Madame Noël no fewer than ninety-seven autograph letters from James Boswell to his lifelong friend and confidant, the Reverend W. J. Temple. The dates of the letters spanned the whole of Boswell's adult life, the earliest being written when he was only eighteen and the last near to his death. Madame Noël had already used a number of letters as wrappers, and had Major Stone not called when he did, the rest would have been used for the same purpose.

The letters had come of course not from Boswell's archives but from the private papers of Temple, and it is possible to suggest how they found their way to France. Temple's eldest daughter, Anne, had married Charles Powlett, a rather worldly clergyman with expensive tastes. Despite a reasonable living of his own and a useful income of some £400 a year from his wife, he was forced to go abroad to escape from his creditors. In 1825, he settled in Outreau, near

---

[114]The decision of the Court of Session is reported in *Session Cases* (XIV Dunlop), 1852, pp. 378–95. The clerk who wrote out the deed of entail had originally written the word "redeemably" and then, after erasing the first three letters, had substituted "irredeemably." The alteration was not properly authenticated and, since the use of the word "irredeemably" was essential under the statute governing the form of entails, the Court decided unanimously that the deed was void.

[115]Thomas Alexander Boswell was the son of JB's brother Thomas David Boswell. In 1852 he was the next heir of entail. By 1857 (the date of Sir James's death), however, he had died without male issue (his only son having died unmarried in India). Thus, had the entail been followed in 1857, the succession would have passed to the descendants of Lord Auchinleck's brother, Dr. John Boswell.

[116]For fuller accounts of this incident, see Introduction to Thomas Seccombe's edition of *Letters of James Boswell to the Rev. W. J. Temple*, London, 1908, and *Literary Career*, p. 275 *et seq.* See also *Edinburgh Review*, April 1857; *Notes and Queries*, second series, III, pp. 381–82; and *The Times*, 6 January 1857.

[117]This is the date conjectured by Pottle. Seccombe states 1850, but gives no authority.

Boulogne. Presumably the family papers were taken to France then and dispersed after his death in 1834.

Major Stone kept his letters until his death in about 1850. They then passed to his nephew, Augustus F. Boyse, a barrister of the Inner Temple, who sold them to a fellow barrister, Edmund G. Hornby. Hornby arranged for their publication by Richard Bentley; he had originally intended to do the editing himself, but the demands of his profession made this impossible, and the task was undertaken anonymously by Philip Francis. The book appeared just before Christmas, 1856, and was very well received,[118] but Hornby's plans for a second edition never came to fruition. The original letters are now in the Pierpont Morgan Library in New York.

The letters contain frequent remarks which make clear the huge scope and interest of the journals, and the richness of the other materials which Boswell collected so assiduously.[119] One might have expected their publication to have inspired fresh efforts to establish the fate of the archives beyond any doubt. No such efforts are known to have been made until about 1874, when *Boswelliana, The Commonplace Book of James Boswell* was published for the Grampian Club, with an extended biographical memoir and annotation by the Reverend Charles Rogers. The manuscript of this collection of anecdotes and witty sayings had come from the sale of the library of James Boswell junior in 1825. After passing through the hands of J. H. S. Pigott (a Somerset bookseller) and Thomas Kerslake (a Bristol bookseller), it was acquired by Lord Houghton, who made it available to the Grampian Club for publication.[120] In his memoir, Rogers writes:

> The three persons nominated as literary executors did not meet, and the entire business of the trust was administered by Sir William Forbes, Bart., who appointed as his law agent Robert Boswell,

[118]*The Times* devoted six whole columns to its review spread over several days from 3 to 8 January 1857.

[119]As early as 1758, JB writes to Temple of keeping an exact Journal and in 1767, when Temple was about to visit Scotland, JB promises him "journals and letters, which you will delight to peruse." Other remarks show that by the end of JB's life his journals must have run to many volumes, and that he contemplated using the material which they contained for publication. On 3 September 1780, he writes: "I hope to see your Journal that you kept; you shall see all my volumes when you come to Scotland"; and on 22 May 1789: "My Journal will afford materials for a very curious narrative. I assure you I do not now live with a view to have surprising incidents, though I own I am desirous that my life should *tell.*"

[120]Lord Houghton had earlier printed a few anecdotes from the MSS. for the Philobiblion Society (*Miscellanies* of the Philobiblion Society, II, London, 1856, No. 15). See *Literary Career*, p. 274.

writer to the signet, cousin german of the deceased. By that gentleman's advice, Boswell's manuscripts were left to the disposal
of his family; and it is believed that the whole were immediately
destroyed.[121]

Rogers offers no authority for his statement, but, in his preface,[122]
he thanks the "representatives of Thomas David Boswell, the biographer's brother, and of his uncle, Dr. John Boswell," who, he says,
"have been most polite and obliging in their communications." He
makes no mention of the family at Auchinleck, who would have been
the most obvious source of information. His reference to Dr. Boswell's
son, Robert Boswell (1746–1804), may indicate that his enquiries were
directed to members of this family. He certainly had plenty of scope,
for Robert Boswell had nine children and no fewer than forty-two
grandchildren.[123]

Robert Boswell, as Rogers tells us,[124] was a pious character, given
to composing hymns and reading the Scriptures in the original
tongues—just the sort of person to be shocked by the journals. His
attitude towards his cousin's indiscretions is apparent from this epitaph
which he wrote for him:

> Bury his failings in the silent grave
> And from unfriendly hands his memory save.[125]

R. W. Chapman, in his essay on Boswell's archives,[126] has suggested
that Robert Boswell may have been a myth-maker: "A man of his
way of thinking might well advise the destruction of his cousin's journals, and might perhaps assume that his advice had been taken." This
probably goes too far. Robert Boswell acted as law agent in the executry
and also for Alexander, the heir. He was in a position to know what

[121]p. 186.

[122]p. xiii.

[123]Robert Boswell, W. S. (1746–1804) was Dr. John Boswell's eldest son and JB's cousin. He
practised as a solicitor in Edinburgh and acted for Sir William Forbes in the administration of
JB's executry. A family tree prepared in 1936 by Messrs. Scott Moncrieff & Trail, W. S. (copy in
my possession) shows him as having 4 sons and 5 daughters, all but one of whom left issue.
The 42 grandchildren are all named. Robert Boswell's eldest son, William, married JB's
daughter Elizabeth and looked after her interests as a beneficiary under JB's will. He died in
1841, but his daughter, Mrs. Williams, was alive when Rogers was making his enquiries.

[124]See *Boswelliana*, p. 198.

[125]Quoted in *Boswelliana*, p. 188.

[126]See above p. 13, n. 70.

happened to the papers without having to make assumptions. It is possible, though, that if he thought the papers *should* be destroyed, this may have evolved into a belief by his descendants that they *had* been destroyed. If that were so, it would explain how his son, William Boswell, might have misinformed Croker; and Rogers's own informant may have been William Boswell's daughter, Mrs. Williams.

Rogers's memoir provided strong support for the legend of destruction. Yet a careful scholar should have questioned the authority for his statement and why he did not mention any approach to Auchinleck. Rogers also printed Boswell's will for the first time. This had been available for public inspection in Edinburgh since Boswell's death, but few were likely to have taken advantage of the fact. The special provisions whereby the papers were entrusted to Forbes, Temple, and Malone now became common knowledge.

After Sir James Boswell's death in 1857, his widow continued to live at Auchinleck until her own death in 1884. The mansion-house then passed to her daughter, Mrs. Mounsey, for her lifetime. It was in 1887, during Mrs. Mounsey's time at Auchinleck, that Hill published his great edition of the *Life*. This contains no reference to any approach to Auchinleck and, in a later publication, he showed that he thought the papers had been destroyed. In 1890, he wrote in his *Footsteps of Doctor Johnson (Scotland):* "How little did he [i.e., Boswell] foresee that his executors, with a brutish ignorance worthy of perpetual execration, would destroy his manuscripts!"[127] It is hard to understand how Hill came to make such an accusation. No one had ever before attributed the destruction of the papers to the executors; it was surely inconceivable that men like Malone and Forbes would have condoned such an act of vandalism.[128] Later in the *Footsteps,* Hill repeated the charges

---

[127]*Footsteps of Dr. Johnson (Scotland)*, p. 285. The belief in the destruction of the papers is also expressed in Leslie Stephen's article on Boswell in the *Dictionary of National Biography* (1886). Hill and Stephen were close friends. (See Seccombe's article on Hill in the DNB, second supplement, II, 1912.)

[128]Malone was the first great editor of the *Life* and JB's papers were essential sources of reference for him. He would have been the last man to destroy the raw material on which his scholarship depended. Forbes was a distinguished Edinburgh banker, much respected by a wide circle of acquaintances. He and JB were close friends and he admired JB's literary achievements. He knew SJ and acted as clerk to the "Round Robin" (*Life*, III, pp. 83–85 and 482–83). He wrote a Life of James Beattie (1735–1803), Professor of Moral Philosophy and Logic at Aberdeen, and some other pieces. In keeping with his profession, he was an extremely methodical man, in the habit of preserving letters and papers of all kinds in carefully sorted bundles. All in all, it would be difficult to think of two men *less* likely to indulge in the wanton destruction of papers of known literary importance.

JOHN WILSON CROKER (1780–1857).
From the portrait by Lawrence.

GEORGE BIRKBECK HILL (1835–1903).
From the drawing by Ellen G. Hill.

against Sir Alexander and Sir James, that they were indifferent to the great achievements of their ancestor. He also expressed the hope that one day the family would throw open the doors of Auchinleck House to strangers.

Hill had in fact made an unsuccessful approach to Auchinleck a year earlier—the first approach of which we have certain knowledge since Croker's sixty years before. He printed an account of the incident in his essay, *Boswell's Proof Sheets,* first published in the *Atlantic Monthly* in 1894:

> I had once tried to penetrate into Auchinleck, Boswell's ancestral home. I had hoped in the library . . . to find many curious memorials. Permission was refused me. My attempt even excited suspicion; for soon after I had made it I received the following letter which, now the venerable writer is dead, may without impropriety be given to the world. "I hope," wrote Boswell in his preface to his 'Account of Corsica,' "that if this work should at any future period be republished, care will be taken of my orthography." This pious care I have taken of the orthography of his granddaughter.
>
> 44 Queen Street, Edinburgh,<br>June 1, 1889.
>
> Dear Sir
> I am told you are about to publish another addition of My Grandfather's book—"Boswell's Life of Johnston," and that you have "some papers from Ayrshire"! May I ask you to be so good as inform me from whom you received them and oblige.
> Yours faithfully<br>M. E. Vassall
> I may tell you that I am daughter of Sir Alexander Boswell
>
> G. Berbick Hill.

The circumstances of Hill's approach to Auchinleck and Mrs. Mounsey's reaction to it are matters of conjecture. Hill obviously felt himself aggrieved, though one may wonder why he chose to take revenge on poor Mrs. Vassall, who was not directly involved and whose polite letter gave him no cause for offence. His experience was certainly very different from that of another outsider who visited Auchinleck about this time. In 1904, Jasper John Boswell (no relation of the Boswells of Auchinleck) published volume I of *The Boswell History*.[129] In his preface, he thanked those who had placed documents at his disposal, remarking:

> The largest number as well as the most important are at Auchinleck House, the seat of Mr. and Mrs. Mounsey, whom I have visited by invitation several times. When at Auchinleck I have had the keys of the Library, the Muniment Chest, &c., which engrossed all my spare time; but even then the time was too limited to look half of them through, there were so many other attractions provided by my host, independent of visits and receptions; their kindness and courtesy could not be exceeded.

Title deeds and other papers bearing on the general history of the Boswells are one thing; the private journals and papers of James Boswell, the Biographer, are quite another. One cannot readily assume that Mrs. Mounsey would have been equally willing to show the latter to an outsider. But Hill's failure to obtain access is still puzzling. In his published account he did not say that he hoped to find any manuscripts in the library—only "many curious memorials." He seems to have taken for granted that Boswell's archives had perished.

In 1893, Mrs. Mounsey sent a large portion of the library at Auchinleck to London for sale by Messrs. Sotheby Wilkinson & Hodge. The printed catalogue[130] includes the original manuscript of Allan Ramsay's *The Gentle Shepherd,* which had been presented to Boswell by Ramsay's patroness, Susannah, Countess of Eglinton; Sir Robert Sibbald's manuscript autobiography; Boswell's files of the *Scots Magazine* and the *London Magazine* in which his own contributions were probably marked;[131] some proof sheets of the first edition of the *Life* with manuscript correc-

---

[129]Jasper John Boswell: *The Boswell History,* vol. I, 1904. This is a rare book. It is listed in the British Museum Catalogue, but the National Library of Scotland has no copy. There is a copy in the Edinburgh Public Library. Volume II was never published, but F. A. Pottle tells me he is in touch with the author's descendants, who have the completed printer's copy. J. J. Boswell also had among his papers two unpublished letters from JB to Margaret Montgomerie (1769) and a fragment of the journal of JB's brother, Lt. John Boswell. It is not known how he got them, but they may have come from Mrs. Mounsey.

[130]*Catalogue of the Selected Portion of the Celebrated Auchinleck Library, Formed by the late Lord Auchinleck, The Property of Mrs. Mounsey* (Sotheby Wilkinson and Hodge, 23, 24, and 26 June 1893).

[131]Both these files were sold to dealers and their present whereabouts is unknown. The *Scots Magazine,* vols. 7–71, was sold to Thin of Edinburgh for £ 5.5/– and the *London Magazine,* 1732–1783 (wanting 1778) was sold to A. Jackson for £ 3.3/–.

tions by Boswell;[132] and many printed books with annotations by him or bearing his signature. There was nothing, however, to suggest that Boswell's journals or other papers might have survived.

Mrs. Mounsey's sister, Emily, died in 1898, survived by her husband, the fifth Lord Talbot, and by one son, the Honourable James Boswell Talbot, who inherited her one-half share of Auchinleck estate. He succeeded to the other half share on Mrs. Mounsey's death in 1905, but he continued to make his home at Malahide. For the next twelve years, Auchinleck stood empty except for periodical visits by the Talbot family. During this time, the books and furniture were gradually cleared and disposed of at various auctions. One hundred and eleven lots from the library were sold at Sotheby's in March 1916, but the only reference in the catalogue to manuscript material is a single letter to Boswell from Capel Lofft.[133] The remnants of the Auchinleck library were included in a sale of "Valuable Libraries" and postage stamps held in the rooms of Alexander Dowell in Edinburgh on 28, 29, and 30 May 1917. No manuscripts are listed in the catalogue,[134] but, at the end, are a number of unidentified miscellaneous lots which may have contained some items from Boswell's archives, the provenance of which is otherwise unexplained.[135] The 1917 sale certainly included Johnson's diary for 1782, containing an interesting account of his last visit to Brighton with Mrs. Thrale. It was purchased by Miss E. H. Dowden and is now in the Bodleian Library.[136]

The furniture and other contents of Auchinleck were also sold at auction by Dowell's. Forty-four items were included in a mixed sale in Edinburgh on 17 March 1906, shortly after Mrs. Mounsey's death, and a large sale was held at Auchinleck on 4 and 5 April 1917, presumably to complete the clearance of the mansion-house, because the Talbots had decided to dispose of the property. In 1918, the

[132]Now in the Hyde Collection.

[133]*Catalogue of Valuable Books & Manuscripts, the Property of the Honble. James Boswell Talbot, of Auchinleck House* (two other owners) *and other properties* (Sotheby Wilkinson and Hodge, 29, 30, and 31 March 1916). Lofft's letter accompanied a presentation copy to JB of one of Lofft's books (Lot No. 19).

[134]*Catalogue of Valuable Libraries . . . including that from Auchinleck House, Ayrshire . . . to be sold by Auction by Mr. Dowell . . . 28th, 29th and 30th May 1917.*

[135]See *Literary Career*, p. 134. Pottle quotes a letter from his friend Dr. Robert McKinlay, Congregational minister, Stonehouse, Lanarkshire. McKinlay wrote that his friend Glen, a bookseller in Glasgow, bought "at the Auchinleck sale some years ago" some bundles of oddments which contained a quantity of loose sheets of Boswell's *Ode by Dr. Johnson to Mrs. Thrale upon their supposed approaching Nuptials* (1788), and his *No Abolition of Slavery* (1791). Although this was printed material, manuscripts may have been dispersed in other miscellaneous lots.

[136]Bodleian MS.Don.f.6. Purchased from Miss Dowden's estate by the Friends of the Bodleian, 1938. See *Life*, IV, p. 504.

mansion-house was let to Robert McCrone,[137] and in 1920 the whole estate was put up for sale. The mansion-house and policies were purchased (subject to McCrone's tenancy) by a distant relative, Colonel John Douglas Boswell of Garallan, who was descended from the very branch of the Boswell family (the Craigston line) which Boswell's father had insisted on excluding from the entail.[138] McCrone remained as Colonel Boswell's tenant until May 1923, when his lease expired.

By 1918 it should have been clear that if the papers had survived at all, they would no longer be at Auchinleck—unless some oddments remained which had been overlooked.[139] Belief in the destruction of the papers was still widespread. The only evidence, if it can be called evidence at all, lay in Malone's obscure footnote and the unsupported statements of Croker, Rogers, and Hill. The world's lack of curiosity may to some extent have been due to the influence of Macaulay, whose notorious essay, first published in 1831,[140] did its work of defamation all too well. People were interested in Boswell not so much for his own sake as for what he had to offer about Johnson. It was not until later that the prospect of recovering manuscripts having no bearing on Johnson seemed worthwhile or exciting.

Interest in Boswell was stimulated by important new editions of the *Life* by Fitzgerald (1874), and Napier (1884). Then came Hill's definitive edition in 1887, followed by his *Footsteps of Dr. Johnson (Scotland)* (1890), in which he castigated Macaulay: "The worst of it is that Macaulay, like Rousseau, talked his nonsense so well that it still passes for gospel with all those who have advanced as far as reading, but have not as yet attained to thinking."[141] Hill's new and more sympathetic approach to Boswell was continued and developed by others, notably

[137]Lease to Robert McCrone dated 28 and 30 January 1918 (TLP).

[138]Disposition in favour of John Douglas Boswell dated 19 and 26 May and recorded in the Division of the General Register of Sasines for the County of Ayr on 1 July 1922. Transfer of ownership to Colonel Boswell was back-dated to 15 May 1920.

[139]Quite a number of oddments *did* remain. Tinker in his edition of *JB Letters* refers to information communicated by McCrone "preserved in manuscript letters at Auchinleck House" (p. 90, n. 1). See also ibid. p. 187, n. 2, where he refers to a letter dated 22 January 1765 from the first Mrs. Boswell to JB's brother John "preserved at Auchinleck House." F. A. Pottle, who has access to some of Tinker's papers, states that in a letter to Tinker of 8 September 1920, McCrone refers to "Account Books" of JB's time still at Auchinleck, and says that he has "quite a number of his Memoranda and Letters of Instructions, but there is a considerable gap prior to his becoming Laird." Items continued to turn up at Auchinleck until a few years ago when the house was completely gutted internally for the eradication of dry rot. As to these more recent finds, see below, Appendix I, p. 305 *et seq.*

[140]*The Edinburgh Review*, September 1831, liv. pp. 1–38.

[141]*Footsteps*, p. 286.

by Professor Chauncey B. Tinker of Yale. Tinker was the first formidable scholar to commit a lifetime of productive work to the study of Boswell the man (not just the *Life*). His book, *Young Boswell* (1922), perhaps more than anything else, created the modern attitude to Boswell. Then came his great edition of the *Letters of James Boswell* (1924) for which he tracked down more than one hundred unpublished letters scattered from Switzerland to California. He was also an inspiring teacher and lecturer. The present strength of Boswellian studies in America is due in no small measure to his influence. Meanwhile, the activities of collectors such as Tinker himself, R. B. Adam of Buffalo, and A. E. Newton of Philadelphia were awakening a keen interest in Boswell manuscripts. Adam specialized in Johnsoniana and Boswelliana, and by 1921 (when a catalogue with an introduction by Professor Charles G. Osgood of Princeton was printed[142]) he had the finest collection in the world. Newton concentrated on the same field and communicated his enthusiasm to a wide public through his popular volumes on book-collecting. It was to be expected that this new interest of scholars and collectors alike would lead to fresh efforts to discover the fate of the archives. But still the old pattern persisted. The few persons who doubted the destruction of the papers either failed to make any enquiry at all or else abandoned their investigations before establishing the truth.

One person to suspect the possible survival of some of the papers was Thomas Seccombe, who edited a re-publication of Boswell's letters to Temple in 1907. In his preface, he writes: "His [i.e. Temple's] letters to Boswell (which may possibly at some future date be rescued) should prove interesting."[143] Unfortunately, Seccombe made no attempt to conduct the rescue operation himself. A. E. Newton got as far as visiting Auchinleck, but he arrived without forewarning or introduction when the family was not in residence. Not surprisingly, the servant who answered the door refused him admission.[144]

So far as we know, Tinker was the only outside scholar to apply to Malahide before 1925, and it was chance which first directed his attention that way. In 1920, he was planning his edition of Boswell's letters and was anxious that it should be as complete as possible. He

---

[142]*Catalogue of the Johnsonian Collection of R. B. Adam.* Introduction by Charles G. Osgood. Privately printed, Buffalo, 1921.

[143]*Letters of James Boswell to the Rev. W. J. Temple with an Introduction by Thomas Seccombe*, London, 1908, p. xv.

[144]The story is told in his book *The Amenities of Book Collecting*, 1918, pp. 181–84.

followed the usual custom of writing to *The Times Literary Supplement* enquiring about letters which might be in private hands.[145] Two replies came almost at once, both advising him to try Malahide. One was anonymous; the other came from Miss Elsie Mahaffy, daughter of the former Provost of Trinity College, Dublin.[146] She wrote: "The last representative of Boswell and owner of Auchinleck is Honble. James Talbot, Malahide Castle, Co. Dublin. He has lately imported here an escritoire of Boswell's which is full of Letters, so far uncatalogued."[147] Tinker wrote immediately to Mr. Talbot, and received this reply: "I am very sorry I am unable to give you any letters of James Boswell's for publication. I regret I cannot meet your views in this respect."[148] This was so discouraging that meanwhile Tinker made no further approach to Malahide. His enquiries at Auchinleck were equally unproductive. Mr. McCrone, the tenant, told him:

> There were a number of documents of one kind and another of the old laird's time, and it is just quite possible that when the present proprietors came in they burnt these along with a great number of other manuscripts which were in the House. That this was done, I know from the old joiner who is still resident on the place. When James Boswell Talbot took possession he cleared out a large number of the Books and Papers which were thrown over the window into the court and he along with this same joiner made a bonfire, so little did the family think of their great predecessor.[149]

McCrone's account was based on hearsay, and it turned out later to be a tissue of inaccuracy.[150] But Tinker was sufficiently deterred

---

[145]*The Times Literary Supplement*, 29 July 1920.

[146]John Pentland Mahaffy (1839–1919). It was he who, when a Fellow of Trinity, invited Oscar Wilde to accompany him on a journey to Greece.

[147]From Tinker's papers. The anonymous postcard is not amongst the papers, but Pottle remembers hearing Tinker mention it. The quotation is from a postcard signed "Elsie Mahaffy late of Provost's Ho. Trinity College Dublin." It bears a Dublin postmark dated 31 July 1920 and the address is 19 Westland Row, Dublin. Tinker never knew who wrote the latter postcard because of the illegibility of the signature. It was not until about 1959 that Pottle was able to identify Miss Mahaffy.

[148]Ibid. Letter dated 5 August 1920, signed "James B. Talbot."

[149]Ibid. Letter from McCrone to Tinker dated 8 September 1920.

[150]Lady Talbot writes: "My husband had one fault, he would never part with anything or destroy anything if he could possibly avoid it. I am quite sure the story of his throwing papers out

to desist from further inquiries, although he may have been uneasy about the possibility of letters existing at Malahide.

A year or two later,[151] whilst working in the Pierpont Morgan Library in New York on the texts of the Boswell-Temple correspondence for his book, Tinker came across the following letter from Malone to Euphemia Boswell:

Foley Place, May 4, 1809.

Dear Madam,

To your first letter there was no date of time, nor any denotation of place; so that an answer could not be easily given: however I should have answered such parts of it as I could read before now, but for some unexpected avocations;—having learned your address from your brother.—you are, I conceive, under some mistake with respect to your father's papers. I was not his Executor,[152] but to the best of my recollection he desired, in his will, that no use should be made of them without the consent of Sir Wm Forbes and myself. They were put into my hands by Sir William, and after an inspection, I was clearly of opinion that they contained nothing fit for the press. I afterwards returned them to Sir William Forbes; and since his death, a large parcel of them was sent from Scotland to London for the inspection & consideration of your brother, James; who, after examining them, clearly co-incided with me, respecting the impropriety of printing any part of them. They are now deposited at Auchinleck; in which repository, I trust, they will be suffered to remain in peace.

I am, Madam,
your most humble and obedient Servant,
Edmond Malone

---

of a window to be burned is untrue. Mr. McCrone was not on very good terms with my Father-in-law. He resented the place being sold over his head." (Corrections sent by Lady Talbot to Pottle for his draft History of the Boswell Papers prefaced to the de luxe edition of the *London Journal*, 1951.)

[151] The chronology is established by a letter from Tinker to Alan G. Thomas dated 17 August 1946 (shown to me by Mr. Thomas). Tinker states that he wrote to Lord Talbot "long before" he came across Malone's letter to Euphemia.

[152] Forbes was JB's sole executor in the strictly legal sense of the term. Forbes, Temple, and Malone are described as "literary executors" because JB entrusted his literary manuscripts to them to determine what should be published. The phrase however is misleading because Temple and Malone were never JB's *legal* executors. A fully detailed account of the executry administration is given below in Chapter VI.

This was immensely significant. The literary executors had *not* burnt the papers, nor had they been destroyed by the family (or not at any rate before 1809). Malone's footnote about the burning of papers was clearly contradicted by his own subsequent letter. Lieut.-Commander Rupert T. Gould, at one time president of the Johnson Club at Lichfield, has suggested that the footnote contained a misprint; that Malone really intended to say: "the original letter being *buried* [not burned] in a mass of papers in Scotland."[153] If Gould is right, as he almost certainly is, the earliest and seemingly the most authentic evidence of destruction of the papers rested for more than a hundred years on the misprint of a single letter in a single word.

Malone's letter to Euphemia suggested that the main bulk of the archives could still be in existence. Tinker might have been expected to follow up his discovery by making further enquiries and perhaps even trying to arrange a personal visit to Malahide. Strangely enough, he took no immediate action and, when his book appeared in 1924, he commented on the disappearance of the journals without expressing any hope for their recovery, nor did he refer to the possibility of any unpublished letters surviving at Malahide.[154]

Shortly after the publication of Tinker's book, rumours began to circulate openly in literary circles that Boswell's archives, or at any rate a large portion of them, had survived. By 1925, these rumours were known to be true. A great mass of journals, letters, and other papers had remained at Auchinleck for more than a hundred years until some time after Mrs. Mounsey's death in 1905, when they were moved to Malahide. There was no single dramatic moment of discovery. The truth became known, not because of skilled detection from outside, but because the Talbot family let it be known. In 1920, when Tinker was making his enquiries, there were already a number of outsiders, from dinner guests to publishers, who knew or had heard of the existence of papers at Malahide, and as years went by the number increased.[155]

---

[153]It is interesting to compare JB's own phraseology in his letter to Temple of 28–30 November 1789: "You cannot imagine what labour, what perplexity, what vexation . . . I have endured, searching for papers, *buried* in different masses . . ." (*JB Letters*, p. 382). Tinker did not in fact know about Malone's footnote at this time. Pottle came across it in 1929 or 1930 and wrote a letter to *The Times Literary Supplement* to which Gould's suggestion was a reply (27 February 1930).

[154]See *JB Letters*, p. 225, n. 2: "Boswell's journals having unfortunately perished . . . . . ."; and p. 372, n. 1: "This journal, like countless others of Boswell's, has disappeared."

[155]Some writers have cast Tinker in the role of literary detective. (See for example "The Boswell Detective Story" by Hamilton Basso in *Life* magazine, 4 December 1950, and "The Secret

The year of Mrs. Mounsey's death,[156] 1905, marks an important turning point in the history of the Boswell papers: until then the papers had lain undisturbed at Auchinleck, but they now became increasingly the focus of attention. In September 1905, the fifth Lord Talbot went to Auchinleck[157] and spent some time going through papers, some of which were packed up and sent to Ireland. Mr. Thomas Drysdale, who was for many years Land Steward at Auchinleck, said (in 1937) that he remembered hearing from other members of the staff that Lord Talbot spent a lot of time working amongst old boxes of papers in an attic room which had previously always been kept locked and he thought that a quantity of papers from this attic was packed up and sent to Ireland. Although Mr. Drysdale's information was obtained second-hand from other employees, he distinctly remembered seeing Lord Talbot coming down from the attic "as black as a miner."[158]

Whatever treasures Lord Talbot may have rescued from the dusty attic, the journals and probably many other papers were at this time housed in the ebony cabinet. Mr. Samuel Gurney, youngest son of Lord Talbot's second wife, Isabel, wrote in a biography of his mother published in 1935: "In a small room on the left [i.e., the morning room at Auchinleck] stood the famous ebony cabinet, containing the manuscript of an unpublished Diary of the Biographer."[159]

Lady Talbot quickly became interested in the journals and, early in 1907, she wrote to her brother-in-law, Henry Lee Warner, for advice as to their publication. Warner replied that the journals had never been published, so far as he knew, and suggested consulting his brother, Philip Lee Warner, who was a partner in the publishing house of Chatto & Windus. This firm, he thought, would offer terms and could

---

of the Ebony Cabinet" by Richard D. Altick from *The Scholar Adventurers*, 1950). Tinker certainly played a role of some importance (as to which see also the next chapter), but it was not that of literary detective. He had in fact several leads which he did not follow up. As to those who knew of the existence of Boswell papers at Malahide about this time, mention has already been made of Miss Elsie Mahaffy and the anonymous postcard writer. Others are named later in this chapter and in Chapter II.

[156]She died on 8 July 1905.

[157]Letter dated 15 August 1905 from Messrs. Howden & Molleson, C. A., Edinburgh, to Lord Talbot (copy in ILP). They state there is no objection to Lord Talbot's proposal to take up residence at Auchinleck at the beginning of September.

[158]Mr. Drysdale was interviewed on 16 November 1937 by the Edinburgh law firm of Steedman Ramage & Co., W. S. The above information comes from a memorandum of the meeting prepared by this firm (copy in ILP).

[159]Samuel Gurney: *Isabel, Mrs. Gurney, afterwards The Lady Talbot de Malahide, 1851–1932*, 1935, Norwich (Jarrold etc.), p. 140.

certainly give a good opinion.[160] Chatto & Windus were not in fact approached,[161] but plans for a possible publication remained under consideration.[162]

By 1908, most of the journals were at Malahide[163] and were seen there by Lord Talbot's younger brother, Colonel Milo Talbot:[164]

> During the Autumn of, I think, 1908 my brother with his family went on a trip to South America. At my brother's request, I stayed at Malahide to look after the Castle, and I amused myself by looking through the family papers. Boswell's Diary was the only Boswell paper that I touched and there were gaps in it. I suggested to my brother that it would be worth while to have it looked at with a view to publication.[165]

Lord Talbot took his brother's suggestion seriously and discussed the possibility of publication at length with his wife.[166] He was not a Boswell himself, which made him anxious not to do anything which might offend his late wife's family. Publication of an unexpurgated version seemed to him out of the question and he therefore arranged for a huge typescript to be prepared from which many passages were censored. This was sent to Sir John Murray, who wrote in reply:[167]

July 2 1911

Dear Lord Talbot de Malahide,
   I have read the Journals of James Boswell which you kindly submitted to me with much care, and, as is my usual practice in the case of important works, I have also in confidence consulted a personal friend of great literary experience so that two independent opinions may be formed.

[160]Letter dated Swaffham, 8 February 1907 (original in possession of Joyce, Lady Talbot de Malahide). Warner writes: "My own impression is that the diary is a discovery. . . . I suppose the value rather depends on whether the diary contains much new matter, not contained in the letters" (i.e., the Temple letters).

[161]Confirmed in a letter by Norah Smallwood of Chatto & Windus Limited dated 7 February 1968.

[162]See Gurney's book referred to above at p. 140: "Lord Talbot would often discuss with Isabel the question of publishing it" (i.e., the diary).

[163]The ebony cabinet, however, did not leave Auchinleck until about 1914. (See below p. 45.)

[164]Milo Talbot was a brilliant soldier, a colonel in the Royal Engineers. He married Eva, a daughter of Colonel John Joicey, M.P., and his son, also called Milo, succeeded to the peerage when the sixth Lord Talbot died on 22 August 1948 without issue. The seventh Lord Talbot died in 1973.

[165]Letter from Colonel Milo Talbot to Joyce, Lady Talbot, dated 19 June 1930 (TFP).

[166]See above p. 39, n. 159.

[167]A letter-press copy of this letter is still in the files of the late Sir John Murray, from which the present copy has been made.

THE FIFTH LORD TALBOT DE MALAHIDE (1846–1921)
and his first wife EMILY HARRIET née BOSWELL (d. 1898), a great-granddaughter of the Biographer.
From miniatures at Malahide.

COLONEL MILO TALBOT
From the portrait by William Carter.

SIR JOHN MURRAY, K.C.V.O.
From the portrait by A. Rivière.

Our opinions agree in almost every detail and I am sorry to say that the prevailing impression left upon both of us is one of disappointment, I had almost said of dismay, at finding how badly Boswell's character shows itself throughout. Macaulay, as you are no doubt aware, formed but a poor opinion of Boswell: "Those weaknesses which most men keep covered up in the most secret places of the mind, not to be disclosed to the eye of friendship or of love, were precisely the weaknesses which Boswell paraded before all the world. . . . He was not ashamed to exhibit himself to the world as a common spy, a common tattler, a humble companion without the excuse of poverty, and to tell a hundred stories of his own pertness and folly, and of the insults which his pertness and folly brought upon him." But Macaulay had not seen these journals: had he done so he would have added that he was an incurable sot and libertine: conscious of his own iniquities: sometimes palliating them as "Asiatic satisfactions quite consistent with devotion and with a fervent attachment to my valuable spouse": sometimes making resolutions of amendment which were not carried into effect, but always lapsing into the slough of drunkenness and debauchery and indolence.

The occasions on which he records that he was intoxicated, and even blind drunk are innumerable, and over and over again he notes that "he ranged the streets and followed whores" or words to that effect.

Many passages have been cut out, I presume on account of their immorality, but if they were worse than many which remain they must have been bad indeed.

He calls his Father "a little wretch," and his brother John "shockingly sulky" and "a man of gloomy horrid ill nature": he records "the abominable unfeeling ill nature" of Lady Auchinleck, who he says "talked with venom."

In writing thus it must not be supposed that I regard the journals as devoid of interest: far from this they contain excellent passages—chief among them being those which refer to Dr. Johnson, but these (so far as I have compared them) are reproduced word for word in the great biography. There are conversations with David Hume, Lord Thurlow and a few other notabilities, which are interesting but small in extent, but by far the larger part consists of trivialities; records of eating and drinking; bare facts and dates; and introspective reflections which rarely tend to raise one's estimate of the writer.

Macaulay wrote "There is not in all his books a single remark of his own on literature, politics, religion or society which is not either commonplace or absurd." This is unjust, but they rarely rise to the point of merit which attracts attention, or calls for permanent record.

If we eliminate the passages which have already been published: those which are unpublishable: and those which are too trivial for permanence, the residuum is I fear very small.

The books would be invaluable to anyone who was engaged in writing Bozzy's life, but if they were to be published as his authentic autobiography, the question would arise how far the editor would be justified in eliminating the true character of the man. If this were fully displayed he must inevitably fall very low in public estimation—altho' he writes of himself "I had faults but was upon the whole one of the best men that ever lived."

Boswell like Byron must ever live as the writer of some of the best English literature: his private life like Byron's is best left to oblivion. I make this comparison from some bitter experience. In my 13 volume Edition of Byron's works I asked the editors to deal almost exclusively with his writings and to leave aside the frailties of his private life. He was dead and it was impossible to pass fair judgment on a man who could not say a word in his own defence. Byron's own grandson, Lord Lovelace, frustrated this purpose by producing a scurrilous and garbled book to vilify his own grandfather. Infinite harm has been done thereby, altho' as time goes on the tide is turning more in favour of Byron and against his detractor.

I confess however that I should be sorry to play the Lord Lovelace to Bozzy: the more so as he would be damaged not merely by inference and innuendo as Byron was but by his own explicit confessions.

And so I am reluctantly driven to the conclusion that I cannot offer to publish this book, but I thank you none the less for having consulted me.

Believe me,
Yours very truly,
John Murray.

Sir John's letter shows how persistent was the influence of Macaulay. Although Hill and many others had exposed the unfairness of Macaulay's essay, it was still Macaulay who coloured the views of an experienced publisher such as Sir John. Lord Talbot, in submitting the journals for publication, was in fact ahead of his time. As a publisher, Sir John had to make his decision on commercial rather than on literary grounds, and from this point of view his decision was understandable. To expurgate the journals would have been to emasculate them and, in 1911, an uncut version would have been impossible.

After receiving Sir John's letter, Lord Talbot abandoned any further thought of publication. He was very conscious of his responsibilities to Boswell's descendants. Some years later, Lady Talbot wrote in a letter to her son, Samuel Gurney, who had again raised the possibility of publishing the journals:

> I will talk to Lord Talbot again about Boswell's Diary, but he is so sensitive about it that I hardly like to refer again to the subject. He thinks it is not fair on James or Boswell relations to see what horrors he wrote! We have now got Boswell's picture here, by Reynolds, and one of his wife. Also the two Raeburns which were at Auchinleck, and Boswell's famous ebony cabinet, mentioned in his will. We thought they would be much safer here, in case the place is let.

Lady Talbot's letter is dated 1 January 1915.[168] By then, the ebony cabinet stood at Malahide in a position of honour inside the front hall, containing the journals and probably many other papers besides. Plans for publication might have been abandoned, but the ebony cabinet was proudly pointed out to visitors, and no secret was made of the fact that it contained Boswell papers.[169] Selected portions were sometimes read to guests after dinner.[170] It is impossible to be certain as to the exact dates on which the papers were taken to Malahide. We do know that they went in several batches; and there was probably a final clearance from Auchinleck in 1917, the year when the remnants of the library and most of the furniture were put up for sale.

[168]Quoted by Gurney in his book, p. 140. (See above p. 39, n. 159.)
[169]Information from "The Boswell Papers" by Joyce, Lady Talbot de Malahide, a 19-page typed narrative in TFP.
[170]Information from the late seventh Lord Talbot.

# II

# *"Col. Isham came to tea"*[1]

ON the death of the fifth Lord Talbot in 1921, James Boswell Talbot succeeded to his father's estates and title. He was a reserved man, already in middle age, still unmarried, and with a strong dislike of publicity. During his father's lifetime, he had never handled the papers and, after his succession, he took little interest in them.[2] He was proud of his descent from the Biographer and did not seek to conceal the existence of Boswell manuscripts at Malahide; but he was still influenced by the views of Sir John Murray and would not have contemplated any publication of the journals without extensive expurgation. The papers therefore continued to lie undisturbed until September 1924, when he married Miss Joyce Gunning Kerr, daughter of Frederick W. Kerr, the distinguished actor.

The new Lady Talbot was a spirited young woman of great charm and intelligence, and she quickly became interested in the family papers. She realized not only that these were of exceptional literary and historical interest, but also that they were likely to be worth a considerable sum of money.[3] She believed that publication of the journals should be seriously reconsidered, and discussed the matter with her father, who was shown some of the manuscripts. He in turn talked to his

---

[1]Quotation from Lady Talbot's journal. See below p. 61.

[2]Letter, Lady Talbot to Pottle, 13 August 1950 (copy in TFP).

[3]The cost of running and maintaining Malahide was very heavy and the monetary value of the papers could not be disregarded (conversation between Lady Talbot and Mr. and Mrs. D. F. Hyde on 5 November 1961, recorded in the latter's private journal).

THE SIXTH LORD TALBOT DE
MALAHIDE (1874–1948). Great-great-
grandson of the Biographer.

JOYCE, LADY TALBOT DE MALAHIDE

MALAHIDE CASTLE

friends in the Garrick Club in London and rumours soon began to circulate that a mass of Boswell papers was lying at Malahide.[4]

In May 1925, the Talbots met Eveleigh Nash of the publishing house of Nash & Grayson to discuss the possibility of publishing the journals.[5] Nash arranged a dinner party to which he invited Lord Dunedin, an eminent Scottish judge, so that he might discuss the legal aspects of copyright.[6] In the end, according to Lady Talbot, Nash "decided, as did Sir John Murray, that the Diary was too improper for his firm to publish as it stood. He pointed out that deleted it was interesting only to scholars, but as it stood it could make a fortune through its indecent appeal. Neither he nor Lord Talbot wished to profit by that class of publication and the scholar's edition he said would be too costly."[7]

This was the second time in the space of fifteen years that the journals had been rejected by a leading publisher, and on both occasions the reasons were similar. The Talbots had hoped to be able to retain the ownership of the manuscripts and at the same time to profit from their publication. They were now told that this was not a practicable proposition—or not at any rate on terms to which they could agree. Even if they were to find a purchaser for the whole collection, there was no guarantee that the papers would not be exploited in just the way they wished to guard against. The asset which they owned was of considerable value, but ownership also brought with it certain responsibilities. These responsibilities they recognized and respected. They could easily have realized a quick profit by selling selected items at auction, but they were concerned that the integrity of the collection should be preserved and that ultimately the papers should be published in a manner which would do them justice. For the moment, therefore, they took no further action. A good many people already knew about the papers[8] and they did not have long to wait before they were approached again.

[4]"My father was shown the contents of the ebony cabinet. He was a member of the Garrick Club and in talking there of the papers he aroused interest." (Spingarn Letter.) Lady Talbot, speaking to Mr. and Mrs. D. F. Hyde on 5 November 1961, confirmed that her father talked freely about the papers and even read excerpts to his friends. Knowledge of the papers was considerable in London literary circles.

[5]"The Boswell Papers" by Lady Talbot (referred to above p. 45, n. 169).

[6]Letter, Nash to Lady Talbot, 4 June 1925.

[7]Spingarn Letter.

[8]Roger Ingpen, in the preface (dated April 1925) to his illustrated edition of the *Life*, published in 2 volumes by George Bayntun in 1925, writes (p. xviii): ". . . a large quantity of his [i.e. JB's] papers, including nearly all of the precious note-books used for his great biography, are said to

Tinker, as we have seen, did not follow up the clue provided by the letter from Malone to Euphemia Boswell, and his edition of the *Letters* (1924) shows that he thought the journals had perished.[9] The rumours which were circulating in 1925 reached the ears of A. E. Newton, who wrote to his fellow collector, R. B. Adam:[10]

> You know the story, perhaps we have discussed it, that the Boswell journals, the material he used in writing the *Life*, an immense mass was not destroyed but was stored in an attic in Auchinleck. When E. V. Lucas[11] was with us, I asked him if there was any truth in the rumor that this material had been discovered and that he was going to edit it, and he said "had there been any truth in the story I would have heard of it from him." I did not pursue the matter, and I did not realize until later that Lucas had not specifically answered my question as to the EXISTENCE of the material. Tinker got very excited, and I urged him to go to Dublin (the material was supposed to be in a castle somewhere outside of Dublin) and run the story down, taking with him every possible credential, and securing the material, if it existed, against all comers.

Tinker also received a report of the existence of Boswell papers at Malahide from Wilmarth S. Lewis.[12] He decided to follow Newton's advice and arranged an early trip to Ireland. He wrote to his friend, Dr. Charles M. Hathaway,[13] the American Consul-General in Dublin, for help and advice in obtaining a suitable introduction. Hathaway gave a small tea-party for Tinker to which he invited Archdeacon Lindsay, an old friend of Lord Talbot. The Archdeacon, himself a book-collector, confirmed that the papers had survived. He was sympathetic towards Tinker and used his good offices to obtain an invitation to tea from Lady Talbot. Tinker's reception at the castle was polite,

---

have been destroyed some years after his death. His *Diary*, though at present unpublished, has survived." The fact that Ingpen, whilst aware of the survival of the journals, did not apparently know that many other papers had also survived suggests that gossip and rumour at this time were centred on the journals.

[9]See above p. 38, n. 154.

[10]Letter, A. E. Newton to R. B. Adam, 13 July 1925 (Hyde Collection).

[11]E. V. Lucas was a member of the Garrick Club and knew Lord Talbot.

[12]According to Pottle, the report originated from Mr. John Drinkwater who told Mr. A. W. Evans who told Dr. Lewis.

[13]This information and the narrative which follows are based on the letter from Tinker to Alan G. Thomas cited above, p. 37, n. 151.

A. EDWARD NEWTON

CHAUNCEY B. TINKER

THE OAK ROOM AT MALAHIDE CASTLE
The ebony cabinet stands where it did at the time of Tinker's visit; it still stands
there today.

but he sensed a certain reserve on the part of Lady Talbot and his gift of a set of his edition of Boswell's letters was less well received than he had hoped. He gathered that the Talbots felt he should have consulted them before allowing so much of Boswell's private correspondence to be published for the first time.[14] Lady Talbot confirmed that there were documents in the castle including "two cases of papers from Auchinleck that had never been opened since their arrival in Ireland";[15] but Tinker's offer of editorial assistance was not accepted. He was permitted to see a few of the papers and some years later he described his feelings when he first glimpsed the contents of the ebony cabinet:

> I was led into an adjoining room, where I found myself standing in front of the famous "ebony cabinet"—a sort of highboy with many drawers. The drawers which I was permitted to pull open were crammed with papers in the wildest confusion. I felt like Sinbad in the valley of rubies. I glanced—panting the while—at a few sheets. One was a letter from Boswell to Alexander, then a schoolboy. At once I realized that a new day had dawned for Boswellians, and that for C. B. Tinker there was a dreadful crisis, the resolution of which would alter the whole of his future life. (I did not sleep that night).[16]

Tinker sent a cryptic postcard to Newton from Dublin: "Everything here and nothing to be touched. I have been on the rack." Newton wrote at once to Adam, remarking testily: "Why in hell's name could he not be more specific? If he meant to say, 'Entire mass of material is in existence and I cannot get at it,' why did he not say so?"[17] Tinker returned to London, dispirited by what he regarded as a futile trip.[18] But his efforts had not been entirely wasted, for he did revive the Talbots' interest in publication.[19] He also verified beyond doubt that a substantial part at least of Boswell's archives had survived at Malahide.

[14]Tinker *had* however informed Lord Talbot by letter of his intention of publishing Boswell letters and Lord Talbot had raised no objection.

[15]Letter, Tinker to R. B. Adam, 9 November 1925 (Hyde Collection). As to these two unopened cases, see below, p. 241, n. 16.

[16]Tinker's letter to Alan G. Thomas, cited above.

[17]Postcard, dated Dublin, 6 July 1925, quoted by Newton to Adam in his letter of 13 July 1925, cited above.

[18]Letter to me from Mr. W. H. Haslam, 24 June 1963. Mr. Haslam writes that Tinker called at his house in Hanover Terrace, Regents Park, "frustrated by a futile visit to Malahide."

[19]"The Boswell Papers" by Lady Talbot (referred to above, p. 45, n. 169).

He was *the* acknowledged expert and he had actually seen and handled some of the papers. Rumour was converted to fact.

In his letter to Adam, Newton had commented: "If Tinker fails, others may succeed. I'll bet a hat someone works this invaluable mine." The news spread, and one person who heard it was the redoubtable Dr. A. S. W. Rosenbach, doyen of American rare-book dealers. Rosenbach's reaction was swift. He was in no doubt as to the importance of the Boswell papers and cabled an immediate offer of £50,000[20] for the whole collection, sight unseen. His unsubtle tactics misfired. Lady Talbot wrote back on 27 August 1925: "We regret that such Boswell papers as are in our possession are not for sale, nor can they be seen by anyone. Lord Talbot was very surprised and annoyed at the matter being opened by telegram."[21] Lady Talbot has since explained why she and her husband were so upset. Telegrams had to pass through the local post office, which might have led to gossip in the village and consequent publicity distasteful to a man so reserved as Lord Talbot.[22] But even if Rosenbach had sent a letter instead of a telegram, it is unlikely that he would have been more successful.[23] It would have helped if he had taken the trouble to get a proper introduction and to observe some of the social amenities before coming so directly to the point, but the problem was not simply one of etiquette. What mattered was to appraise the situation accurately before making *any* proposal: to grasp how Lord and Lady Talbot *felt* about the papers and what sort of arrangements they might agree to. Whoever was to succeed at Malahide would need patience, perception, and skilled strategy.

Newton also spoke of the papers to his friend Lt.-Col. Ralph Heyward Isham, who, like himself, was an enthusiastic Johnsonian collector. He met Isham by chance during a transatlantic voyage on board the *Majestic,* and tried to persuade him to go to Malahide.[24] Isham's imagination was immediately fired by the prospect of recovering such a rich haul and making it available to the world. His character and background

---

[20]The cable itself is missing, but the amount is confirmed in a letter of 21 March 1942 from Lady Talbot to Isham (copy in TFP).

[21]Letter in files of the Philip H. and A. S. W. Rosenbach Foundation.

[22]Confirmed to me by Lady Talbot (July 1971).

[23]In her files, Lady Talbot has a letter from Rosenbach from the Carlton Hotel, London, dated 29 August [1925] apologizing for the offence given by his telegram and stressing that he would always be interested in the papers if the Talbots should ever consider selling.

[24]Told to me by Mrs. Persifor Frazer of Newport, who in 1925 was Isham's second wife and who accompanied him on the voyage.

made him uniquely fitted for the task. Born in New York in 1890, the son of Henry Heyward and Juliet Calhoun Isham, he was descended through his father from Jonathan Trumbull, Colonial Governor of Connecticut. He attended Cornell and Yale universities and it was at Yale that his interest in Boswell was first aroused:

> I began studying Boswell at Yale and my interest became keen because Boswell made me feel one of the party, as it were. His characters seemed to live for me and I decided then that I wanted to get closer to them, so I started to collect their works. That's when I started on the "downward" path.[25]

In 1915, before America entered the First World War, he enlisted in the British army as a private soldier. He was later commissioned second lieutenant in the Royal Engineers and served on the staffs of Field Marshals Robertson and Lord Haig. After the armistice, as a lieutenant-colonel, he performed valuable service in restoring morale amongst disaffected troops, in recognition of which he was made a Commander of the British Empire.

After the war, he returned to a business career in America.[26] He also started collecting rare books and manuscripts with a special interest in Boswell and Johnson. In 1925, he was thirty-five years old and, despite his American birth, his bearing and manner of speech were British. He had a wide circle of British friends, many of them persons of distinction and influence. In the negotiations he now planned, it was important to know the right sort of people and to speak with the right sort of accent. His strikingly handsome physical appearance was combined with great charm of manner and formidable powers of persuasion. Newton described him as "a fascinating devil."[27] He could and occasionally did act outrageously, but the persons offended seldom harboured resentment for long; and his behaviour in these cases was dictated not so much by selfish motives as by financial necessity, the demands of literary scholarship, or, occasionally, by an explosion of his own volatile temperament. He was a man who loved good company and good living, and his wit and skill as a *raconteur* made

[25]Reported in the *Cape and Islands Sunday Standard-Times*, 2 September 1951 (New Bedford, Massachusetts). Clipping in IFP.

[26]He became president of Trumbull Securities Corporation, and later was involved in various other business ventures.

[27]Letter, Newton to Adam, 23 July 1926 (Hyde Collection).

LIEUT.-COLONEL RALPH HEYWARD ISHAM

him widely sought after. "Rafe Isham," wrote his friend Christopher Morley, "is one of the most entertaining narrators that ever lived; one of the few men I have ever known who could have given Dr. Johnson tit for tat in dialogue, though he would have been too courteous to do so."[28] He was adept at handling people and had the ability to communicate something of his own enthusiasm and vitality to others. He knew when and how to take swift and effective action, but he also understood the value of patience and tactical delay, and that sometimes an indirect approach might be more successful than a direct one.

Lady Talbot has said that Isham gave her the impression he was a millionaire.[29] He was in fact a man of considerable wealth, but much of the capital from which he derived his income was locked up in a family settlement and could not be touched. In relation to the prize which he hoped to win, his resources were meagre enough. It is not surprising, though, that Lady Talbot formed the impression she did, for Isham always thought and acted in the grand manner. Perhaps this explains why he was immediately attracted to the Boswell papers. To recover them in their entirety and to present them to the world in impeccable form would be one of the greatest literary coups of all time. Yet even Isham might have hesitated if he had been able to foresee that to achieve this goal would take him most of the rest of his life, and involve him in a series of surprises, set-backs, and financial pressures which would consume his personal fortune and all but shatter his resolve to continue. Later, he used to remark wryly that when he first interested himself in the Boswell papers he had grasped a bear by the tail and couldn't let go.[30]

Isham knew better than to make the same mistake as Rosenbach. Preliminary reconnaissance and patient negotiation were essential before making any direct proposition. At the same time, he could not afford any delay for fear of possible competitors. He was convinced that his first step must be to obtain a suitable introduction to Malahide, and in February 1926 he sent a cable to his friend Major Nesbitt in London, asking if he knew Lord Talbot and, if so, whether he would approach him about the Boswell papers.[31] He promised "will

---

[28]From The Library Associates of Haverford College Bulletin, No. 21, 23 November 1948.

[29]Spingarn Letter.

[30]A favourite remark of Isham's confirmed by his son, Heyward.

[31]There is an undated draft of the cable scribbled in Isham's hand on a page of New York hotel notepaper (in IFP). It is only by Nesbitt's return cable that we know he was the addressee and can fix the date. According to Mrs. Persifor Frazer, Major Nesbitt was an army friend of Isham's.

dance at your wedding if you can help." He also warned "American
dealer sailing today on chance purchasing manuscripts but does not
know Malahide." The identity of the American dealer remains uncertain. There must have been one, for Isham refers to him again, but
whoever he was, he never got so far as Malahide.[32]

Unfortunately, Major Nesbitt was unable to help. He did not know
Lord Talbot himself and on 6 March he cabled Isham to say he had
been unable to find anyone else who did. As he was leaving London
that day, there was little more he could do.[33] Isham remained positive
that the right approach to Malahide was through someone who knew
the Talbots and, the same day, he sent this cable to his London solicitors,
Messrs. Denton Hall & Burgin:

> Lord Talbot de Malahide of Malahide Castle, Dublin, inherited
> large quantity manuscripts of James Boswell all or part of which
> am extremely anxious acquire for my collection. Can you find
> anyone suitable approach him to request first refusal for me at
> his own valuation if he decides to sell. One American dealer
> offended him by cabling direct another is on way to see him.
> Speed is most important. If you cannot find person known to
> Talbot proceed see him yourself fortified with all possible creden-
> tials. From information judge value approximately twenty
> thousand pounds. Will give you one thousand pounds bonus if
> you can arrange my purchase of manuscripts otherwise charge
> me expenses and fees. Cable your plans.
>
> Isham[34]

Mr. Harold Burgin, a partner in the firm, crossed to Dublin on 9
March 1926[35] and arranged an early meeting with the Talbots through
their solicitors.[36] On 11 March, Burgin cabled Isham to report on his
"very lengthy and valuable interview" the day before with Lord and

---

[32]Mr. Michael Papantonio, of the Seven Gables Bookshop, New York, is confident that the
dealer was E. Byrne Hackett of the Brick Row Bookshop, New York. He mentions that Isham and
Hackett were very friendly at the time (letter from Papantonio to Mrs. Donald F. Hyde, 29
January 1969). However, there is evidence that Hackett sailed or planned to sail for Dublin in
both January and December 1927 (see below p. 78, n. 112). He may have made more than one
trip or he may have postponed his sailing on more than one occasion. Lady Talbot tells us that
he never got so far as Malahide.

[33]Cable, Nesbitt to Isham, 6 March 1926 (IFP).

[34]Copy in IFP.

[35]Cable, Burgin to Isham, 9 March 1926 (IFP).

[36]Cable, Burgin to Isham, 10 March 1926 (IFP). The meeting took place on 11 March 1926.

Lady Talbot and their solicitor, Mr. A. J. Robinson.[37] He had received a verbal assurance that Isham would be given "equal right of purchase with anyone else" of any manuscripts which might be sold, including possibly the journals after publication.[38] He warned that some time might elapse before a sale, but was convinced that he had induced the Talbots to sell sooner or later. Perhaps the most valuable thing which he achieved was a definite assurance that no one else would be interviewed or communicated with in the meantime. The so-called "equal right of purchase with anyone else" did not amount to much and presumably meant that if and when the Talbots decided to sell, Isham would be notified and given the opportunity to make an offer along with anyone else who was interested. The significant point was that the Talbots had no immediate inclination to sell, although they still contemplated publishing the journals.

Isham was far from satisfied, despite Burgin's enthusiasm. Too many points were left vague. What were the rights which Burgin was supposed to have secured for him? How long would it be before the Talbots would consider a sale? What plans, if any, did they have for publishing the journals?[39] The time had clearly come for him to visit Malahide personally and he realized his approach would have to be carefully planned. He must present himself, not as a prospective buyer, but rather as an enthusiast who only wished to see and admire the treasures contained in the ebony cabinet. Burgin was instructed to write to Lord Talbot to ask if Isham might call. Lord Talbot's reply of 30 May 1926 was not encouraging:

The position is still the same as when we saw you in Dublin. I do not wish to sell any Boswell Papers and I shall frankly be too busy to be able to show Colonel Isham any of them as they have recently been moved and are now somewhat difficult to get at.[40] We have in the house one or two specimen papers, such as the one I showed you, which I should be very pleased to show him, but there are only one or two of these. I must also point out that if Colonel Isham came over it would have to be entirely of his own wish and the position will remain unchanged; that

[37]Cable, Burgin to Isham, 11 March 1926 (IFP).

[38]This indicated that the Talbots were at this time still thinking of arranging publication of the journals themselves and *then* selling the manuscripts.

[39]Isham cabled back to Burgin immediately asking for clarification of these points (copy of cable in IFP).

[40]This presumably refers to the deposit of papers in the bank as a security measure following receipt of Rosenbach's cable.

if the Boswell Papers are to be sold, we will advise Colonel Isham and give him as good a chance as anyone to buy them.[41]

Lord Talbot agreed that Isham might call after 10 June if he wished, but felt it would hardly be worth his trouble.

Isham now went to Newton, and suggested that they should join forces on a fifty-fifty basis. Newton declined. Amongst Isham's papers is a brief note from Newton which reads: "Dear Ralph, For me to go to Ireland would be as mad as for you not to. Greetings. A.E.N."[42] Shortly afterwards, Newton told his friend R. B. Adam about Isham's offer: "Ralph Isham, who has London assurance and knows his Johnson and Boswell well, cooked up a plan by which he and I were to buy it [i.e., Boswell material at Malahide], or a part of it. I confess that it was very plausible, and three weeks ago, when I saw him in New York, he suggested that he and I sail the day following and attempt to secure at least a part of the collection. His plan had been carefully matured. I was staggered. . . . I told him I would let him know, and upon returning to my hotel, wrote him that it would be as mad for me to go as for him not to."[43] According to Newton, Isham made a similar proposition to Rosenbach, who also refused.[44]

Isham was on his own, but he had the courage and determination to go ahead, despite his limited financial resources, and despite the unpromising nature of Lord Talbot's letter. He wrote to Malahide direct for the first time, explaining that he desired to see Lord Talbot in no sense to persuade him to sell the manuscripts. He added, characteristically: "I should gladly go much farther than Dublin to see even one letter of James Boswell. Perhaps in this I have something akin to the religious fervour that moves the pilgrims to get out on their journeys to Mecca!"[45]

A visit to Malahide was fixed for Tuesday, 15 June,[46] and Isham set sail from New York. To fortify his credentials, he arranged for a letter of recommendation from Lord Ivor Spencer-Churchill to precede his arrival.[47] He tells us: "The journey seemed interminable, the most nerve-racking part being the hours I spent in Dublin, awaiting

[41]Letter, Lord Talbot to Burgin, 30 May 1926 (copy in TFP).

[42]Letter (undated) in IFP. The note-paper is that of The Plaza, New York.

[43]Letter, Newton to Adam, 24 June 1926 (Hyde Collection).

[44]Letter, Newton to Adam, 9 November 1927 (Hyde Collection).

[45]Letter, Isham to Lord Talbot, 7 June 1926 (TFP).

[46]Letter, Lord Talbot to Isham, 10 June 1926 (copy in TFP), agreeing to see him on "Tuesday, June 14th." In 1926, 14 June fell on a Monday. The actual date of the visit was Tuesday 15 June, confirmed by the entry in Lady Talbot's diary (see below).

[47]Letter, Lord Ivor Spencer-Churchill to Lord Talbot, 11 June 1926 (TFP).

the time appointed for the short motor trip to Malahide."[48] Lady Talbot's diary for 15 June reads simply: "Col. Isham came to tea"[49]—a brief enough entry for a meeting more significant for Boswellian literature, perhaps, than any since the famous first meeting between Boswell and Johnson. Unfortunately, we have no detailed account of how Isham handled his visit, but his subsequent correspondence with Lady Talbot gives us an idea of what took place. He must have used his charm and powers of persuasion to the full; and he was quick to realize that Lady Talbot was already partly on his side. If he could only reach agreement with her, she might in turn be able to persuade Lord Talbot. Lord Talbot was not prepared to sell the journals at this stage, nor was he particularly interested in selling anything else; he would have been content simply to leave the papers lying as they were, although he was not averse to publication of the journals under proper control. The main obstacle to any sale was the Talbots' fear that commercial exploitation of the wrong sort might follow. Lady Talbot was fascinated by the papers and believed that the journals should be published; but although Lord Talbot was glad to leave her to deal with all practical details concerning the papers, she was not willing to act in any way which might meet with his disapproval. From then on, Isham conducted his correspondence and other negotiations with Lady Talbot and she in her turn sought to win over her husband. Sufficient acknowledgement has not been made of the vitally important role which Lady Talbot played in this connection: without her tact and diplomacy, Isham could not have hoped to succeed.[50]

Soon after Isham, another visitor called at Malahide. This was S. C. Roberts (later Sir Sydney C. Roberts), who in 1926 was already an established Johnsonian and Secretary of the Cambridge University Press. Roberts published an account of his visit in which he erroneously claimed to have *preceded* Isham at Malahide.[51] He later confirmed[52] that the actual date of his visit was 22 June 1926 (exactly a week after Isham's), and provided the following revised account:[53]

[48]Isham's account for B.B.C. broadcast on 12 August 1951 (copy typescript in IFP).

[49]Diary of Lady Talbot, shown to me in November 1967.

[50]In a letter of 15 April 1930 (copy in TFP), Lady Talbot wrote to him: "You, and only you, are in a position to know that publication [i.e., of the Boswell papers] could not have been without my efforts."

[51]*Doctor Johnson and Others* by S. C. Roberts, Cambridge University Press, 1958, chapter entitled "Pepys and Boswell."

[52]Letter to Mrs. D. F. Hyde, 16 March 1966.

[53]Sent to Mrs. Hyde with the above letter. Roberts also published a similar corrected account of the incident in his book *Adventures with Authors* (1966).

I had been deeply interested in Tinker's *Young Boswell* (1922) and in his edition of Boswell's *Letters* (1924). In 1925 I met Tinker in Yale, but it was not until the following year that rumours about the Malahide treasure reached me and it was from M. R. James, Provost of Eton, whom I had known well as Provost of King's, that I heard them. Accordingly I asked my sister-in-law, then living in Dublin, whether she could put me up for a few nights in June. She agreed and I was with her from 20 to 23 June. Monty James kindly gave me an introduction to J. H. Bernard, Provost of Trinity College, with whom I had lunch on, I think, 21 June. He, in his turn, introduced me to the Rector of Malahide[54] and after lunch on 22 June, the Rector escorted me to the castle and presented me to Lord Talbot.

I was courteously received; Lady Talbot, I was told, was not very well but on a refectory table I was shown a considerable number of Boswelliana. What I particularly noted was Goldsmith's reply to Boswell's letter of congratulation on the production of *She Stoops to Conquer,* but I made no attempt at compiling a list. I was simply on a personal voyage of discovery. At the back of my mind was the bare possibility of making some arrangement to publish the Boswell papers at Cambridge, but I had no definite proposal to make. I did however emphasise that I should be deeply interested in helping to edit or publish the papers, if it were decided to make them known to the world.

Roberts was certainly excited by what he saw. The moment he got home, he dashed off a letter to Lord Talbot repeating the offer of his services as editor and publisher.[55] He also offered to introduce certain collectors who might be interested in purchasing any papers which were for sale. He suggested that publication might be arranged on the basis of a royalty payment, and he advised that publication would not destroy the sale value of the original manuscripts.[56] Roberts was a serious contender for the papers and his British nationality and

[54]Roberts must mean Archdeacon Lindsay (who also introduced Tinker). In a letter of 4 August 1926, Lady Talbot wrote to Isham that Roberts "was brought here by the then Archdeacon of Dublin, a very old friend of my husband's, and has become one of many people most anxious to manage the collection for us!!!!!" (Letter in IFP.)

[55]Letter, Roberts to Lord Talbot, 25 June 1926 (TFP).

[56]The validity of this advice may be questioned, but it is worth noting that in a letter to Lady Talbot dated 12 July 1926, Eveleigh Nash advised "that the value of good letters is generally enhanced after publication." He strongly recommended that Lord Talbot should sell the whole original manuscript only after it had been published, and that publication rights should be reserved in making any sale (letter in TFP).

Dr. A. S. W. ROSENBACH

SIR SYDNEY C. ROBERTS

63

scholarly reputation gave him certain advantages over Isham. The fact that he was never really in the running says much for the force of Isham's personality, and emphasizes the strength of Lady Talbot's tacit commitment to him.

At Malahide, Isham had been shown, amongst other things, the same Goldsmith letter which later attracted Roberts's attention. He had felt sure enough of his ground to offer the Talbots £120[57] for it, and to express keen interest in buying any other items which they might be prepared to sell. Most of the papers were lying in the bank (where they had been transferred for safe custody after Rosenbach's cable) and even the Talbots did not know exactly what they comprised. Lady Talbot promised that she would consider Isham's offer seriously and would go through the miscellaneous papers as soon as she had time. She was also sufficiently impressed with his literary *savoir faire* to ask his advice about the problem of publishing the journals.[58] Isham wrote with detailed suggestions a week or two later and it is worth quoting his letter at length because it shows how exactly he judged the situation and contrived to produce a formula aimed at allaying Lord Talbot's misgivings, whilst at the same time leaving the way open to achieve his chief object, which was to acquire the journals:

I have given much thought to your question about ways and means of publishing the Diary. I agree entirely with you that it should be published. But the work of preparing it for the press—of arranging each thing in proper order and with proper references—is so huge and laborious that I know it would seriously tax your strength and your patience. On the other hand I sympathise with your desire to suppress certain passages. With all these considerations in mind I have thought that the best solution of the problems was this; provided of course you are willing to dispose of the Diary you would sell it to someone of substantial means and honour and you would make the purchase consideration consist of three things—first, the amount of money involved; second, a signed undertaking to publish the Diary; third, an undertaking to submit to you a copy of what it was proposed to publish and to allow only that which met your approval to be used. Your

[57]The amount is confirmed in the Spingarn Letter.
[58]See letter from Isham quoted below. Also "History of Papers," a 3-page typed document by Lady Talbot (in TFP): "Lord Talbot, subsequently to his talk with Mr. Nash, had begun to realise how intricate and costly such a publication would be. He had decided not to attempt it himself, and he was impressed with Colonel Isham's qualifications for doing so."

Solicitors could easily prepare a document embodying these princi-
ples, which would safeguard you and would have the effect of
nullifying the sale with the loss to the buyer of the money paid
in case the undertakings were not carried out. I need hardly
say that I would myself be glad to purchase the Diary on this
basis although I am appalled at the work involved. You asked
my opinion of the value of the Diary and I said I thought it
about £2,000. On thinking it over I have come to the opinion
that it is worth four or five thousand.[59]

It is interesting to notice Isham's very low valuation. He must
have known that the journals were worth much more than £5,000,
just as the Goldsmith letter was worth more than £120. He undoubtedly tried to buy the Boswell papers as cheaply as possible, but who
can blame him? As a collector of limited means, he had little option,
and Lady Talbot was well able to look after herself. One of the first
things she did after Isham's visit was to obtain independent expert
advice. In July, she and Lord Talbot went to London taking with
them the Goldsmith letter and several others.[60] Eveleigh Nash was
consulted and he strongly advised her to hold on to all the letters
until they had been published and then to send them for auction
at Sotheby's.[61] At the end of the month, she wrote to Isham in these
terms:[62]

We have been over to London for a few days and took some
of the letters with us meaning to get a valuation. There was not
time however to leave them for a proper written valuation, as
they would have kept them some days. We were very strongly
advised however to sell by auction. . . . In 1911 a very inferior
letter from Goldsmith fetched £265, which since that was at a
time when there was "little demand for him" to quote the valuers,
and his letters are now greatly sought after, leads us to the supposition that this letter is worth at least £400. . . . I mention all this,
since now that there is the question of an auction, you might
care to make a quick offer for this letter, and we shall take no
steps about it until we hear from you. But I do not think Lord
Talbot will sell this letter privately for less than £400. It seems
a great deal, but one cannot get away from its great superiority

[59]Letter, Isham to Lady Talbot, 5 July 1926 (TFP).
[60]Letter, Lady Talbot to Isham, 27 July 1926, quoted below (IFP).
[61]Letter, Nash to Lady Talbot, 12 July 1926 (TFP).
[62]Letter of 27 July 1926, referred to above.

over the £265 letter. Apparently he is of especial value, and
this letter really is a gem!

The Chatham correspondence[63] also seems to be of great
value, tho' no precedent was mentioned, or in fact exists I suppose,
to give us any idea of a price. When we see this firm again to
arrange an auction of some of our papers (mostly earlier ones)
we will also get a valuation of some of Boswell's own letters and
in most cases I expect my husband will be willing to sell them
privately to you, if you wish, at the valuation put upon them.
But in the cases of the Goldsmith and Chatham letters, unless
a very substantial private offer came along, it seems that we may
lose heavily by not putting them up to auction, since their value
is, as it were, a fancy one and they are more than likely to go
for an immense sum of money.

Regarding the diary. We thank you very much for all your
kind offers of help and your suggestions. We will remember your
willingness to buy it, and to publish it subject to our approval.
For the time being however we cannot take any steps about it.

*If* you care to buy the Goldsmith letter, I can get it taken
out to New York to you I think.

I hope you are "quite recovered of" your cold, as Boswell
would put it.

Isham *did* care to buy the Goldsmith letter and despatched his
cheque at once.[64] By early September, the letter was in his hands.[65]
He had every reason to feel pleased. He had succeeded in buying
one important item from Boswell's archives and there was an excellent
chance that more would soon come his way. Most exciting of all, his
proposals about the journals had been well received. It was now a
question of time and patient negotiation.

Letters from Lady Talbot throughout the late summer and autumn
continued to be friendly and encouraging. On 21 August, she wrote:[66]

I am so glad the letter has gone to you. It will encourage my
husband to give more attention to the papers. So far he has not
done very much about them. But I like to go into them, and
they should be placed where they will be appreciated! ... We

[63]Letters from William Pitt, 1st Earl of Chatham, to JB, Nos. 502 and 503 of *Malahide
Catalogue.*
[64]Letter, Isham to Lady Talbot, 9 August 1926 (TFP).
[65]Letter, Isham to Lady Talbot, 3 September 1926 (TFP).
[66]Letter, Lady Talbot to Isham, 21 August 1926 (copy in TFP).

shall be doing some work on all the papers this Autumn and I will write to you when we have any finds that may interest you. We bear in mind your suggestions about the Diary. For the moment we are *very* busy with house parties!

Lady Talbot was as good as her word and, before leaving Ireland in late November to winter in the south of France, she went through all the papers and separated the letters from the remainder. She did not find time to read each one thoroughly or to make a complete list with details as she had intended, but she came to the conclusion that the letters formed "an uncommonly nice collection" which if published would sell.[67] On 30 November, she wrote to Isham from Menton reporting on her progress and said: "Lord Talbot is very undecided whether to sell all, some or none!"[68] She was clear that all the letters should be published together, but she and her husband were not keen to part with Boswell's love-letters to his wife. She suggested tentatively that if Isham were to acquire the whole collection other than the love-letters, he might be allowed to publish these too, although the manuscripts would not be his property. She gave a very brief and rough description of what the letters comprised, and said:[69]

If you feel inclined to make an offer on such slender information, it would probably hurry things up! ... My valuation [ £10,000 ] is entirely my own and this letter must not be taken as saying that Lord Talbot would accept that sum. If however you did offer it, it would as I said hurry matters because we could soon let you have an answer. ... However you may prefer to wait until you can see the letters, but it lets in other people. So many seem to be after them! We shall be back in Ireland in February; perhaps you will let us have a line to Menton in the meantime.

Lady Talbot was acting largely on her own initiative and hoped that a substantial cash offer from Isham might spur her husband into a definite decision. She also showed that Isham was not the only one who understood the psychology of bargaining! Isham was now placed in the difficult position of having to make an offer blind. He had only the briefest information about the letters and, exciting though

[67]Letter of 30 November 1926, referred to below.
[68]Letter, Lady Talbot to Isham, 30 November 1926 (copy in TFP).
[69]Ibid.

they sounded, his prime object was to buy the journals. He wrote back offering the suggested figure of £10,000, but to include not only the letters (other than the love-letters), but also the journals and any other papers. He stressed that if the journals were published he would respect Lord Talbot's wishes as to censorship.[70] Some two months elapsed before Lady Talbot replied to say that Lord Talbot would not entertain the idea of including the journal, and she added, discouragingly: "It will be some years before that can be dealt with." She explained that in arriving at her valuation she was taking into account profits from "side shows" such as publication in American newspapers.[71] She promised to go through the letters properly and to make a detailed list. Her progress was slow and by mid-July 1927 she had listed only about a quarter of the total number.[72] She borrowed Maggs catalogues from her friend, the Archdeacon, and from these she placed a rough value on each item as she went along.[73] On 18 July, she wrote to Isham to say that her valuation already exceeded £5,000 and there was little chance of Lord Talbot accepting less than £10,000 for the whole collection of letters. She suggested that if Isham were interested, he should come to spend a week-end at Malahide to discuss the matter.[74]

This was the opportunity Isham had been hoping for and, on Friday 19 August, he arrived at Malahide for the second time. For three days, Lady Talbot and he spent almost every available moment working their way through the mass of letters and other miscellaneous papers, agreeing on a value for each item as they went along.[75] A hand-written list still in the possession of Lady Talbot shows that they reached a total figure of £13,585.[76] Even without the journals, the

[70]Letter, Isham to Lady Talbot, 17 December 1926 (TFP).

[71]Letter, Lady Talbot to Isham, 14 February 1927 (copy in TFP).

[72]Letter, Lady Talbot to Isham, 18 July 1927 (copy in TFP).

[73]Spingarn Letter.

[74]Letter, Lady Talbot to Isham, 18 July 1927 (copy in TFP).

[75]The entries from Lady Talbot's diary are: "Friday 19 August 1927: I. arrived—went through letters all day. Saturday 20 August 1927: Worked at letters all day except for a drive to Howth. Sunday 21 August: Church. I. left in the evening." In a letter to F. A. Pottle dated 17 May 1958 (copy in TFP), Lady Talbot refers to her "three days close work" with Isham.

[76]The list indicated *inter alia* a price of £1,200 for the MS. of the *Account of Corsica*, £450 for the fragment of the MS. of the *Life*, £400 for JB's account of his meeting with Mrs. Rudd, £2,000 for Themes in French (see *Malahide Catalogue*, No. 274), and £4,265 for what is described as "Catalogued Bundle." This bundle was inventoried in a separate 18-page typed list of letters (now in IFP) prepared by Lady Talbot with a price marked by her against each item. Almost every price has been scored out and a lower figure substituted resulting in a total for the "Catalogued Bundle"

richness of the material was remarkable. There were about 150 letters (or copies or drafts of letters) by Boswell; more than 200 letters to Boswell and others from various correspondents, including Edmund Burke, Robert Burns, Chatham, Goldsmith, Johnson, Rousseau, Sir Walter Scott, Voltaire, and Horace Walpole; almost the whole of a holograph manuscript of *An Account of Corsica,* apparently a fair copy of Boswell's draft with corrections and additions; 16 leaves of the manuscript of the *Life* with a 4-leaf paper apart; Boswell's account of his interview with the dying David Hume; and a wealth of other material. The most serious gap was the bulk of the manuscript of the *Life,* which was thought to have "perished to powder."[77]

The purchase was completed and, when Isham returned to London, he took with him the entire collection of Boswell papers then known to exist at Malahide, with the exception only of the journals. He was also offered a present of one of Lady Talbot's Irish wolfhounds, a breed in which he developed a sudden interest after discovering Lady Talbot's own enthusiasm![78] The sale of the papers was evidenced by a document drawn up by Isham and signed by Lord Talbot which was later to become of some importance:

---

of £4,265, as against Lady Talbot's original total of over £10,000. The reduced prices suggest some hard bargaining by Isham. The highest price for an individual letter is £600 for JB's remarkable letter to Temple telling of his meeting with Voltaire (*Malahide Catalogue,* No. 129). The only item on the detailed list which is not a letter is the account of JB's interview with David Hume, priced at £150 (*Malahide Catalogue,* No. 288).

[77]In a letter to *The Times* (published 17 September 1927), Geoffrey Scott, after a brief look through the papers, wrote: "While it would be premature to give any list before the papers have received closer and more particular study, I may say at least they surpassed all expectations and satisfied nearly every hope. Unfortunately the great bulk of the Boswell manuscript was found by Lord Talbot to have perished to powder. This appears to have been the manuscript of the life of Johnston [sic], of which only about 30 pages survived the effects of damp. But this disappointment is compensated by the richness of variety of the new material, comprising, for example, a poem by Goldsmith and an intensely vivid description of Voltaire written by Boswell when he was his guest at Ferney. Rousseau, Pitt, Burns—almost every handwriting that could be wished is represented. Considerable light is thrown on Boswell's methods of work. With the exception already named, the papers are in perfect preservation." For full details of Isham's purchase from Malahide, see *Malahide Catalogue.* As to the manuscript of the *Life,* see below Appendix III, pp. 330–33.

It was during this visit that Lady Talbot, according to Isham, threw into the fire 6 leaves from JB's journal notes containing an account of his amour with Rousseau's mistress, Thérèse Le Vasseur. The publicity and controversy attaching to this incident has been such that it is fully considered below in Appendix IV, p. 334 *et seq.*

[78]Letter, Lady Talbot to Isham, 9 September 1927 (copy in TFP).

August 21st 1927
Malahide Castle, Co. Dublin.
For a price agreed upon, receipt whereof is hereby acknowledged,
I have this day sold and delivered to Lt Col. Ralph Isham the
collection of papers, manuscripts and letters, by, or belonging
to James Boswell, inherited by me as his great-great-grandson
and otherwise. For value recieved [*sic*] I likewise sell and assign
to the said Lt Col. Ralph H. Isham whatever rights of Publication
of said papers and Manuscripts that are vested in me.
Talbot de Malahide[79]

Isham again raised the question of the journals, and with such
success that Lady Talbot agreed to go through them a section at a
time as soon as she could; and then, if Isham wished to acquire them
and terms could be agreed, she promised to try to persuade her husband
to let her send them to him in batches until he had the whole.[80] It
was arranged that she would make a start with the Ashbourne journal,
most of which had already been printed in the *Life* and which Lord
Talbot might therefore be more willing to sell. She insisted, however,
that no part of the journals could be delivered to Isham until it had
been effectively censored and that her husband would never agree
to a sale unless this were done.

On arrival at London with the papers, Isham immediately began
to consider plans for their publication. In this, as in everything else,
he thought on a grand scale and he conceived the idea of a magnificent
private edition, financed by himself, edited by a distinguished scholar,
and impeccable as to design and typography. At first, he thought he
had the editor in Tinker. Tinker was the obvious choice and, quite
by chance, Isham encountered him in a London bookshop. He invited
him to see the papers in his room at Claridge's. There, after a day-long
session during which the wealth of material was laid before the bemused
Tinker, he shocked Isham by declining the editorship. The atmosphere
was highly charged as the pair made their way to the hotel lift, accompanied by Mrs. Isham. Together they descended to the crowded lobby
and, as the lift doors opened, Tinker raised his fist and exclaimed
in ringing tones, quite heedless of the consternation he was causing:
"You have stolen my mistress!"[81]

[79]Copies of this document in both IFP and TFP.
[80]Letter, Lady Talbot to Isham, 19 November 1927 (copy in TFP).
[81]Told to me by Mrs. Persifor Frazer (then Mrs. Isham), who witnessed the incident, and confirmed by Isham's son, Heyward. Mrs. D. F. Hyde also tells me that she heard the story both from

Tinker's decision is perhaps more easily understood if we bear in mind the intense disappointment he had suffered over the Malahide papers. His edition of the *Letters* was already hopelessly incomplete and his visit to Malahide had only served to frustrate him. His main reason for refusing was not the excuse of poor eyesight given to Isham,[82] but, as he himself explained some years later to his friend Alan G. Thomas:

It was an amazing experience for a scholar to go through. In my case it meant that if I were to continue in the field, I must give up all my other work as a professor of English here at Yale, and devote myself exclusively to the editing and interpretation of the Boswell papers. This I was unwilling to do. ... It was a harsh decision I had to make, involving the surrender of my reputation as a productive scholar, and I still smart under it."[83]

For an alternative editor, Isham approached his friend T. E. Lawrence, whom he had known for a number of years. On the face of it, no choice could have been more inappropriate. Lawrence was no literary scholar and knew nothing about Boswell, but he had made a deep impression on Isham. He was a man of action, and he also had insight and literary flair. These were qualities which appealed strongly to Isham.[84] Lawrence, at this time, was serving with the R.A.F. in Karachi and was officially known as Aircraftsman T. E. Shaw. Lawrence declined the invitation, saying that he was not "a literary bird" and admitting that he had never "seen or read a line of any of Boswell's books."[85] Isham probably had little hope of an acceptance because, before Lawrence's refusal was even received, and in the three weeks which remained until his voyage home, he found his editor and arranged for him to come to America. Isham has left his own vivid account of how this happened:

On the day, in late August, 1927 when I returned to London with James Boswell's papers from Malahide, I took it into my head, for no apparent reason, to lunch at Simpsons in the Strand.

---

Isham and from Tinker, although Tinker's version differed slightly in the details. Tinker used the "mistress" metaphor again in a letter to Newton: "Why then should I worry myself into the grave because Isham bought my mistress with his money?" (This letter is quoted in full in a letter by Newton to Adam of 9 November 1927, in the Hyde Collection.)

[82]Information from Heyward Isham.

[83]This letter has already been quoted in part above. See above p. 51.

[84]Reported to me by Isham's son, Heyward.

[85]Letter, T. E. Lawrence to Isham, 22 November 1927 (IFP).

I had not been there in perhaps five years. As my wife and I were leaving, an excited hand was clapped on my shoulder and I was wheeled around to face my old friend, A. Edward Newton, who had only returned that day from his travels on the continent. I told him of my good fortune at Malahide and, ardent Boswellian that he is, his excitement was as keen as his desire to view the papers at the earliest possible moment. We fixed upon dinner that night in my rooms at Claridge's, where, with the papers waiting to be seen, I am afraid dinner was a tedious ceremony for both of us.[86]

In the small hours, after their perusal, we sat back and considered, silently. At last Newton said "It's a great responsibility. What are you going to do with them?" I said "Obviously, publish them." He asked me whom I would ask to prepare and edit them. I was undecided. After a moment he said "Of course you have read the 'Portrait of Zélide,' by Geoffrey Scott. That, my friend, is one of the most exquisite books in the English language."

Then and there it leapt to my mind that Geoffrey Scott was the ideal man for this work. He would bring to it both genius and scholarship. But how to find him? Neither Newton nor I had ever met him, nor had we the slightest idea as to his whereabouts. Both of us had a notion that he was living in Italy and was probably highly unobtainable.

In point of fact Geoffrey Scott had been living in London for some time. He had long had it in his mind to write a Life of Boswell and the publishers of the "British Men of Letters" series had proposed that he write it for them. From time to time he had visited his friend Mr. J. G. Wilson, the bookseller in London, and Mr. Wilson had invariably asked him how he was getting on with the projected work, and it had become a standing joke with them, Geoffrey having done very little, for the reason that he had learned of the existence of the papers at Malahide and had decided not to proceed with his Life until they had been revealed.

Two days after my evening with Mr. Newton, a sudden urge came over me to call on Mr. Wilson. I dropped work and went. I told him of my acquisition. He popped with excitement and said "I wish you had been in here fifteen minutes earlier. Geoffrey Scott was here then." It was incredible. In a very few minutes

---

[86]Newton wrote to Adam on 27 September 1927 (letter in Hyde Collection): "I met Isham and his wife quite by chance in London and saw the material. . . . It is certainly a choice lot."

he had Geoffrey on the telephone, introduced me to him over it, and I told him the Boswell "news." At this moment I had my first glimpse of his brilliant enthusiasm.

He dined with us that night. I was much impressed by his erudition, his vivid conversation, and by his romantic appearance. He was of great height and heavy build. His head was large and fine, his face sensitive,—at times beautiful in expression. His black hair, which he wore long, was vigorous and untidy. His manner was gentle and sympathetic.

We sat up all that night in our eagerness to get a full idea of the importance of the treasures we were examining. In late dawn he taxied home for a change of clothes. He was back soon. That day I pressed him to come to live at Claridge's where he would be closer to the papers. From that time until my sailing in mid-September we were scarcely separated during our waking hours. By that time we had made plans. He was to come to America to edit the papers as soon as his personal affairs could be arranged.[87]

Geoffrey Scott's friend, W. H. Haslam, gives another account of the same incident:

Geoffrey was occupying the Mews of my house at 8 Hanover Terrace when one morning in the Summer of 1927 Mr. Wilson of Bumpus's called him by telephone. "Mr. Scott," said Mr. Wilson in his clear Scottish tones, "Would you like to meet the owner of the Malahide papers?" Geoffrey's hand shook with excitement as Colonel Isham came to the telephone and invited him to his suite at Claridges. He took the call in his dressing gown, threw on his clothes and left by taxi for the hotel. He had no wherewithal but it was 48 hours before he returned, excited and dishevelled. Those two days he spent handling the collection, elated in particular by the fact that the hitherto missing correspondence between Boswell and Belle de Zuylen was so precisely as he had inferred in the *Portrait of Zélide*. I know that he was charmed by Colonel Isham's trust in throwing the papers to him unlisted, and it was during those two days that he agreed to edit the documents.[88]

[87]Typed narrative by Isham in IFP, printed in *The Saturday Review of Literature*, 24 August 1929.
[88]Letter from W. H. Haslam, published in *The Times Literary Supplement* on 15 July 1955.

In a letter of 24 June 1963, Mr. Haslam adds an amusing rider to his account:

> I could have added that Isham over the telephone invited Scott to Claridge's, but added "you had better bring some money with you." As a result of which Scott slipped a few notes into his pocket, being unable to appreciate Isham's sense of humour. Scott told me that what endeared Isham at that moment was the confidence shown. He was given free and unsupervised access to the papers, and could easily have purloined any.[89]

Isham was determined, if he could, to include the Ashbourne journal in the papers he was to take back to America. He postponed his sailing date by a week and wrote to Lady Talbot urging her to complete her work on it and, if it "passed," to send it to him before his departure.[90] Four days later the manuscript was delivered to him at Claridge's.[91] Lady Talbot wrote to say that she had ruled out with black paint a few passages relating to incidents which Lord Talbot wished censored. Other deletions were Boswell's own and could be deciphered. She suggested a price of £2,000 but agreed that, since this was (in her opinion) the best portion of the journals, the rest would be valued at a lower figure. Alternatively she was prepared to take £1,250 (equivalent to just over £10 per page), provided the rest of the journals were valued at approximately the same rate.[92] Isham agreed to the figure of £1,250, which brought the total price of the Boswell papers so far acquired by him to just under £15,000.

Isham's financial courage and self-confidence during the autumn of 1927 were quite remarkable. He did not yet own the bulk of the journals which were essential for his scheme of publishing the papers and editing them comprehensively. He had not even agreed upon definite terms with Lady Talbot and there was no knowing where her views on censorship might lead, or whether she would succeed in persuading her husband to sell. Yet he acted almost as though the journals were already his. He brought Geoffrey Scott to America in October 1927 as his full-time editor, although he knew that progress

---

[89]Letter from Mr. Haslam to myself.

[90]Letter, Isham to Lady Talbot, 6 September 1927 (TFP).

[91]The Talbots handed the Ashbourne journal in to the head office of the Royal Bank of Ireland in Dublin on 9 September 1927. The bank sent it care of their agent, Mr. H. J. Wiley, who delivered it personally to Isham at Claridge's at 10 A.M. on Saturday 10 September 1927 (correspondence in TFP).

[92]Letter, Lady Talbot to Isham, 9 September 1927 (copy in TFP).

would be seriously impeded until he had all the journals. Arrangements were made in December with William E. Rudge whereby Rudge was to print a limited edition of the collection almost in its entirety and Isham, though reserving the publishing profits, was to meet the whole printing costs and to relieve Rudge of all financial responsibility.[93] Bruce Rogers was employed to design the layout and typography at a fee of $250[94] a volume and given *carte blanche* to ensure that the presentation was beyond reproach. Isham's plan was to let Bruce Rogers and Rudge produce a de luxe edition in twelve volumes limited to 490 sets, all done in the best possible manner and replete with facsimiles of the more interesting manuscripts. He anticipated having to charge $500 a set and expected to follow up the private edition with a public edition in three volumes by Doubleday.[95] He appreciated that the cost to himself would be enormous, but commented: "It is so necessary that the thing should see the light of day in impeccable form."[96] Later, the plan of twelve volumes was expanded to eighteen volumes plus a catalogue and an index. The number of sets was increased to 570 and each of the eighteen volumes was priced at $50, making a total of $900 for a set; even so, the receipts from sales were nothing like sufficient to cover the cost of printing, editing, and other overheads, which by 1935 came to nearly a third of a million dollars.[97] Bruce Rogers commented: "The publication was undertaken as something a little more splendid than was absolutely necessary to give significance to the importance of the discovery and acquisition. It was our feeling that Boswell himself, with his love of fine things and magnificence, would have approved his works being brought out with considerable show."[98]

[93]Copies of a short Memorandum of Agreement dated 23 December 1927 signed by Isham, Scott, and Rudge and a long letter from Isham to Rudge of 28 December 1927 are in IFP. The work was published as *Private Papers of James Boswell from Malahide Castle in the Collection of Lt-Colonel Ralph Heyward Isham.* It is elsewhere cited and referred to as "private edition."

[94]There is in IFP a copy letter of 16 March 1932 from Isham to Rogers sending $750 for designing Vols. X, XI, and XII.

[95]The public edition by Doubleday never materialized.

[96]Letter, Isham to F. A. Pottle, 18 November 1927 (copy in IFP).

[97]A draft account in IFP analyses costs and credits on the production of the private edition from the beginning of the project to 30 June 1935. Total charges came to $304,827.99, including printing, binding, commission, handling, packing, shipping, advertising, mailing, loan interest, editorial salaries (excluding payments to Geoffrey Scott), secretarial salaries, and numerous miscellaneous charges. Cash collected from subscribers came to $285,839.34, indicating that some 320 out of the total of 570 sets of books were sold. Isham had of course many other costs to meet not included in the account.

[98]Letter, Bruce Rogers to F. A. Pottle, 16 March 1930 (now in IFP).

Isham's plan was more than just a splendid flourish to proclaim his own success to the world. He hoped and expected that he would ultimately reap a substantial profit, both from the private edition and from subsequent trade publication. The financial commitment involved was massive, but, in 1927, he believed it was commercially justified. He also believed that the texts of the papers should be made accessible to scholars and others who might be interested, at the earliest possible opportunity. This could best be achieved by issuing a finely printed edition of the texts with facsimiles and introductions, whilst at the same time making progress on the necessary editorial work and research for a definitive public edition. To R. W. Chapman, he wrote: "Although this de luxe edition will inevitably be costly, I feel that its existence, even in a few of the principal libraries, will go far towards giving those who are urgently in need of any particular information, access to the new material."[99]

He was always generous and courteous to scholars. Many applied to him and few were refused the use of the papers, even though this might have operated to his financial disadvantage. Amongst those to whom he gave help and materials were F. A. Pottle for *The Literary Career of James Boswell, Esq.*, L. F. Powell for his revision of Hill's edition of the *Life*, and R. W. Chapman for his edition of Johnson's *Letters*. He hoped that eventually the complete archives would pass to a university or other scholarly institution. In the meantime he was determined to make them available to the world in the best possible manner, and to avoid impairing the integrity of the collection. Few realize the sacrifices which this involved, in terms both of money and of his private life. He undertook financial commitments beyond his means, and he was later driven to desperate measures to keep his project afloat. If he later had to sell a few carefully selected items from the archives, this was not through choice, but necessity.[100] In 1927, he wrote that his wife's peace of mind was already disturbed by his "infatuation with non-income bearing manuscripts,"[101] and eight years later Pottle wrote to him: "I can easily understand how a man like yourself, beset by financial and domestic worries so long and so constantly, should be in a mood approaching desperation."[102]

[99]Letter, Isham to R. W. Chapman, 8 February 1928 (copy in IFP).
[100]See below pp. 80 and 108.
[101]Letter, Isham to Lady Talbot, 30 November 1927 (TFP). Mrs. Persifor Frazer has confirmed this to me.
[102]Letter, Pottle to Isham, 24 May 1935 (IFP).

In 1927, Isham's plans depended on one vital factor: being able to purchase the journal material still at Malahide. Soon after his return to New York, he wrote urging Lady Talbot to go through the journals and to let him have such parts as appeared to her to be publishable.[103] This produced no response and he decided to force the pace a little. On 28 October, he wrote again to say that Geoffrey Scott had now joined him in America and no progress could be made with his plans for publication until he had the diary.[104] This was followed up with a cable stressing the urgent need for action.[105] Lady Talbot replied, rather startled: "I am very sorry to hear that you have Mr. Scott with you waiting for the Diary. It never occurred to me that you would even feel so sure of getting it that you would make any plans to combine it with the Letters."[106] She reminded him of the very tentative arrangements made during his week-end visit[107] and warned: "No more cables; they thrill the village and make me feel hustled." She estimated that it might take nearly a year to hand over the journals complete. She explained that four-fifths were in quite good order, and had been typed out (for Sir John Murray), but the remainder was in complete confusion. She suggested a price of £10 per page of Boswell's handwriting with an overall maximum of £20,000, anything over 2,000 pages being thrown in for nothing. Regarding censorship, she said: "I intend to leave in a good many rather coarse things, and only to take out anything to which Lord Talbot takes great exception. It is too good a work to have its personality disturbed, tho' I repeat that anything that would tend to giving it a bumper sale *on account of impropriety* must come out."

Lady Talbot now got down to work on the journals in earnest. Two days later, she deposited 334 pages of manuscript with her bank in Dublin and sent the corresponding portion of the Murray typescript to Isham, suggesting a price of £2,500.[108] Within another week, she had been through a further 900 pages which she valued at £5,700, and again she sent the corresponding typescript to Isham, promising

[103]Letter, Isham to Lady Talbot, 26 September 1927 (TFP).
[104]Letter in TFP.
[105]The cable is not traced but is referred to in Lady Talbot's reply.
[106]Letter, 19 November 1927 (copy in TFP).
[107]Ibid. "I remember the gist of what I said with regard to the Diary when you were here, and that was as soon as I could I would begin to go through it and then if you wished to acquire it on terms we approved I would try to get my husband to let me send it out in fragments until you had the whole."
[108]Letter, Lady Talbot to Isham, 21 November 1927 (IFP).

to deposit the manuscript as soon as terms were agreed upon.[109] It was clear by now that the number of pages would total about 4,000 without counting the jumble of loose sheets, and on the basis of £10 a page the overall maximum of £20,000 would be far exceeded. Isham wrote to say that he regarded the price as reasonable and agreed to the figure of £20,000 for the whole journal.[110] He was, however, beginning to feel the financial strain of his purchases. In the space of a year, he had already spent nearly £15,000 on manuscripts and had incurred heavy travelling and other expenses. He was also about to embark on one of the most costly schemes of private publication ever undertaken. He therefore asked Lady Talbot if he might defer payment of half the price for a year. He also sought an assurance that he should now be considered to have purchased the entire collection of manuscripts and private papers of James Boswell inherited by Lord Talbot, except for the few specimens the Talbots wished to retain.[111] Unfortunately for Isham, Lady Talbot had received a cable from her brother, Geoffrey Kerr, in America only a few days before to say that Byrne Hackett, the leading Johnsonian bookseller, was enormously interested in the journals and prepared to pay a fair price. Hackett was due to sail on 30 December and Lady Talbot was strongly advised to delay.[112] She decided, however, that this would not be fair to Isham and Hackett's approach was choked off.[113] She wrote to Isham regretting that she could not agree to his request for deferred payment and defined the scope of his purchase:

> Lord Talbot cannot agree to any contract which arranges that you possess the entire collection of papers inherited by him from the Boswells. . . . I am genuinely under the impression, strengthened by careful search, that no other papers exist. At

[109]Letter, Lady Talbot to Isham, 28 November 1927 (IFP).

[110]Letter to Lady Talbot, 30 November 1927 (TFP).

[111]Letter to Lady Talbot, 19 December 1927 (TFP).

[112]The cable (copy in TFP) was received on 23 December 1927, presumably a day or two before Isham's letter. There is evidence that Hackett sailed for Ireland on three separate occasions, but if he did, he never reached Malahide. See above p. 58, n. 32, for the possibility that he may have been planning a trip in February 1926. On 31 January 1927, Newton wrote to Adam: "I hear Byrne Hackett has sailed for Dublin with an idea of buying that Boswell material." The present cable indicates the third instance.

[113]Letter, Lady Talbot to Isham, 4 January 1928 (IFP): "Another offer came too, a week or so ago, and thinking all settled, we choked it off. If however you are worried at parting with such a sum, don't hesitate to change your mind. We are quite certain we can get it. But it would be sad after all our present transactions."

the same time in view of the immense value of the stray papers of that period, he cannot enter into any contract. . . . £20,000 covers the whole Diary, of that be assured. But beyond that Lord Talbot will not go.[114]

Isham could only accept Lady Talbot's terms. He had been living on a very lavish scale and his problem was to find the money.[115] Fortunately his friend, James H. Van Alen, came to the immediate rescue with a short-term loan of $124,000.[116] Van Alen, a brilliant sportsman and member of a wealthy Newport family, had no particular literary bent, but he was struck by the rightness of what Isham was trying to do. His own expression is that Isham "had a Rolls-Royce without an engine."[117] Van Alen's loan covered the cost of the journals with something to spare, but it did not provide a long-term solution of the financial problems which were beginning to loom. The costs of the private edition were mounting, arrangements for Geoffrey Scott's remuneration had to be settled, and of course Van Alen would have to be repaid. Isham was compelled to seek other means of raising money.

The story is told in Edwin Wolf's and John F. Fleming's biography of A. S. W. Rosenbach that Isham called to see Dr. Rosenbach in New York shortly after his return from Malahide.[118] He is said to have brought a large bundle of the papers with him and invited Rosenbach to offer for them at an impossibly high valuation. Although Rosenbach declined to consider a purchase at Isham's price, he seems to have thought Isham was in earnest about wanting to sell. This was almost certainly not the case: it was not the attitude of a man for whom, in the words of his wife, the Boswell papers had become an obsession which he consistently placed before everything else.[119] As a collector, Isham could not resist showing off his prize to Rosenbach

---

[114]Ibid.

[115]Letter, Newton to Adam, 9 November 1927 (Hyde Collection): "Isham seems to be living at a pretty good clip. He has bought an island off the coast of Florida, a part of an island off the coast of Georgia, an apartment at Fifth Avenue and 72nd Street, New York, and a very well established place not far from Oyster Bay, Long Island—for this he tells me he paid a hundred and seventy-five thousand dollars."

[116]Information from G. Campbell Becket, Van Alen's attorney. There were 3 promissory notes: 3 December 1927 for $106,000; 4 December 1927, for $6,000; and 14 January 1928 for $24,000. Isham repaid $12,000, making a net loan of $124,000.

[117]A remark made at a private dinner-party, noted by Mrs. D. F. Hyde.

[118]Edwin Wolf and John F. Fleming: *Rosenbach: A Biography*, 1960, pp. 276–78.

[119]Told to me by Mrs. Persifor Frazer.

and pulling his leg into the bargain. After all, Rosenbach had approached Malahide before him and failed. If Isham had really wanted to do business, he would not have started by asking an unrealistic price, nor would he have entered into his commitments with Scott and Rudge.

Isham was, however, in earnest in trying to sell a few carefully selected items from the papers. These were manuscripts which had already been published and which could therefore be separated from the collection without prejudice to the private edition. The two most valuable items of this nature were the fragment of the manuscript of the *Life* and the manuscript of *An Account of Corsica,* both of which were offered to Rosenbach. Isham put $23,000 on the *Corsica* manuscript, which Rosenbach declined,[120] but he did agree to buy six leaves from the manuscript of the *Life,* together with a paper apart of four leaves, and two fine letters from Boswell to his wife for a total of $17,000.[121] Rosenbach offered the *Life* manuscript to Newton at $4,000 a page, but Newton was not interested.[122] It seems that Rosenbach eventually sold five of the leaves, each laid inside a first edition of the *Life,* to separate purchasers. The sixth leaf and the paper apart were not sold and are now in the Rosenbach Foundation.[123]

Isham also considered what profits might be extracted from commercial publication. He planned a trade edition to follow the private edition, and thought of offering it to Doubleday Page & Co. (later Doubleday, Doran & Co.). He met Nelson Doubleday several times late in 1927 to discuss terms.[124] Doubleday was able to obtain an attractive offer of $10,000 (plus 50 percent of syndicate profits) for world newspaper publication rights from *The New York Herald Tribune.*[125] Unfortunately, the *Tribune* wanted to serialize in fifty-two weekly articles and to postpone publication of the books until the serialization was complete. Apart from the delay, this might have injured book

---

[120]Letter, Newton to Adam, last cited: "Rosy tells me that Isham offered him the manuscript of the Corsica book for twenty-three thousand dollars. . . ."

[121]Files of the Philip H. and A. S. W. Rosenbach Foundation. Isham reserved the right to publish the two letters, and they were printed in the private edition, XVII, pp. 141–47. The letters are dated 28 January 1789 and 9 February 1789, and both are now owned by the Rosenbach Foundation.

[122]Letter, Newton to Adam, last cited: "Rosy asked me what I would say if he offered to sell me some pages of Boswell's Life of Johnson in Boswell's hand. . . . the price was to be four thousand dollars per page."

[123]See below Appendix III, p. 331.

[124]Correspondence in IFP.

[125]Letter from the managing editor of the *Tribune* to Isham dated 30 September 1927 (in IFP).

sales. Isham refused to commit himself and negotiations petered out.[126] Newton was highly sceptical of Isham's publication plans. He told Adam that they sounded "almost impossible," but added: "Isham is a very remarkable man, he has no end of effrontery and resource, and he may get away with it."[127]

Lady Talbot sent the manuscript of the journals to Isham in several batches during the months of December 1927 and January 1928, but only after she had censored it extensively. It is easy to blame her for the censorship, but it must be remembered that she was only able to persuade Lord Talbot to sell on the understanding that she would delete everything which the fifth Lord Talbot and Sir John Murray had considered too improper to publish.[128] She was able to deduce the views of her father-in-law and Sir John from the many passages which had been inked over in the Murray typescript.[129] Her method was to go through the journals with the corresponding pages of typescript and to blot out on the original manuscript those passages which had already been inked over in the typescript.[130] She also generally gave effect to a number of notes written by the fifth Lord Talbot directing that certain passages be expunged. She did not, however, remove any pages of the journal, although there are many gaps in the manuscript. The Murray typescript, about half of which is still preserved, indicates that, with a few exceptions, the same gaps already existed in 1911.[131] She had a typescript prepared for most of those portions of the journals not covered by the Murray typescript, and to these she applied similar standards of censorship. Her main concerns were to spare descendants of people about whom Boswell recorded matter that might be embarrassing, to expunge any "very frank passages

[126]Correspondence in IFP.

[127]Letter, Newton to Adam last cited.

[128]Spingarn Letter.

[129]Ibid.

[130]Some of the blottings were made by Lady Talbot herself and some by her secretary on her instructions (information from F. A. Pottle).

[131]What remains of the Murray typescript is now at Yale. As to the exceptions, F. A. Pottle has kindly supplied the following note: "One leaf of the journal, containing part of the record for 25 Mar. 1768, which was missing when Isham received the MS., had been in existence when the Murray typescript was made. The corresponding leaf of the typescript had been removed too, but not destroyed, and it somehow got sent to Isham by accident. See *Boswell in Search of a Wife*, Eng. edn. pp. 153–54; American edn. pp. 143–44. In the entry for 31 Mar. 1775, five leaves (versos blank) were *in situ* when the Murray transcript was made but were missing when Isham received the MS. Three leaves of the Murray typescript, corresponding to this lacuna, were absent from the typescript when Isham received it, and have never been recovered. See *Boswell, The Ominous Years*, p. 110, n. 5."

about the mad brother,"[132] and to cut out anything which might appeal to "that section of the public, at present so much in the majority, who will run after anything of a particularly nasty nature."[133]

As she completed each section of the journals, she posted the censored typescript to Isham and deposited the corresponding manuscript, also censored, with her bank pending settlement of the price.[134] When he received the first batch of typescript, Isham was shocked by the extent of the deletions and wrote urgently to Lady Talbot: "I am . . . seriously alarmed by the thought that the actual manuscript when I receive it may be as mutilated as the typescript."[135] His worst fears were later confirmed when the manuscript was delivered and he found it defaced by numerous deletions in black paint or carbon ink.[136] Although he had promised to respect the Talbots' wishes as to censorship, he had not anticipated that the censorship would be

---

[132]Boswell's younger brother, John. He was kept in St. Luke's House, Newcastle-upon-Tyne, a small hospital for the mentally ill, run by Dr. John Hall.

[133]Letter, Lady Talbot to Isham, 9 December 1927 (IFP).

[134]Correspondence in IFP and TFP.

[135]Letter, 29 December 1927 (TFP).

[136]Before Isham acquired the journals they had been subjected to censorship by other hands than those of Lady Talbot and many of the deletions are JB's own. The most serious was the removal of a number of leaves from the journals bound in notebooks, resulting in gaps of anything up to nine consecutive leaves. We do not know when or by whom this was done. Several persons may have been involved. Whoever was responsible worked through the bound journals to 19 April 1776, skipped to 7 May 1780 and gave up altogether after 21 March 1784. The censorship was not systematic and many outspoken passages were left untouched. The typist who copied the diary for submission to Sir John Murray in 1911 specifically indicated where pages of the manuscript were missing. These may have been removed by the fifth Lord Talbot beforehand or they may already have been missing. The ink deletions on the typescript which Lady Talbot later used as a guide for her own censorship were presumably made by the fifth Lord Talbot before the typescript was sent to Sir John Murray; but it is uncertain whether he made any deletions on the actual manuscripts. Apart from JB's own deletions, the manuscripts have been blotted at some time with three different materials: ordinary blue-black ink, black carbon ink, and black paint. Lady Talbot has confirmed that she used the last two materials and these blottings can probably be attributed to her. It is less likely that she had anything to do with the ordinary ink blottings as she evidently took pains to ensure that anything she wished censored was properly obscured. The fifth Lord Talbot may have been responsible, but we cannot be certain. We do know, however, that although he jotted down a number of notes that certain passages were to be expunged, he did not in fact give effect to these on the original manuscripts. His directions were later carried out in a number of cases by Lady Talbot. About half of the Murray typescript survives at Yale and in this portion there is only one sheet which contains material not matched in the manuscript (see above p. 81, n. 131). F. A. Pottle found the sheet of typescript in Isham's house after vol. VII of the private edition had been printed. Apart from this single sheet and Isham's account of the burning of six leaves from the journal notes (see below Appendix IV p. 334), there is no evidence that any of the original manuscript of the journals was lost, destroyed, or removed at Malahide after 1911.

so radical. Yet if Lady Talbot had not acted as she did, her husband would not have agreed to the sale. On 21 January 1928, after depositing the last consignment of the manuscript in the bank, she wrote to Isham:

> I am afraid it has been impossible to avoid mutilating some of the oddments [i.e. loose journal sheets and notes]. It will be very difficult for you to realise what I was up against and I only hope you will not resent my cutting[137] it up so much. . . . I have really tried to consider your point of view and safeguard your investment for you, but don't forget that it has been very difficult to persuade Lord Talbot to see it at all, so that I could only do my best to please all parties.[138]

Lady Talbot's censorship presented Isham with one of his most difficult decisions. It proved possible by various means[139] to make out most of what she had obscured and he was strongly urged to permit publication. Scott and the other scholars whom he consulted all advised him that to give effect to Lady Talbot's deletions would seriously impair the historical and literary value of his publication.[140] Isham shared this view, but he was at the same time very conscious of the many assurances he had given to the Talbots.[141] He had the choice now of either breaking his word or sanctioning a publication which he knew, and Geoffrey Scott knew, would be unsatisfactory. For Isham there was only one possible decision—to permit publication. His action was no doubt indefensible so far as the Talbots were concerned, but he consistently placed the Boswell papers and their proper publication before any other consideration.

Lady Talbot was bound to discover the truth sooner or later, and in September 1929 she wrote to Isham taxing him with failure to respect her censorship.[142] Isham could only write back admitting the

---

[137]"Cutting" (i.e., inking). Lady Talbot did not physically cut this manuscript.

[138]Letter in IFP.

[139]Blottings made with ordinary writing fluid could generally be read through the blotting from the back side of the leaf when held up to a strong light. The black paint could be removed with turpentine. Ordinary ink on the typescript could be removed with ink eradicator. Carbon ink on the original manuscript was more difficult. Infra-red photography proved useless, and most of the deciphering was done by careful scrutiny under a good light and the sparing use of ink solvent and an ordinary pencil eraser.

[140]See letter quoted below p. 84.

[141]Repeatedly given in letters (copies in TFP).

[142]Letter, 27 September 1929 (copy in TFP).

charge, and trying to explain the difficulty of his position:

> When Mr. Scott and I subjected the manuscripts to a careful study, we discovered that, in a bright light, it was perfectly possible in many instances to read Boswell's writing through the substances with which you had covered it. We were not a little surprised to discover that you had censored many paragraphs which Boswell himself had published verbatim in his Life of Johnson, and with which, therefore, the world has been familiar since 1791. It was discovered, furthermore, that you had blacked out many of his sentences or single words in which we could discern no offensive meaning or suggestion. . . . As we are dealing with manuscripts of great age and of the utmost historic and literary importance, both Mr. Scott and I felt very strongly that our duty was not one that would admit of a general suppression of such words and passages as we found deleted. We believe that such a frequent recurrence of omissions as would be entailed by following this course could only deceive the reader into unfortunate surmises regarding Boswell and his circle, for of course it is incumbent upon an editor to indicate by suitable printer's marks wherever any word in the manuscripts has been omitted in type.
>
> We therefore after consulting many of the foremost scholars of England and this country and on their urgent advice adopted the procedure of either printing or not printing the censored portions, wherever we could decipher them, according to the standards usually followed in a scholarly publication of historic manuscripts.[143]

Lady Talbot could hardly be expected to condone Isham's action, but to her immense credit, she was able to forgive him for taking a step which she would have had every justification for regarding as unpardonable. In future dealings, she and her husband continued to show Isham courtesy and consideration. They remained sympathetic to his endeavours and any resentment they may have felt over the censorship matter was not allowed to obtrude.

With the arrival of the journals in America, Geoffrey Scott was able to make swift progress. He stayed with Isham at his home in Long Island and the intense enthusiasm with which he worked is best told in Isham's own words:

> He commenced work almost immediately and became completely absorbed in his intellectual activities,—and charmingly absent-

---

[143]Letter, 28 January 1930 (TFP).

minded about everything else. It soon became difficult to persuade him to leave his work long enough for exercise or recreation.

His usual method was to write or dictate during the day, which began for him about ten o'clock. When the secretaries had gone he would write on until the last moment before dinner. If it was a family dinner the work would be discussed and he would tell us eagerly of progress and discoveries. After dinner we customarily went straight back to the library, from which Boswell seldom let us emerge before morning hours.[144]

Mrs. Persifor Frazer, who in 1927 was Isham's wife, recalls Scott's stay with less enthusiasm. She says that she never saw her husband except for meals. He and Scott only detached themselves from the Boswell papers to eat, sleep, or indulge in Scott's favourite pastime, which was playing poker half the night. The irregular hours drove her to distraction, and they were besieged by publishers who telephoned constantly.[145]

It was about this time that two batches of letters from the Malahide papers were lost. The more important was a collection of at least eighteen manuscript letters from Margaret Montgomerie to Boswell. Scott thought he might have left them on the luggage rack of a Long Island train! Fortunately, before the letters went amissing, they had been carefully copied and collated, so the texts are preserved.[146] The other group of letters was part of James Bruce's correspondence with Boswell, consisting of letters from Bruce to Boswell on which Boswell had jotted down minutes of his replies. Bruce was overseer at Auchinleck and his letters related mainly to estate matters. According to Isham a considerable number of them was sent to a dealer to be sold if a suitable offer could be obtained, and the dealer subsequently reported that the manuscripts had been lost.[147] The identity of the dealer has not been established.

By the summer of 1929, Scott had completed the first six volumes of the private edition, and much of the text of volumes VIII, IX, X, and XI was in galley proof. As the volumes appeared, they were

---

[144]From narrative partially quoted above pp. 71–73.
[145]Told to me by Mrs. Frazer, May 1969.
[146]See Pottle's "Editorial and Textual Note" in private edition, VIII, p. v. Pottle, in a memorandum to me, says that he helped to search Dr. Murphy's house in New York where Scott lived, without finding the missing letters. Eighteen letters were copied by the typist, of which fifteen ranged in date from 1 October 1767 to 7 February 1770, the other three being written in 1784. One letter escaped loss. This was Margaret Montgomerie's acceptance of Boswell's proposal (22 April 1766) which, along with the proposal itself, Isham kept in a special morocco case.
[147]Pottle thinks there may have been some 30 or 40 letters.

widely acclaimed for their presentation and content. It is a measure
of the recognition which Scott received that Harcourt, Brace & Company, with whom he had contracted to write a biography of Boswell
after completing the private edition, were able to ask $30,000 for the
advance sale of the serial rights.[148] Under his contract with Isham,
drawn up in May 1929, he was to receive total remuneration of $75,000
for his work on the private edition, with additional remuneration for
editing any public or trade edition. The royalties and profits derived
from his biography of Boswell were to be divided equally between
Isham and himself.[149]

After signing his contract, Scott took his first break from his
labours. He returned home to Britain for two months' holiday, during
which he remained preoccupied with Boswell. He visited Auchinleck,
where he saw the portrait of Paoli, the "romantic grotto," and the
Gothic bridge, and he also called on various members of the Boswell
family, including the Boswells of Crawley Grange. He hoped, in vain,
that he might turn up some more papers to fill the gaps in those
which had come from Malahide.[150] On 27 July 1929, he sailed back
to America, eager to return to his work.

[148]This was a more extended biography than the projected one for the English Men of Letters
series. Harcourt, Brace and Company were negotiating to sell the serialization rights of the
biography to the Curtis Publishing Company.

[149]Memorandum of Agreement dated 20 May 1929 between Isham and Scott (IFP).

[150]On 24 July 1929, Scott wrote to Isham from London giving an account of his stay in Britain
(copy letter in IFP).

# III

# *"Long of Books, Short of Money"*[1]

T HE completion of the private edition was now in sight. Isham looked forward to recovering some of his huge financial outlay from the profits of a public edition, and ultimately to selling the collection as a whole to a learned institution. His hopes were soon shattered. Scott had returned from his trip to Europe on 4 August in excellent spirits and keen to resume work, but only three days later he became ill with pneumonia. On 14 August, after a week's struggle for life, he passed into unconsciousness and died.

His early death was a tragic loss for English Literature. His work on the private edition, especially his brilliant introductions and his definitive study on the making of the *Life,* had already shown that in temperament and intellect he was perfectly equipped to interpret his subject. Desmond MacCarthy wrote in his obituary for the *Manchester Guardian* that "his 'Life of Boswell,' which he would have written when his task of editing 'The Boswell Papers' was finished, would have been one of the most remarkable biographies in the English language." MacCarthy commented on the strong temperamental affinity between Scott and Boswell and lamented the loss of "a very fine book."[2]

Isham's immediate problem was to find a new editor. One possible choice was Frederick A. Pottle, who in 1926 had been appointed Assistant Professor of English at Yale at the early age of twenty-eight.

[1] Quotation from letter, Newton to Adam, 22 October 1929 (Hyde Collection). (See below p. 93.)

[2] A loss which is now happily made good by Pottle's fine biography of Boswell. The first volume, *James Boswell, The Earlier Years 1740–1769*, was published in 1966 and the remaining volume is eagerly awaited. MacCarthy's obituary for Scott was published in the *Manchester Guardian* on 15 August 1929.

GEOFFREY SCOTT
From the portrait by the Chevalier de Bouvard.

FREDERICK A. POTTLE

Pottle, a protégé and former student of Tinker's, was fast establishing a reputation for himself as an outstanding Boswellian. In 1926, a year after taking his Ph.D. degree, he had written to Isham on Tinker's introduction explaining his plans to publish an extended Boswellian bibliography and asking permission to verify a number of points from Isham's collection.[3] This was the start of a friendly and extended correspondence in which Scott was also involved. Both Isham and Scott were impressed by the young man's perception and grip of his subject. They helped him all they could by answering his queries, reading his proofs, and allowing him to examine and quote from the Malahide papers. In 1929, the bibliography was published by the Clarendon Press under the title *The Literary Career of James Boswell, Esq.* It was immediately recognized as a definitive work.

Strangely enough, it was Geoffrey Scott who to a large extent determined the choice of his own successor. Only a few days after his death, a letter was found in a pocket of the suit which he had worn before his illness. It was addressed to Pottle, but had never been posted. It began as follows:

Dear Mr. Pottle,

I have just returned to New York after a couple of months in England, in which I took the first holiday I have been able to afford time for since Boswell's resurrection. In the course of it I was able to *read* your bibliography (which hitherto I had only consulted on specific points in your proofs) and I cannot refrain from writing to express my profound admiration—amazement, rather—at the total achievement, which sets an altogether new standard in a field of scholarship already exacting enough. No one is better able, perhaps, than I to appreciate one particular aspect of the miracle—namely, your faculty of forestalling evidence. I am exceedingly glad you have left your original reasoning as it stood before the Malahide MSS. confirmed your conclusions. I look forward to paying more adequate tribute to your extraordinary divination and comprehensiveness, when I come to deal with Boswell's periodical journalism in one of the next prefaces, for there you have forestalled the diary point by point.[4]

---

[3] Letter dated 12 September 1926 (IFP).
[4] Story told and letter quoted in printed Announcement circulated amongst subscribers to the private edition.

The letter was shown to Isham whilst he was pondering the choice of a new editor. Later he wrote: "I cannot describe the effect which the reading of this letter produced upon me. The choice of Professor Pottle as Scott's successor would in any case have had to be seriously considered, but in my perplexity and distraction the letter seemed to be nothing less than the voice of my friend from the tomb directing me."[5] Isham telegraphed to Pottle at once[6] and at the meeting which followed invited him to complete Scott's work. After a brief period of deliberation, Pottle accepted, with the approval of his associates at Yale. Tinker wrote to congratulate Isham on his choice: "The world does not hold a better man for the purpose."[7]

It was arranged that Pottle would continue to meet his classes at Yale for three days a week until June 1930, after which he was to devote himself to the papers full-time until the private edition had been completed.[8] His principal incentive for accepting the editorship was that, after completing the private and trade editions and also a short popular biography of Boswell for Harcourt Brace, he would be entitled to prepare a fully annotated scholarly edition and also to make use of the materials for a massive and definitive Life of Boswell in two or three volumes.[9] His contract[10] allowed him only two years (until 1 October 1931) to complete the remaining twelve volumes of the private edition as well as doing the editorial work for some sort of trade publication. He was then to have the exclusive use of the papers until 1 October 1933 for his popular biography, followed by a non-exclusive right to use them for writing a definitive biography and preparing the scholarly annotated edition.

Pottle undertook this onerous time-table without any prior opportunity to estimate the bulk of material still to be published in the private edition;[11] nor did he know how much work the so-called "trade edition" would involve, for nobody had yet defined its scope. He only

[5]Draft of the above Announcement (IFP). The draft differs slightly from the printed version.
[6]Telegram dated 23 August 1929 (copy in IFP).
[7]Letter dated 6 October 1929 (IFP).
[8]Memorandum of Agreement among Isham, Pottle, and Rudge dated 1 October 1929 (copy in IFP).
[9]Letter, Pottle to Isham, 8 September 1929 (IFP).
[10]i.e., the Memorandum of Agreement cited above.
[11]Note to me from F. A. Pottle (1972). Pottle reports that when he took over the editorship, the papers were uncatalogued, were not even filed in order, and some of the most difficult bits of the journals had not been transcribed. An adequate working estimate of the bulk of publishable material would have taken a lot of time which was just not available.

knew that Isham and Scott had contemplated "a single volume of brilliant extracts from the journal—a scissors-and-paste job with an introduction and next to no annotation."[12] "I was perhaps rash," he now says, "in thinking that in two years I could complete twelve volumes of the size of Scott's vols. 1, 2, 3, 4, and 5, plus one trade volume, but nobody will ever know, because I had no chance to try. The work began to expand from the very beginning. As soon as I got into the manuscripts, I found myself disagreeing with Scott's policy of omitting great quantities of memoranda and journal notes. These notes, though abbreviated, elliptical, and cryptic, I found often to be more revealing than the fully written journal. It seemed to me that we had been entrusted with a great coherent human document which was misrepresented by anything less than full publication. I spoke to Isham of this and found that for some time he had felt just as I did. He concurred heartily in my decision to print all the journal from the point where I took over."[13]

This decision involved a considerable expansion in the size of the remaining volumes of the private edition, and hence in the time needed for their completion. To assist Pottle in this task, Isham agreed to employ Miss Helen Cohan as a full-time secretary. She had previously worked for Scott, starting with him at the age of only eighteen, with no other training than a secretarial qualification. She had a quick intelligence and soon became expert at reading deleted passages in the papers. Some years later, Pottle was to acknowledge to her "an indebtedness that amounts to co-editorship."[14]

Pottle's appointment solved Isham's editorial problem, but financial worries remained. His purchase from the Talbots had seriously stretched his resources and the costs of the private edition were mounting alarmingly. He was also faced with a settlement of $22,500 to Geoffrey Scott's estate.[15] Pottle's salary was his responsibility (although Rudge was advancing it meantime) and he had Miss Cohan's wages

[12]Ibid.

[13]Ibid.

[14]See private edition, XVIII, p. viii. In working on the deleted passages, Miss Cohan and Pottle would each make independent decipherments and, if they agreed, they reckoned they were probably right. Miss Cohan continued to work for Pottle until completion of the index to the private edition in 1936 (see below p. 109). The successful completion of the private edition owes much to her devoted labours.

[15]Payable under Scott's contract. The settlement was $22,500 plus legal costs of $1,022.60. (General Release Melville H. Cane to Isham, 16 June 1931 (now at Yale) and bill of legal costs in IFP.)

to meet.[16] His decision to support Pottle's new editorial policy was an expensive one. He was under no obligation to his subscribers to publish the journal notes and memoranda in full. By doing so, printing costs were increased, the rate at which the volumes could appear was retarded, and the intended time-table of publication was frustrated.

The easy solution would have been to sell some of the manuscripts, but he was determined not to impair the integrity of his collection more than was absolutely essential. In view of the financial pressures, which intensified as the years went by, and the ease with which only a few manuscripts could be converted into large sums of money, it is remarkable that he sold so little.[17] It was his intention that the Boswell papers, preserved as complete as possible, should ultimately pass to a university or other learned body, and he continually had in mind the possibility of a sale to such a body on terms which would not interfere with his publication plans. As early as September 1927, Frank Halsey of Princeton University had approached him: "This is just the sort of stuff that a university press would like to publish and of course from your point of view the imprint of the Yale, Harvard or Princeton University Press is not entirely to be snickered at." He added dryly: "I haven't any idea what sort of promises I could make you but in any case most publishers are over-optimistic and all printers are liars."[18] By 1929, Harvard was keenly interested and its interest was inspired to no little extent by its rivalry with Yale. On 30 March 1929, George P. Winship wrote to Professor R. P. Blake of Harvard:

Dear Mr. Blake:—

There is of course no possible doubt about the extraordinary importance of the Boswell documents which Colonal Isham has, either from a literary point of view, or the very high value from that of book collectors. I can imagine no greater tragedy for literary scholarship, nor one which would for all time be increasingly regarded as a reflection on the far-sightedness of American benefactors, than to have this collection broken up and dispersed through the sale of the individual pieces at auction. Taken as a whole, as it now stands, I doubt if there has ever yet come upon the market a collection which touches a greater range of

---

[16]Miss Cohan's salary in December 1932 was running at $50 a week (see below p. 102). Under his contract, Pottle was to be remunerated at the rate of $5,000 for his first year, and $8,000 for his second.

[17]Isham always reserved publication rights in anything he sold.

[18]Letter, Halsey to Isham, 22 September 1927 (IFP).

perennial, human and literary interests. The people who wrote these papers have an assured place in literary annals and as a group they make up for falling just below the topmost rank of fame by the unequalled appeal of their personalities as human beings.

One special reason would make it particularly delightful if we could get these papers for Harvard. This is the fact that for many reasons Yale wants them very much indeed. The man on the Yale faculty whom we envy Yale more than anyone else is Chauncey Tinker; could we make Tinker come up to the Harvard Library for the material which he can interpret better than anyone else now living, it would give some of us a very pleasant feeling. We who know the Harvard Library best have no serious fear of the rivalry of Yale, but the new Yale building is going to give them a great impetus and Yale men are frankly determined to make their collection better than ours if they possibly can. I cannot think of any single thing of any sort which would put us further ahead and make the stern chase more hopeless than these Boswell papers.

Very sincerely yours,

George P. Winship[19]

On 9 October 1929, the Wall Street market crashed. All hopes of a sale to Harvard or Yale receded for the time being. Nobody had any money for books and manuscripts and the value of the Boswellian collection plunged. Isham's private fortune, already under severe pressure, dwindled further. The future of the private edition was in jeopardy. It had always been under-subscribed and the chances of finding more subscribers now became remote. There was even a risk that some existing subscribers would be unable to afford the remaining volumes. Newton reported to Adam that Isham was "in an awful jam. Long of books, short of money, short of editors, and I fear, short of friends."[20]

Fortunately for Isham, one friend did stand by him in his predicament. This was Van Alen, whose 1927 loan was long over-due for repayment. By the end of 1929, Isham's debt stood at $122,836,[21] including interest, and Van Alen, with remarkable forbearance, agreed to waive repayment on the understanding that the money would be

[19]Original letter in IFP.

[20]Letter, Newton to Adam, 22 October 1929 (Hyde Collection).

[21]Letter, G. Campbell Becket to Gordon S. Murphy, 27 February 1950. This figure was taken as the principal sum in the agreement cited below.

treated as his personal investment in the papers until they could be sold. A contract was drawn up under which Isham retained control of all sale negotiations.[22] He thus left himself in a position to ensure that the collection would not be broken up and that, if sold, it would go to an institution worthy to receive it—even though it might have been more profitably disposed of to others. Meanwhile, Isham was to have complete discretion over all matters relating to publication. In the event of a sale, the proceeds were to be applied first in meeting all expenses, including costs of editing and publishing, and only then was Van Alen to receive repayment of his investment out of the balance. Van Alen's support kept the project afloat. The terms to which he agreed were exceptionally generous and, without his friendly backing, Isham could never have continued.

Isham now negotiated an agreement with the Viking Press for publication of the trade edition which would follow the private edition.[23] Viking was given the exclusive right to publish the Malahide papers in book form in the United States of America and a non-exclusive right to publish and sell the work in Canada. The first publication was planned in a set of not less than six volumes, to be followed by other forms of publication including, possibly, cheaper trade editions, text book editions, derivative volumes, and so forth. A volume on the making of the journals was also contemplated. Pottle was to prepare a suitable manuscript for delivery to the printer between the spring of 1932 and the spring of 1934.

Pottle was not a party to this contract and the programme of work proposed for him was quite unrealistic. The "trade edition" had suddenly expanded from a single volume of extracts to a possible publication of the entire collection of Malahide papers. He was told that the first six volumes, to be completed by 1934, might contain all the fully written journals, with notes and an index.[24] This represented a more onerous task than the whole private edition. Since he was due to return to his teaching duties at Yale in the autumn of 1931, adherence to the stipulated time limits was impossible. Nevertheless, the terms negotiated with Viking provided Isham with a measure of badly needed relief. Viking agreed to publish at its expense and to pay $7,500 immediately on account of advance royalties. A similar payment of $7,500 was to be made by William Heinemann

[22]Agreement dated 1 January 1930 between Isham and Van Alen (IFP).
[23]Agreement between Isham and the Viking Press, Inc., dated 1 May 1930 (copy in IFP).
[24]Note to me from F. A. Pottle (1972).

Ltd., who were offered exclusive publishing rights in the British Empire (except Canada) and a non-exclusive right to publish and sell in Canada.[25] The time needed for preparation of copy and related editorial work was seriously underestimated, but there was at least a prospect of substantial royalties at the end of the day.

By the beginning of April 1930, volumes VII, VIII, and IX of the private edition were in press and the formalities of the Viking and Heinemann contracts were nearly completed. It seemed as though Isham had weathered both the editorial and the financial crises.

Then, on 15 April 1930, Lady Talbot wrote from Ireland with startling news. She had found a box full of additional Boswell manuscripts in a cupboard which she had never supposed to contain any papers. The box had formerly been used for croquet balls and the papers inside were wrapped in newspapers of 1907.[26] She thought that they must have been brought to Malahide along with other papers by the fifth Lord Talbot and stowed away to dry out in the cupboard which was heated from a nearby fireplace. She gave little indication of the size or importance of her find, which she described as being chiefly notes for publications, a portion of an attempted Life of Lord Kames, and many pages of rough notes. She added: "The papers are in a very bad state, a most forceful example of Boswell's own mutilations and of secondary value. I think Lord Talbot would only want a nominal sum for them, but of course he cannot say for certain until we have been through them."

Isham replied at once to express his interest, but warned that his financial position was such that he might not be able to meet the Talbots' price.[27] He asked for details and promised to do all he could to make a purchase. Two further letters soon arrived from Lady Talbot.[28] She explained that the papers were in very bad confusion, but she had been through them and discovered, besides some fragments of the journals, a further portion of the manuscript of the *Life*, and what she described as "notes for the Tour of the Hebrides" with "a certain amount of unpublished matter in them crossed out by Boswell." She also referred to letters from Boswell and other oddments which Isham might wish to offer for. The fragments of the journals were

[25]Agreement between Isham and William Heinemann Ltd. (copy in IFP, dated 1930, no day or month mentioned).

[26]Letter to Isham, 15 April 1930 (copy in TFP).

[27]Letter to Lady Talbot, 6 May 1930 (TFP).

[28]Dated 26 May and 14 June 1930, both to Isham (copies in TFP).

as many as would fit into an envelope twelve inches by nine and this she promised to send to Isham immediately as being included in his earlier purchase. For the "Hebridean Notes" she asked £ 500 and said that Lord Talbot had decided to auction the portion of the *Life* manuscript on the assumption that Isham was not in a position to buy it.

Lady Talbot's discovery presented Isham with serious practical problems. Unless he acquired *all* the new papers, his collection would be incomplete and the prospects for its eventual sale would be impaired. The subscribers to the private edition had been told that "Boswell's Papers in their entirety" had passed to his collection.[29] It was important to maintain his reputation of owning all the Boswell papers from Malahide, even though he had never undertaken to print them all. Scott's volume VI had been largely devoted to interpreting Boswell's biographical method as revealed by the sixteen pages of the manuscript of the *Life* included in the original purchase, and this subject might have to be reassessed in the light of the new discovery. The journal material was also important because of Pottle's decision to print the journals in full from volume VII onwards. As to the remaining items, some of them would be required for the private edition, and all or most of them for the proposed trade and scholarly editions.

Isham was thus confronted with the need to make a further major purchase. The completion of the private edition would inevitably be delayed, which would cost money, and he would also have to pay for any expansion in the size of the remaining volumes by the inclusion of additional material. On 21 July, he wrote urgently to Lady Talbot explaining his difficulties and asking to be allowed to acquire all the new papers, including the manuscript pages of the *Life*. He pointed out that his earlier purchase of sixteen pages had been priced at £ 450 on the assumption that no more of the manuscript had survived, but now that a much larger portion had come to light, his own purchase had depreciated.[30] (He did not add that Rosenbach had paid him $17,000 for only six leaves, a "paper apart," and two Boswell letters.)

On 27 July, Lady Talbot sent Isham all the new journal material (about 150 pages), without charge. Very correctly, she regarded it as being covered by his previous purchase of the entire journals. She also gave brief details of the rest of the find. The so-called "notes

[29]Prospectus for the private edition.
[30]Letter in TFP.

for the Tour of the Hebrides" turned out to be nothing less than the original manuscript of the Hebridean journal with the extensive revisions by which Boswell and Malone had prepared it for the printer in 1785. Besides the journal fragments, there were no fewer than 110 pages of the *Life* manuscript,[31] letters to and from Boswell, materials for writing a Life of Lord Kames, legal notes, and other miscellaneous items.

As soon as Lady Talbot's package arrived, Isham informed Pottle, who was then on vacation.[32] Pottle agreed that it was vital to acquire the whole of the new find, but suggested that Lady Talbot might be persuaded to hand over the Hebridean journal for nothing as being included, like the other journal material, in the original purchase.[33] Despite a transatlantic telephone call from Isham,[34] Lady Talbot would not accept this argument, pointing out that had the existence of the Hebridean journal been known in 1927, it would have been singled out for special treatment as in the case of the Ashbourne journal.[35] Her price of £ 500 was, however, extremely modest—far less than the open market value. She asked £ 3,000 for the 110 manuscript pages of the *Life* and £500 for all the remaining items. She also offered to buy back the portion of the *Life* manuscript already sold to Isham for what he had paid, if he did not wish to give as much as £ 3,000 for the larger portion. She did not of course know that this was impossible because of his previous sale to Rosenbach.[36]

The figure of £4,000 set by Lady Talbot on the new papers brought the total price for all the Malahide papers to just under £ 40,000 (equivalent to $200,000 at the prevailing rate of exchange[37]). Once again Isham faced the problem of raising money, and once again the good-natured Van Alen came to the rescue. He agreed to increase

[31]See Appendix III, pp. 331–32.
[32]Telegram dated 8 August 1930 (copy in IFP).
[33]Letter, Pottle to Isham, 10 August 1930 (IFP).
[34]Referred to in letter, Lady Talbot to Isham, 17 September 1930 (copy in TFP).
[35]Letter, Lady Talbot to Isham, 17 October 1930 (copy in TFP).
[36]See above p. 80.
[37]Actually £39,235, made up as follows:

| | |
|---|---:|
| Goldsmith letter (1926) | £ 400 |
| Miscellaneous papers and letters (1927) | 13,585 |
| Ashbourne journal (1927) | 1,250 |
| The whole of the journal (1927–28) | 20,000 |
| The croquet box find (1930) | 4,000 |
| | £ 39,235 |

his investment in the papers by another $20,000, which provided Isham with just the sum he needed to pay Lady Talbot. He also agreed that his investment would not extend to the newly found portion of the *Life* manuscript, which Isham could therefore deal with as he pleased.[38] This was extremely generous on Van Alen's part, but, for Isham, it was essential. The publication costs of the private edition were a continual drain on his resources, the deficit on the first nine volumes amounting in September 1930 to more than $51,000.[39] He seriously considered changing to another publisher who might be able to complete the work at a lower price, but was deterred by the enormous practical difficulties involved.[40] He had to be free to turn the acquisition of the *Life* manuscript to profitable account and this he achieved with his usual resourcefulness.

In October 1930, he entered into a private agreement with Harold K. Guinzburg of the Viking Press under which Guinzburg advanced $20,000.[41] The understanding was that Isham would complete the purchase of the croquet box find and that the 110 manuscript pages of the *Life*[42] would be Guinzburg's property. These pages were to be at Isham's entire disposal for the purpose of the publication of his collection and, so far as the public was concerned, were to be kept with and treated as part of his collection. Isham also reserved the right to include the pages at a figure of $50,000 in any sale of the entire collection to a public institution within two years. After two years, Guinzburg was to be entitled to sell, but Isham reserved a right of pre-emption. On any sale, Guinzburg was to receive back his $20,000 plus interest and expenses, and one half of any additional profit. At the same time, the earlier agreement with Viking was extended to give Viking the right to publish the *Tour* from the newly discovered manuscript after completion of the private edition. Viking was also given an exclusive world-wide right to publish a limited edition of the *Tour*, subject to Isham's approval as to handling and format.[43]

Soon the whole contents of the croquet box were in Isham's hands, and a circular was sent out to his subscribers:

[38]Copy Memorandum of Agreement, February 1931, between Isham and Van Alen (IFP).

[39]Cost statement (in IFP) for vols. I to IX, W. E. Rudge to Isham, 12 September 1930. Total costs were $154,907.26, against which cash received from subscribers was only $103,555.08. A cash payment of $17,500 from Isham still left a net deficit of nearly $34,000.

[40]Letter, Pottle to Isham, 10 August 1930 (IFP).

[41]Agreement dated 31 October 1930 between Isham and Guinzburg (copy in IFP).

[42]The agreement mentions 107 pages. There were in fact 110. (See Appendix III, p. 332.)

[43]Agreement dated 18 October 1930 between Isham and the Viking Press, Inc. (copy in IFP).

According to the terms of the contract with subscribers, Colonel Isham was under no obligation to include any of this material, nor had Professor Pottle any obligation to edit it. But they both decided that its interest and importance were such that it should be made a part of this edition. Consequently all the new material following in date later than the ninth volume will be included without extra expense to subscribers. This has meant a virtual doubling of the size of the volumes as originally planned. Even so, it now appears that there will not be space in volume XVIII to include the index. For this reason we announce an additional volume No. XIX, which will go to subscribers without cost.[44]

This statement typifies Isham's attitude to the private edition. He was determined that it should be beyond reproach as to completeness, scholarship, and presentation, whatever sacrifices might be involved. Sacrifices he certainly had to make. His preoccupation with the Boswell papers and the depletion of his private fortune in acquiring them was leading to the break-up of his second marriage.[45] In 1927, he had sold many of the most valuable items from his collection of seventeenth- and eighteenth-century books[46] and, in June 1930, he put up eighty-four lots (mostly Goldsmith) for sale by auction at Sotheby's.[47] Early in 1931, he sold his beautiful home at Glen Head,

[44]The "virtual doubling of the size of the volumes as originally planned" was not primarily due to the inclusion of extra material from the croquet box, although Isham's generosity in giving his subscribers more for their money is not in doubt. In his five volumes of texts covering the period 1762–65, Scott omitted a mass of journal notes and memoranda (*Malahide Catalogue* Nos. 1, 3, 4, 5, and 7) and also the "Themes in French" and "Ten Line Verses" (*Malahide Catalogue* Nos. 275 and 276). It was Pottle's decision, approved by Isham, to print the journals in full which chiefly caused the enlargement of the volumes from VII onwards. When the croquet box material arrived, volumes VII, VIII, and IX were already in print and it was decided not to go back and pick up journal material of earlier date than the end of volume IX (21 September 1774). This meant that *Malahide Catalogue*, Nos. 20, 21, 22, 26, 31, 33, 34, and 35, all from the croquet box, were excluded from the private edition. No. 33, the Hebridean journal, was later to be published as a separate book, but the others, apart from extracts in the Yale trade edition, have still not been fully published. In total, the croquet box find added perhaps 100 printed pages to the private edition, consisting of journal material after 1774, the materials for a Life of Lord Kames, JB's "Address as Recorder of Carlisle," and a few letters. (I am indebted to F. A. Pottle for providing me with the detailed information contained in this note.)

[45]It ended in divorce in 1933. See below p. 106.

[46]Catalogue of American Art Association, Inc.: *The Important Collection of XVIIth & XVIIIth Century English Books formed by Lt.-Colonel Ralph H. Isham, C.B.E.*, 7 January 1927 (priced copy in IFP).

[47]Mixed sale at Sotheby's, June 16–19 1930. Lots 1–84 were Isham's (lots 1–75 being Goldsmith material).

Long Island, and the papers were moved to the New York Public Library for safe-keeping.

Before the move, the whole collection was exhibited at the Grolier Club, New York, and a catalogue was compiled by Pottle and his wife, Marion S. Pottle.[48] Pottle prefaced the catalogue with a historical account of the papers which contemporary readers must have found exceptionally thought-provoking. He exploded the myth that the literary executors had neglected their duty, and quoted letters by Forbes and Malone to show that the exact reverse was true. Temple had died before he could play any active part in the literary trust, but Forbes and Malone had gone carefully through the papers at Auchinleck and in London and had decided against publication. Malone's letter to Euphemia Boswell of 4 May 1809 was also published for the first time to show that Malone believed all the papers to have been returned to Auchinleck. Pottle then traced the family history to establish how the papers were finally taken from Auchinleck to Malahide.

Perhaps the most interesting fact to emerge was that an enormous bulk of material was still missing. After the croquet box discovery, Malahide had been searched from top to bottom without yielding anything more, and yet the list of established losses was, in the words of Geoffrey Scott, "long, tragic, and irrational." Pottle commented that there were no letters of Johnson, Wilkes, and Garrick; and many documents referred to in the *Life* and copies of Boswell's own letters which he was known to have made were also missing. The journals were more complete, but the London Journal of 1762–63 was a serious gap. Pottle sought to explain the losses as "what one would expect in a large, miscellaneous, and untidy collection, left probably by its owner in complete confusion, moved several times, subjected at least once to a house-cleaning (in which various particularly disreputable looking scrawls were burned without any reference to their contents), improperly handled, imperfectly protected from dust and damp, and submitted (probably more than once) to censorship of a capricious

---

[48]*The Private Papers of James Boswell from Malahide Castle in the Collection of Lt.-Colonel Ralph Heyward Isham, a Catalogue* by Frederick A. Pottle & Marion S. Pottle, published by the Oxford University Press, New York, 1931 in a binding to match the rest of the private edition. The catalogue was also issued in paper under the imprint of the Grolier Club, without the preface, under the title: *Catalogue of an Exhibition of the Private Papers of James Boswell from Malahide Castle. Held at the Grolier Club, New York, December Eighteenth, 1930, to February Seventh, 1931.* The catalogue is elsewhere cited in this work as *"Malahide Catalogue."*

and arbitrary nature."[49] Pottle also suggested that James Boswell junior might have removed dossiers of correspondence in which he was particularly interested. Neither of these explanations entirely satisfied him and he wrote: "The situation is excessively complicated, and no one theory seems completely to fit the facts."[50]

The possibility obviously existed that further riches might still remain to be discovered. But Malahide and Auchinleck had apparently been exhausted, and if there *were* any other papers, there was no clue to suggest where they might be.

After the exhibition at the Grolier Club closed in February 1931, Pottle worked daily on the papers in the New York Public Library and made good progress in preparing the copy for the remaining volumes of the private edition. Volumes X, XI, and XII were all brought out in 1931. In August of that year, he wrote to Isham that volume XIII was in galley proof, volume XIV nearly so, and most of the copy for volume XV and 100 pages of the copy for volume XVI had been sent to the printer.[51] Even so, it was clear that he would not be able to complete the eighteen volumes by the deadline of 1 October 1931 stipulated in his contract. This was because of the decision to print the journals in full, the enlargement of the collection by the croquet box find, and the period of more than three months needed to prepare the catalogue. He had undertaken this additional work without asking for extra remuneration, but inevitably had been thrown behind schedule. His leave of absence from Yale was due to expire at the end of September and he would then have to resume his teaching duties at New Haven. This meant not only that he would be able to devote less time to the papers, but also that access to them in the New York Public Library would be inconvenient. To overcome this problem, the Library offered to make negative photostats of the entire collection at their own expense and to supply positives which could be paid for as and when needed.[52] In the spring of 1932, the Department of English at Yale gave a grant for a complete duplicate set of photostats which made Pottle largely independent of the New York Public Library.

What Pottle now requested, reasonably enough, was a relaxation

[49]*Malahide Catalogue*, p. xxiv.
[50]Ibid., pp. xxiv–xxv.
[51]Letter dated 16 August 1931 (in IFP).
[52]Ibid.

of the time limits set in his contract and the continued services of Helen Cohan.[53] Isham could hardly refuse, for he had concurred in the decision to expand the scope of the private edition and it was at his request that valuable time had been spent on preparing the catalogue. The prospect of getting some return from his outlay was still remote and in the meantime publication costs continued to mount. Even Helen Cohan's salary became an embarrassment. In December 1932, he wrote to Pottle: "By the way, how much longer do you think Helen will be necessary for you? Of course I am very fond of her but the $50 a week is piling up against me frightfully."[54] So acute was the financial pressure that, in April 1932, he asked Pottle to find out if Yale were interested in buying his whole collection. Pottle approached W. S. Lewis, Tinker, and President Angell, but the response was not encouraging. He wrote to Isham: "Everybody wants to sell MSS. dirt cheap just now.[55] . . . [Yale's] regular appropriation is very small normally, and has been severely cut because of the deficit."[56] He did not think that an appeal to the rich alumni at the moment would be likely to bring results. After further negotiation, one rich alumnus was found who might have been prepared to finance the purchase, but only at a price considerably below what Isham had paid.[57] Not surprisingly, Isham did not pursue the matter.

A few days after these negotiations had fallen through, Isham was shocked to receive a letter from Pottle giving details of an important batch of papers, apparently from Boswell's archives, to be sold by auction at Sotheby's on 1 and 2 June 1932.[58] The catalogue described them simply as "The Property of a Lady." They comprised three fine letters by Boswell to his son Sandy, a draft of a letter "to a Peer" concerning the murder of Mungo Miller at Mauchline, an autograph notebook of eleven pages, containing amongst other things a draft of a dedication of Wanley's *Wonders* to the Earl of Eglinton and an

[53]Ibid.

[54]Letter, Isham to Pottle, 2 December 1932 (copy in IFP).

[55]Isham's chances of selling were not enhanced by the fact that, in December 1931, R. B. Adam offered Tinker a six-months' option for the purchase of his superb Johnsonian collection by Yale. No price was stipulated, but Rosenbach, as Adam's agent, indicated $1,000,000 (letter, Tinker to Adam, 20 December 1931). Tinker wrote to Adam on 13 February 1932 releasing the option because of the difficulty of raising the money.

[56]Letter, Pottle to Isham, 24 April 1932 (IFP).

[57]The alumnus was Edward Harkness. Pottle thought he might be able to interest Harkness at a figure of $150,000 to $200,000 (letter from Pottle to Isham dated 26 April 1932 in IFP). This might have covered the bare cost of purchasing the papers, but none of Isham's huge outlay on editing, publishing, travelling, and so forth.

[58]Letter dated 18 May 1932 (IFP).

account of Boswell's dream at Carlisle in 1785; an autograph account of how his daughter Euphemia had thrashed a boy for ill-treating a little child; an autograph manuscript of an epitaph by Lady Cochrane on Lord Dundee and an anecdote of the Earl of Argyll; an autograph manuscript entitled "Uxoriana, or My Dear Wife's excellent sayings"; a certain amount of autograph material by Sir Alexander Boswell; autograph manuscripts of verses by Samuel Johnson; letters to Boswell from Sir Alexander Dick, Francis Gentleman, Margaret Montgomerie (afterwards Boswell's wife), and Rousseau; and a few other items, including a letter from Sarah, Duchess of Marlborough, to Mr. Rudd with an autograph endorsement by Boswell, and a fine letter from Sir Walter Scott to Lady Boswell on the death of her husband, Sir Alexander.

Pottle wrote to Isham:

> This lot of MSS. must have come from Malahide Castle; no other collection could have furnished them. Lady Talbot has either found another croquet box, or, as I fear, held them out of the MSS. she sold you in 1930. I must say that I find the review of them very disheartening. The letter from Rousseau is important, but we could hardly print it in our remaining volumes. The same is true of the letter by Peggy Montgomerie and the various scraps of Boswelliana. But the three letters to Sandy surely ought to go in our last volume; it will be a sad thing to have to admit that your fine series does not contain *all* the letters now preserved which Boswell wrote to his heir. All the items listed should, of course, be in your collection to preserve its integrity, but I am thinking of the situation from the position of an editor of the Boswell Papers.[59]

For the second time, Isham found himself seriously embarrassed by the unexpected appearance of important new material. Pottle's advice was that he should cable a strong expostulation to Lord Talbot protesting at the unfairness of selling the manuscripts at public auction.[60] Isham followed this advice and dispatched a rather hotheaded cable to Lord Talbot who replied immediately, denying all knowledge of the new papers.[61] Newton was asked if he could help and he made an indirect approach to Sotheby's, who refused

[59]Ibid.
[60]Ibid.
[61]Cable dated 20 May 1932 and copy letter from Lord Talbot to Isham dated 20 May 1932 (TFP).

to disclose the name of their client.[62] Newton did not, however, think that Lady Talbot was involved.

Isham lacked the means to bid himself and could only wait for the sale to take place in the hope that the purchasers would allow him to print the more important items. The three letters to Sandy, the draft letter concerning the murder of Mungo Miller, and the letters from Peggy Montgomerie and Rousseau were all bought by Alwin J. Scheuer, the New York bookseller. Scheuer retained the two best letters to Sandy (for which he paid a total of £ 55), but allowed Isham to print them. The other four letters (for which he paid a total of only £ 27.10/–) he resold to Isham and they were all printed in the private edition.[63] The autograph notebook and the manuscript of "Uxoriana" both went to Tinker, by whose permission the account of Boswell's dream at Carlisle was printed in a footnote in volume XVI.[64] Isham was not able to print any of the remaining lots from the sale, but he had at least been able to obtain or print the more important ones. He later discovered[65] that the anonymous lady seller was Mrs. Laurence Eliott, a great-great-granddaughter of the Biographer.[66]

Meanwhile, Pottle continued to devote every moment which could be spared from his professorial duties to completing his work on the private edition. His progress was inevitably slower than before, but he managed to bring out volumes XIII, XIV, XV, and XVI by the end of 1932. During this year, he also succeeded in solving the puzzle of the shorthand which Boswell sometimes used in his journals and

---

[62]The approach was made on Newton's behalf by Elkin Mathews Ltd., the London booksellers (copy letter Elkin Mathews Ltd. to Sotheby & Co. dated 20 May 1932 and reply dated 23 May 1932, both in IFP).

[63]Scheuer resold to Isham at cost plus 10 percent commission (invoice dated 11 June 1932 in IFP).

[64]The information about purchasers and prices in the 1932 sale comes from a priced copy of the catalogue, photostats of which were kindly sent to me by Gabriel Austin, formerly Librarian of the Grolier Club. Tinker paid £90 for the autograph notebook and £27 for "Uxoriana." Ellison bought the autograph account of Euphemia for £15, the epitaph on Lord Dundee and the anecdote of the Earl of Argyll for £11, the autograph material by Sir Alexander Boswell for £3.15/– and an autograph copy letter from JB to M. Sommelsdyck for £3.10/–. The autograph manuscript of Johnson's verses *"Festina lente"* and "Upon the Feast of St. Simon and St. Jude" were sold to Hay for £40 and £52 respectively and are now in the Hyde Collection. The letter from the Duchess of Marlborough to Mr. Rudd went to Patch for £1.10/–, who also bought a letter from Dr. Edward Jenner to Mrs. Cuming for £2.10/–. Quaritch bought the letter from Sir Walter Scott to Lady Boswell for £15. The letters from Sir Alexander Dick and Francis Gentleman to JB fetched only 5/– apiece from Cash and Dobell respectively.

[65]The information came from Scheuer.

[66]Her grandmother was Janet Theresa Boswell, Sir Alexander Boswell's elder daughter who married Sir William Eliott, seventh Baronet of Stobs and Wells. (See Table IV, p. 355.)

which until then had defied decipherment. In the autumn of 1931, he had begun to teach a course called "The Boswell Papers" in the Yale Graduate School. Each student was given a photostat portion of the journals from which to prepare an annotated text with introduction and index. One of these students, Charles H. Bennett, worked on the London memoranda of 1763, which contained several cipher passages of considerable length. He thought that these passages looked like shorthand—probably an eighteenth-century system. He investigated Mason's system, but found Boswell was not using this. Another student, Hale Sturges, worked on the Dutch memoranda of 1763 to 1764 which also contained some sentences in cipher. Whilst checking Sturges's work, Pottle noticed from the photostat of the original manuscript that at one place Boswell had written out a longhand passage below a passage in cipher and he guessed, correctly, that both passages said the same thing. This gave him the key to the greater part of the shorthand alphabet which he was able to complete by referring to the cipher passages in the London memoranda. On consulting old manuals of shorthand in the Yale library, he was able to identify the cipher as the shorthand system of Thomas Shelton, first published in 1641 in a book called *Tachygraphy*.[67] By a remarkable coincidence, the system was the same as that used by Pepys in his diary.[68]

By the end of 1932, volume XVII of the private edition was in galley proof and two-thirds of the copy for volume XVIII was nearly ready. Pottle estimated that he would have both volumes ready to publish in June 1933. In the meantime, a start had been made on the immense task of preparing slips for the index to be published as volume XIX. Pottle was, of course, under no obligation to compile this index, but because of its importance, he agreed to undertake the task, provided he had help with the preparation of the slips. His aim was to have all the slips ready by the time volume XVIII was published.[69]

Pottle's forecast of publication dates was over-optimistic. Volume

[67]See Pottle's letter on "Boswell's Shorthand," *The Times Literary Supplement*, 28 July 1932.

[68]Letter, Pottle to Isham, 2 August 1932 (IFP). Pottle reported that the cipher passages were about what one would expect. Some of them were quite innocent and must have been written for practice rather than secrecy. Others were of an atrocious nature such as "swear no more rogering before you leave England, except with Mrs L." Many of the passages concerned Temple's brother Robert: "Behave distant to Bob," etc. (JB was in the habit of showing his journals to Temple so it was an obvious precaution to put such passages in cipher.) On one occasion he debated whether or not he had time to have a girl in the park before an appointment with Johnson at the Mitre at 9 o'clock.

[69]Letter, Pottle to Isham, 4 December 1932 (IFP).

XVII appeared in the autumn of 1933 and it was not until 22 December 1933 that he was able to write to Isham:

> On Thursday night I returned the last bit of corrected proof for Volume XVIII and can at last say that the work I undertook so jauntily four years and more ago is finished. Of course there is still the index volume, but I don't feel that as such a responsibility. ... I know that the set has taken too long to finish and that everything has changed since those hectic days when you and Scott and Rudge planned it. But it *is* done, and it is a great achievement. Whatever its defects, it is a landmark in the history of literature. As time goes on people will come to realize more and more what a courageous and generous act it was to publish such a set of books—as I have realized ever since I became editor.[70]

The index proved to be a much more formidable undertaking than expected. The final number of slips was about 50,000, double Pottle's original estimate.[71] Their preparation was undertaken by Mrs. Pottle, Miss Cohan, and Dr. Charles H. Bennett. Bennett was also responsible for going through the slips and adding the necessary identifications—a huge task, because in the private edition the texts had been printed without annotation.[72] Pottle and his wife contributed their services for nothing and Bennett was able to work for at least a year without cost to Isham, thanks to a grant from the General Education Research Board at Yale.[73] Even so, Isham's financial sacrifice was considerable, for progress on a profitable trade edition was inevitably delayed. Although he was under no obligation to present his subscribers with a separate index volume running to more than 350 pages,[74] he supported the project because he realized that a comprehensive index would be an essential tool for future research on the papers.

Meanwhile, his troubles continued. In 1933, his second marriage finally ended in a divorce. His income from the family trust which in 1932 had been $29,400 plunged in 1933 to $17,050 and in 1934

[70]Letter, Pottle to Isham, 22 December 1933 (IFP).

[71]*Malahide Index*, p. viii.

[72]Ibid. Bennett was greatly helped in the references down to 1773 by the collections of the graduate students named on p. viii, but none of them, except Foladare and Kirby, worked directly on the index. From 1773 to 1795, Bennett had to research each name himself. (Note from F. A. Pottle.) As to Foladare's and Kirby's participation, see below, pp. 108–09.

[73]Bennett received a stipend of $1500 a year (later $1800) and worked full-time on the Boswell papers under Pottle's direction for six or seven years from 1933 onwards. (Note from F. A. Pottle.)

[74]He had originally intended to include a simple index at the end of volume XVIII, although the prospectus advertising the private edition does not mention any sort of index.

to $7,396.[75] To raise funds, he undertook an arduous programme of broadcasts and lectures. His weekly radio series "The Romance of Literature," went out over the "Red Network" and was heard by more than eighty stations from coast to coast. As a lecturer on the Boswell papers he was brilliant. Louise Richardson, Librarian of Florida State College, told him: "All our speakers are rated now by you. Not infrequently do we hear remarks like the following: 'Oh yes, he was all right but not in the class with Colonel Isham.' "[76] By 1936, he could command an average fee of $200 a lecture and it was not unusual for him to deliver as many as seven lectures within the space of a fortnight.[77]

Broadcast and lecture fees eased financial problems, but did not remove them. In 1933, shortage of money compelled him to put up for auction a further large portion of his library, including Johnson manuscript material and important first editions.[78] Market prices were depressed and for a collector such as Isham it is difficult to imagine a bigger sacrifice. After the sale, A. E. Newton wrote to R. W. Chapman: "I am sending for your edification and horror a priced catalogue of the Isham slaughter."[79] Later, he told his fellow collector R. B. Adam:

Isham's books were thrown away literally. There was a time when he could have had as much as he received for the lot for the

[75]Isham's trust income for the years 1928 to 1934 was:

| | |
|---|---|
| 1928 | $28,280 |
| 1929 | $21,780 |
| 1930 | $36,350 |
| 1931 | $30,400 |
| 1932 | $29,400 |
| 1933 | $17,050 |
| 1934 | $ 7,396 |

Information obtained by W. L. Payne from Messrs. Carey and Jardine (1928–30) and from documents found in State House Annex, Trenton, New Jersey (1931–34).

[76]"Comments on Colonel Ralph H. Isham" (undated) issued by Clark H. Getts (copy in IFP).

[77]For example his schedule for two weeks in April 1936 was as follows:

| | | |
|---|---|---|
| April 13 | Pittsburgh | $200 |
| 15 | Philadelphia | 200 |
| 18 | Cleveland | 50 |
| 21 | Columbus | 250 |
| 23 | Minneapolis | 200 |
| 27 (A.M.) | Yellow Springs | 100 |
| 27 (P.M.) | Chicago | 200 |

[78]Sale Number 4041, May 4, 1933, of the American Art Association, Anderson Galleries, Inc. Priced Catalogue (*The Renowned Library of Lieutenant-Colonel Ralph H. Isham, C. B. E.*) in IFP.

[79]Letter dated 31 May 1933.

presentation Johnson.[80] I am very sorry for Isham, he is very erratic and in terrible trouble, trouble from which no one can extricate him.[81]

In February 1935, Isham sold the 110 pages of the manuscript of the *Life* found in the croquet box to Rosenbach for $35,000.[82] Under his agreement with Guinzburg,[83] he had to repay the latter $20,000 with interest at 6 per cent from October 1930. Guinzburg was also entitled to a further $7,500, being one half of the amount by which the price paid by Rosenbach exceeded the sum of $20,000. The balance left for Isham was not much more than $2,000.

There was little hope of any further financial relief until the profits started coming in from the publication of the complete version of the *Tour*, Pottle's popular biography of Boswell, and the trade edition of the papers. Progress on these projects was held up while so much work remained to be done on the index. Two years earlier, Isham had agreed that Pottle might have unlimited time to complete the biography, despite the deadline set in his contract.[84] Pottle, for his part, had offered to economize by dispensing with the services of Miss Cohan when working on the biography;[85] but even this saving could not be achieved so long as her help was required for the index.[86]

By the end of 1934, Pottle needed a full-time paid assistant to compile the copy for the index under his direction, and Dr. Joseph Foladare was employed at Isham's expense[87] for a spell of six months. In May 1935, Pottle reported that Foladare could not complete his work within the time allowed and would, in any event, be unable to continue when his six months were up.[88] Isham agreed to the employ-

[80]Lot No. 27. A copy of the first edition of the *Life* (1791) presented to Wilkes, sold for $2,250. The following are examples of the pathetic prices realized: Lot 17, Sir Alexander Boswell's copy of the first edition of the *Tour*, $25; Lot 13, Boswell's rare pamphlet, *A Letter to the People of Scotland, on the Present State of the Nation* (1783), $15; Lot 32 a fine extra-illustrated presentation copy of James Boswell junior's *A Biographical Memoir of the late Edmond Malone* (1814), $15; and Lot 70, a first edition of Johnson's *An Account of the Life of Mr. Richard Savage* (1744), $17.50.

[81]Letter, Newton to Adam, 7 July 1933 (Hyde Collection).

[82]Correspondence in files of the Philip H. and A. S. W. Rosenbach Foundation.

[83]See above p. 98.

[84]Letter, Isham to Pottle, 23 February 1933 (copy in IFP).

[85]Letter, Pottle to Isham, 4 December 1932 (IFP).

[86]Letter, Pottle to Isham, 2 April 1934 (IFP).

[87]Isham was fortunate to obtain the services of Foladare, and also those of his successor, Kirby, at the very modest salary scale of $1,500 a year.

[88]Letter, Pottle to Isham, 6 May 1935 (IFP).

ment of a successor and Pottle obtained the services of John P. Kirby, who had already had experience of indexing for *The Encyclopaedia Britannica*. Kirby also ran out of time but, after a further short extension, Pottle reported, on 22 August 1935, that the copy for the index was finished, apart from the articles on Boswell and Johnson which he intended to write himself.[89] A month later he had completed these, revised the entire copy, and sent it off to the publishers. He thought the volume could be issued early in 1936.[90]

The private edition was still seriously under-subscribed. In November 1931, Isham had complained to Newton that ninety of the subscribers refused to take the volumes still to be issued;[91] and by 1934, when all eighteen volumes had appeared, a large number of sets lay unsold in Rudge's warehouse. W. E. Rudge had died in 1931. He had collaborated with Isham and Scott in planning the private edition and had taken a close personal interest in the project. For Pottle, his death meant the loss of "a friend such as we are not likely to find again."[92] Afterwards, relations with his firm became much more impersonal and gradually deteriorated until the firm itself went out of business in May 1936. Pottle criticized the firm strongly for not lifting a finger to get additional orders and even failing to answer letters from prospective purchasers.[93] He stressed the need for an active selling policy, pointing out that times had improved and that the completion of the set had focussed public attention on the books.[94] The publication of the index would also help push sales, but it was imperative to get rid of as many sets as possible before the appearance of the cheaper trade edition.[95] With the help of Pottle, Isham managed to sell off a number of additional sets to American universities and others, but only at very much reduced prices which averaged less than half the original price of $900.[96] Final evidence of the disorganized state of Rudge's after the death of W. E. Rudge came when the firm terminated business in 1936[97] when Isham instructed an inventory of all volumes on hand to be made: 412 volumes were found to be

[89]Letter to Isham (IFP).
[90]Letter, Pottle to Isham, 23 September 1935 (IFP).
[91]Information from letter, Newton to Adam, 21 November 1931 (Hyde Collection).
[92]Letter, Pottle to Isham, 14 June 1931 (IFP).
[93]Letter, Pottle to Isham, 2 April 1934 (IFP).
[94]Letter, Pottle to Isham, 26 May 1934 (IFP).
[95]Letter, Pottle to Isham, undated, but probably October 1934 (IFP).
[96]e.g., University of Minnesota, $500; Ohio University and Colgate, each $350.
[97]On 1 May 1936.

missing and it was discovered that they had been accidentally removed by an employee in the bindery and destroyed with surplus stores.[98] Isham was thus left with a large number of broken sets which were virtually unsaleable.

The printing of the index was undertaken not by Rudge, but by the Oxford University Press. Isham was reluctant to take the work away from Rudge, but in his straitened circumstances he could not afford to disregard the very favourable terms which Pottle was able to negotiate with R. W. Chapman. Chapman was of course familiar with the private edition and recognized its importance to all workers in the field of eighteenth-century biography and literary history. The original intention had been to issue the index only to subscribers for the complete set of eighteen volumes; but Chapman felt there were many who could not afford the complete set who would wish to own the index. He therefore arranged to print additional copies in sheets and to buy these back from Isham for public sale. In this way, Isham's net outlay for printing, binding, and delivery to the subscribers was kept to the minimum.[99] The work was eventually published in 1937 and, in his preface, Pottle paid "grateful tribute to Colonel Isham for his generosity and public spirit."[100] In a private letter, Pottle wrote: "That book is very much to your credit, for you planned and executed it with no prospect of any financial return, simply to make the Papers accessible to the scholarly public."[101]

Meanwhile, Guinzburg of Viking and A. S. Frere-Reeves of Heinemann were becoming restive about the delay in fulfilling their contracts. The delay was due to Isham's decision to produce both a catalogue and an index, the arrival of the new material from the croquet box, the policy of printing the journals in full from volume VII onwards, and the greatly expanded scope of the trade edition. Isham had undertaken to deliver the copy for the trade edition over a period of two years between the spring of 1932 and the spring of 1934. He was clearly in breach of contract and, by the autumn of 1934, Frere-Reeves in particular had become very impatient. Guinz-

---

[98]Deposition of Melvin Loos dated 23 September 1940 (IFP).

[99]The arrangements for publishing the index are discussed at length in the Pottle-Isham correspondence in IFP. The net cost for printing 1,250 copies, including the binding of 607 copies, after allowing for 250 copies bought back by the publisher at 21/– each, was £208.3/–.

[100]*Index to the Private Papers of James Boswell from Malahide Castle in the Collection of Lt-Colonel Ralph Heyward Isham* (1937), Preface, p. ix. The index is cited elsewhere as "*Malahide Index*".

[101]Letter to Isham, 23 December 1936 (IFP).

burg, perhaps because he was on the scene, had more sympathy with Isham's difficulties. He seems to have become reconciled to the fact that the delay was inevitable and that it might take years for Pottle to complete the text of the public edition. He did feel, however, that it should be possible to publish the complete version of the *Tour*, which would entail relatively little work and which was likely to be the most valuable single volume from a commercial point of view. So far as the rest of the publication was concerned, he accepted that Pottle would proceed with his work as rapidly as possible and that in the meantime it would be foolish to make any further plans. He knew, too, that Pottle would have to face a problem of priorities, because he had an independent agreement with Alfred Harcourt to write a biography of Boswell and this agreement predated Isham's agreements with Viking and Heinemann. Guinzburg realized that such a biography would be an extremely important book and felt that it should be written; but if Pottle took a year off for the job, his own publication would be further delayed. In October 1934, he wrote to Frere-Reeves explaining the situation at length.[102] Frere-Reeves replied that he wanted a much better assurance.[103] He felt that as Isham had committed himself to certain dates, he should obtain the necessary assistance to enable him to meet his obligations. He warned that Isham "should realize that our patience may not be inexhaustible." He was also furious that the biography was to go to another publisher and suggested that Pottle be told that "we will resist every attempt to publish it elsewhere until our own *complete* edition of the Boswell Papers has been published."[104]

Isham was seriously worried by his position and sought Pottle's advice. "James Boswell will be the death of us," he wrote.[105] Pottle was reassuring. He did not believe that Frere-Reeves would ever bring suit for fulfilment of the contract and suggested that Isham should just continue to temporize as tactfully and apologetically as he could.[106] There was little that either Guinzburg or Frere-Reeves could do but to accept the situation, and in the meantime Pottle promised to do the work well and conscientiously, and as fast as he could.

At the beginning of 1935, Pottle made a start on preparing the text of the *Tour* from the manuscript. He found it much the best

[102]Letter dated 23 October 1934 (copy in IFP).
[103]Letter dated 1 November 1934 (copy in IFP).
[104]Ibid.
[105]Letter, Isham to Pottle, 23 November 1934 (copy in IFP).
[106]Letter, Pottle to Isham, 26 November 1934 (IFP).

thing in Isham's whole collection and thought that a popular edition should be successful. It was clear, though, that it would make a very big book, for the typescript of the text alone ran to 450 pages.[107] Bennett collaborated in the editing and the work progressed rapidly with assistance from Kirby, who worked on a preliminary index.[108] The Viking Press announced with a considerable flourish that a limited edition of the work[109] would be issued in November 1936, which would have "the unique distinction of being the first edition, published 163 years after it was written, of a work that has been famous for generations." The printed announcement (which contained an exceptionally misleading and inaccurate history of the papers) also promised that all the other Boswell material from Isham's collection would be published, beginning in 1937.[110]

---

[107]Letter, Pottle to Isham, 1 January 1935 (IFP).

[108]Letter, Pottle to Isham, 28 October 1935 (IFP).

[109]Limited to 790 copies.

[110]This announcement was written by someone at the Viking Press and was never approved by Pottle. Viking also suppressed a brief history of the papers by Pottle which constituted the first half of his preface, and substituted a "Publisher's Note." Pottle explains that this is why his preface as printed begins so abruptly.

# IV

# *"Operation Hush"*

BY the early spring of 1936, most of Isham's difficulties seemed to be over. The magnificent private edition was complete except for the index, which was in the hands of the printers and soon to be published. He had weathered the financial pressures which followed the stock market crash of 1929, the death of his first editor, the embarrassment of coping with a mass of new material, and above all the seemingly endless delays. The integrity of his collection of Boswell papers had for the most part been preserved and the private edition was properly comprehensive.

The cost had been high: he had sacrificed his home, his marriage, his fortune, much of his cherished collection of books, and also, unavoidably, a few items from the papers themselves;[1] but now he was poised to reap the rewards of years of endeavour. The Viking-Heinemann edition was about to be launched with the complete version of the *Tour*, and Pottle's biography of Boswell for Harcourt would follow. These publications were expected to yield a profit and Isham looked forward to getting back at last some part of his enormous outlay.

The first hint that all was not well came in a cryptic telegram from Chapman to Pottle:[2]

1936 MAR 9.

TIMES 9 MARCH ANNOUNCES DISCOVERY SCOTLAND MANY MISSING BOSWELL PAPERS STOP AM SENDING YOU COPIES WITH LETTER—

CHAPMAN.

[1]See above pp. 80 and 108.
[2]In IFP.

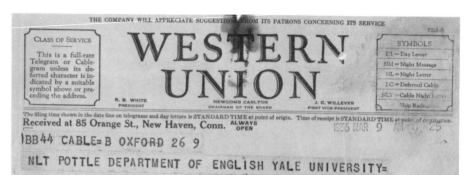

BB44 CABLE=B OXFORD 26 9

NLT POTTLE DEPARTMENT OF ENGLISH YALE UNIVERSITY=

NEWHAVENCONN=

TIMES 9 MARCH ANNOUNCES DISCOVERY SCOTLAND MANY MISSING

BOSWELL PAPERS STOP AM SENDING YOU COPIES WITH LETTER=

CHAPMAN..

*Received this this morning. I suppose the N.Y. papers will have something to-morrow — can't imagine what has turned up, but I suspect its letters.*

*FAP*

R. W. CHAPMAN'S CABLE TO F. A. POTTLE
Breaking the news of the Fettercairn discovery.

The telegram arrived without forewarning and Pottle was understandably perplexed. He sent it straight to Isham with this scribbled comment:

> Received this this morning. I suppose the N.Y. papers will have something to-morrow—can't imagine what has turned up, but I suspect it's *letters*.
>
> FAP.

Nothing was to be discovered from the American newspapers the following day and it was not until Chapman's promised letter arrived on 20 March that Pottle and Isham learnt the devastating truth.[3] The announcement in *The Times* took the form of a letter to the editor from Professor C. Colleer Abbott of University College, Durham, which began as follows:

> Sir,—It was my privilege, in 1930–31, while a lecturer in the University of Aberdeen, to be allowed to examine the miscellaneous documents scattered through a Scottish country house. I had particular reason for wishing to make the search, but, though I went with high hopes, the result bettered my expectation. The full story of the finding must be left till later; but I am now free to make public the more important results of it.

What Abbott had discovered, as his letter went on to make clear, was a mass of Boswell papers (in bulk perhaps about half the size of Isham's entire collection) which included the vitally important London journal of 1762–63, part of the journal for 1778, the Northern Circuit journal for the autumn of 1788, two registers of letters sent and received, the correspondence between Boswell and Forbes, 287 drafts or copies of letters from Boswell, 1,030 letters to Boswell, and 119 letters from Johnson to various correspondents. Abbott asked to be excused any correspondence on the subject, but indicated that a detailed catalogue of the entire find would be published later in the year by the Oxford University Press.

---

[3]Letter, Pottle to Isham, 20 March 1936 (IFP), partly quoted below, p. 143.

The catalogue appeared eight months later, in November 1936,[4] and Abbott's introduction gives a fascinating account of what was perhaps the most remarkable discovery in the whole history of the Boswell papers. It was a discovery in the true sense of the word. Unlike the papers acquired by Isham from Malahide, which had always been known to the family, most of those found by Abbott had lain forgotten at Fettercairn for generations.

His story is an extraordinary one.[5] In 1928, when a lecturer at the University of Aberdeen, he became interested in a collection of papers relating to James Beattie (1735–1803), Professor of Moral Philosophy and Logic in the Marischal College at Aberdeen. The Beattie papers had come into the possession of the University after being used by Margaret Forbes as the basis of her book *Beattie and his Friends*, published in 1904. A century earlier, a life of Beattie had been written by Sir William Forbes, Boswell's friend and executor.[6] Abbott went through the papers to compare the materials used for the two books and discovered that many of the manuscripts which had been available to Forbes were missing. In the course of his work, he became increasingly interested in Forbes for his own sake rather than merely as the biographer of Beattie:

It began to seem strange that he made so small a figure in literary history. He was, for example, not only Boswell's friend, but also his executor and the guardian of his children. Yet in Professor Tinker's excellent edition of Boswell's *Letters* there was no letter to him. In a century so fully documented how had it come about that more had not been heard of a man so active and considerable, who had won from Walter Scott affectionate poetic tribute? He must have left papers. He certainly left an heir. My inquiries, which were not methodical, gave me no satisfaction.[7]

---

[4]*A Catalogue of Papers Relating to Boswell, Johnson & Sir William Forbes Found at Fettercairn House a Residence of the Rt. Hon. Lord Clinton 1930–31*, Oxford at the Clarendon Press, 1936. Elsewhere cited and referred to as "*Fettercairn Catalogue*."

[5]It is told in Abbott's introduction to the *Fettercairn Catalogue*. Since this is a scarce book, inaccessible to most readers outside a large library, it is retold here. Much of the narrative which follows is based on Abbott's own account. The extensive quotations are by kind permission of the Clarendon Press and C. C. Abbott's literary trustees.

[6]Sir William Forbes of Pitsligo, Bart.: *An Account of the Life and Writings of James Beattie, LL.D. . . .*, Edinburgh, 1806, 2 vols.

[7]*Fettercairn Catalogue*, Introduction, p. xiv.

Abbott investigated Pitsligo, the country seat of the Forbes family, but found nothing. Then came an essential clue, provided by the late Alistair Tayler, who, with his sister Henrietta, published in 1930 *Jacobite Letters to Lord Pitsligo, 1745–46, preserved at Fettercairn House.*[8] Fettercairn House was the Kincardineshire home of Baron Clinton of Maxtock and Saye, at whose desire Tayler edited the letters. Whilst at Fettercairn, Tayler either saw or was told of the existence there of certain Beattie papers. He was also aware that Fettercairn contained Forbes material. In the preface to his book, dated 1 February 1930, he describes how the Jacobite letters were in a packet docketed on the outside in Forbes's hand; he also knew that Lord Clinton was Forbes's great-great-grandson. When Forbes died in 1806, his title passed to his elder son, William, who became the seventh Baronet. In 1797, the young William had married Sir Walter Scott's early love, Wilhelmina Wishart Belsches Stuart, only child of Baron Sir John Stuart of Fettercairn House. Fettercairn thus came into the Forbes family and passed by marriage and descent to Lord Clinton.[9]

Lord Clinton married Lady Jane Grey McDonnell, whose book *Happy Hours in a Scottish Home* (1902)[10] hinted at exciting discoveries to be made at Fettercairn:

Part of the quaint feeling which pervades the house is, no doubt, owing to the fact of its being so full of old-world contents, things having remained in the same place for generations, old bundles still tied with faded ribbons by fingers at rest for many an age. Some one jokingly remarked that you are lucky if you pick up a paper published in this century. . . .[11]

and in a later passage:

I often go and hunt among the funny old cupboards and unused rooms and have found many treasures.[12]

[8]*Jacobite Letters to Lord Pitsligo, 1745–1746, Preserved at Fettercairn House*, ed. Alistair and Henrietta Tayler, Aberdeen, 1930.
[9]See Table VI, p. 357.
[10]Jane Grey Forbes Trefusis, Baroness Clinton: *Happy Hours in a Scottish Home*, 1902, privately printed by William Brown, 26 Princes Street, Edinburgh.
[11]Ibid., p. 29.
[12]Ibid., p. 33.

Lady Clinton's book was privately printed and hence little known. Fettercairn remained unexplored by scholars and, even when the Taylers were invited there to work on the Jacobite papers, they did not attempt any systematic search.

Alistair Tayler learned of Abbott's interest in Beattie from his friend, the late Dr. Douglas Simpson, Librarian of Aberdeen University, to whom he reported that there was Beattie material at Fettercairn. Simpson passed this information on to Abbott and, at Abbott's request, wrote to Lord Clinton asking that any papers of interest might be sent to Aberdeen.[13] Towards the end of January 1930, a box arrived from Fettercairn and Abbott set to work on the contents:

[13]It has been alleged that Tayler, and not Abbott, was the first man to discover Boswell material at Fettercairn. Certainly Tayler preceded Abbott at Fettercairn and it was his report of Beattie material there that provided Abbott with the clue he needed. This Abbott is at pains to acknowledge in his introduction. Dr. Simpson had no recollection of Tayler saying anything to him about Boswell material and no reference to any is made in the preface to Tayler's book. Before publication of the *Fettercairn Catalogue*, Tayler made no public claim to have discovered any Boswell papers. Yet on 12 February 1937, after the catalogue had appeared, he said in an address to a meeting of the Clan Chattan Association: "At another house when searching for and finding Jacobite material, I was delighted to discover a collection of letters from James Boswell, which has proved a somewhat important literary discovery." (*Clan Chattan . . . Journal of the Clan Chattan Association*, I, No. 4 (1937), pp. 99–100.) Tayler may have seen some Boswell papers at Fettercairn, but if he did so, he did not make it known publicly until 1937, nor was he sufficiently interested to make a proper search. The bulk of the papers catalogued by Abbott were found in repositories which had clearly been undisturbed for many years. Tayler could not have had the slightest idea of their existence. He probably saw the same portfolio which was shown to Abbott on his first evening at Fettercairn and which contained amongst other things a few letters *to* JB (see below). He may also have seen the papers laid out for Abbott on his first day at Fettercairn, which were readily accessible and which included JB's London journal 1762–63 and letters to JB from his children. But Tayler did not claim to have seen any of these items. Professor Pottle reminds me that the first parcel which Abbott handled amongst those laid out for him was labelled by Sir William Forbes: "Letters from Mr. Boswell of Auchinleck, and from his brother Mr. James." Pottle suggests very plausibly that Tayler may have seen this parcel and had it in mind when reporting his discovery of "a collection of letters from James Boswell"; although if Tayler had opened the parcel he would have discovered that "Mr. Boswell of Auchinleck" was Alexander and not JB, and if he had read the label carefully he would have realized that "Mr. Boswell of Auchinleck" who had a brother James could not be JB himself. As Tayler's research concerned Jacobite papers, he may well have left the parcel unopened and retained an inaccurate recollection of the label as indicating that the contents were letters from JB. It is certain however that Tayler did not find any such letters. The only collection of letters *from* JB (those addressed to Forbes) was found by Abbott at the bottom of a chest where they had lain untouched for years (see below); and most of the letters *to* JB were found in the furthest recess of an attic behind lumber so massive that it could not be moved without a man's help (see below). Tayler died on 8 November 1937 without enlarging on his claim, but I am inclined to accept Pottle's suggested explanation. At any rate, the main discoveries at Fettercairn were undoubtedly Abbott's and his alone; Tayler's significance in the history of the Boswell papers is that he provided Abbott with an essential clue.

FETTERCAIRN HOUSE

THE LIBRARY AT FETTERCAIRN HOUSE

The bulkiest package was part of the manuscript of Sir William Forbes's *Life* of Beattie, with the letters in it as he had sent it to the printer, and unopened since it was wrapped up. . . . It was Beattie material of the first rank; but of far more importance was the indication that where this had been found, other papers of Sir William might be, including his correspondence. . . . It was essential now to know what papers were at Fettercairn House, and I was eager to be there.[14]

Abbott had no idea at this stage why Fettercairn should have come to house Forbes's papers. It was only later that he learned of Lord Clinton's direct descent from Sir William.[15] Nevertheless, it did not occur to him "to doubt that there were discoveries to be made."[16] His main quarry was Forbes's correspondence, which might well include letters from Johnson, Boswell, and the Boswell children.

Simpson again wrote to Lord Clinton asking permission for Abbott to investigate the papers at Fettercairn for himself. Lord Clinton agreed, but as the house was only opened up for about two months each year, it was not until Monday, 6 October 1930, that Abbott arrived there for his first short visit. The story of this visit is best told in his own words:

A room overlooking the garden and adjoining the library had been set aside for the hunt, and, after a little, I was left to my job.

Most of the floor space was filled with a variety of boxes, metal and wood, open and unopened, attended by noble bunches of keys. Great piles of papers were stacked on a side table. A blazing log fire made the room bright. I started with the boxes and soon had clear evidence that my surmise was right. For here, in stout wrapping-paper, was a package marked in Sir William's bold flowing hand "Letters from Mr. Boswell of Auchinleck [i.e. Alexander], and from his brother Mr. James," and in another box were "Letters from Miss Veronica and Miss Euphemia and Miss Elizabeth Boswell."[17] But these seemed to have strayed, for

---

[14]*Fettercairn Catalogue*, Introduction, p. xv.

[15]Ibid., p. xv, n. 1.

[16]Ibid., p. xv.

[17]All these letters from JB's children to Sir William Forbes are now in the Fettercairn Papers deposited in the National Library of Scotland. There are some 87 letters from Alexander, 45 from James junior, 86 from Euphemia, 13 from Elizabeth, and 4 from Veronica; also some 27 draft replies (or copies of replies) by Forbes. These numbers are subject to adjustment when the Fettercairn Papers have been fully sorted and listed.

the other papers in these boxes were mainly estate accounts or letters of business. . . . From the boxes came no considerable result except one great reassurance. Traces of Sir William Forbes were everywhere. It was evident that he was a most careful man of business who kept practically every letter written to him and a copy of all he wrote, and that he destroyed nothing, not even visiting-cards. Moreover, he docketed or parcelled most things. There was great hope in this. Any disorder or loss there might be would not be due to him. I was already finding, here and there in docketed packets, drafts of letters to various Boswells, and wished I knew exactly what the Ebony Cabinet contained. . . .

When I knew, roughly, what was in the boxes that would open, I turned to the stacked papers. They were of all kinds, and mainly belonged to Sir William. There was more manuscript of the Beattie *Life*, interleaved with letters as before, with a packet of materials used for the *Life*, and miscellaneous Beattie papers. And, at the bottom of one pile, was a stout bundle whose cover had almost disappeared, though the writing on what remained of it was still legible. It was "My Journal," and for a moment I thought it must be Sir William's. The top page was browned. But when I looked at the writing there I knew it at once for Boswell's, and stared in excited astonishment at the truth. The manuscript seemed to be complete: it was certainly in excellent preservation. In this respect, as will be seen, fortune favoured me throughout.

Boswell's Journal from 15 November 1762 till 4 August 1763 was thus in my hands. It was a delight to turn the pages and know there was still a major Boswell MS. in Scotland.[18]

Abbott had not expected to find any part of Boswell's *own* archives at Fettercairn. At best, he had hoped to unearth Boswell's letters to Forbes. But now he had recovered one of the most important portions of the entire journals. Inevitably he thought, "If this is here, well, anything not in the Ebony Cabinet may be here too."[19] He realized that a systematic search of the entire house was essential and, resisting the temptation to read the journal at once, he and Lady Clinton went through every room. His attention was particularly attracted to a long double attic "tremendous with lumber of all kinds, the accumulation

---

[18]*Fettercairn Catalogue*, Introduction, pp. xv–xvii.
[19]Ibid., p. xvii.

of generations," and to a large cupboard at the foot of the stair leading to the attic, which was full of papers "in immense disorder, in boxes, sacks, and loose."[20]

Before dinner that night, Lord Clinton produced, to Abbott's astonishment, a portfolio of letters containing, amongst other things, letters *to* Boswell including one from Johnson—of 11 July 1784—partially printed in the *Life*[21] and a copy made by Johnson (for Reynolds) of his letter to Macpherson.[22] This confirmed Abbott's belief that what he would find might largely depend on "the gaps in the Ebony Cabinet":[23]

Here was a hunt worth following, and I was all eagerness to pursue Sir William and Boswell and perhaps even Johnson through the house.[24]

Next morning, as there was insufficient time left to search the long attic properly, Abbott set to work on the cupboard at the foot of the attic stair. After going through a mass of papers without discovering anything of interest, he came upon two large dusty sacks which were carried down to a covered courtyard to be emptied. There he made some of his most remarkable finds:

Here I saw two large wooden chests standing one upon the other. The top lid was lifted, damp canvases that looked as if they were village stage-properties were cleared aside, and there, in neat piles,

---

[20]Ibid.

[21]*Life,* IV, p. 351. The letter is printed as 11 June, but Hill's note correctly suggests that 11 July is the right date.

[22]*Fettercairn Catalogue,* Introduction, p. xvii. These items and some other contents of the portfolio are now included in the Fettercairn Papers. How these letters, which were Boswell rather than Forbes papers, ever got into the portfolio is not known. Perhaps Alistair Tayler found them. Or perhaps the Forbes family were not entirely ignorant of the Boswell treasures lying at Fettercairn, and someone at some time sorted out a few choice specimens to display in a portfolio. The fact that one bundle of Boswell material discovered by Abbott was wrapped in a copy of *The Times* of 1874 (see below) indicates at least one sorting by the family after the papers first came to Fettercairn. The survival of a single fine letter from SJ to JB is of exceptional interest. Apart from three small scraps, no other letters from SJ to JB have been found to this day. See below Appendix II, p. 319 *et seq.*

[23]Abbott uses the phrase "Ebony Cabinet" in this context to mean the Boswell papers from Malahide, which, or many of which, were housed there in the Ebony Cabinet before Isham acquired them. JB did *not* use the Ebony Cabinet himself for the general storage of his papers. See above pp. 11–12.

[24]*Fettercairn Catalogue,* Introduction, p. xvii.

lay Sir William's correspondence, each batch in stout wrapping-paper on which he had written the year or the name of his correspondent. "The main box," I said to myself, "and here I shall find Boswell's letters to him." But first I had a fright. My heart sank when I found that the corner on which I started was damp-sodden. Part of each packet there had already been eaten away. Mercifully these were of comparatively small importance (select letters of various early years) and the vicious damp was confined to that one spot. The opposite side was unharmed, and there, right at the bottom, was the packet marked "Letters from Mr. Boswell."[25]

The rest of Abbott's short stay was comparatively uneventful. The second chest contained only discarded books and none of the other sacks and boxes he searched yielded anything of interest. It was impossible to prolong his visit as the Clintons were soon leaving and he was due back in Aberdeen:

So ended three days more full of dust and excitement than most. I had no doubt that other finds would follow. I came away carrying with me the Journal, the letters to Sir William, and a packet of miscellaneous letters which Lord Clinton had entrusted to me to copy and edit, and wondering why no one had tackled Sir William before.[26]

Abbott returned to Fettercairn on Saturday, 15 November 1930. In the meantime, he had been worrying lest the chest in the courtyard had not been thoroughly emptied. He remembered that in his delight at finding the Boswell-Forbes correspondence, he had gone at once to his room with the letters, leaving the servants to follow with the other files. A doubt now nagged at his mind that he might have overlooked something important lying at the bottom of the chest. On his second visit, he went straight to the courtyard, expecting to find the chest empty underneath the theatrical canvases:

But it was not empty. There were four shabby bundles of papers at the bottom, and, luckily, not at the damp end. By this time I had become used to wonders, but it was difficult now to believe my eyes and horrid to think how serious my carelessness might have been. The largest bundle was loosely wrapped in a tattered page of *The Times* of 21 August 1874. Inside that was another time- and dust-stained cover. And inside that again, bent double

[25]Ibid., p. xviii.
[26]Ibid., p. xix.

and with some edges damaged by wear and exposure, were wads of letters from Johnson to various correspondents. Langton, Windham, Lucy Porter, Reynolds, Brocklesby: I caught names at random. There were dozens of letters in that most characteristic handwriting.[27]

The Johnson letters catalogued by Abbott numbered 119[28] and coincided almost exactly with the letters from Johnson sent to Boswell by various correspondents for use in the *Life* and which he did not

[27]Ibid.

[28]*Fettercairn Catalogue*, Nos. 1472–1590, all now in the Hyde Collection. For some reason, Abbott did *not* include in his catalogue the letter from SJ to JB of 11 July 1784, nor the copy made by SJ for Reynolds of SJ's letter to Macpherson. (The piece of paper on which this copy is written is endorsed on the back "say as little of this as you can.") Yet he mentions both these items in his introduction as being included in Lord Clinton's portfolio. They must have come originally from JB's archives and their omission from the catalogue is not explained. Other papers from JB's archives which Abbott saw at Fettercairn but which are neither catalogued nor mentioned in the introduction are as follows:

1. A letter from SJ to Reynolds (undated) correcting an error made by him in the text of his copy of the letter to Macpherson. This establishes that the copy was in fact made for Reynolds.
2. A letter from Reynolds to JB dated 18 February 1784.
3. Copy (in Mrs. Boswell's hand) of a letter from JB to Reynolds dated 23 December 1784. This is the only text of a long and important letter in which JB refers to SJ's death and requests the return of his letters to SJ. Readers of *Correspondence etc. re Life* may wonder why JB did not write to Reynolds for material for his *magnum opus*. This letter, which was unfortunately not available in time for inclusion in the book, supplies the deficiency.
4. A letter from Joseph Warton to JB dated 9 April 1791.
5. A note of invitation from Mrs. David Garrick to JB dated "Thursday 19th April."

All the above items were contained in a box of papers mostly relating to JB, removed by Abbott from Fettercairn to Durham with Lord Clinton's permission, and only returned to Fettercairn in 1968. They are now (with the other contents of the box) in the Fettercairn Papers. On p. xxii of his introduction, Abbott also describes the discovery of what he "had long been looking for, and knew must be somewhere—Johnson's letter to Sir William." Tantalizingly, this letter was also omitted from the catalogue, although all JB's letters to Forbes were included; nor did Abbott explain why he should have expected to find this letter. Forbes sent it to JB with his letter of 19 October 1787 (*Fettercairn Catalogue*, No. 357), but JB did not use it in the *Life*, presumably because SJ expressed whole-hearted disapproval of his plan of removing his family to London. JB wrote to Forbes on 7 November 1787: "Dr. Johnson's letter to you is a very good one but from its subject cannot appear for some time" (letter in Fettercairn Papers). JB's words were unwittingly prophetic. Chapman did not print the letter in his edition of SJ's *Letters*, but it is listed and dated in Mary Hyde's article, "Not in Chapman," in *Johnson, Boswell and their Circle*, Oxford: Clarendon Press, 1965. Happily, this letter (which is undated, but docketed 7 August 1784 on the back) is now also included in the Fettercairn Papers. These papers generally include all manuscripts from Fettercairn (forming part of the Forbes rather than the Boswell archive). In addition to the items mentioned above, there are:

JB's letters to Forbes (*Fettercairn Catalogue*, Nos. 1320–60).

Copies or drafts of various letters from Forbes to JB listed in the *Fettercairn Catalogue*, including Nos. 365, 366, 373, and 381.

Nos. 1411, 1414, and 1430 of the *Fettercairn Catalogue*.

return. Abbott hoped that one of the other bundles would contain the richest prize of all, Johnson's letters to Boswell.[29] In this, he was disappointed. Two of the bundles contained Forbes papers of little interest, but the last bundle was marked by Boswell "Sir William Forbes" and held letters to Boswell from Sir William and also certain rough drafts of Boswell's replies.[30] It formed the other side of the correspondence which Abbott had been so pleased to discover during his first visit.

Abbott spent most of the next two days going through a cupboard in the nursery. This contained a very mixed assortment of papers, none of which seemed likely at first sight to be of much importance. His painstaking and systematic search was however again rewarded. In a box otherwise full of estate papers of the time of Lord Clinton's grandfather, he found a bundle containing an important miscellany relating to the *Life* and the projected second edition, including a number of draft letters from Boswell. There was no wrapper, but on the outside of the bundle were pages of notes from Isaac Reed on the first edition, docketed by Boswell. The only other find during this visit was the draft of Boswell's *Criminal Opera* which had strayed into a bundle of Sir William's papers.[31]

Abbott was again at Fettercairn from Friday to Monday, 28 November to 1 December 1930. This time he concentrated on the long attic, which so far had not been touched. It was crammed with lumber including many heavy boxes which, with the aid of a man, he systematically opened and searched. Several of the larger boxes contained only bric-à-brac, whilst others held estate papers of no interest. On the first day, only one box was found to contain papers which looked promising. Abbott emptied these into baskets and brought them downstairs to examine. Among them he found, in two bundles, nearly 140 miscellaneous letters to Boswell, mainly belonging to the years

---

Many letters to Forbes from JB's children (Alexander, James junior, Euphemia, Elizabeth, and Veronica) along with a number of Forbes's draft replies.

Correspondence with various persons including W. Cumming, Malone, Dilly, Dr. Barnard, Paoli, Reynolds, John Boswell (JB's brother), Claud Boswell of Balmuto, T. D. Boswell, William Boswell (who married JB's daughter Elizabeth), Robert Boswell, and W. J. Temple.

A mass of non-Boswellian papers, including Beattie material.

All these papers are being arranged and catalogued in the National Library of Scotland where they have been deposited by their owner.

[29]*Fettercairn Catalogue*, Introduction, p. xx. See above p. 123, n. 22, and Appendix II, p. 319 *et seq.*

[30]Now in Fettercairn Papers.

[31]*Fettercairn Catalogue*, Introduction, pp. xx–xxi.

1785–93. Correspondents from whom there were several letters included the Rev. Thomas Warton, Bennet Langton, Wilkes, Malone, and the Bishop of Killaloe. One of the bundles also contained a number of drafts of Boswell's replies. Amongst the papers from the same box, Abbott also found, stuffed into the middle of a small bundle of Pitsligo papers, copies of two letters from Boswell to Paoli, two long letters from Malone to Boswell, and a loose packet marked by Boswell on the wrapper, "Concerning Ladies." That evening he opened the packet and found a collection of letters and notes to Boswell from ladies of his acquaintance:

> Among these was a tiny package marked by Boswell "Selena."
> I opened it expecting to find a short note, and was startled when the light fell on a coil of fair hair, as bright now as when it was cut off. What had happened to the Hon. Miss Selena Eardley, I wondered?[32]

Abbott spent most of Saturday and Sunday examining "multitudes of confused papers from the attic." He was disappointed to find nothing of much importance, but had the consolation of discovering on a shelf in the library a letter from Johnson and two letters from Malone, all to Sir William.[33] On Sunday, the far end of the right-hand side of the attic still remained to be searched, but the lumber there was too heavy for him to manage by himself. He could only wait until the following morning when a man's help would be available.

On Monday 1 December, Abbott and his helper attacked the furthest recesses of the attic:

> Nothing had been touched there for years, and of papers there was no sign. A great wooden box, extricated with difficulty, held nothing but rolls of wall-paper. But when I removed the next up-sided table I saw, wedged in between other furniture, a small sack, rather like a small mail-bag, with rents here and there from which letters were ready to drop. Quickly I dragged it out. A loose letter fell. It was written to Boswell. Down the winding stairs

[32]Ibid., p. xxii. The Hon. Selena Eardley married Colonel John Walbanke Childers of Cantley near Doncaster and was mother of John Walbanke Childers, M. P. for Cambridgeshire in 1833 and for Malton from 1835 to 1852, and of the Rev. Eardley Childers (d. 1831). The wrapper with JB's inscription (and the lock of hair) is now in Fettercairn Papers.

[33]Ibid. All of these letters are now in the Fettercairn Papers. As to the letter from SJ, see above p. 125, n. 28.

I hurried the sack, wondering whether all the contents could possibly concern Boswell. Before emptying the papers I drew out another loose letter. The omen was favourable. Soon I knew the truth. The sack was stuffed tight with Boswell's papers, most of them arranged in stout wads, torn here and there, and dirty, but for the most part in excellent order. Neither damp nor worm nor mouse had gnawed at them.[34]

Abbott was due back in Aberdeen that afternoon and had no time to examine his incredible find properly. He put all the papers into padlocked boxes and left them in a store-room to be returned to when he had the opportunity. Only when he revisited Fettercairn on 12 and 13 December 1930 did he realize the riches he had found. The contents of the "mail-bag" are separately listed in the introduction to his catalogue, which must be referred to for details.[35] The following brief summary was given by Abbott in an article about his discoveries, printed in *The Times* on 21 November 1936:

These [i.e. the contents of the "mail-bag"], besides a great number of miscellaneous letters, include letters to Boswell (parcelled by him and often with drafts of his replies) from his friend W. J. Temple (a long series), Burke, Godfrey Bosville, Sir Alexander Dick, General Oglethorpe, Sir John Pringle, Lord Bute, Paoli, Edward Dilley [sic], the Earl Marischall, Wilkes, the Earl of Pembroke, and the Bishop of Killaloe. A bundle marked "Johnsonian Letters" contains two letters from Mrs. Thrale to Johnson, but is chiefly concerned with requests for letters written by Johnson, or for information about him. The chief Boswell manuscripts are his Journal from March 20 to May 28, 1778, his Journal of Northern Circuit from July 1 to July 28, 1788, and two Registers of Letters sent and received from June, 1769, to the end of December, 1777, and from January 1, 1778, to August 26, 1782.

Abbott mentions two further visits to Fettercairn in January and March 1931.[36] During the first, he discovered a sack of papers in a recess in the library which contained a few Boswell items of minor importance. Finally, on 28 March 1931, Lord Clinton took Abbott again through the whole house, in case anything had been missed:

[34]Ibid., p. xxiii.
[35]Ibid., pp. xxiv–xxvi.
[36]Ibid., pp. xxvi–xxvii.

The search revealed little. In a cupboard were a few of Sir William's papers, and among them a copy of the Bishop of Killaloe's letter to Boswell concerning the Sacrament; and in the thirteenth drawer of a bureau was, to make a fitting end, Sir William's copy of the "Round Robin."[37]

Here Abbott's narrative ends. No full account has previously been given of the events which occurred between his last visit to Fettercairn and his announcement in *The Times* in 1936, nor has any convincing explanation been offered as to why secrecy should have been necessary for more than five years. These are matters which cannot be side-

---

[37]Ibid., p. xxvii. See *Life*, fourth edition (1804), III, p. 84, n. 1. This footnote by Malone indicated that what Sir William sent to JB was only a copy, the original remaining in the possession of Dr. Barnard, Bishop of Limerick. The background to this footnote is an amusing interchange of letters (now in the Fettercairn Papers) between Malone and Forbes. On 3 March 1804, Malone wrote to Forbes: "I conceived that you had sent Mr. B. the original, and stated the matter so, some time ago at Mr. Metcalfe's, in the presence of the present Bp. of Limerick (Barnard). But he said it was in his possession; and was so piqued at the contrary supposition, that he immediately got into his carriage which was then at the door, went to his lodgings, & brought it to us in his hand.—I suppose therefore that which you sent to Mr. B. was a copy. But as the facsimiles cd. not be engraved without the original, it seems strange that he shd. desire a copy from you, if he were possessed of the original. Perhaps the solution is, that at the time of his corresponding with you on this subject, he had not obtained the original, and procured it from Bishop Barnard at a subsequent period." Forbes replied on 9 March 1804: "As to the *Round Robin*, I request you will do me the honour of presenting my respectful compliments to My Lord Bishop of Limerick, and assure his Ldshp. that I had not the most distant intention by what I said in my letter transmitting the Copy of it to Mr. Boswell to deprive the Bishop of the property of the original or to arrogate the possession of it to myself. The history of the matter was shortly this. When I was in Dublin in the year 1785, at which time I had frequently the opportunity of being with the Bishop of Limerick, at that time Bishop of Killaloe, while we were talking of our mutual London friends, & of incidents that had happened to us in our intercourse of society there a few years before, the Round Robin was mentioned among other things, of which the Bishop told me he was in possession. As a literary curiosity in which we had both had a concern, I requested his Ldshp.'s permission to take a Copy, which I brought home with me. In my mentioning this to Mr. Boswell the first time I saw him, who was at this time engaged in his Life of Johnson, he beg'd I would make a Copy for him also, which I did, & sent it to him in the letter to which you refer. I did not, indeed, in the letter call it a Copy, because he knew it perfectly well to be one. And it must have been after that period, that the Bishop had lent him the original to get the *fac simile* of the subscriptions done from it." (Draft letter in Fettercairn Papers.) Forbes's copy of the Round Robin is now in the possession of Mrs. Somervell at Fettercairn House. There is a copy of it in Fettercairn Papers. The original Round Robin is owned by the present Earl of Crawford and Balcarres. L. F. Powell comments that few documents have given rise to such confusion as the Round Robin; he explains the position briefly thus: "Barnard wrote the original address. Burke dictated the revised address, which Forbes copied. Reynolds carried it to SJ. SJ apparently returned it to Dr. Barnard—or somebody did—and it remained in Barnard's possession, transmitting through his descendants to the Earl of Crawford." The Round Robin was used as an illustration in the *Life*, first edition, II, facing p. 92. Forbes's letter transmitting his copy of it to JB is dated 19 October 1787 (*Fettercairn Catalogue*, No. 357).

stepped in a detailed history of the Boswell papers. The consequences of concealment for Isham and the publication of his collection were disastrous, and his was not the only scholarly project to suffer.[38]

At Abbott's suggestion, Lord Clinton consulted Humphrey Milford, Publisher to the University of Oxford, and, in early April 1931, a meeting took place, attended by Lord Clinton, Abbott, Milford, and Chapman (as Secretary to the Delegates of the Press).[39] Milford was prepared to consider publication, provided the question of copyright could be cleared. Later that month, he discussed this problem with Sir Frank MacKinnon, then a judge of the King's Bench in England. MacKinnon advised that the matter was governed by Scots Law and suggested that an opinion should be obtained from Sir Wilfrid Normand, K.C., Solicitor General for Scotland.[40]

Meanwhile, Chapman took over direct responsibility on behalf of the Clarendon Press for the Fettercairn project, which was given the code-name "Operation Hush." During May and June 1931, discussions about possible publication plans continued and Abbott's working catalogue was studied by Chapman.[41] In August, Chapman saw Normand and discussed informally the problem of copyright. Normand explained that he was not an expert on copyright law, but he doubted whether Lord Clinton was entitled to physical ownership of the papers.[42] It was essential to obtain a formal written opinion dealing with both copyright and legal ownership. With Lord Clinton's approval, a written "Case" was submitted on 5 October 1931 for the joint opinion of Normand and A. C. Black, K.C.[43]

This "Case" is of great interest because it shows that by the autumn of 1931 Milford and Chapman were fully aware of the issues involved and, in particular, that other interests might be affected. Counsel's attention was drawn to the terms of Boswell's will and the difficulty in interpreting them. Reference was also made to volumes I to XII of the private edition (which had already been published), and the *Mala-*

---

[38]See below p. 140.

[39]"Fettercairn Papers," a five-page memorandum prepared in 1962 from the files of the Clarendon Press by D. M. Davin, then Assistant Secretary. The files themselves have not been made available to me for perusal. The memorandum is cited below as "Davin Memo."

[40]Ibid.

[41]Ibid.

[42]Ibid.

[43]A copy of this "Case" along with a copy of Normand's and Black's opinion has been supplied to me by Mr. Davin.

*hide Catalogue* for the information which it contained about the actings of the literary executors. Counsel were told:

> The bulk of the papers undoubtedly were sent to Auchinleck, and there remained until they were removed to Ireland by Boswell's lineal descendant the present Lord Talbot de Malahide, who in the course of the last five years sold them to Lt. Col. Isham, an American gentleman. It has hitherto been assumed that many papers, seen to be missing from the collection, had perished. It now appears that some of them had remained in Forbes' hands.
>
> Unless Lord Clinton has acquired a title by prescription,[44] it would seem *prima facie* that Lord Talbot may have a claim.

Counsel were asked to advise about copyright as well as ownership. Their opinion was clear and to the point:

> In our opinion Lord Clinton has not an exclusive title to the MSS. and other papers now in his possession in virtue of which he can deal with them as his own property. While that is so, he is, in our opinion, under a distinct duty to regard himself as a trustee of the papers under obligation to make them forthcoming to the persons, of whom he may be one, who have legal rights to, or in, them.
>
> The difficulties of both fact and law which surround the matter make it impossible for Lord Clinton without the authority of the Court, to undertake the task of discharging the obligation which is incumbent upon him, and in our opinion the proper course for him to adopt is to apply to the Court of Session in Scotland for the appointment of a Judicial Factor. . . . It will be the duty of the Judicial Factor, who is an officer of the Court, to take the necessary steps to ascertain who are the persons interested and what are their respective rights. . . .
>
> In the questions with which the Memorialist [i.e., Milford] is more immediately concerned we have experienced great difficulty and are not wholly at one. This however is of no moment, as it is obvious that the matters cannot be dealt with on Counsel's Opinion but must be made the subject of judicial decision.

[44]A principle of law whereby certain rights may be acquired by lapse of time.

Normand's and Black's opinion is dated 23 November 1931, and, although their advice was plain enough, more than four years elapsed before it was acted upon. It is difficult to justify this delay in the face of the explicit statement as to where Lord Clinton's legal duty lay; more so in that Lord Talbot's possible interest (and hence Isham's) was clearly recognized. It was not necessary, as has been suggested, that Abbott should complete his catalogue before any positive steps were taken. The papers had, of course, to be listed in sufficient detail to identify what was to be entrusted to the care of the Judicial Factor; but this did not require a detailed and scholarly catalogue which would take years to prepare. As early as January 1931, Abbott had made a rough catalogue of most of the papers[45] from which a suitable inventory could have been compiled. The important thing was to transfer the responsibility for the papers to a Judicial Factor as soon as possible, so that other interested parties might not suffer from being kept in ignorance. Then, if the Judicial Factor had felt that a more elaborate catalogue were needed, he could have arranged accordingly.

Lord Clinton, Abbott, Milford, and Chapman met again in London on 30 December 1931 to consider counsel's opinion and to decide future action.[46] According to Chapman, Lord Clinton dominated the discussion. In his memorandum of the meeting, he noted: "C. made nearly all the running; and though he very politely asked you [i.e., Milford] for your advice (as a friend), his mind was pretty well made up."[47] Lord Clinton apparently decided that a further opinion should be obtained from counsel before petitioning for the appointment of the Judicial Factor,[48] although why he should have thought this necessary is not clear. What is clear is that he was against any early disclosure of the discovery.[49] It must have come as a shock for him to learn that the papers might not be his and he probably wanted to take stock of the situation. In his view, the evidence at Fettercairn had not yet been fully explored, and what had been read had not been digested.[50] He felt that Abbott should continue with his catalogue and that no further action should be taken until it had been completed

---

[45]Davin Memo.

[46]Ibid.

[47]Letter to me from Davin dated 8 November 1962, amplifying his memorandum and providing much detailed information including quotations from correspondence and memoranda in the files of the Clarendon Press. This letter is cited below as "Davin Letter."

[48]Ibid.

[49]Ibid.: "Clinton did not feel there was any obligation to haste."

[50]Davin Memo.

CLAUDE COLLEER ABBOTT

THE RT. HON. LORD CLINTON

R. W. CHAPMAN

SIR HUMPHREY MILFORD

and published. According to Chapman: "This has always been C.'s view, and A. is being converted to it. We supported it."[51]

With Lord Clinton's approval, the whole of the papers were removed from Fettercairn to Aberdeen University Library and there Abbott worked on them from 1931 to 1934 during most of his spare time in term and vacation.[52] He was assisted in the immense task of copying and indexing by Miss A. M. Davidson of Aberdeen (who refused to take any remuneration for her work[53]), and by two of his students, Mr. Alexander Macdonald and Mr. A. D. Adam. Every document was copied (with the exception of the journal from 20 March to 23 May 1778, part of which was in Boswell's most abbreviated and elliptical style of journal-writing) and checked and card-indexed with a summary. From the card index, the catalogue was prepared.[54] Progress was slow, because the time which Abbott could spare from his professional commitments was limited.[55] On 22 April 1935 (more than four years after the discovery), the completed text was at last deposited with the Clarendon Press, who were to publish it at their expense if approval could be obtained from Lord Clinton and the Court.[56]

There was now no excuse for any further delay and, on 24 July 1935, Lord Clinton, Abbott, Milford, and Chapman met again. Lord Clinton promised to see his solicitors about the appointment of a Judicial Factor and, if they approved, he would seek authority to print (not publish) the catalogue. The solicitors advised that the Judicial Factor would have to apply to the Court for directions and that the Court would probably order him to advertise for claims. They thought that the catalogue should be printed so that it might be available for reference and, on 12 September, Lord Clinton gave authority to print.[57]

On 12 December, Chapman sent a set of proofs to Lord Clinton, suggesting that Isham and Pottle should now be informed, as he did not wish them to learn of the matter from outsiders. Lord Clinton

[51]Davin Letter. The quotation is from a memorandum from Chapman to Milford of 30 December 1931.

[52]"Note of Expenses incurred to Professor Abbott in connection with the Boswell papers referred to in the Action of Multiplepoinding and Exoneration at the instance of the Judicial Factor on the Estate of the late James Boswell. . . ," 1939 (copy in ILP). Abbott estimated that he spent at least 4,000 hours working on his catalogue from 1931 to 1936.

[53]Ibid.

[54]*Fettercairn Catalogue*, Preface, p. ix.

[55]He was appointed to the Chair of English Language and Literature at the University of Durham in 1932.

[56]Davin Memo.

[57]Ibid.

replied that other interests could be informed as soon as a Judicial Factor had been appointed and, after further discussion, it was decided that this could best be done by a formal letter from Abbott to *The Times*. It was also to be left to the Judicial Factor to decide whether the catalogue should be published.[58] The late Ernest M. Wedderburn (afterwards Sir Ernest), a prominent Edinburgh solicitor and Deputy Keeper of His Majesty's Signet, was invited to take the office of Judicial Factor. He agreed, and the petition for his appointment was lodged on 5 March 1936.[59] Abbott was authorized to publish his letter to *The Times*, which appeared on 9 March. As we have seen, Chapman cabled Pottle the same day with news of the discovery and followed up immediately with a letter containing a more detailed account. So ended "Operation Hush."

The final authority for decisions during the five years of secrecy lay with Lord Clinton. The papers were found in his house and he was ostensibly their owner. Neither Abbott nor Chapman could act nor make any disclosure without his approval. Although a kindly and responsible man, he was not the sort of person who could be hurried. He was elderly and had many important commitments and responsibilities. He was the twenty-first Baron, second on the list of peers in the House of Lords, representative of four families with seats in Devonshire and Scotland, owner of nearly 35,000 acres, and his houses were full of papers which had been accumulating for centuries. When the Boswell papers came to light at Fettercairn he did not doubt that they were his. The idea of publishing a complete edition of "The Clinton Papers" appealed to him and, despite Normand's and Black's opinion, he remained hopeful that he would be able to establish a legal title to the manuscripts.[60] He also owed a loyalty to Abbott, the discoverer of the papers, and wished to afford him the opportunity to complete his catalogue. For these reasons, he did not want to pre-

[58]Ibid.

[59]Petition to the Court of Session, Scotland, of Lord Clinton for Appointment of Judicial Factor. A print of the petition is in ILP.

[60]Pottle was in Britain in the summer of 1936 and spent a day with Chapman in Oxford. He also had a long luncheon with Abbott. On 3 August, after his return to America, he sent Isham a long report (letter in IFP). Abbott told him that a complete printing of the Fettercairn papers (in eighteen volumes!) was proposed, to which Chapman and Milford agreed if the ownership question could be resolved. Pottle got the impression that Lord Clinton balked at decisive action after the Normand-Black opinion was issued: "He saw no reason why he should bother himself and it didn't suit him then to open the legal issue." According to the Davin Memo, in September 1934, Lord Clinton "was still thinking of a complete edition of 'The Clinton Papers' and evidently had little doubt the legal decision would be in his favour."

cipitate matters by applying at once for the appointment of a Judicial Factor. He needed time to consider the question of ownership with his lawyers[61] and Abbott needed time for the catalogue. His decision at the meeting in December 1931 to do nothing until Abbott had finished his work must have seemed to him justified since it was supported by two such eminent publishers as Milford and Chapman. But even when the catalogue was ready three years later, Lord Clinton was in no hurry. The text was deposited with the Clarendon Press on 22 April 1935, but nearly a year passed before he petitioned the Court for the Judicial Factor's appointment. Meanwhile Pottle and Isham remained in ignorance.

Lord Clinton was not, of course, familiar with the world of books and publishers, and he probably knew little of the activities of scholars in the field. Almost certainly he did not realize how grievously Isham and others would be hurt by concealment. If Chapman and Milford had pointed out to him the extent to which other interests were involved and insisted as forcefully as possible that the legal advice should be followed at once (which apparently they did not), he might have been influenced. They, after all, were vastly more experienced than he in such matters, and they did acquiesce in delay, at least until the catalogue was ready.

Abbott, as discoverer of the papers at Fettercairn, naturally wanted the opportunity to catalogue them. After they were taken to Aberdeen, his main concern was to progress with his catalogue as fast as his rather limited time permitted. He was also interested in editing the papers for publication and his advice that the Clarendon Press should be consulted was obviously sensible. He did not doubt at this stage that the papers belonged to Lord Clinton, nor did he fully appreciate the extent to which others would suffer from prolonged secrecy. Later, when the problems of legal ownership and copyright became apparent, it was for the lawyers and the publishers rather than for him to advise what should be done. Lord Clinton had consulted persons of the greatest eminence and there was no reason why Abbott should doubt the soundness of their advice. At the meeting in December 1931, Lord Clinton, Milford, and Chapman all thought that Abbott should forge ahead with his catalogue with a view to publication.[62] It is not surprising that he readily agreed. In 1932, the need for silence actually operated

[61]According to the Davin Memo., Lord Clinton wanted a further legal opinion before applying for the appointment of a Judicial Factor.
[62]Davin Memo. and Davin Letter.

to his disadvantage when he was a candidate for the Chair of English Language and Literature at Durham and was unable to say anything about his find.[63] He was, of course, vitally concerned that the questions of ownership and copyright should be resolved in favour of Lord Clinton; otherwise he stood to lose the opportunity of editing the planned publication. But in the whole circumstances, he had little choice short of withdrawal but to leave matters in the hands of Lord Clinton and his expert advisers.

Even so, as the years passed, Abbott became increasingly worried about the continued secrecy. The Library of Aberdeen University purchased for his use a set of the private edition and he realized how serious his own discovery would be for Isham. There was also the possibility that Lord Talbot might be the legal owner of the papers. In September 1934, he wrote to tell Chapman that he was planning to send him a specimen of the catalogue and he hoped that soon "this absurd holding back will come to an end and the book be rushed on."[64] It seems, therefore, that for at least eighteen months before his letter appeared in *The Times,* Abbott wanted to end the secrecy, even though he must have realized that to do so could result in his being deprived of all further work on the papers.

Chapman's role is the hardest to evaluate. As early as 1923, he had written to Isham explaining his interest in publishing a new edition of Johnson's letters and asking if he might inspect Isham's Johnsonian collection.[65] Isham readily granted this request and, from then on, he and Chapman were in frequent and friendly communication.[66] In October 1927, Chapman was in New York where Isham entertained him hospitably and allowed him to examine all the papers which he had just acquired from Malahide.[67] Chapman's chief interest was letters or copies of letters from Johnson. Although there were only a few of these from Malahide, he wrote to thank Isham for a "charming evening and a real thrill."[68] Shortly afterwards, he wrote from London, offering to review the private edition for the *Review of English Studies,* admitting that his ulterior motive was to be able to own a set of books

---

[63]Letter, Abbott to H. W. Liebert, 23 April 1949 (copy in IFP): "When I was a candidate for the Chair here, in 1932, I was able to say nothing whatever about the find. One doesn't withhold so good a card as that on purpose."

[64]Quoted in the Davin Memo.

[65]Letter, Chapman to Isham, 28 May 1923 (IFP).

[66]Correspondence file in IFP.

[67]Ibid.

[68]Letter, Chapman to Isham, 12 October 1927 (IFP).

which would otherwise be beyond his means.[69] He assured Isham of his willingness to assist his work in any way, whether by checking or otherwise, and asked if he might tell the Johnson Club (of which he was then Prior) something *"ex cathedra"* of Isham's plans.[70] Isham responded with typical generosity. He presented Chapman with a set of the costly private edition and he also took the trouble to send a detailed account of his publication plans so that Chapman might have something to tell the members of the Johnson Club.[71] Chapman wrote back:

> As for the books, when they come I shall feel it incumbent upon me not merely to feel humbly and profoundly grateful, but to do my utmost to promote the great enterprise if I have any power to do so. I think your plan of publication admirable.[72]

In April 1929, Chapman was again in New York, where he met and exchanged notes with Geoffrey Scott.[73] Isham marked the occasion by giving a further set of the private edition to be presented to the library at Johnson House in London. Once again, Chapman acknowledged his generosity and commented that nothing could have given "our infant library a better send off."[74]

Between 1929 and 1936, Chapman remained closely in touch with the progress of Isham's plans. In a number of ways he was directly involved himself. He wrote reviews, corresponded with Pottle (who sent him proofs for correction and advice), and he became Isham's publisher when he undertook publication of the index to the private edition. He was also Pottle's publisher, having accepted the *Literary Career* for the Clarendon Press.

Chapman certainly found himself in a very difficult position when asked to handle the Fettercairn project. He was naturally keen to obtain publication of such important manuscripts for the Clarendon Press with its strong tradition of service to Johnsonian studies; and from a personal point of view, the 119 new letters from Johnson were vital for his projected edition of Johnson's letters. But he was soon to be Isham's publisher and indebted to him for much kindness and generosity. He had promised to do his utmost to promote Isham's "great

[69]Letter, Chapman to Isham, 23 December 1927 (IFP).
[70]Ibid.
[71]Letter, Isham to Chapman, 8 February 1928 (copy in IFP).
[72]Letter, Chapman to Isham, 27 February 1928 (IFP).
[73]Letter, Chapman to Isham, 15 April 1929 (IFP).
[74]Letter, Chapman to Isham, 27 July 1929 (IFP).

enterprise," and yet he must have known at once that Abbott's find would vitiate it and that the longer the facts were kept secret, the more serious would be the consequences. He also had his friend and colleague, Dr. L. F. Powell, to consider. Powell had been working for many years on a revision of Hill's edition of the *Life,* and the Fettercairn papers contained material of vital importance for him. It was at Chapman's suggestion that Powell had embarked on this great undertaking which was promoted and paid for by the Delegates of the Clarendon Press. His first four volumes were published in 1934,[75] without his having had the benefit of seeing the Fettercairn papers or even being told of their existence. Chapman's view was that by keeping one of his own authors in ignorance, in the same way as Pottle and Isham, he was demonstrating his complete impartiality and good faith. And so, when he read Powell's proofs, he passed over in silence gaps which the new material might have filled. In 1935, Powell was taken through the Library of Aberdeen University by Dr. Simpson. There, he saw the bags which, unknown to him, were crammed with papers from Fettercairn. He was given no hint of their contents. Like Pottle, he was kept in complete ignorance of the discovery until Abbott's letter appeared in *The Times.*

Several persons who knew Chapman have described him as a man who enjoyed a devious and romantic approach to a subject. He delighted in secrecy.[76] Herein, perhaps, lies the key to his handling of "Operation Hush." The Fettercairn discovery was the biggest and choicest literary secret imaginable. It opened up so many fascinating questions, not least of which was what would happen to the Johnson letters in which he was so keenly interested for his own work. Here was a secret to be savoured and enjoyed. In case this assessment should seem far-fetched, one should consider that in 1932 he published an essay entitled "Boswell's Archives."[77] Although he knew about the Fettercairn papers, he was not at liberty to make any disclosure. It is astonishing that a scholar such as he should have *chosen* to publish a learned essay on a subject about which he had vital information which he was temporarily unable to use.

[75]*Boswell's Life of Johnson, together with Boswell's Journal of a Tour to the Hebrides and Johnson's Diary of a Journey into North Wales,* edited by George Birkbeck Hill, D. C. L., revised and enlarged by L. F. Powell, Oxford 1934. The two remaining volumes appeared in 1950.

[76]Pottle, writing to Isham on 3 August 1936, said, "Chapman loves schemes and intrigues" (letter in IFP).

[77]Cited above p. 13, n. 70.

Chapman was also motivated by strong nationalistic feelings. He frankly admitted to Pottle, when they met in the summer of 1936, that he deeply regretted the loss of the Malahide papers to America and he felt bound to support any action which might help to keep the Fettercairn papers in Britain. The further legal investigation which Lord Clinton proposed seemed to him that sort of action. In deciding amongst conflicting loyalties, he felt he had to opt for national loyalty, much as he regretted the consequences for Isham and Pottle. It was just because he could not notify them that he felt obliged to treat Powell in the same way, even though one of Oxford's own publications might suffer.[78]

By 1934, however, Chapman had begun to worry about the prolonged secrecy. A memorandum of his of the spring of that year shows that he was coming to think that Pottle might be brought in as co-editor and that in any event the journal material from Fettercairn should be handed over later to Pottle for inclusion in his own edition. He was also beginning to doubt whether there was much case for publishing a complete edition of "The Clinton Papers" as such. Nevertheless, he was still prepared to leave matters over until Abbott had finished his catalogue and the Judicial Factor had been appointed. Then, he wrote: "Perhaps the Beneficiaries will swoop down like Harpies and release us from the trouble of a decision."[79]

By 1935, the catalogue was ready and Chapman was anxious to let Isham and Powell into the secret. He raised the question with Lord Clinton in July and again in December 1935, but, as we know, on both occasions Lord Clinton wanted to wait until the Judicial Factor had been appointed. As soon as Abbott's letter appeared in *The Times*, Chapman wrote to Pottle and Powell. Powell immediately doubted that Lord Clinton had a title to the papers and Pottle thought they were obviously Lord Talbot's and should have been handed over.[80] This reaction worried Chapman and, in a series of letters to Milford, he sought to justify their handling of the matter. On 11 May 1936, he wrote that the possibility that the papers belonged to Lord Talbot "dawned on us only by degrees";[81] but had not Milford referred to this very possibility in his "Case" for counsel's opinion in 1931? On

---

[78]Note from F. A. Pottle with impressions of his meeting with Chapman in 1936.
[79]Davin Memo.
[80]Ibid.
[81]Ibid.

13 May 1936, he wrote again to Milford: "Even if Clinton's moral duty was plainly something else, that was not your affair or mine. It was open to us to do the best for learning, consistent with our duty to him as having consulted us."[82]

Lord Clinton's "moral duty" may or may not have been Chapman's proper concern, but he faced a moral issue himself which he could not side-step. This arose from the conflict between his commitment to Lord Clinton and his earlier loyalties to Pottle, Isham, and Powell. Instead of supporting Lord Clinton's policy of delay, he might have urged the importance of following the lawyers' advice at once; and if Lord Clinton had remained adamant, he could have refused to have anything further to do with the project. In acting as he did, he seems to have been influenced by a genuine anxiety for the safe preservation of the papers and their retention in Britain.[83] He feared that they might be lost to America or dispersed once their existence was made known. His first concern therefore was that they should be accurately transcribed and catalogued. By supporting a course of action which would allow Abbott to complete his work without interruption, he no doubt believed quite sincerely that he and Milford were doing their "best for learning." At the same time, one cannot but wonder at his willingness to condone five years of secrecy which dislocated Isham's plans (which he had pledged himself to support in every way possible) and impaired Powell's work on the *Life* (which he had officially initiated and otherwise actively supported).

[82]Ibid.

[83]When Pottle met Chapman in 1936, Chapman spoke with great earnestness of the need to insure the papers against loss by having them transcribed and catalogued. Photography was little used by English scholars at that time and it did not occur to Chapman to use it. (Note to me from F. A. Pottle, 1972.)

# V

# *Action of Multiplepoinding*

"NOT since the discovery of the Ebony Cabinet have good Boswellians enjoyed such a thrill as they will get from Professor Colleer Abbott's letter this morning." So ran *The Times* leader on 9 March 1936.

Isham could scarcely be expected to share the writer's enthusiasm. For him, Abbott's discovery was a disaster and its disclosure could not have come at a worse time. On 20 March, Pottle wrote to him:

> This discovery is overwhelming. Though it does not affect our limited edition in which we professed to print only Malahide MSS., it obviously affects our popular edition. . . . Even a selection from Boswell's Journal which does not contain the London Journal for 1762–63 will be hard to defend. And as the owner of the Malahide Papers you are very definitely concerned.[1]

In saying that the private edition was unaffected, Pottle meant only that Isham could still fulfil his legal commitment to the subscribers. Financially, the effect was most damaging. Sales had languished during the years of the depression and Isham had hoped that completion of the set would attract buyers for the large stock of unsold volumes. This hope was dashed now that he could no longer claim to own virtually all the surviving Boswell papers. About a third of the bulk was in other hands and nobody knew for certain to whom it belonged. To prospective purchasers, it must have seemed that the private edition had become seriously incomplete.

[1]Letter in IFP.

143

This was not altogether true. In spite of the new discovery, the private edition remained a "massive and influential work of scholarship."[2] The chief literary importance of Boswell's papers lay in his journals. Isham's collection from Malahide contained all his surviving journals except for the three portions found at Fettercairn—the London journal of 1762–63 and fragments of the journals for 1778 and 1788.[3] Apart from these and some early journal notes omitted by Scott from his first five volumes, the private edition provided a complete, accurate, well-indexed text of all surviving journal material. Its importance and integrity was thus assured; but the appearance in 1936 of so many new papers was fatal to its commercial success and to the planned trade edition.

Pottle's forecast that Isham would never be taken to court for breaking the time limits set in his agreements with Viking and Heinemann[4] had proved accurate. Guinzburg and Frere-Reeves had both eventually accepted the situation and, in February 1936, a new agreement had been drawn up which waived all claims against Isham for delay in delivery of the material. Against this, the terms of the original agreements as to royalties and editorial costs were modified. Isham was not to receive any further advance of royalties, and an advance of $2,500 towards the remuneration of Pottle and an assistant for editing the *Tour* was to be deducted from his royalties when earned. The finished manuscript for the entire set of the public edition was to be delivered to the printer not later than 1 October 1939.[5]

The Fettercairn discovery completely dislocated this arrangement. In December 1936, Isham met Guinzburg and it was agreed that Isham would make every possible effort to acquire the new papers. If he succeeded, Viking were to have all publication rights in the United States and Canada. Isham was to receive royalties at rates similar to those already agreed upon for the Malahide papers and Viking were to have the privilege of incorporating the new material in a limited edition or in the proposed trade edition. In return, Isham received a further advance of $5,000 against future royalties.[6] Meantime, the

[2]The description is Pottle's. In a note to me (1972) he writes of the private edition: "It has been the basis of an enormous amount of effective research (I will wager that no new work in English letters appearing in the last forty years has been so much cited) and will continue to be avidly used by scholars until the Yale Research Edition is completed."

[3]*Fettercairn Catalogue*, Nos. 1361, 1362, and 1363.

[4]See above p. 111.

[5]Agreement between Isham and the Viking Press, Inc., dated 10 February 1936 (copy in IFP).

[6]These terms are set out in a letter from Guinzburg to Isham of 18 December 1936. The copy

trade edition had to be shelved until the fate of the Fettercairn papers was known. The new edition of the *Tour*, based on the complete manuscript found in the croquet box, was fortunately not affected. It appeared in November 1936 and met with considerable success; but Isham had to content himself with the profits of this one volume instead of the whole series which had been planned. The financial return for which he had waited since 1927 was still a long way from being realized.

No future publication of the journals could be contemplated without the London journal of 1762–63; and any edition of Boswell's correspondence depended on the availability of the letters from both collections. Malahide yielded some four hundred letters to and from Boswell, and Fettercairn more than three times that number. The important registers in which Boswell recorded letters sent and received were split between the two collections. The two registers found at Fettercairn ran from June 1769 to 26 August 1782 and dovetailed with a similar register from Malahide covering the period 27 August 1782 to the year of Boswell's death.[7] It was clear that a unified scheme of publication and editing could never be undertaken until all the papers were reunited. In the meantime, Isham's collection was seriously devalued and his plan that one day the entire archive would find a home in a great university library looked to be a lost cause. Tinker was most sympathetic and thought Isham had been given "a very raw deal";[8] and A. E. Newton wrote to R. B. Adam in April 1936:

That new and important discovery of Boswell-Johnson material in Scotland, too long a story to tell, has thrown a monkey wrench into all the scholarship of the last twenty-five years. As Tinker writes "we are all undone." . . . It may be years before the courts decide to whom it belongs.[9]

Isham could not have been blamed if he had given up at this stage. To achieve his ultimate purpose, he was faced with the necessity of acquiring the Fettercairn papers and adding them to his collection.

of this letter in IFP is docketed "agreed and accepted: Ralph H. Isham. Dec. 18th, 1936."

[7] See *Fettercairn Catalogue*, Nos. 1364 and 1365. The register of letters from Malahide is not included in the *Malahide Catalogue*, because it did not come to light until 1937 (see below p. 162).

[8] So reported Pottle in his letter to Isham of 24 March 1936 (in IFP).

[9] Letter dated 18 April 1936 (Hyde Collection).

The difficulties were formidable. No one as yet fully understood how the papers had come to Fettercairn or why they had been allowed to lie there in oblivion for so long. The question of legal ownership was even more obscure. Pottle thought that Lord Talbot could probably establish title by tracing his inheritance through the intervening generations.[10] Isham's best hope, therefore, was through the Talbots, but relations with them had been somewhat strained ever since he had disregarded their wishes over censorship.[11] Besides, Lord Talbot, with his horror of publicity, was unlikely to want to pursue a claim in his own name through the courts.

Isham had to consider whether the original sale document, which Lord Talbot had signed on 21 August 1927,[12] entitled him to claim in his own name as deriving right from Lord Talbot. In this document, Lord Talbot acknowledged that he had sold and delivered to Isham "the collection of papers, manuscripts and letters, by, or belonging to James Boswell, inherited by me as his great-great-grandson and otherwise." At first sight, this seemed to cover future finds such as that at Fettercairn, but unfortunately the wording equated what had been sold with what was actually delivered in 1927. The document had been written out by Isham at the time of his first major purchase and signed by Lord Talbot without much consideration of its implications. It was certainly not the intention of the Talbots to sell anything more than the letters and papers which Isham actually took away with him on this particular visit. When the document was signed, Isham had not yet even negotiated the purchase of the journals. Later, after he had acquired the journals, Lady Talbot made it quite clear in correspondence that the price would include any scraps of journal material which might turn up later, but not any other papers. Isham accepted this and, in 1930, he paid an additional price for the croquet box find.

The cooperation of the Talbots was therefore essential. Even granted this, Isham's chance of success was very uncertain. There were

[10]Letter from Pottle to Isham of 20 March 1936 (in IFP). Pottle pointed out that Lord Clinton was the eldest direct descendant of Sir William Forbes, but, in his view, Forbes never had a shadow of a title to the manuscripts and he did not see how Lord Clinton could have acquired one. He drew Isham's attention to JB's will, the effect of which, he considered, was to carry the papers to Sir James Boswell as last heir of entail and he thought that Lord Talbot had inherited everything from Sir James. Pottle admitted that the question as to whether Isham's earlier purchase from Lord Talbot covered the Fettercairn papers presented "a nice legal puzzle," but his conclusion was that if Isham was not the owner of the new papers, Lord Talbot certainly was.

[11]See above pp. 83–84.

[12]See above p.

bound to be a number of competing claims which could only be resolved after lengthy court proceedings. A decision could not be expected for at least a year and, whatever the outcome, the legal costs could be ruinous. Yet, despite the risks and uncertainties, Isham made up his mind to fight. This was a remarkably brave decision, considering the set-backs and financial pressures to which he had been subjected since 1927. Nowhere in his whole struggle does he show to better advantage than at this moment. To the task of recovering the Fettercairn papers he brought those qualities of energy, courage, and enthusiasm which equipped him so well to undertake the salvage of Boswell's archives. He had good reason to feel ill-used, but he refused to indulge in rancour or self-pity. He maintained friendly relations with Chapman, despite the latter's involvement in "Operation Hush," and when Chapman was bringing out his edition of Johnson's letters some years later he was allowed to print any unpublished letters from Isham's own collection.[13]

Having made his decision, Isham moved swiftly. He sailed immediately for England after cabling Lord Talbot from New York:

Sailing today Steamer *Paris*. Account report published in London Times regarding Lord Clinton Manuscript. Believe these yours and think essential we meet London 29th. Work out plans avoiding possible legal complication. London address, Garrick Club.[14]

On his arrival in London, a letter was waiting for him from Mr. A. J. Robinson, Lord Talbot's Dublin solicitor, to say that the Talbots were in Italy and would not return before the end of May at the soonest.[15] Isham telephoned to Robinson to explain that all he wished was to assist Lord Talbot in any way possible to recover the Fettercairn papers and, for this purpose, to place his specialized knowledge at Lord Talbot's disposal. He added delicately that if Lord Talbot were to succeed in obtaining any of the documents and were disposed to

---

[13]A good example of Isham's magnanimity. He must have been upset that Chapman had given no hint of the existence of important new material which he had known about since 1931. Isham's friends thought he had been badly used and told him so. Nevertheless, in 1945, he allowed Chapman to use and publish any portion or all of his letters of SJ, whether previously published or not. Chapman wrote on 21 November 1945 to acknowledge this generosity, remarking: "I had hardly ventured to hope for the unpublished letters" (letter in IFP).

[14]A typed copy of the cable is in TFP. It is undated but must have been sent about the last week of March 1936. A letter from Pottle to Isham of 24 March wishes him Godspeed and by 1 April Isham was in London.

[15]Letter dated 30 March 1936 (copy in TFP).

sell, he would be very interested in making a purchase. Robinson refused to commit himself in the absence of the Talbots, but promised to report to them what Isham had said.[16] Isham, realizing that there was nothing to be achieved by staying on in London, returned at once to the United States.[17]

News of the Fettercairn discovery reached the Talbots at their villa in Italy soon after publication of Abbott's letter to *The Times*. John M. Howden, their accountant in Edinburgh, wrote on 13 March to say that he had consulted with the family's Scottish solicitors, who thought that Lord Talbot had a direct claim. He advised that a claim should be lodged when the Judicial Factor had been appointed.[18] A few days later, Lady Talbot heard from Sir Gilbert Eliott, tenth Baronet of Stobs and Wells, who was descended from Sir Alexander Boswell's elder daughter, Janet Theresa.[19] He reported that he had already instructed his solicitors to claim on his behalf, and suggested that Lord Talbot might like to combine with him in a joint claim.[20] Absence abroad made it difficult for the Talbots to take active steps, but they instructed their solicitors to intimate to the Judicial Factor their intention of claiming, and this was done on 30 March.[21] Meanwhile there were others busily engaged in checking their descent from Boswell who were soon to emerge as claimants.

Wedderburn was confirmed by the Court as Judicial Factor on 27 March 1936,[22] and so became entrusted with the physical custody of the papers and the task of determining who was legally entitled to them. The petition for his appointment[23] attempted to explain how the papers had come into Lord Clinton's possession by recording his direct descent from Sir William Forbes[24] and giving a brief historical survey which included a summary of the relevant provisions of Boswell's

---

[16]Reported in a letter from Robinson to Lady Talbot of 1 April 1936 (TFP).

[17]Ibid. Robinson mentions Isham's intention of returning to America.

[18]Letter dated 13 March 1936 (TFP).

[19]See Table IV, p. 355.

[20]Letter dated 21 March 1936 (TFP).

[21]Letter, Scott Moncrieff & Trail to E. M. Wedderburn, 30 March 1936 (copy in S. R. & Co.'s papers).

[22]Extract Decree of the Court of Session in favour of Ernest Maclagan Wedderburn dated 27 March and extracted 27 April 1936.

[23]Petition of the Right Honourable Charles John Robert Hepburn Stuart Forbes Trefusis, Baron Clinton of Maxtock and Saye, Fettercairn House, Fettercairn, Kincardineshire for Appointment of Judicial Factor on the Estate of the late James Boswell of Auchinleck (print in S. R. & Co.'s papers).

[24]See Table VI, p. 357.

will. Lord Clinton made it clear that he still regarded himself as the owner of the papers, but had decided to petition for appointment of a Judicial Factor to obtain a definitive ruling on the questions of ownership and copyright. At this stage, there were thus already three contenders: Lord Talbot, Sir Gilbert Eliott, and Lord Clinton.

Pottle was due to visit Scotland in the summer of 1936 to receive an honorary degree from Glasgow University. This gave him a chance to find out for Isham how the situation was developing and to speak to the various persons involved. On 11 July, he had a meeting in Edinburgh with Wedderburn, who told him that he had been unable to adjudicate between the competing claims and would have to raise an action so that the Court of Session might decide. The Court would insist on public advertisement for claims and further claimants would probably appear. The Court had already given permission for the publication of Abbott's catalogue to enable interested parties to define their claims. The case was unlikely to open before Christmas or to be decided in less than a year. Pottle enquired about expenses and received the unwelcome information that Wedderburn's whole costs and probably also those of the other claimants would have to be met by the successful claimant.[25] Meanwhile the manuscripts were held on Wedderburn's behalf locked up in the strong-room of Aberdeen University Library in the charge of Dr. Douglas Simpson. Pottle went to see Dr. Simpson, who received him courteously, but "shut up like a clam" after admitting the papers were in his safe.[26]

The following week, Pottle met first Chapman and then Abbott. Chapman, he found "almost embarrassingly friendly, but deliberately vague"; Abbott, he thought "very frank and honest." Chapman seemed hurt when Pottle told him what construction everybody placed on his conduct, and pointed out that he was pledged to secrecy and could not have made any disclosure without Lord Clinton's permission, which was not forthcoming. Pottle accepted that Chapman had not been deliberately false, but told him bluntly that he was certainly to blame, being Isham's publisher and under great obligation to him,

[25]Reported in a letter from Pottle to Isham of 14 July 1936 (IFP). Pottle attended the meeting with his friend T. B. Simpson, who as an advocate at the Scottish bar and a Boswellian enthusiast was well qualified to advise. Isham had earlier written on Pottle's recommendation to ask Simpson to act for him, but Simpson had to decline as he was already retained as counsel for Lord Clinton (letter Simpson to Isham, 27 March 1936 in IFP). In the Court action which followed, Simpson in fact represented the Judicial Factor and not Lord Clinton whose counsel was J. F. Strachan.

[26]Ibid.

for entertaining plans for a rival publication. He told both Chapman and Abbott that the present situation was the worst that could have been devised for everybody except the lawyers, and suggested that Lord Clinton should have been informed that he had no moral right to the papers and ought to hand them over to Lord Talbot.[27]

On his return to the United States at the beginning of August, Pottle sent Isham a detailed report.[28] The most ominous news was that Chapman and Abbott had both spoken of the possibility of a claim by the descendants of Boswell's "younger children." As previously explained, Boswell used this phrase loosely in his will to mean all his children except Alexander, his elder son (although Veronica and Euphemia were both older than Alexander). Veronica, Euphemia, and James junior all died unmarried and Pottle had thought that Elizabeth's line failed before 1900.[29] It now seemed that she might have surviving descendants after all[30]; even if this were not so, the "younger children" might still have inherited some right to the papers under Boswell's will which could have transmitted to their heirs or executors. There was also the possibility of a claim by descendants of Janet Theresa Boswell, of whom Sir Gilbert Eliott was one.[31] Pottle commented:

> The whole thing is a nightmare, and when you add the question of copyright to that of ownership, you have one of the most promising cases from a lawyer's point of view that the world was ever blessed with. . . . The lawyers so far have done literally nothing. They haven't looked at the Catalogue. For Boswell's will, they have gone no further than Rogers,[32] though the original is in the Register House at Edinburgh, twenty steps from Simpson's daily round, and contains two important codicils which Rogers didn't print. Some one must work up a real brief for Talbot and you, and if Talbot's lawyer is no more active than Clinton's, I fear I shall have to work it up. I will try to write something, but it will be a long document, and will take time.[33]

Lady Talbot returned from Italy in the early summer and began to take stock of the situation. Her husband's main desire was not to

[27]Letter, Pottle to Isham, 3 August 1936 (IFP).
[28]Ibid.
[29]Ibid.
[30]See Table III, p. 354.
[31]See Table IV, p. 355.
[32]See above, p. 29.
[33]Letter, Pottle to Isham, 3 August 1936 (IFP).

become involved,[34] but she could not ignore Isham's position. Isham had written to Robinson in mid-April explaining in detail why he believed that Lord Talbot was the rightful owner by inheritance of the newly discovered papers. He also put forward his own claims with some force:

> It was always my understanding that I was purchasing the entire collection, as left by Boswell in so far as it survived. Indeed, had this not been so, it is questionable whether I should have purchased them at all, and it is certain that the price I agreed upon was largely influenced by this consideration; for publication rights, which were part of my purchase, gained their main value from the completeness of the collection.

After quoting the 1927 sale agreement,[35] Isham went on to say:

> I have now spent over eight years of work on these manuscripts. In addition to my own efforts, I have engaged and paid for the services of the most eminent scholars to assure their being presented to the world in the most scholarly and accurate manner. During this time, we have produced in a private printed edition eighteen volumes. The nineteenth and final volume is now being printed by the Oxford University Press. The cost of editorial and secretarial work alone, entirely paid for by me, has been, to date, over $70,000, no part of which has been recovered by the sale of the private edition. . . .[36]

Lady Talbot had lost her copy of the 1927 agreement and was somewhat alarmed by the possible extent of Isham's legal rights. An anxious correspondence with Robinson ensued. She decided to arrange a meeting with Isham, but first she had investigations of her own to make. She came to the conclusion, quite correctly, that the persons entitled to the papers were those who could deduce ownership by legal transmission through the various generations back to Boswell himself. She realized that mere relationship did not matter; what counted was who at each stage was legally entitled to inherit. She believed that Boswell's will had the effect of passing his papers to the "younger children" and that the descendants of Elizabeth were

---

[34]See letter quoted below p. 152.
[35]Quoted above p. 70.
[36]Letter, Isham to Messrs A. J. & A. Robinson, 17 April 1936 (copy in IFP).

therefore the persons truly entitled to benefit.[37] Her interpretation was certainly open to question and it did not seem to occur to her that it was not consistent with her husband's ownership of the Malahide papers.

Lord Talbot's claim was formally intimated to the Judicial Factor on 17 September 1936[38] and, on 7 October, Lady Talbot wrote to Sir Gilbert Eliott, hinting that he should withdraw his own claim:

> James is very anxious to withdraw from the case, but at present his solicitors have persuaded him to continue. I have asked one of Elizabeth Boswell's descendants for a complete list of the other descendants and I have asked her to try to find out whether Elizabeth left her property and to whom it ultimately descended. If . . . nobody can prove their legal right to Elizabeth's property, it would be better for James to continue as chief claimant. . . . He can then do what he thinks fair to any descendants of Elizabeth Boswell who in spite of being morally the people whom the Biographer meant to benefit, are unable to prove any legal claim. . . . Above all, I think that we should all combine to keep out Lord Clinton, if possible, as there can be no moral justification for his claiming the papers.[39]

The descendant of Elizabeth Boswell mentioned by Lady Talbot was Miss Elena Hailey, Elizabeth's great-great-granddaughter.[40] From Miss Hailey, Lady Talbot learnd that three great-grandchildren survived: Mrs. E. M. Hailey (Elena's mother), and Mrs. Hailey's brother and sister, Mr. C. E. Cumberlege Ware and Mrs. E. C. Marriott. Another sister had died only a few months before.[41] Somewhat arbitrarily, Lady Talbot decided that Mr. Cumberlege Ware and his sisters were entitled to the Fettercairn papers.[42] Lord Talbot was only too ready to withdraw

[37]All this is explained in a letter from Lady Talbot to Sir Gilbert Eliott of 7 October 1936 (copy in TFP).

[38]Letter, Scott Moncrieff & Trail to Wedderburn, 17 September 1936 (copy in S. R. & Co.'s papers).

[39]Copy letter in TFP.

[40]She is mentioned in a letter from her uncle, C. E. Cumberlege Ware, to Lady Talbot of 30 October 1936 (TFP).

[41]See Table III, p. 354. The other sister was Miss K. A. Cumberlege, who died on 21 February 1936.

[42]Writing to Mr. Cumberlege Ware on 30 October 1936, Lady Talbot said that she and Lord Talbot did not think that anyone other than he and his sisters should benefit by the papers if JB's intentions could be fairly interpreted (copy letter in TFP).

his claim in their favour, but Lady Talbot felt that Isham should be informed before any positive action was taken. She was also a little afraid that Isham might be provoked into legal action, and her lawyer warned her to tread carefully.[43] On 12 October, she wrote to Isham suggesting a meeting.[44]

Isham had been waiting for this cue ever since his fruitless trip to London in the spring. He travelled immediately to Dublin and, after a preliminary talk with Robinson, he met the Talbots and Robinson at Malahide on 29 October. The emergence of the unknown Mr. Cumberlege Ware as a contender was an unwelcome complication and he felt it necessary to take a firm line. He brought up the subject of the 1927 sale agreement, and persuaded the Talbots that it could be interpreted as assigning to him any right which Lord Talbot might have in the Fettercairn papers. So far as Mr. Cumberlege Ware was concerned, Isham convinced Lady Talbot that her interpretation of Boswell's will was wrong and that it was Sir Alexander and not the "younger children" who inherited the papers. The person with the best legal claim, he argued, was Lord Talbot himself by virtue of his descent from Sir Alexander. He conceded that the publication rights might conceivably have transmitted to Elizabeth's descendants, although both he and Robinson doubted this.

The upshot of the meeting was that Lord Talbot agreed to withdraw his own claim and to assign his rights to Isham, leaving Isham free to prosecute the claim in his own name. Isham was to meet the whole costs and to indemnify Lord Talbot against any expense he might incur.[45] The astute Robinson strongly suspected that the 1927 agreement did not in fact confer on Isham the rights which he claimed,[46] but Lady Talbot told him: "It is worth a good sum of money to have Colonel Isham as a friend instead of an enemy. He behaved well on the whole—I think he enjoys behaving well, although he is capable of behaving very badly."[47] Some months later, Lady Talbot wrote in a letter to Sir Gilbert Eliott:

[43]Correspondence between Lady Talbot and Robinson (TFP).
[44]Copy letter in TFP.
[45]All this information about the meeting with Isham comes from the long letter from Lady Talbot to Cumberlege Ware of 30 October 1936 (copy in TFP). Lady Talbot wrote that Isham managed to convince herself and Lord Talbot that owing to earlier correspondence and "a rather rough and ready contract with him" he could probably claim the papers away from Lord Talbot if Lord Talbot became the possessor of them.
[46]Letter, Robinson to Lady Talbot, 28 October 1936 (TFP).
[47]Letter, Lady Talbot to Robinson, 30 November 1936 (TFP).

James, as you know, has made over rights to the Clinton manuscripts he might have to Colonel Isham. He was moved to do this by a feeling that Colonel Isham's collection would be practically ruined in value if it were not the complete collection of the Biographer's letters and works which we thought it was when we sold it to him. It seems fairer therefore to give him the opportunity to acquire these new papers at no further expense than it would cost him to pay all the legal expenses. James therefore gave him his claim as a gift but he has relieved James of all expenses in connection with it. . . . As you know, a great deal of matter has been published we did not wish, but I do not think that he has ever been prompted by any wish for personal gain which made us feel we ought to treat him as generously as possible as he is no longer a rich man.[48]

Lady Talbot still insisted that Mr. Cumberlege Ware was morally entitled to some financial benefit. Isham offered, therefore, to make him an *ex gratia* payment of £500, provided he made no claim.[49] Cumberlege Ware did not respond with much enthusiasm. He told Lady Talbot that before accepting Isham's offer, he intended to go very carefully into his chances of making a successful claim.[50] He would have done better to have taken the money. He had in fact no right, legal or moral, to benefit from the papers and, for reasons soon to be explained, he ended up with nothing.[51]

By now, five more possible claimants had emerged: the Dowager Lady Forbes, of Alford, Aberdeenshire, Dr. Henry St. George Boswell, of Roxburgh, Mrs. Louisa Scott, Mrs. Emily Eliott, and Mr. Charles W. Eliott.[52] The last three, like Sir Gilbert Eliott, all traced their descent from Boswell through Janet Theresa Boswell.[53] Dr. Henry St. George Boswell was a great-great-grandson of Robert Boswell, W. S., cousin of the Biographer. He claimed, correctly, to be the senior male representative of Boswell's family to whom the estate of Auchinleck would

[48]Letter, Lady Talbot to Sir Gilbert Eliott, 21 April 1937 (copy in TFP). Lady Talbot mentions another reason for treating Isham generously: "He is I believe being financed by an exceptionally nice American whose money I would hate to be squandered more than is necessary." Lady Talbot presumably refers to Van Alen.

[49]Letter, Lady Talbot to Cumberlege Ware, 30 October 1936 (copy in TFP).

[50]So Lady Talbot reported in her letter to Isham of 9 November 1936 (copy in TFP).

[51]See below p. 172.

[52]Information in copy letter of Baillie & Gifford of 6 October 1936, addressee unknown (TFP). Presumably this was sent to Lady Talbot by Sir Gilbert Eliott, whose solicitors were Baillie & Gifford.

[53]See Table IV, p. 355.

have passed had the entail not been broken by Sir James Boswell in 1852.[54] Lady Forbes's only interest was apparently to trace certain documents said to have been handed to Boswell by her great-grand-father, Sir Alexander Dick of Prestonfield.[55]

As Lord Talbot's assignee, Isham was at last able to join battle. He went immediately to London, where he saw his lawyer, Humphrey Thackrah, of the firm of Denton Hall and Burgin. Before leaving Dublin, he had arranged for Robinson to instruct Lord Talbot's Edinburgh lawyers, Scott Moncrieff & Trail, to withdraw Lord Talbot's claim and to prepare a suitable assignation in his favour. He was anxious to have this completed as quickly as possible as he was due to sail on the *Normandie* on 4 November to fulfil a remunerative engagement for a series of lectures at Northwestern University. Thackrah told him he would have to instruct a lawyer in Edinburgh as the whole matter was governed by Scots Law on which he was not qualified to advise. The first step was to find out the latest forecast of when the court case would begin. Wedderburn was told guardedly that Isham was interested because he had some important documentary evidence he wished to lay before the Court; no hint was given that he would himself be a claimant. Wedderburn was reassuring and thought that Isham might safely return to America meantime. He explained that he had decided to see what claims emerged following the publication of Abbott's catalogue later in the month and that the court action would not begin until after Christmas at soonest.[56]

Isham was nevertheless reluctant to return home at this stage. The Talbots were shortly leaving for Italy and would be away until the following spring.[57] He felt it was important for him to stay until the assignation had been properly completed and intimated to the Judicial Factor. There was also a great deal of groundwork to be done in preparing his claim and briefing his lawyers. Although he could ill afford to lose his fee of $2,500 from Northwestern University, he decided that the wise course was to cancel his lectures and to remain in England.[58]

[54]See Table V, p. 356.

[55]Information from Judicial Factor recorded in letter, Steedman Ramage & Co. to Denton Hall & Burgin, 1 December 1936 (copy in S. R. & Co.'s papers).

[56]Information in this paragraph comes from a memorandum dated 3 November 1936, by Thackrah, made available to me by Messrs. Denton Hall & Burgin.

[57]Ibid. The Talbots planned to leave on 10 November and to return about the beginning of the following May.

[58]Ibid.

Thackrah now asked Eric P. Buchanan, a partner in the Edinburgh firm of Steedman Ramage & Co., to act as Isham's lawyer in Scotland. This was a happy choice because Buchanan, who found most of his day-to-day legal work rather dull, was immediately gripped by the story of the Boswell papers. He fell under the spell of Isham's personality and performed prodigies of painstaking research in helping to build up the case. Much of the material on which this book is based is the direct result of that research.

Buchanan's first task was to complete the assignation by Lord Talbot. He strongly advised Isham to let him negotiate for the assignation to include Lord Talbot's rights to any papers which might be found in the future.[59] Isham decided, however, not to press this point lest it cause delay or even jeopardize the whole arrangement.[60] In so doing, he made a serious error which was later to cost him dearly.

The assignation was finally signed and delivered to Buchanan on 28 November after Isham had paid the bills of Lord Talbot's lawyers in Dublin and Edinburgh.[61] On 30 November, it was formally intimated to the Judicial Factor and, on 3 December, a carefully worded announcement appeared in the press.[62]

Isham was now openly in the saddle, but he had to be careful of public opinion. Pottle had warned him of the existence of anti-American feeling in certain quarters and that the removal of Boswell manuscripts to America had caused resentment.[63] It was important that these feelings should not be allowed to prejudice his chances. The press notice deliberately avoided mentioning his nationality and referred to his working with scholars from "both British and American universities." Later, in the court proceedings, he made a point of adding "C.B.E." after his name to draw attention to his British honour.[64]

Abbott's catalogue was published on 26 November 1936.[65] Isham

---

[59]Letter, Steedman Ramage & Co. to Denton Hall & Burgin, 10 November 1936 (copy in S. R. & Co.'s papers).

[60]Reply from Denton Hall & Burgin to Steedman Ramage & Co., 11 November 1936 (S. R. & Co.'s papers).

[61]The total was £83.18.5d (S. R. & Co.'s papers).

[62]In *The Scotsman, The Glasgow Herald,* and other newspapers.

[63]Pottle wrote to Isham on 17 December 1936 (letter in IFP): "If you and I had not been Americans, there would not have been this conspiracy of silence. Britons are *very* sore about the removal of papers from Britain."

[64]He claimed as "Lieutenant-Colonel Ralph Heyward Isham, C. B. E."

[65]See above p. 116, n. 4.

read it through at once and found that although most of the documents listed must originally have formed part of Boswell's archives, there were others which had probably been Forbes's property. He came to the conclusion that he could not reasonably claim Sir William's copy of the Round Robin nor the letters from Boswell to Sir William.[66] This was a common-sense point of view, but his lawyers feared it might weaken his position and pressed him to claim everything in the catalogue as a *"unum quid"* without any exceptions.[67] Isham decided on a compromise: he would contend that all the documents in the catalogue should be treated as a whole, but he would not ask for Boswell's letters to Forbes, apart from five doubtful ones.[68] Strangely, neither Isham nor any of the other parties tried to claim the important manuscripts which Abbott mentioned in his introduction but failed to list in the catalogue itself. These included the only surviving letter of substance from Johnson to Boswell.[69]

Isham now had to complete his team of lawyers for the forthcoming lawsuit. Buchanan, as a solicitor, could not appear for him in court, and he would need a senior and a junior counsel. On Buchanan's advice, J. R. Wardlaw Burnet, K.C., one of the ablest advocates at the Scottish Bar, was briefed as senior counsel, and W. R. Milligan (now Lord Milligan, recently retired as a judge of the Court of Session) was chosen as junior counsel. Milligan was already familiar with the background as he had represented Lord Talbot until the latter had withdrawn his claim.

Pottle's strictures on the inertia of the Edinburgh lawyers were not justified in the case of Scott Moncrieff & Trail, who acted for Lord Talbot. By June 1936, they had traced the wills of all the persons through whom Lord Talbot claimed, from Boswell himself to Mrs.

---

[66]*Fettercairn Catalogue*, No. 1604 and Nos. 1320–60.

[67]It was argued that JB was in the habit of collecting all the letters and papers he thought might be useful in his literary work, and that his letters to Forbes might have been given back to him during his lifetime or added to his papers by Forbes after his death. Lord Clinton, moreover, had withheld correspondence found at Fettercairn addressed to Forbes by the "younger children" after JB's death. By placing JB's own letters to Forbes in the hands of the Judicial Factor, he was tacitly admitting that his right of ownership to them was not clear. The lawyers also feared that if the whole papers were not claimed as a *unum quid,* it might be argued that other items listed in the catalogue were also separable.

[68]The five doubtful ones were *Fettercairn Catalogue*, Nos. 1324, 1339, 1340, 1345, and 1346. Isham eventually decided to include the copy of the Round Robin in his claim.

[69]See above p. 123, n. 21, and below Appendix II, pp. 323–24.

ERIC P. BUCHANAN

W. R. MILLIGAN

J. R. WARDLAW BURNET, K.C.

Mounsey. They had also prepared a useful family tree and a memorandum analysing Lord Talbot's chances of success.[70] As soon as the assignation in favour of Isham was completed, they turned this material over to Buchanan, along with a mass of other papers which they had unearthed.[71] Most of these related to a bitter dispute between Alexander and the "younger children" as to the interpretation of their father's will, a dispute which was only settled after protracted arbitration. A number of important documents were missing, but Buchanan was able to trace these and, after spending many hours searching the public records at the Register House in Edinburgh, he reconstructed the whole history of the dispute.[72] This was important, because if the Court were to find that the papers passed under the will to the "younger children," the circumstances of the family quarrel and the way in which it was settled would become a crucial issue.

Pottle, too, had been busy thinking about Isham's claim. He knew that the will was capable of several interpretations and he rightly concluded that the actings of the literary executors, if they could be reconstructed, would shed important light on the problem. Another key to interpretation was Boswell's personal circumstances when he made the will (and a subsequent codicil), because from these his intentions could be deduced. It would also be necessary to explain how the archives came to be split and how a third of the total bulk found its way to Fettercairn.

Pottle's unrivalled knowledge of Boswellian studies enabled him to give valuable help. In April 1936, he wrote to Isham drawing his attention to the correspondence between Forbes and Malone, containing information about the execution of the literary trust.[73] In December 1936, he wrote again with more detailed information about the literary trust, and he analysed possible interpretations of the will.[74] He also dealt with the physical whereabouts of the papers between the dates of the will and Boswell's death and suggested how a part of them had come to rest at Fettercairn.[75] Pottle's help was vital in building

[70]Both these documents are with S. R. & Co.'s papers.

[71]Letter, Steedman Ramage & Co. to Denton Hall & Burgin, 28 November 1936 (copy in S. R. & Co.'s papers).

[72]Fully documented in S. R. & Co.'s papers.

[73]Letter dated 17 April 1936 in IFP.

[74]Letter dated 17 December 1936 in IFP.

[75]Ibid. Pottle surmised that the papers were in Forbes's hands as executor when he died in 1806 and that his son and heir overlooked to return a third of the total bulk to the family at Auchinleck. This third was taken to Fettercairn when young Sir William Forbes's wife succeeded to the property. See above p. 117.

up Isham's case. His reputation as a scholar was such that his views on a number of points were later accepted by the Court without challenge or proof.[76]

Isham returned home for Christmas, but was back in London in time to attend a conference with Buchanan and Thackrah on 6 January 1937.[77] Buchanan reported that Wedderburn had opened the court proceedings the day before by raising an action of multiple-poinding in the Court of Session in which Lord Clinton, Isham, and Sir Gilbert Eliott were called as defenders. Buchanan explained that "multiplepoinding" was the name given to a special type of action in Scotland in which the Court was asked to decide the ownership of disputed property. The action was raised by the person holding the property (in this case the Judicial Factor) and the defenders were the persons claiming to be entitled. The property in dispute (in this case the Fettercairn papers) was known technically as "the fund *in medio.*" Buchanan thought there was no immediate urgency about completing and lodging Isham's claim. The Court would first order advertisement for claims to be inserted in the leading newspapers and would then fix a date by which claims had to be lodged. This was unlikely to be sooner than May and the time limit might very well be extended. Once all the claims had been lodged, each claimant would be allowed to adjust his pleadings in the light of the other claims and the "record" would then be "closed," that is to say the pleadings would become final.[78] A hearing would then be fixed and the Court, after consideration of the points of fact and law involved, and after hearing counsel for the parties, would give its decision.

Isham assured Buchanan and Thackrah of his determination to do anything necessary to give his claim the best possible chance of success, and he promised to make himself available in Edinburgh whenever he might be needed. After detailed consideration of the case, he arranged to travel to Edinburgh for a consultation with Buchanan, Wardlaw Burnet, and Milligan. This took place on 18 January

[76]Lord Stevenson, for example, accepted Pottle's statement in his introduction to the *Malahide Catalogue* "as an accurate account of the location of Boswell's papers at the date of his death" (opinion of Lord Stevenson, 19 August 1938, S. R. & Co.'s papers).

[77]"Note of Conference held at 14 Pall Mall on Wednesday January 6th, 1937. Present: Col. R. H. Isham, Mr. E. P. Buchanan, Mr. Thackrah" (copy in S. R. & Co.'s papers).

[78]In Scottish lawsuits, the pleadings of the parties are set down prior to the hearing in a written document known as a "record." A period of time is allowed for the parties to adjust their pleadings in the light of one another's arguments. Thereafter the record is closed and is known as a closed record.

1937.[79] The existing evidence was minutely scrutinized, various weaknesses were pin-pointed, and many avenues for further research and enquiry were opened up. Buchanan was instructed to try to fill in the gaps in Scott Moncrieff & Trail's dossier on the arbitration proceedings and also to find out when the "younger children" died and to whom they left their estates. There was also the need to scrutinize the Fettercairn papers themselves and certain letters between the "younger children" and Forbes, which, although found by Abbott at Fettercairn, were not included in his catalogue. Buchanan promised to communicate with Lord Clinton's solicitors to see what he could arrange.[80]

Isham, for his part, said he would write to Lady Talbot immediately to ask if she had any information or papers which might be helpful. Lady Talbot replied to his letter from Italy, unable to give him any of the required information.[81] He decided therefore that he must remain in London until her return and then try to visit her at Malahide. At the same time, he planned to see Robinson in Dublin to get details about the estates of Mrs. Mounsey and Emily Lady Talbot.[82]

Early in March, the Talbots passed through London on their way home. Isham met them and asked if he might visit Malahide to search for correspondence and other papers having a bearing on his case. Lady Talbot was confident that there was nothing to be found, but she agreed that Isham might come as soon as she and her husband had had a few days to settle in.[83] On the day set, Isham arrived at the castle and the search began. He knew enough of the Boswell papers by now to realize that he could not afford to neglect any hiding place, however unlikely. In the words of Lady Talbot's secretary "he nearly

[79]Date confirmed by S. R. & Co.'s papers (business ledger). Also "Note for Lt.-Col. R. H. Isham" of 5 February 1937 prepared by Wardlaw Burnet and Milligan, considering in detail the matters discussed at the consultation (copy in S. R. & Co.'s papers).

[80]Information from S. R. & Co.'s papers.

[81]Isham's letter is dated 19 January 1937 (TFP). He asks about how the papers were transferred to Malahide, whether Mrs. Mounsey gave any to the sixth Lord Talbot during her lifetime, and whether there is any correspondence amongst JB's children at Malahide which might shed light on the interpretation of JB's will. Lady Talbot's reply is referred to in a letter of 3 March 1937 from Denton Hall & Burgin to Steedman Ramage & Co. (S. R. & Co.'s papers).

[82]Information from correspondence in S. R. & Co.'s papers.

[83]The meeting is referred to in a letter from Isham to Lady Talbot of 5 March 1942 (TFP) as being in the spring of 1937. The exact date is unknown. It must have been early March, because Lady Talbot invited Isham to come to Malahide in a few days' time (ibid.). On Friday, 12 March 1937, Thackrah telephoned to Buchanan to say Isham was going to Ireland "that week-end" and would then be returning to America (business ledger entry, S. R. & Co.'s papers).

ate the whole castle." Two full days were spent on the search. Accompanied by the butler, he started with the strong-room and then worked his way systematically through every other room in the castle. Not even the kitchen quarters escaped and every cupboard or receptacle which could contain papers was checked.[84] The result of the search was startling. Chapman, when he heard of it, wrote to Isham:

> That even you should have done it again is almost incredible—but I suppose you make a rule of never visiting a house without finding a manuscript. I wish I could acquire the habit.[85]

Isham had indeed unearthed yet another cache of Boswell papers, which were found in a tin dispatch box in the strong-room.[86] The most important item was a small diary of Samuel Johnson containing seventy-two pages written in his hand. Very spasmodically, it covered events from 1 January 1765 to 8 November 1784, the last part being *"Aegri Ephemeris,"* a history of his final illness.[87] Also important were Boswell's "Book of Company at Auchinleck"[88] and his register of letters for the period 1782 to 1790. This last item was a continuation volume of the registers of letters from 1769 to 1782 found at Fettercairn. Other finds included Johnson's D.C.L. diploma at Oxford,[89] more fragments of the journals, a few letters, and miscellaneous items of Boswelliana. Lady Talbot also produced a document discovered in the office of her Edinburgh lawyer and sent to her some months previously. It was the original grant of £500 by Boswell to his daughter Veronica in consideration of her "infantine attention to my illustrious Friend Doctor Samuel Johnson." Its recovery was specially pleasing because, until now, there had been no evidence that Boswell had ever fulfilled his intention, expressed in the *Tour*,[90] of giving £500 of additional fortune to Veronica in recognition of her fondness for Dr. Johnson.[91]

[84]Information from Spingarn Letter and letter, Isham to Lady Talbot, 5 March 1942 (TFP).

[85]Letter, Chapman to Isham, 20 March 1937 (IFP).

[86]The tin dispatch box is mentioned in Lord Talbot's letter to *The Times*, published on 6 April 1937.

[87]Now in the Hyde Collection. It is published in *Samuel Johnson: Diaries, Prayers and Annals*, ed. E. L. McAdam, Jr., with Donald and Mary Hyde, 1958.

[88]Also now in the Hyde Collection.

[89]This was the original document, written on vellum in 1775. In 1938, Isham presented it to the Bodleian Library, Oxford, which still owns it (MS. Lat. misc. c.61, fols. 1 and 2). See *The Times*, 21 March 1938, p. 17, and 25 March 1938, p. 15, and also the *Bodleian Quarterly Record*, viii, 458. A copy of the diploma (the printer's copy for the *Life*) was later acquired by Isham and presented by him to the Bodleian in 1947. See below p. 261.

[90]See *Life*, V, p. 26.

[91]See "Notes on the Importance of Private Legal Documents for the writing of Biography and

Isham also turned up a large bundle of correspondence and other papers covering the period 1884 to 1917 which gave valuable information about the relationship between Mrs. Mounsey and the Talbot family and the disposal of her personal estate and effects after her death.[92] Included in these papers were a number of old sale catalogues which showed how the library at Auchinleck was finally broken up.[93] A good deal of information also came to light about the settlement of Sir Alexander Boswell's affairs after his death. It looked as though it might be very difficult to establish that the papers passed from Sir Alexander to Sir James. This was disturbing, for Isham's whole case depended on Sir James's succession to the papers.

The Talbots generously gave all the newly found Boswell papers to Isham with the exception of the grant to Veronica and a few other mementoes which they decided to keep for sentimental reasons.[94] They also allowed Isham to borrow all the other papers relevant to his case.[95]

Immediately after his visit to Malahide, Isham had to return to America to deliver his postponed lectures at Northwestern University. He sailed on 17 March 1937 on the *Queen Mary* and on arrival in New York was besieged by reporters who had got wind of his latest

---

Literary History," by F. A. Pottle (*Proceedings of the American Philosophical Society*, vol. 106, No. 4, August, 1962). Isham did not discover the grant as he told Pottle and as Pottle stated in his article. It was found by Messrs. Scott Moncrieff & Trail in their office in Edinburgh. They sent it to Lady Talbot on 9 July 1936 (letter in TFP). She showed it to Isham when he visited Malahide in 1937.

[92]Copies of these are in S. R. & Co.'s papers.

[93]The sales are described in Chapter I above.

[94]The grant to Veronica remained at Malahide at least until the death of the seventh Lord Talbot in 1973. The other mementoes retained by the Talbots were:
1. A small paper packet labelled by JB and containing his wife's wedding ring, still owned by Lady Talbot.
2. A small packet labelled by JB, containing a lock of his wife's hair, still owned by Lady Talbot.
3. A packet labelled by JB, containing his wife's purse, still owned by Lady Talbot.
4. A letter from SJ to Mr. Cave, January 1756. Printed by Chapman in his edition of SJ's *Letters*, No. 89, from the text in *Gentleman's Magazine*, Jan. 1793, i, 19. This letter was sold in November 1967 by Lady Talbot to Mrs. Donald F. Hyde and is now in the Hyde Collection.
5. Two small leather-bound notebooks containing notes on law-court proceedings in JB's hand. One of these, containing ten pages of notes by JB as Recorder of Carlisle, relative to the case of Bennet v. the Mayor and Corporation of Carlisle, 7 December 1789, was also purchased by Mrs. Donald F. Hyde from Lady Talbot in November 1967 and is now in the Hyde Collection. The other notebook is now unaccounted for unless it is the notebook now in the National Library of Scotland (see below p. 305). As to the few other mementoes still owned by Lady Talbot, see below Appendix I, pp. 313 and 317.

[95]All of these were forwarded to Buchanan and there are copies in S. R. & Co.'s papers.

find.[96] Isham, knowing Lord Talbot's intense dislike of publicity, refused to give any interviews until a number of unauthorized and speculative accounts had appeared. He was then persuaded to receive representatives from three leading newspapers with his secretary present. He stressed that he had made no payment to the Talbots and the American press so reported. The press coverage in England, however, was less responsible. On 18 March, Buchanan and Thackrah had released a brief and carefully worded announcement (avoiding all reference to the court proceedings) to the main Scottish newspapers and to three London press agencies. The announcement was published in Scotland, but completely ignored in London. Only when the news broke in America did *The Times* of London pick up the story. This was followed by a number of wildly inaccurate articles in other papers. The worst offender was *The Daily Sketch,* whose headline on 27 March ran: "DOCTOR JOHNSON'S LOST DIARY FOUND IN DUNGEON. It tells great man's secrets to within five minutes of his death." Isham was described as making his discovery "after days of search in the gloomy dungeons of Malahide Castle." It was implied that the diary was a major manuscript: "The Diary, begun in 1765, holds Doctor Johnson's secrets till five minutes before his death in 1784." Isham was also said to have paid Lord Talbot more than £60,000 for his collection of Johnson relics. Not to be outdone, *The Daily Telegraph* cited a figure of £100,000. *The Sunday Dispatch* printed its version of the story on 28 March and, realizing perhaps that it was last with the news, tried to give the impression that it was first. "Lady Talbot de Malahide made this disclosure exclusively to me today," wrote its Dublin reporter, "when discussing the discovery of the Johnson diary, announced late last night in a cablegram from New York." The tin dispatch box in which the diary had been found was imaginatively transformed into a padlocked iron chest which the butler had had to force open. Yet another account referred to an "immense iron casket . . . so heavy that it required two men to open the lid."

The Talbots were most upset by all this inaccurate publicity. As Lady Talbot later remarked, it was tiresome to have her correspondence swollen by letters of congratulation from friends over a payment of £60,000 (or even £100,000 in the case of *The Daily Telegraph* readers)

---

[96]This information and the account of the press publicity which follows come from the correspondence file between Buchanan and Thackrah and the press clippings file in S. R. & Co.'s papers.

which did not exist. Lord Talbot, highly agitated, cabled Thackrah, who cabled Isham, who cabled back to Lord Talbot protesting innocence. Corrections and apologies were demanded from the offending newspapers and were not generally forthcoming. Lord Talbot's lawyers advised him that he had no grounds for action and he had to be content with publishing a letter in *The Times* of London on 6 April correcting the inaccuracies "typical of the exaggerated stories about my great-great-grandfather's papers so frequently published during the last ten years."

During Isham's absence, Buchanan had plenty to keep him occupied. Sir Gilbert Eliott's solicitors sent him a deed by which Sir James Boswell had renounced his succession to the estate of his father, Sir Alexander.[97] This was a bombshell because unless it could be proved that the papers passed into the ownership of Sir James, Isham's claim would fail. Buchanan immediately got in touch with Scott Moncrieff & Trail, who were able to lend him a mass of papers relating to the hopeless tangle in which Sir Alexander's affairs were left at his death. These papers were soon supplemented by those which Isham had found at Malahide. Buchanan spent many days at the Register House checking the old court records and noting anything which might have a bearing. His enquiries were inconclusive, and it remained uncertain to whom the papers passed from Sir Alexander. He did, however, succeed in tracing the vital decree in the arbitration proceedings between Sir Alexander and the "younger children."[98] This was not with the other papers sent by Scott Moncrieff & Trail and proved very elusive because of a wrong entry in the index at Register House.[99] He also searched the official records for the will of James Boswell junior, but without success.

The Court ordered claims to be lodged by 4 May 1937,[100] but no one was ready by then and a second order was made extending the time limit to 19 June.[101] Buchanan was most anxious that Isham should return to Scotland to discuss the drafting of his claim, on which

[97]The solicitors were Baillie & Gifford, W. S., who reported the discovery of the renunciation to Buchanan by telephone on 9 March 1937 (S. R. & Co.'s papers—business ledger). The renunciation is dated 22 October 1831 and registered in the Books of Council and Session on 10 December 1832. The original is preserved at Register House in Edinburgh.

[98]Decreet Arbitral issued on 7 and registered in the Books of Council and Session on 8 February 1805.

[99]The index is now corrected.

[100]Interlocutor of Lord Stevenson dated 17 March 1937.

[101]Interlocutor of Lord Stevenson dated 8 May 1937.

counsel had been working since early April. He also felt that Isham should see for himself the letters in Lord Clinton's possession between Alexander, the "younger children," and Forbes. In March, Buchanan had written to Lord Clinton's solicitors about this correspondence and they in their turn had written to Abbott for information.[102] Abbott replied to say that the locked boxes containing the Fettercairn papers were in the strong-room of Aberdeen University Library and he had all the keys. He knew approximately what each box contained and thought that the letters from Boswell's children to Forbes were all in one box (he did not know which), uncatalogued and uncopied. He also mentioned that there were hundreds of uncatalogued letters to Sir William of various years at Fettercairn. He offered to go himself to Aberdeen to examine the relevant correspondence.[103] Buchanan felt that Isham would not be too happy about employing Abbott, but he was reluctant to ask for a court order to compel Lord Clinton to produce the documents. This would antagonize Lord Clinton, whose good will might be important if the Court finally decided in his favour.[104]

By 21 May, Isham was again in London[105] and he promised to go to Edinburgh as soon as Buchanan could arrange for him to inspect the Forbes correspondence.[106] After further negotiation, the correspondence was brought to Edinburgh so that Isham could examine it in the office of Lord Clinton's solicitors. He arrived in Edinburgh on 16 June and that afternoon attended a lengthy conference with Buchanan and counsel to discuss his claim and put the finishing touches to it.[107] By the 19th, when the time limit set by the Court expired, only two other claims had been lodged: one by Lord Clinton and one by Charles W. Eliott, Mrs. Louisa Scott, Mrs. Emily Eliott, and Thomas E. Forrest, who claimed jointly as descendants of Sir Alexander's elder daughter, Janet Theresa Boswell.[108] Sir Gilbert Eliott had decided to withdraw from the action[109] and nothing further was heard from either the Dowager Lady Forbes or Dr. Henry St. George Boswell.

[102]Correspondence in S. R. & Co.'s papers.

[103]Copy letter, Abbott to Mackenzie & Kermack, in S. R. & Co.'s papers.

[104]Correspondence between Buchanan and Thackrah, March 1937 (S. R. & Co.'s papers).

[105]Letter, Thackrah to Isham in London, of this date (IFP).

[106]Telephone call, Isham to Buchanan, 28 May 1937 (business ledger entry, S. R. & Co.'s papers).

[107]Recorded in business ledger (S. R. & Co.'s papers).

[108]See Table IV, p. 355.

[109]Largely in compliance with the wishes of Lady Talbot.

Buchanan warned Isham that even now he could not safely regard the list of claimants as final. At any time up to the actual hearing the Court would probably admit additional claims from persons who could show reasonable grounds. Mrs. Mounsey's will[110] could be interpreted in two ways and one of them meant that her interest in the papers passed to a hospital in Carlisle known as the Cumberland Infirmary. This institution, to which Mrs. Mounsey left the residue of her estate, was still quite unaware that it might have a claim. The irony of the situation was that had Mrs. Mounsey known of the existence of family papers at Fettercairn, the last thing she would have wanted was for them to fall into the hands of outsiders. Still, the problem of the Cumberland Infirmary had to be faced sooner or later. If Isham did not inform them, the Court probably would and would blame him for not having done so.

Before leaving Edinburgh, Isham spent a day[111] in the office of Lord Clinton's solicitors, reading through all the Forbes correspondence. A number of important letters to Forbes came to light including one from Alexander and two from James junior.[112] All of these supported the interpretation of Boswell's will which Isham wanted to establish. The next day he returned to London and by the beginning of July was back in New York.[113]

The Court now ordered a record containing the various claims to be printed and allowed the parties until 13 October to adjust their pleadings.[114] This was longer than usual because the Court's long summer vacation ran from mid-July to the end of September. Buchanan, however, was glad of the extra time as he still had much to do. The merits of the competing claims were carefully considered with counsel and many further lines of enquiry were suggested. One of the most difficult problems was to clarify the transmission of the papers on Sir Alexander's death. Buchanan was able, with the help of Scott Moncrieff & Trail, to unearth still more documents which disclosed the interesting fact that Sir Alexander's widow had purchased the library and furniture at Auchinleck from her husband's creditors. Her own will[115] was also traced in which she left everything to her younger

[110]Cited below p. 212, n. 128.
[111]19 June 1937. Business ledger entry (S. R. & Co.'s papers).
[112]As to these, see below p. 185, n. 37.
[113]Information from files in S. R. & Co.'s papers.
[114]Interlocutors of Lord Stevenson dated 23 June 1937 and of Lord Robertson dated 7 July 1937.
[115]Disposition and Settlement by Dame Grace Cuming or Boswell dated 5 April, 1860 (copy in S. R. & Co.'s papers).

daughter, Margaret Amelia (who became Mrs. Vassall). This was disturbing, for it seemed to open the door for a claim by the descendants of Mrs. Vassall. It was also discovered that Sir James had tried to settle part of his father's debts and Buchanan went to great pains to try to find out whether any creditors remained whose claims still entitled them or their successors to a share of the papers.[116]

There were many other matters still to investigate. Buchanan was determined not to neglect any enquiry, however far-fetched, which had the slightest chance of yielding useful information. He read through the eighteen volumes of the private edition and various other Boswell works in the National Library of Scotland. He re-read Pottle's and Abbott's catalogues and again went over all the Forbes correspondence belonging to Lord Clinton. He scrutinized all the available Auchinleck estate accounts and in one of them he discovered a clue which enabled Thackrah to trace the will of James Boswell junior in London.[117] Much time was spent combing the various public registers: the Books of Council and Session (the principal Scottish register) were searched from 1800 to 1920, also the Sheriff Court Books in Ayr from 1800 to 1937 and the Ayr Commissary Court records from 1824 to 1917. Every document or entry that might have a possible bearing was carefully noted, and details of the inventories of the estates of the various generations of the Boswell family were obtained to see whether they contained any mention of the manuscripts. Scott Moncrieff & Trail were also asked to provide full information, supported by the necessary documents, about the Talbot family succession following the death of Emily Lady Talbot.[118]

Towards the end of September, Buchanan arranged another conference with counsel to discuss the results of his labours and to decide what still remained to be done.[119] Counsel strongly advised that Wedderburn should now be told of the possible interest of the Cumberland Infirmary; if this were not done, the Court was bound to realize at the hearing that the Infirmary had an interest and would probably

[116]For detailed consideration of the problem of transmission of the papers on Sir Alexander's death, see below p. 203 *et seq.* where the relevant documents are cited and discussed.

[117]Holograph will dated 15 September 1818 and proved at London 19 March 1822. In looking through some Auchinleck estate accounts, Buchanan found an entry of 15 July 1835 for the sum of £601.11.6d received from the London firm of Sladen, Glennie & Sladen as the proceeds of the late James Boswell Esquire's estate. This prompted a search for the will in London which was successful.

[118]All these labours are fully documented in S. R. & Co.'s papers.

[119]"Memorandum for Counsel with reference to Consultation to be held on 21 September 1937" (S. R. & Co.'s papers).

hold up the proceedings to enable them to lodge a claim.[120] Isham accepted this advice and Buchanan wrote to Wedderburn,[121] who in turn wrote to the Infirmary. As a result, the Infirmary decided to come into the action.[122] Isham authorized Buchanan to lend the Infirmary's solicitors any documents they wished to see and, for the most part, their claim rode astride his own, making use of all his own arguments and research. Where they differed was in their interpretation of how the papers transmitted after the death of Sir James Boswell's widow in 1884.[123]

The intervention of the Infirmary left Buchanan with still more enquiries to make. The documents which Isham had found at Malahide in the spring showed that, during Mrs. Mounsey's lifetime and for some years afterwards, Auchinleck estate was factored by the Edinburgh firm of Howden & Molleson. They also showed that, after Mrs. Mounsey's death, her furniture and effects were listed and valued by Dowell's of Edinburgh who later handled the sale of the remnants of the library.[124] Buchanan interviewed representatives of both these firms because he realized that it was important to try to reconstruct when and in what circumstances the Malahide papers were taken to Ireland. If he could prove that Mrs. Mounsey made a gift of the papers to her nephew during her lifetime and that they left Auchinleck *before* she died, the interpretation of her will would cease to matter and the Infirmary's claim would be defeated.

Howden & Molleson were unable to help, but, at their suggestion, Buchanan traced and interviewed Thomas Drysdale, who was Land Steward at Auchinleck from 1896 to 1920.[125] Unfortunately, Drysdale was fairly certain that no papers had been removed during Mrs. Mounsey's lifetime.[126] The information from Dowell's was also unhelpful. They found their detailed inventory and valuation of Mrs. Mounsey's

[120]"Memorandum as to points dealt with at consultation with Counsel. 21/9/37" (S. R. & Co.'s papers).

[121]Letter dated 20 October 1937 (copy in S. R. & Co.'s papers).

[122]On 9 November 1937, Buchanan heard from Messrs. J. & J. Galletly, solicitors in Edinburgh, that they had been instructed to lodge a claim for the Cumberland Infirmary. Reported to Thackrah this date (copy letter in S. R. & Co.'s papers).

[123]For a full consideration of these differing interpretations, see below pp. 212–14.

[124]See above p. 33.

[125]Letter, Buchanan to Thackrah, 10 November 1937 (copy in S. R. & Co.'s papers).

[126]"Memorandum re Meeting with Mr. Thomas Drysdale on 16th November 1937" (S. R. & Co.'s papers).

personal estate, but although it contained no reference to papers of any kind, they thought it likely there had been bundles or boxes of papers which, on being glanced at by the valuer, would have been pushed aside as worthless.[127]

Buchanan also made further strenuous efforts to find wills by Euphemia and Elizabeth Boswell. He met with no success and it was assumed that both sisters died intestate. No one seems to have spotted the reference to Euphemia's will in Rogers's *Boswelliana*.[128]

The time allowed by the Court for the parties to adjust their claims was due to expire on 13 October 1937. By the end of September, nobody had made any adjustments at all.[129] Each claimant wanted to see the adjustments of the others before making his own. Nobody wanted to be first. Buchanan also had to consider that, before the record was closed, Isham would have to see the adjustments for the other claimants and approve his own. This would take time, as he was still in America. When the case came before Lord Stevenson on the 13th, he extended the period for adjustments until 10 November;[130] and this was again extended to 8 December because of the intervention of the Cumberland Infirmary.[131]

In view of the uncertainty as to when the record would be closed and the case heard, Isham crossed to Europe in mid-November.[132] He arranged to spend the winter in France, but was ready to travel to Edinburgh as soon as he was needed. He was becoming seriously worried by the enormous intricacy of the case and the extent of his financial involvement. He had been warned that the cost of *all* the claimants might be awarded out of the fund *in medio*. This meant in effect that if he were successful, he would either have to sell some of the papers or pay the entire costs of the action out of his own pocket. Each fresh claimant meant additional expense and he was worried by the thought that even at this late stage other claims might emerge. He was therefore desperately anxious to have the record closed and the hearing fixed as soon as possible.

[127]"Memorandum for Counsel re Enquiries made at Messrs. Dowell's . . . March 1938" (S. R. & Co.'s papers).

[128]See above p. 7, n. 39. The will, however, is still untraced.

[129]Letter, Buchanan to Thackrah, 24 September 1937 (copy in S. R. & Co.'s papers).

[130]Interlocutor of Lord Stevenson, dated 13 October 1937.

[131]Interlocutor of Lord Stevenson, dated 10 November 1937.

[132]Isham arrived in Britain on 10 November 1937. Letter, Thackrah to Buchanan, 11 November 1937 (copy in S. R. & Co.'s papers).

The Infirmary's claim was not received until 8 December 1937 and all the other claimants, Isham included, needed time to reconsider their pleadings. Lord Stevenson allowed a further period for adjustment until 5 January 1938,[133] and Buchanan hoped that this would be the last continuation; but when 5 January came round, counsel for the Infirmary argued that he needed more time and yet another continuation was allowed, this time until 2 February.[134]

To avoid further delay, Buchanan arranged a meeting with the solicitors for the Judicial Factor and Lord Clinton, and they agreed that the period for adjustment had dragged on far too long and that Lord Stevenson should be strongly pressed to close the record when the case next came before him.[135] Buchanan was rather taken aback therefore when, a few days later, major alterations were made to Lord Clinton's claim and four new letters from Malone to Forbes were produced.[136] This in itself, although unexpected, was not enough to delay the closing of the record, especially as the letters were, if anything, favourable to Isham's case.

On 31 January, Buchanan received the news that Charles W. Eliott and those claiming with him had decided to abandon their claim in favour of the trustees of Mrs. Vassall.[137] This was bound to cause more delay and, on 2 February, Lord Stevenson allowed the Vassall trustees to enter the proceedings in place of Eliott and his co-claimants. He also granted a further continuation until 2 March to enable them to adjust their claim.[138] When these adjustments were received, it was clear that Isham was in effect facing a completely new claim. The old claimants traced their descent from Janet Theresa, Sir Alexander's elder daughter; the new claimants were the representatives of Margaret Amelia, his younger daughter.

Buchanan's hope that the record would at last be closed when the case came before Lord Stevenson on 2 March was dashed by a letter received from Wedderburn's solicitors on 15 February:

> You will be interested to hear that a Mrs. Hailey, who is a great-great-granddaughter of Elizabeth Boswell, Boswell's youngest

[133]Interlocutor of Lord Stevenson, dated 8 December 1937.
[134]Interlocutor of Lord Stevenson, dated 5 January 1938.
[135]Letter, Buchanan to Thackrah, 25 January 1938 (copy in S. R. & Co.'s papers).
[136]As to these letters, see below pp. 186 and 189 *et seq.*
[137]Letter, Buchanan to Thackrah, 31 January 1938 (copy in S. R. & Co.'s papers).
[138]Interlocutor of Lord Stevenson, dated 2 February 1938.

daughter, has been in communication with Professor Abbott and it may be that she will lodge a claim.[139]

   A week later, it was certain that Mrs. Elizabeth M. Hailey[140] would be claiming and Lord Stevenson allowed two further continuations, the first to 23 March and the second to 4 May, so that her claim might be prepared.[141] It seemed inconceivable that anything else could happen to delay the closing of the record beyond 4 May, but on that very morning, Buchanan received a cryptic letter from Mrs. Hailey's solicitors warning that other potential claimants, represented by the Edinburgh firm of Messrs. Thomson Dickson & Shaw, were in the offing.[142] Buchanan had a hurried consultation with Milligan before going into court later in the day and stressed that matters must be brought to a head at once, especially as Mrs. Hailey's claim had still not been lodged. On Milligan's representations, Lord Stevenson agreed to close the record unless Mrs. Hailey's claim was tendered at the bar of the Court that same morning; later in the morning, her counsel was able to hand over her claim and at the same time he asked for a further two weeks' continuation. Lord Stevenson refused to allow more than one week, and the case was continued till 11 May.[143]
   Isham never discovered the identity of the other "potential claimants." Whoever they were, they did not put in a claim. Even so, as the result of Mrs. Hailey's intervention, Isham had to contend, at the last moment, with a claim by a descendant of the "younger children." This was serious because, until now, none of the other claimants had tried to argue that Boswell left his papers to the "younger children." One interesting point which emerged from Mrs. Hailey's claim was that her brother, the same Mr. Cumberlege Ware whom Lady Talbot had wished to benefit, was shown to have no right whatever to any share of the papers which might have belonged to Elizabeth, and Mrs. Hailey herself claimed only half of Elizabeth's share.[144] The

---

[139]Letter in S. R. & Co.'s papers.
[140]Mrs. Elizabeth Mary Cumberlege or Hailey. See Table III, p. 354.
[141]Interlocutors of Lord Stevenson, dated 2 and 23 March 1938.
[142]Letter J. & R. A. Robertson to Steedman Ramage & Co (S. R. & Co.'s papers). The letter does not name the other potential claimants.
[143]Interlocutor of Lord Stevenson, dated 4 May 1938. Also information from business ledger entries (S. R. & Co.'s papers).
[144]See Table III, p. 354. Mrs. Hailey's argument was that under JB's will a one-fourth share of the papers passed to each of the "younger children." Elizabeth's share was increased to five-sixteenths when Veronica died intestate. This share, or at any rate half of it, passed to Elizabeth's

unfortunate thing from Isham's point of view was that the interpretation of Boswell's will would now become a contentious issue at the hearing and it would be necessary to drag in the mass of complicated evidence relating to the dispute between Alexander and the "younger children," the subsequent arbitration, and the arrangements for the final disposal of Boswell's personal estate. This would inevitably lengthen the hearing and increase costs. Mrs. Hailey's own costs would also probably be added to those of the other claimants as a charge on the fund *in medio*.

On 11 May, to Isham's enormous relief, the record was finally closed[145] and at last it became possible to fix a definite date for the hearing. Several days were needed for a case so complex and the Clerk of Court doubted whether sufficient time could be found until October, after the long summer vacation. Isham, dismayed at the prospect of another long wait, instructed Buchanan to press urgently for a hearing before the Court rose. Somehow or other the time was found, and the hearing was arranged to begin on Tuesday, 12 July 1938.

daughter, Mrs. E. M. Williams, who by her will left the residue of her estate to Mrs. Hailey and her sister Miss K. A. Cumberlege. Miss Cumberlege died in 1936 leaving everything to Mrs. Hailey, so Mrs. Hailey claimed a half of whatever share of the papers might have belonged to her great-grandmother, Elizabeth Boswell. Mr. Cumberlege Ware had no claim to the papers under Mrs. Williams' will.

[145]Interlocutor of Lord Keith, dated 11 May 1938.

# VI

# *Problems of Succession*

THE final brief prepared for Isham's counsel at the court hearing ran to over a thousand pages. It was distilled from materials of much greater length.[1] The result of two years of laborious research was a remarkably complete account of the transmission of the papers after Boswell's death and a detailed family legal history covering more than 140 years.

The starting point for every claimant was Boswell's will, which alone governed the transmission of his papers on his death.[2] For a trained lawyer, he made a very bad job of expressing himself clearly. In a codicil made on 30 May 1785, only two days after the will, he added bequests of mourning rings to his friends General Paoli and Dr. Barnard, commenting "as it frequently happens that there are strange and unaccountable omissions in Wills so it has happened in mine."[3] A much stranger and more unaccountable omission than these was his failure to make clear to whom the property in his precious archives was to pass. The codicil in question did nothing to put this right.[4]

The will began with the appointment of Sir William Forbes as executor. It did not deal with the family estate of Auchinleck, for

---

[1]Most of which or copies of which are in S. R. & Co.'s papers or ILP or both.

[2]Holograph will dated 28 May 1785 and registered in the Books of Council and Session (Durie) on 7 August 1795. See p. 6, n. 31, above and also illustration facing this page.

[3]The codicil is also registered along with the will.

[4]In referring to "strange and unaccountable omissions in Wills," JB may have had in mind the omission of himself from SJ's will. Brocklesby wrote to him shortly after SJ's death: "He [i.e., SJ] was so agitated till the day I pronounced he could not live, that he forgot to mention in his Will made in that time of perplexity the names of Boswell Strahan Murphy etc. whom he lovd sincerely but forgot their mention." (Letter, 27 December 1784, MS. at Yale.) SJ made his will on 8-9

I James Boswell Esquire of Auchinleck having already settled every thing concerning my landed Estate so far as is in my power as an heir of entail so that my mind is quiet respecting my dear wife and children do now when in perfect soundness of mind, but under the apprehension of some danger to my life, which however may prove a false alarm, this make my last will and testament

Furthermore as my late honoured Father ... a very curious collection of the Classicks and other Books which it is agreeable shall be preserved for ever in this Family of Auchinleck I do by these presents dispose to the successive heirs of entail of the Barony of Auchinleck Greek and Latin Books, as also all Manuscripts of whatever kind lying in the House of Auchinleck under the same conditions and under the same forfeiture as I have mentioned with regard to the Ebony Cabinet and dressing Plate

and I hereby leave to the said Sir William ... the Reverend Mr Temple and Edmund Malone Esquire all my Manuscripts of my own composition and my letters from various persons to be published for the benefit of my younger children as they shall decide that is to say they are to have a discretionary power to publish more or less

**EXTRACTS FROM BOSWELL'S WILL**
The passages most directly affecting the transmission of his papers.
From the original manuscript at Register House, Edinburgh.

the succession to this had already been settled from generation to generation by a deed of entail,[5] and Boswell was only concerned with the lands which he had himself purchased and also his personal estate, which included his books, papers, and other effects. These are the provisions of the will relevant to the disposal of the papers:

> And whereas my honoured and pious Grandmother Lady Elizabeth Boswell devised to the Heir succeeding to the Barony of Auchinleck from generation to generation the Ebony Cabinet and the dressing plate of silver gilt which belonged to her Mother Veronica Countess of Kincardine leaving it however optional to her son my Father to ratify that Entail thereof or not, as he should think fit, and he having neglected so to do, whereby the said Ebony Cabinet and dressing plate are now at my free disposal, I do by these presents dispone the same to the heir succeeding to the Barony of Auchinleck from generation to generation and I declare that it shall not be in the power of any such heir to alienate or impignorate the same on any account whatever . . . in case any of them shall alienate the said Ebony Cabinet and dressing plate, the person so alienating shall forfeit the sum of one thousand pounds sterling which shall be paid to the next heir succeeding by the Entail. . . . Furthermore as my late hon-

---

December 1784 and died on 13 December. JB had written to Brocklesby on 18 December asking for materials for the *Life:* "I shall be vexed if he has burnt all his Manuscripts, more especially if he has destroyed two volumes of Memoirs of his life a considerable part of which I have read. He knew that I was for many years assiduous in collecting materials for his life; and I have a large stock which I shall in due time arrange and publish." (MS. at Yale.) JB also asked Brocklesby for the return of his own letters to SJ referring to correspondence for more than twenty years in which he wrote to SJ as a confessor. JB got back his letters, which SJ had sealed up in a bag for return to him shortly before his death. But JB must have been dismayed to learn from Brocklesby that SJ had "burnt all written memoirs of himself and his life" (letter of 27 December 1784 cited above). JB put a brave face on being omitted from SJ's will, but Temple was indignant and wrote to him on 6 January 1785: "I have read his *Will* in the News Papers and am disappointed and angry at not seeing your name in it. Your partial and even enthusiastick attachment to him well deserved some fond memorial. I fully expected he would have left his Papers to your care, and desired as the last act of a long friendship that you would be his editor and historian." (MS. at Yale.) There can be little doubt that JB was influenced by all of this when he made his own testamentary writings. The role of Forbes, Malone, and Temple as literary executors under his will resembles closely the role which Temple considered he should have played in relation to SJ's papers. Unfortunately JB still left unclear to whom physical ownership of his archives was to pass.

[5]Disposition and Deed of Tailzie by Alexander Boswell of Auchinleck with consent of James Boswell in favour of himself and the Heirs of Tailzie and Provision within mentioned, dated 7 August 1776 and registered in the Books of Council and Session (Durie) on 5 March 1777.

oured Father made a very curious collection of the Classicks and other Books which it is desireable should be preserved for ever in the Family of Auchinleck I do by these presents dispone to the successive heirs of entail of the Barony of Auchinleck [here there is a word torn off][6] greek and latin Books, as also all Manuscripts of whatever kind lying in the House of Auchinleck under the same conditions and under the same forfeiture as I have mentioned with regard to the Ebony Cabinet and dressing Plate and all my other moveable Estate or executry, I leave equally among my younger children. . . . And I hereby leave to the said Sir William Forbes the Reverend Mr. Temple and Edmund[7] Malone Esquire all my Manuscripts of my own composition and all my letters from various persons to be published for the benefit of my younger children as they shall decide that is to say they are to have a discretionary power to publish more or less. . . .

This could be interpreted in several ways. The phrase "all Manuscripts of whatever kind lying in the House of Auchinleck" seemed wide enough to carry the whole collection of papers to Alexander as heir of entail; but did it cover papers whose normal repository was Auchinleck, but which had temporarily been taken elsewhere? The whereabouts of the papers at the date of the will and at Boswell's death might be of vital importance. And if Boswell meant to leave his personal manuscripts to Alexander, why did he preface the bequest

[6]The lacuna exists on the original holograph will preserved at Register House in Edinburgh. It is written on both sides of a single large sheet of paper, one of the top corners of which has been torn off. The missing fragment is very small, being a triangle measuring approximately 1½" × 1" × ¾". On side *recto*, only a single letter appears to be missing as indicated by square brackets in the following passage: "I James Boswell Esquire of Auchinleck [h]aving already settled every thing concerning my Landed Estate . . ." On side *verso*, the passage is as follows, missing words or letters again being indicated by square brackets: "I do by these presents dispone to t[he] successive heirs of entail of the Barony of Auchinleck [    ] greek and latin Books, as also all Manuscripts of" (the letter "f" is partly missing) "whatever kind lying in the house of Auchinleck under th[e]" (the letter "h" is partly missing) "same conditions. . . ." The missing word is likely to have been "the" or "all." It must have been short because of the dimensions of the torn fragment. The will was in London when JB died and his brother T. D. Boswell had it copied a few days later. This copy (which is in TLP) supplies "the" as the missing word and does not indicate any lacuna. T. D. Boswell docketed the copy: "Compared and found to agree with the original this copy has been immediately sealed up. London 25 May 1795. T. D. Boswell." The lacuna certainly existed by the time the will was lodged soon after for registration in Edinburgh and I am inclined to think it also existed when T. D. Boswell's copy was made, the word supplied being simply a rather obvious guess.

[7]Properly "Edmond"; the mis-spelling is JB's.

with a reference to his father's collection of the classics and other books, and link the manuscripts with Greek and Latin books? Pottle believed that the manuscripts to which Boswell referred were not his own archives, but his father's collection of mediaeval manuscripts.[8] This interpretation was reinforced by the fact that later on in the will "Manuscripts of my own composition and all my letters from various persons" were specifically distinguished.

The question also arose as to what interest Forbes, Temple, and Malone were to receive. Were they to be regarded merely as trustees appointed to determine what, if anything, should be published, and to apply the proceeds for the "younger children," or were they to receive the actual *property* in the papers? Lord Clinton, whose basic claim was that the papers had been abandoned by the family at Fettercairn and now belonged to him by prescription,[9] argued alternatively that Boswell bequeathed the property in the papers to Forbes, Temple, and Malone and that he, as Forbes's descendant, was entitled to a one-third share.[10]

A further possibility was that the property in the papers passed neither to Alexander nor to the literary executors, but to the "younger children" under the bequest of moveable property. From the beginning, Isham feared a claim based on descent or entitlement from the "younger children." This fear was realized when, at the last moment, Elizabeth Boswell's great-great-granddaughter, Mrs. Hailey, came into the proceedings.[11]

[8]Pottle wrote to Isham on 17 December 1936 (letter in IFP): "When he says that he 'dispones to the successive heirs of Entail of the barony of Auchinleck all Greek and Latin books, as also all manuscripts of whatever kind, lying in the house of Auchinleck,' I am afraid he was not referring to his own 'archives,' but to the numerous fine medieval MSS. which Lord Auchinleck had collected. (See the Catalogue of the Auchinleck Sale, Sotheby, June 23, 1893.) I fear that the only reference to *your* papers and those at Fettercairn is in the famous clause, 'I hereby leave to the said Sir William Forbes, the Reverend Mr. Temple, and Edmund Malone, Esq., all my manuscripts of my own composition, and all my letters from various persons,' etc." Pottle may well have been right. Four years after JB's death, Alexander wrote to Forbes: "I have perused some very curious collections of old Papers made by my Grandfather. He was very expert at reading old hands & fond of studying them so that he copied what he thought interesting. I have a volume of what he styles the Antiquities of Ayrshire which have been extracted with much care & labour from old Manuscripts & Registers. And I see he had taken the trouble to make out a list of all the Religious Houses in Scotland, which was much for a 'Presbyterian true blue.'" (Letter dated 19 April 1799, Fettercairn Papers.)

[9]"Prescription," i.e., uninterrupted possession for a period of time.

[10]Condescendence and claim for Lord Clinton from print of closed record in S. R. & Co.'s papers.

[11]See above p. 172 and Table III, p. 354, and also below p. 202.

The unsatisfactory nature of Boswell's testamentary writings gave rise to a bitter dispute among his children. The outcome of this dispute was of some importance, because although ownership of the papers was not a major issue, it was nevertheless involved. To solve the puzzle of transmission of the papers on Boswell's death, it was necessary to go beyond the terms of the will itself: to consider Boswell's personal circumstances when he made the will; to establish the whereabouts of the papers at this time and at his death; and to find out how the literary executors interpreted their trust, how Sir William Forbes administered the estate, and how the children's disputes were finally settled.

WHEN BOSWELL MADE his will on 28 May 1785, he believed his life to be in danger. In the preamble, he wrote that he was "under the apprehension of some danger" to his life, "which however may prove a false alarm." Pottle explained the reason for this in a letter to Isham of 17 December 1936:

> One thing is clear to me. When, in 1785, Boswell made his will, and made provision for the possible publication of his papers, he had in mind his Johnsonian materials and probably not much else. It must be remembered that on the date of the making of that will he had only just got ready to put the "Hebrides" in shape, and of course he had done nothing on the "Life." He was afraid that he would be challenged by Henry Dundas or Sir Adam Fergusson for remarks in the "Letter to the People of Scotland," just published, and would be killed before he had converted his valuable Johnsonian materials into copy for the printer.[12]

On 18 December 1784, five days after Johnson's death, Boswell had received a letter from his publisher, Charles Dilly, pressing him for a volume of Johnson's conversations.[13] On 20 and 25 December, two more letters had come from Dilly, strongly urging him to go ahead with his work on the *Life*.[14] There was great public interest in anything to do with Johnson, and Boswell must have realized that the publication value

[12]Letter in IFP.
[13]JB's journal for 18 December 1784.
[14]Information from JB's register of letters 1782–95, found at Malahide in 1937 and now at Yale.

of his Johnsonian materials was considerable. He decided not to rush his *magnum opus*, but on 23 December he wrote to tell Dilly that he intended to publish the *Tour* in the spring as "a good Prelude" to his large work.[15] He arrived in London on 30 March 1785[16] and got down to preparing the text for the printer. He was still in London on 28 May when he signed his will.[17] Presumably his chief object in appointing literary executors was to entrust them with the task of seeing the *Tour* through the press, and exploiting the publication value of the rest of his Johnsonian material, in case of his sudden death.[18]

The challenge which Boswell feared never materialized. He completed the *Tour* himself and published it on 1 October 1785. Its great success emphasized the value of his other Johnsonian materials. These amounted to a formidable bulk because, in addition to his own journals and correspondence, he had been for some time assiduously collecting letters, anecdotes, and every other possible scrap of information from Johnson's friends. His register of letters[19] at this time is filled with entries of his own letters asking for information about Johnson and the replies received from the Doctor's friends, many of whom sent him material.[20]

He returned to Scotland on 29 September 1785, but was back in London on 17 November. He lodged for a few days with Dilly and then moved to General Paoli's house, where he stayed until he left again for Scotland on 22 December.[21] On this visit, he probably brought from Auchinleck any material needed for writing the *Life* so that it would be available in London for reference when needed. The *Life*, of necessity, had to be written in London where Johnson's friends could be consulted.

On the day of his departure for Scotland, he added a codicil to his will, giving precise instructions as to the whereabouts of his Johnsonian materials in London, and entrusting them to the care of Malone. It was

[15]Ibid.

[16]See private edition, XVI, p. 79.

[17]The testing clause at the end of the will indicates that it was signed at London. JB even gets this clause wrong referring to the first witness as Edward Dilly whereas the signature is that of Charles Dilly. It had to be Charles because Edward had died in 1779.

[18]No doubt he was also influenced by the irretrievable loss of so many of SJ's papers, and SJ's failure to establish any literary trust in his will. Also Temple had given him the idea of leaving papers to the care of a literary executor. See above, p. 174, n. 4.

[19]Cited above.

[20]Just how massive this material was is now made clear in *Correspondence etc. re Life*. To Dr. Hugh Blair, he wrote: "The Bullion will be immense, whatever defects there may be in the workmanship" (letter dated 21 April 1786, MS. at Yale).

[21]Information from the journals. See private edition, XVI, p. 148.

only prudent to make some such provision for their safety before setting out on the journey to Auchinleck. He recorded in his journal for the same day: "Met Dr. Johnson's Frank[22] in the street, and he promised to search for every scrap of his Master's handwriting and give all to me. It vexed me to be told that he had burnt some letters from Dr. Johnson to Mrs. Johnson."[23] Perhaps this meeting had something to do with the codicil, in which he sought to ensure that a similar fate would not overtake *his* papers:

> Having entire confidence in the discretion honour and talents of my friend Edmond Malone Esqr. I in case of my death leave to him the care of all my Collection of papers and letters and memorandums for writing the life of Dr. Johnson in token whereof I now deliver to the said Edmond Malone Esqr. the key of my Bureau in the house of General Paoli in which Bureau he will find the key of a drawer belonging to it in which are several parcels of the said materials, as also the key of a Trunk belonging to me which is at Mr. Dilly's, in which Trunk are many volumes of a Journal or Diary kept by me, from which a variety of passages concerning Dr. Johnson may be excerpted,—I trust that he will not divulge any thing he may find in the said volumes which ought to be concealed, and as I have already by my Will left what profits may arrise from the publication of any of my papers, to my younger children I depend on my friends attention to their interest in what is hereby committed to him.[24]

This codicil ceased to have any practical effect when Boswell completed the *Life* himself in 1791; but it remained an important key to the interpretation of the will. It was only the *care* of his Johnsonian materials which he left to Malone and this suggested that when, by his will, he left his papers to Forbes, Temple, and Malone, he had in mind a similar entrustment of care. The codicil made it clear that he meant his "younger children" to have the profits of publication, but it said nothing about their succeeding to the actual property of the papers. His instruction to Malone not to divulge anything which ought to be concealed showed that he never contemplated complete

[22]Francis Barber, SJ's Negro servant and chief beneficiary under his will.
[23]See private edition, XVI, p. 148.
[24]Like the will, the codicil was registered in the Books of Council and Session (Durie) on 7 August 1795, but, unlike the will, the original document was not deposited at Register House for preservation. The document at Register House (which provides the text quoted) is an official copy prepared from the original. There is a note on the backing of the copy that the original was returned to Robert Boswell, W. S. The wording of the testing clause indicates that the original, like the will, was entirely in JB's own hand.

publication of his journals, although, until his death, he planned to publish selected portions.[25] It seemed as though the literary executors had been named, not as the recipients of a bequest, but to carry out the necessary task of sifting, selecting, and turning to account.

The success of Isham's claim, as also that of the Cumberland Infirmary and Mrs. Vassall's trustees, depended on establishing that Alexander succeeded to the papers under the will. This interpretation was supported by the circumstances surrounding the making of the will and codicil, and by Boswell's known attitude to his archives. If he was so anxious to preserve his father's collection of books and manuscripts at Auchinleck, it was reasonable to suppose that he intended his own collection, by which he set such high store, to be similarly preserved. To divide the papers after his death among the literary executors or among the "younger children" would have been to disperse them, perhaps irretrievably, and to make publication of the *Tour* and the *Life* difficult, if not impossible.

Presumptions of this kind could not, however, override the express terms of the will; and the papers left to Alexander were clearly limited to those "lying in the House of Auchinleck." It was therefore necessary to establish the whereabouts of the papers both at the date of the will and at the date of Boswell's death. Pottle thought it likely that all the papers (except the materials for the *Tour*) were at Auchinleck when the will was made.[26] There was no evidence to the contrary and the will, although executed in London, made no reference to the papers being anywhere but at Auchinleck. If they had been elsewhere, Boswell might have been expected to say so as he did in the subsequent codicil. He had presumably sent the papers mentioned in the codicil to Mr. Dilly's house after making his will, in anticipation of moving his family to London. He had come to London on 12 November 1785 with that intention, though he had immediately wavered. The storage of his papers at Mr. Dilly's was a necessary expedient until he had a house of his own.[27]

It was impossible to be certain what was done with the papers after 1785, but the reasonable assumption was that from time to time, as Boswell journeyed to and fro between London and Auchinleck, he moved such papers as were necessary for his literary projects. When he died in London in 1795, he had many of his papers beside him,[28]

[25]In a letter to Forbes of 24 October 1793 (*Fettercairn Catalogue*, No. 1357, now in Fettercairn Papers), JB refers to "the Account which I am to publish of my Travels."

[26]Typed notes on whereabouts of the papers prepared in 1938 (S. R. & Co.'s papers).

[27]He did not move into his London house until 16 May 1786. See private edition, XVI, p. 188.

[28]See above p. 6.

but they had only been temporarily removed from Auchinleck which he always regarded as the true repository of his archives. Thus, in a letter to John Wilkes of 25 June 1791, he wrote: "You said to me yesterday of my *Magnum Opus*, 'it is a wonderful book.' Do confirm this to me, so as I may have your *testimonium* in my archives at Auchinleck."[29]

Forbes, Temple, and Malone were Boswell's close friends as well as his literary executors. They were in the best position to know how he intended his papers to be dealt with, and it was therefore vital to reconstruct their actings after his death in the fullest possible detail.

Pottle had already pieced together part of the story in his preface to the catalogue of the private edition, published in 1931.[30] The letters to Forbes from Alexander and young James, found by Isham in 1937,[31] and the letters from Malone to Forbes, produced by Lord Clinton in 1938,[32] filled in further details. In recent years, more letters have come to light.[33] These were not available to the claimants in 1938, but they do not alter the conclusions on which Isham based his claim. They are therefore included in the account which follows. It was clear to Isham that Forbes and Malone had undertaken their responsibilities seriously. Temple's diaries, published in 1929, showed that he had corresponded with Forbes about the papers shortly before his death in 1796, but Isham was unable to trace any of this correspondence.[34] One letter from Temple to Forbes has since been recovered[35] and it shows that he, too, played his part in the literary trust.

After Boswell's death, the papers in London, including most of the journals, were immediately taken by Malone into his charge.[36] The remaining papers were at Auchinleck, where they were sorted out by Alexander before being forwarded to Forbes for perusal. On 8

[29]*JB Letters*, No. 303, p. 437 (original in the British Museum).

[30]See above p. 100. Pottle's material in 1931 was limited to a letter from Forbes to Malone of 14 August 1795 belonging to Isham (but not from Malahide), another letter from Forbes to Malone of 30 June 1796 (in the R. B. Adam Collection), and Malone's letter to Euphemia Boswell of 4 May 1809 in the Pierpont Morgan Library (see above p. 37).

[31]See above p. 167. There were one letter from Alexander dated 8 July 1795 and two letters from James junior dated 2 January 1796 and 5 March 1796.

[32]See above p. 171. There were four letters dated 25 April 1796, 3 March 1804, 2 May 1804, and 4 May 1804. See below in this chapter where these letters are quoted from or referred to.

[33]Details are given below in this chapter.

[34]*Diaries of William Johnston Temple* (ed. Bettany), Oxford at the Clarendon Press, 1929. Temple records writing to Forbes on 27 February and 27 April 1796 and having received a long letter from Forbes about the papers on 19 July 1796. Temple died on 13 August 1796.

[35]The letter of 27 April 1796 referred to in Temple's diary. See previous note.

[36]See above p. 6.

SIR WILLIAM FORBES, 6th Bart. (1739–1806)
From the portrait by Raeburn.

EDMOND MALONE (1741–1812)
From the portrait by Reynolds.

BOSWELL'S LITERARY EXECUTORS
No picture is traced of the third literary executor, the Rev. W. J. Temple.

July 1795, Alexander wrote to Forbes to say that he would be in Edinburgh at the beginning of the following week and promising: "All letters that can possibly concern litterary subjects I likewise bring with me & you can chuse such as are fit for publication."[37] If Alexander brought only letters which he regarded as of literary interest, some of his father's other papers may have remained at Auchinleck and may never have been seen by Forbes. It is also significant that Alexander did not offer to bring the letters because Forbes, Temple, and Malone were the beneficiaries to whom they belonged, nor did he indicate that they belonged to the "younger children" rather than to himself. He was the person who handled the letters, which was to be expected if he were the true owner.

On 14 August 1795, Forbes wrote to Malone:

> Mr. Boswell [i.e., Alexander] has left with me a large parcel of his Father's letters & papers; being a part of that Collection, with the charge of examining which, Our late Worthy friend, by his Will, has honoured Mr. Temple, & you, & me; A task, this, it must be owned of very considerable delicacy.—Yet, I think we may lay down to ourselves certain Canons or principles, by which to judge whether any, or what part, of the papers may be proper for publication. . . .
>
> I am busily employed in perusing the whole, which, as soon as I have gone thro' them, I shall pack up in a Box & forward to you by the Waggon; and in the same manner, when you have perused those letters & papers that are in the house in London, I shall be much obliged to you to take the trouble of forwarding them to me by the same mode of conveyance: They shall be afterwards carefully returned to you.[38]

Malone was in Oxford when Forbes's letter arrived and he did not receive it until some time after his return to London in December 1795. He started to go through the papers already in London, but his attention was soon diverted by the appearance of Ireland's Shakespeare forgeries.[39] Young James Boswell, who was spending his Christ-

---

[37]This letter was picked out by Isham from the batch of uncatalogued correspondence examined by him at the office of Lord Clinton's solicitor in June 1937. The same applies to the letters of 2 January and 5 March 1796 from James junior referred to below. All letters are now in the Fettercairn Papers.

[38]This letter was in Isham's collection in 1938, although it did not come from Malahide. It is now the property of his son, Jonathan T. Isham.

[39]Information from James junior's letter of 2 January 1796 and Malone's letter of 25 April 1796 referred to below.

mas holiday from Westminster School at Malone's house, wrote to
Forbes on 2 January 1796, apologizing for the delay and explaining
that Malone was now completely absorbed in his pamphlet exposing
Ireland. He promised that Malone would write as soon as he could
and, in a further letter to Forbes of 5 March 1796, he wrote: "Mr.
Malone I fancy will now have it in his power to answer your letter
as he has now finished his work."[40] On 25 April 1796, Malone finally
sent his reply:

> I have carefully examined all his papers, but I do not find any
> thing intended or proper for publication. He had meditated a
> Life of Lord Kaims, for which materials were collected, but nothing
> written. His Journals are extremely curious, and at some future
> period, I mean eight or ten years hence, his second son, who
> is a very promising young man, when his education is finished,
> and his mind more mature, might I think make an entertaining
> work out of them, sifting and garbelling them properly; for in
> the freedom of his heart, he put down many things both of himself
> and others that should not appear. They are very numerous,
> for he continued to journalize till the year 1794, though latterly
> less copiously and with less vivacity than formerly.—As these Jour-
> nals are the only MSS. of any value that he has left, and their
> loss would be irretrievable, I would submit to you, Sir, whether
> it would not be more prudent to let them remain here than run
> the risk of their transmission to Scotland, as probably business
> or pleasure may draw you hither ere long, when you can have
> an opportunity of examining them all. I have looked into some
> of them, and always with pleasure, but it was so mixed with
> melancholy at reviewing scenes in many of which I was myself
> engaged, that several of them have been still unexamined.—There
> are some letters and minutes concerning Voltaire, Rousseau, and
> other celebrated men, while he was abroad, that would render
> some little account of his travels curious: but that must also be
> hereafter the work of his son James.[41]

Almost simultaneously with the receipt of Malone's letter, Forbes
heard from Temple. Temple had discussed possible publication of
the papers with Malone and with Bennet Langton during a visit to

---

[40]As to these two letters from James junior, see above p. 185, n. 37.

[41]This letter was produced by Lord Clinton shortly before the court hearing in 1938, along with
the letters from Malone to Forbes of 3 March, 2 May, and 4 May 1804 referred to below. All four
letters are now in the Fettercairn Papers.

London, but in his letter, dated 27 April, his chief concern seems to have been to retrieve his own letters to Boswell:

> Our distance prevented our meeting so often as we wished but our Letters were frequent & written with unreserved confidence. Hardly a thought arose in our minds that we did not communicate. As Letters of such a nature are scarcely fit for any eyes but our own, we mutually agreed that whoever had the misfortune to survive the other, should be put in possession of the whole of our correspondence. If you & Mr. Malone require it, I can send you Extracts of those Letters, in which this is particularly mentioned, or the Letters themselves. With regard to those written to me while he was abroad, when he & the Miss Boswells visited me here in the Autumn of 1793, he desired I would allow him to take them with him, with a view to make Extracts from them for his intended Travels engaging to return them. To this I readily consented, but our loss prevented his carrying his design into execution & they are probably now at Auchinleck. You, Mr. Malone, & the Family will determine what use may be made of them, & whether it will be expedient to publish them at all, or now, or some time hence. As to myself, I am ready to concur in whatever may be thought for the good of the Family, only I could wish that the originals, with my own, might be returned according to our stipulation. It may seem a weakness, but it will be a consolation & comfort to me to read them often in his own hand writing.
>
> When I saw Mr. Malone & Mr. Langton in London in October last, I had some conversation with them respecting his Papers (not with them together, but separately) & it was doubted whether it would be better to select & publish them while his parts & talents were fresh in every one's memory, or to wait till his sons were of age. Various intentions & purposes are mentioned to me in his Letters, but I fear he made little progress in any of them. Probably much interesting matter may be picked out of his Journals, but regard to living names may make great caution necessary in the use of them.[42]

[42]See above p. 183, n. 35, and below p. 315. In 1968, I was permitted to inspect a box of papers at Fettercairn recently returned from Durham where they had been kept by Professor Abbott for many years. Amongst these was this letter from Temple. Its existence is generally unknown, although Abbott and a few others must have seen it. It is now included in the Fettercairn Papers. It may be mentioned that Temple's recollection of dates is not accurate. JB's visit was in the autumn of 1792, not 1793. Temple saw Malone in London in July on his way to a three-months' visit in Suffolk, and Langton in London in October on his way back to Cornwall. See Temple's *Diaries* (cited above), pp. 127 and 147.

Temple made no claim to be a legatee of the papers himself, and his request for the return of his own letters was based on his informal understanding with Boswell, not on entitlement under the will. He apparently interpreted his role simply as one of advice and consent in matters affecting publication of the papers.

That Forbes replied at length to Temple's letter is known from the entry in the latter's diary for 19 July 1796: "Recd a long letter from Sir Wm. Forbes respecting my dear Boswell's Letters and Papers."[43] Unfortunately Forbes's letter has never been recovered and, within a month, Temple's participation in the literary trust was brought to an end by his death.

Forbes's reply to Malone's letter of 25 April 1796 *does*, however, survive:

I much approve of your idea of our doing nothing in regard to the publication of any of our late much regarded friend's papers at present; but rather to wait till his second son be of an age fit for selecting such of them as may be proper for the publick eye. Of those which were brought to me from Auchinleck house, I have read a considerable part; but find them to consist almost entirely of letters from his private friends, by no means fit for the press, but highly valuable & interesting to his family; as they contain the most striking memorials of the high degree of estimation in which he was held by as numerous & respectable a Circle of Acquaintance, as almost any private Gentleman, I believe, could boast of. Besides these, there is one & but one Journal of a Circuit. After I have gone thro' the whole, I will carefully send them to you, in order that the papers may be altogether. His journals are, indeed, exceedingly curious; for it was a faculty he possessed & had cultivated far beyond any man I ever knew. He used occasionally, during our uninterrupted intercourse while he resided in Edinburgh, to favour me with a perusal of these; and they ever afforded me a rich entertainment. I therefore look forward with great expectation to my having the opportunity of seeing those now in your possession. Altho I have no immediate, I may rather say, scarcely a remote view of being in London, I cannot urge you to send them to me, if you are impressed with any idea, that they would be exposed to danger by the way; Altho I do not myself entertain the smallest doubt of their arriving here very safely, if packt in a Box & sent by the Waggon.[44]

[43]See above p. 183, n. 34.

[44]Letter dated 30 June 1796, first quoted by Pottle in his preface to *Malahide Catalogue*, pp. xii and xiii, from a letter in the R. B. Adam Collection. The letter is now in the Hyde Collection.

Malone's suggestion to do nothing until young James was mature enough to decide about publication for himself was obviously sensible. The nature of the journals was such that it was difficult for any outsider to decide as to their publication, even in part, independently of the opinion of a responsible member of the family. In 1796, James, at the age of seventeen, had already developed strong literary interests and, at the end of the eight or ten years proposed by Malone, he ought to be well equipped to make a sensible decision and to undertake any work of editing required. Alexander's literary talent and his respect for his father's achievements as an author would have qualified him also for the task,[45] but the profits of publication were to go to the "younger children" and this made James the more suitable choice.

No further letters were found to establish what happened in the literary trust during the next few years; presumably both Forbes and Malone regarded the matter as settled until James was at least eight years older. It is likely that Forbes and Malone exchanged their respective batches of papers[46] and that eventually all the papers came into Forbes's hands. On 5 June 1799, Alexander wrote to Forbes from London to say: "I called on Mr. Malone today. He knows of no more journals he however means to search & write to you soon."[47] This suggests that, by 1799, Forbes considered that all the journals ought to be in his custody, and had written to Malone to make sure this was the case. By 1804, the materials for writing the *Life* were no longer in London and Malone believed them to be either in the care of Forbes or at Auchinleck. This is clear from the three letters written by him to Forbes in 1804 which Lord Clinton produced shortly before the court hearing.

The main interest of these letters is the light which they shed on Malone's work on the fourth edition of the *Life*, but they also lent helpful support to Isham's argument.[48] In the earliest, dated 3 March 1804, Malone asked Forbes to confirm that the Round Robin sent by him to Boswell and mentioned in the *Life* was in fact a copy and

[45]See above p. 11 *et seq.*

[46]Forbes did not however send all the papers delivered to him by Alexander (see below p. 190, n. 49).

[47]Letter in Fettercairn Papers.

[48]See *Correspondence etc. re Life,* pp. 600–05 where the three letters are quoted in full and annotated. The letters are examined and selectively quoted from here only in so far as they shed light on the legal transmission of the papers, their physical movements, and the manner in which Forbes and Malone carried out the literary trust. For more detailed information and references on other matters concerning these letters, see Waingrow's book. The letters themselves are now included in the Fettercairn Papers.

not the original. He also referred to three letters from Johnson to Boswell, which he suspected were misquoted in the third edition, and he asked Forbes to hunt out the originals. He wrote: "Perhaps after all, the letters may not be in your possession, but in the hands of Mr. Boswell at Auchinleck; if so, I beg the favour of you to forward these enquiries to him. . . ." This implied that Malone regarded Alexander as the owner of the letters and Auchinleck as their natural repository.

Malone appended two further enquiries to the same letter. He was anxious to trace a letter from Johnson to an unknown addressee, incompletely quoted in the *Life,* and wondered whether Forbes could trace it amongst the papers in his hands. He thought that Boswell could not have many original letters from Johnson to persons other than himself.[49] The other enquiry concerned a copy of Johnson's famous letter to Macpherson in Boswell's hand and corrected by Johnson, and also a slip of paper written by Boswell to Johnson's dictation, recording a change in the text of *The Vanity of Human Wishes.*[50] Malone explained that it was clear from the *Life*[51] that Boswell had intended to deposit the former in the British Museum and the latter in the Bodleian Library, but this had never been done. In accordance with Boswell's wishes, he had himself deposited in the Museum a copy of Johnson's letter to Lord Chesterfield, and he felt that if the other two documents could be found, they should also be deposited.[52]

Forbes replied on 9 March answering Malone's query about the Round Robin and promising to write again soon.[53] On 23 April, Malone

[49]The letter to the unknown addressee was a letter to Dr. John Mudge of 9 September 1783. Since it turned up at Fettercairn (*Fettercairn Catalogue,* No. 1545), it was probably in Forbes's possession when Malone wrote, although whether he was able to find it for Malone is not known. Apart from this particular letter there were at Fettercairn many other letters from SJ to various correspondents. *Fettercairn Catalogue* lists 119 (Nos. 1472 to 1590, now in the Hyde Collection). Malone's remark suggests that he did not know JB had retained so many of these letters and that they were not in London with the other materials for writing the *Life* when JB died. It also suggests that Forbes did not send to London for Malone's perusal all the letters which Alexander brought from Auchinleck.

[50]In his letter, Malone writes *"London",* but it is *The Vanity of Human Wishes* to which the slip in fact refers.

[51]See *Life,* III, p. 358, n. 1.

[52]Another 143 years elapsed before the slip was deposited in the Bodleian as JB intended. In 1947, Isham, into whose possession the slip had come, presented it to the Bodleian (see below p. 261 and also *Bodleian Library Record,* 1947, ii, 179).

[53]Draft letter in Fettercairn Papers. The promise to write again soon is not in the draft, but was apparently added in a postscript (see next note).

sent Forbes a reminder[54] which crossed with a letter from Forbes dated 25 April. Forbes's letter has not been traced, but his search seems to have been unsuccessful or partially so for, on 2 May, Malone wrote to him again:

I had the favour of yours of the 25th of April a few days ago, and am sorry to find that my inquiries occasioned you so much trouble.—The Materials from which Mr. Boswell formed his book is an immense mass; but I conceive the paper we are in quest of (I mean Dr. Johnson's original letter to Mr. Boswell, dated Ashbourne Sep. 1 1777,) will not be found among them. I apprehend he kept all Dr. Johnson's letters to himself in one bundle, and arranged in the order of time; and this bundle must be either in your possession or at Auchinleck.[55]

Only two days later, on 4 May 1804, Malone wrote again to Forbes asking him to look for a letter by Johnson to Lucy Porter of 2 December 1784, and also remarking:

I had conceived, as I believe I mentioned in my last, that Mr. Boswell had kept Dr. Johnson's Letters addressed to himself in a distinct parcel; but if this is not the case, & they are blended with the other materials of his work, wd it not be adviseable to take them *all out*, and arrange them in chronological order, to be preserved as an honourable testimony to the Author, in the Library at Auchinlecke?[56]

[54]Letter in Fettercairn Papers. Malone writes: "I should long since have thank'd you for your obliging letter of the 9th of March; but that, as you mentioned in the postscript your intention of writing again soon, I have been in daily expectation of hearing from you."

[55]Letter in Fettercairn Papers. The precious bundle of letters from SJ to JB has never been found. One day they may come to light and a further chapter in the history of the Boswell papers can be written (see below Appendix II, p. 319). It is not known why Malone should refer in this letter only to a single paper, whereas on 3 March he had asked Forbes to hunt for three letters and also for the papers to be deposited in the British Museum and the Bodleian. This suggests that Forbes found the other items and so reported in his letter of 25 April. But this is not borne out by Malone's subsequent editing of the *Life*. Mention has already been made of his famous footnote in the fifth edition, 1807, III, p. 391, to the effect that he could not verify the text of SJ's letter to JB of 3 July 1778, "the original letter being burned [or buried?] in a mass of papers in Scotland." This was one of the letters Malone asked Forbes to find, and he was obviously unsuccessful.

[56]Letter in Fettercairn Papers. SJ's letter to Lucy Porter was probably in Forbes's hands at this time because it later turned up at Fettercairn (*Fettercairn Catalogue*, No. 1562). It is now in the Hyde Collection.

The loss of Forbes's letters reporting on his search makes it impossible to be certain whether he found any of the documents about which Malone enquired. So far as Isham and the other claimants were concerned, the point was immaterial. The significance of the letters was that Malone made no suggestion that the literary executors or the "younger children" had any right of ownership in the papers. He regarded Johnson's letters to Boswell as family heirlooms which ought to be preserved as such in the library at Auchinleck (and Auchinleck was of course Alexander's property).[57] Isham's argument was thus further strengthened.

ISHAM HAD TO BE PREPARED also for the possibility that the Court might accept Mrs. Hailey's interpretation of the will. She argued that the bequest to Alexander was limited, by implication, to Lord Auchinleck's "curious collection" of books and manuscripts and that Boswell's personal collection formed part of the general moveable estate which passed to the "younger children."[58] She claimed that when Veronica died intestate in September 1795, her quarter share of the papers was divisible amongst her brothers and sisters, so that Elizabeth, Euphemia, and James each came to have a five-sixteenths share, and Alexander a one-sixteenth share.[59]

Isham's problem was to establish that, even if Mrs. Hailey were correct, Alexander later acquired for himself all, or at any rate some, of the shares which originally passed to the "younger children." This made it necessary to find out how the children had acted in relation to the division of their father's general estate and how that estate had been administered by Forbes as executor;[60] and also to trace the wills of all of the "younger children" or, if no wills could be found, to identify their heirs in intestacy. The crux of the matter was that Isham could not claim any papers except those which he could prove had belonged to Alexander at his death; and the Cumberland Infirmary and Mrs. Vassall's trustees were in the same position.[61]

[57]If this was Malone's view as to the SJ-JB letters, he could not logically have differentiated the other papers, at least so far as their legal transmission was concerned.

[58]The will provided: "And all my other moveable Estate or executry, I leave equally among my younger children." This wording would include any papers not otherwise specifically bequeathed.

[59]Condescendence and claim for Mrs. Elizabeth Mary Cumberlege or Hailey from print of closed record (S. R. & Co.'s papers).

[60]Although Forbes, Temple, and Malone were appointed to act jointly in the literary trust, Forbes was the sole executor for all other purposes.

[61]All three claimants traced their entitlement from Alexander.

Boswell's will was found in London after his death. His brother, T. D. Boswell, who lived in London,[62] took possession of it and copies were sent to Forbes. On 26 June, Forbes wrote to T. D. Boswell: "We found no will at Auchinleck House nor any other papers except the Bond of Annuity & the Nomination of Guardians. It will be obliging that you send me the will found in London & I will return to you the certified copies wch. your nephew brought down with him, to lie by you."[63]

Forbes must have been quick to perceive the unsatisfactory nature of the will. If Euphemia is to be believed, Boswell himself was unhappy about it and meant to draw up a new one. In a letter to Forbes, she wrote that her father during his illness "blamed himself much" that "he had not made a will for many years," and that he wrote "a little time before he was taken ill to Mr. Temple and said he meant to make a new will."[64] No new will was found and Forbes had to give effect to the one sent from London along with the other testamentary writings. These consisted of the codicils of 30 May and 22 December 1785, the nomination of guardians and bond of annuity mentioned in Forbes's letter to T. D. Boswell, and the grant of £500 to Veronica.[65] Of these, only the will directly affected the transmission of the papers.

[62]He worked in the Naval Pay Office in London.

[63]Draft letter, dated 26 (or 27) June 1795, in Fettercairn Papers. As to the Nomination of Guardians and the Bond of Annuity, see below, n. 65.

[64]The letter is in the Fettercairn Papers. It bears no address and the only date is "Monday ye 9th." The year was probably 1796.

[65]Boswell's testamentary writings thus comprised six separate documents:
  (i) The will itself.
  (ii) The codicil of 30 May 1785, referred to above p. 174, which simply provided additional bequests of gold mourning rings to General Paoli and the Bishop of Killaloe, but contained nothing bearing on the papers.
  (iii) The codicil of 22 December 1785, quoted above p. 181.
  (iv) A holograph document, dated 4 January 1780, appointing his wife and Forbes "Tutors and Curators" (i.e., legal guardians) of his children. There are two later additions to the same document. The first, dated 8 January 1780, provided that the guardians should not be liable for any omissions in their actings. The second, dated 12 October 1791, appointed T. D. Boswell as a guardian in place of JB's wife, who had died. The whole document is registered in the Books of Council and Session on 7 August 1795.
  (v) The bond of annuity, mentioned in Forbes's letter to T. D. Boswell, is a document dated 19 March 1785 and 12 October 1791, whereby JB provided annuities in favour of the "younger children" to be paid out of the estate. The amounts were £150 a year to young James and £100 a year each to Veronica, Euphemia, and Elizabeth. He also made certain liferent provisions in favour of his wife which became inoperative when she predeceased him. The document is also registered in the Books of Council and Session on 7 August 1795.
  (vi) Grant by James Boswell of Auchinleck to his daughter Veronica of £500 dated 3 March 1795. Seen by Isham at Malahide in 1937 (see above p.162). This document was still at Malahide at the death of the seventh Lord Talbot de Malahide in 1973.

Alexander automatically succeeded to the entailed estate, as elder son, and Boswell also left him his unentailed lands under condition of bringing them within the fetters of the entail and settling his debts. Unfortunately, he did not make clear whether by this he meant *all* his debts or only the debts secured over the lands (i.e., heritable debts). The heritable debts alone came to two-thirds of the value of the unentailed lands and, if the other debts were added, Alexander would have had to find over £10,000 out of his own pocket.[66] He could not sell the unentailed lands to raise the money, because it was a condition that they must be brought into the entail. On the advice of his lawyers, he declined the succession to these lands and obtained the Court's authority for them to be sold.[67] The prices realized were better than expected so that, in November 1801, Forbes was left with a balance in hand of £2,103. 8. 6d after paying off the debts.[68]  £1,730 came

---

[66]In July 1795, the problems of interpreting JB's settlements and administering the estate were so great that Robert Boswell, W. S., as law agent for the executry, prepared a lengthy memorial on behalf of (a) Alexander, (b) the "younger children," and (c) Forbes and T. D. Boswell, as guardians of the "younger children." A copy of this document is in S. R. & Co.'s papers. The memorial was submitted to two distinguished advocates, Robert Blair and Adam Rolland, who were asked to reply to a number of specific queries. Copies of their answers dated respectively 29 July and 4 August 1795 are also in S. R. & Co.'s papers. From these documents it is clear that when JB died the value of the unentailed lands was estimated at £7,680 and bonds secured over these lands came to £5,400. After adding other debts, "the sum of debt for which the entailed estate would in this view be liable" was stated in the memorial to be £10,422.10/-. The memorial was important evidence for Isham, because it showed how Robert Boswell interpreted the literary executorship clause in the will, which he summarized as follows: "By the same deed Sir Wm. Forbes, Mr. Temple and Mr. Malone are entrusted with the care of all manuscripts of his own composition . . ." etc. The will did not in fact mention the word "care" but that is how Robert Boswell read JB's intent. Later in the memorial, he included in his list of JB's assets "The value of any publication of Mr. Boswell's manuscripts left with the executors for the use of the younger children—suppose—£500." Note that he says *left with* and not *left to* the executors and it is only the *use* of the papers he supposes the "younger children" to have.

[67]Information from "Memorial and Abstract in the Process of Sale and Ranking, brought at the instance of Alexander Boswell of Auchinleck, as Apparent Heir of the deceased James Boswell of Auchinleck, Esq., his Father;—For the sale of the unentailed Lands and Estate. . . ." 20 June 1798 (copy in S. R. & Co.'s papers). Alexander was served as heir *cum beneficio inventarii*, a procedure open to an apparent heir who was doubtful whether the value of his inheritance would cover his ancestor's debts; the effect was that he became liable for the debts only up to the value of the lands shown in a sworn inventory and no further. As a result of the process of sale and ranking, the Court of Session authorized the sale of the lands, some of which were purchased by Alexander himself.

[68]Narrated in "Memorial and Queries for Alexander Boswell Esqr. of Auchinleck," February 1802 (copy in S. R. & Co.'s papers), another lengthy memorial in which Alexander sought further guidance on numerous points relating to his succession. It was submitted to Matthew Ross, whose answers are dated 22 March 1802 (copy in S. R. & Co.'s papers). Forbes's statement of intromissions showing the balance of £2,103.8.6d, was dated 26 November 1801.

from the sale of the lands and was claimed by Alexander, but Forbes thought that in bringing the lands to a sale Alexander had rejected his father's settlement and was not entitled to the money.[69] There was also a disagreement between Alexander and the "younger children" as to the calculation of their annuities and as to whether certain other annuities were a burden on the moveable or the entailed estate.[70]

Forbes wanted to settle these difficulties in court,[71] but Alexander and James were both averse to the family differences being dealt with in so public a manner. It was therefore agreed to submit the whole matter to the arbitration of the Lord Advocate, Charles Hope.[72]

The "younger children" argued that Alexander in bringing the lands to a judicial sale had frustrated Boswell's intention that the lands should be entailed and remain with successive heirs forever, and that in rejecting his father's settlement so far as the lands were concerned, he had forfeited the right to accept it in respect of the moveables left to him, namely the ebony cabinet, the dressing plate, the Greek and Latin books, and the manuscripts at Auchinleck; as heirs entitled to the moveable estate, they would have succeeded to the cabinet, plate, books, and manuscripts if Boswell had not left them to Alexander under certain conditions; but, as Alexander had failed to comply with these conditions, his bequest lapsed and their right revived. Even if these arguments were not accepted, they pointed out that the bequest to Alexander was expressly confined to Greek and Latin books and manuscripts of whatever kind at Auchinleck, and could not extend to books and manuscripts outside this description. They claimed the whole balance held by Forbes, the ebony cabinet, dressing plate, and the Greek and Latin books and manuscripts at Auchinleck; if the Arbiter rejected this, they still asked for all the books other than Greek and Latin ones, wherever situated at Boswell's death, and all letters, copies of letters, and manuscripts not lying at Auchinleck at Boswell's death, and all other moveable property.[73]

---

[69]Ibid.

[70]Ibid.

[71]Ibid.

[72]"Submission between Alexr. Boswell Esqr. of Auchinleck and his Brother and Sisters &c.," 1802 (copy in S. R. & Co.'s papers). Arbitration was suggested by Matthew Ross in his answers to the memorial and queries for Alexander. James wrote to Forbes on 8 May 1802: "The opinion of Mr. Ross has fully convinced me (if I wanted any conviction before) that a Lawsuit must appear now as repugnant to good sense as it always was to delicacy of feeling. . . . Arbitration is the only proper & the only prudent way of settling the business." (Letter in Fettercairn Papers.)

[73]Memorial and claim in the arbitration for the "younger children," January 1803 (copy in S. R. & Co.'s papers).

Alexander maintained that he was entitled to the ebony cabinet, dressing plate, books, and manuscripts under the condition stipulated in the will; if these items were not allowed to go to him, they could never go to the "younger children" in view of the interest of successive heirs of entail; in any event, the fact that he did not take up the succession to the unentailed lands did not affect his right to the moveables bequeathed to him, and he had never rejected the whole of his father's settlement. He also argued that his father intended him to have all the books at Auchinleck, and not merely the Greek and Latin ones.[74]

The arbiter pronounced an interim decree on 19 March 1804. He held that Boswell's whole debts were a burden on the lands, and that Alexander was therefore liable for them up to the full value of the lands to which he succeeded. The intended entail was defeated, not by Alexander in repudiating the settlement, but by Boswell himself in burdening the lands with debts the amount of which he was probably unaware of. In other respects the will should have effect so that Alexander would take "as an heirloom"[75] the ebony cabinet and dressing plate and also the Greek and Latin books at Auchinleck; the other books, wherever situated at Boswell's death, would fall to the "younger children," but Alexander should be entitled to have them at a valuation if he pleased. All other moveable property was to go to the "younger children" along with the money held by Forbes.[76]

The arbiter made no reference to the manuscripts. This is surpris-

[74]"Answers and Claim for Alexander Boswell to the Memorial and Claim for the younger children," 15 February 1803 (copy in S. R. & Co.'s papers).

[75]JB's attempt in his will to secure the transmission of the ebony cabinet, the dressing plate, and the books and manuscripts to successive heirs of entail was of doubtful efficacy. The statutory basis for entails in Scotland was the Statute of 1685 (act 1685, c.22) which was expressly confined to heritable (i.e., landed) property. The conception of a piece of moveable property as an "heirloom" belonged to English rather than Scots Law. Since an entail of moveables in Scotland could not be entered in the "Register of Tailzies" set up under the Statute of 1685, it could be defeated if the object of the entail were acquired by a creditor or a *bona fide* purchaser. However, as amongst the heirs themselves, any clause of prohibition, penalty, or forfeiture was enforceable. (See E. D. Sandford, *A Treatise on the History and Law of Entails in Scotland,* second edition, Edinburgh, 1842, pp. 251–52.) If Alexander succeeded to JB's papers under the bequest of books and manuscripts, he did so on the terms stipulated in the will, although subsequent heirs could not have prevented their sale to *bona fide* purchasers or protected them from creditors; if on the other hand Alexander acquired them under his purchase of moveable property from the "younger children" (see below p. 200), they became his free property. In any event, the point ceased to matter when his son, Sir James Boswell, broke the entail in 1852 (see below p. 211).

[76]"Extract Interim Decreet Arbitral in Submission between Alexander Boswell Esq. and his Brother and Sisters", dated and registered in the Books of Council and Session on 19 March 1804 (S. R. & Co.'s papers).

ing, for his interim decree was obviously meant to dispose of *all* property passing under the will, and the "younger children" had specifically claimed the manuscripts along with the other items bequeathed to Alexander. There was no reason to differentiate the manuscripts at Auchinleck from the Greek and Latin books at Auchinleck. All were part and parcel of the same bequest and subject to the same terms and conditions. If the arbiter awarded the Greek and Latin books to Alexander, he must also have meant him to have the manuscripts, and his failure to say so can only have been an oversight.

The oversight was not rectified in the arbiter's final decree, pronounced on 7 February 1805.[77] This confirmed and gave specific effect to the findings of the interim decree subject to a number of minor corrections, largely necessitated by the fact that on Veronica's death intestate in 1795, Alexander succeeded to a quarter share of her estate as one of her next of kin. The arbiter ordained Forbes as executor to make over "all the unrecovered Executry funds arrears of rent and feuduties goods gear and moveables of whatever nature or description either in his possession or in that of other persons for his behoof as Executor" to Alexander, James, Euphemia, and Elizabeth. Alexander was to receive a one-sixteenth share as one of the next of kin of Veronica. James, Euphemia, and Elizabeth were each to receive a five-sixteenths share (being one-fourth each in their own right and one-sixteenth each as next of kin of Veronica).

Meanwhile Euphemia had got into serious financial difficulties. On 27 March 1805, she entered into an arrangement with her creditors whereby she placed her affairs in the hands of David Wemyss, an Edinburgh lawyer.[78] From then on, Wemyss represented her in all questions as to her rights of succession in Boswell's estate.

During the months which followed, negotiations, often bitter in tone, took place for the final settlement of affairs between Alexander and the "younger children." These negotiations were conducted mainly by Alexander personally and through his law agent, Harry Davidson, on the one hand, and David Wemyss and William Boswell (Elizabeth's husband) on the other hand.[79]

Wemyss and William Boswell pointed out that, since Boswell's

[77]"Extract of Submission and Decreet Arbitral twixt Alexander Boswell Esquire of Auchinleck and his Brother and Sisters", dated 7 and registered in the Books of Council and Session on 8 February 1805 (S. R. & Co.'s papers).

[78]Trust Disposition and Assignation by Euphemia Boswell in favour of David Wemyss. W. S., for behoof of herself and her creditors, dated 27 March 1805 (copy in S. R. & Co.'s papers).

[79]Copies of this correspondence are in S. R. & Co.'s papers.

death, Alexander had had possession of the furniture and other effects now to be handed over to the "younger children." To avoid any unpleasant disputes as to particular articles and the expense of an inventory, they offered to make over everything to Alexander for a reasonable lump sum payment. They proposed a figure of £400, and made it clear that if agreement were not reached, they were ready to haggle over every item. They raised queries about a huge list of articles which showed the sort of trouble Alexander might expect if he did not come to terms.[80] "Books" were mentioned on the understanding that the Greek and Latin books at Auchinleck went to Alexander and all others formed part of the general moveable estate. Nothing was said at this stage of manuscripts, letters, or the like. Alexander was exasperated by the whole affair and gave vent to his feelings when writing to Harry Davidson:

> Never did beings forget all decency so much as Miss B. and that poor creature Mr. W. B. Having acted openly and to the best of my belief and conscience liberally towards the younger children, this abominable business was most irksome.[81]

Davidson met Wemyss and William Boswell to discuss terms, and, on 12 November 1805, he sent Alexander a list of items to be taken over by him with suggested values. The list made no reference to manuscripts but included all books "not entailed" at a figure of £130. The total price came to £300.[82] Alexander must have agreed to this for, on 6 December 1805, Wemyss and William Boswell wrote to Davidson: "We understand everything to be settled between Mr. Boswell

---

[80]All this is confirmed by a long letter from Alexander to his lawyer, Harry Davidson, of 4 November 1805 (copy in S. R. & Co.'s papers). He mentions "a string of Observations on a Minute prepared by Mr. Wemyss." Among the many articles for which the "younger children" asked him to account were: books (other than Greek and Latin ones), a harpsichord, a down bed, coins and medals, impressions by Tassie, jewellery, bed and table linen, wines and spirits, wax fruits, toilets of lace work, painted glass, an antique watch, a writing case, a gold watch case, drinking glasses, a horn, various weapons, two gongs, a quantity of pewter, prisms and optical instruments, shells, stuffed birds ("a humming bird & a Swallow hung by the legs till Moths dispersed the feathers"), snakes in bottles, stones from the Hebrides, a Corsican dress cap, wooden plates, a miniature of General Paoli, prints and caricatures, trunks and chests, visiting cards, plaster busts, court dresses, silver baubles and Chinese jars. No wonder Alexander lost patience. He was even expected to remember what wines were at Auchinleck ten years previously. The "younger children" arbitrarily valued these wines at £40. Nevertheless, Alexander was at fault in not keeping a record of moveable property at Auchinleck which he did not inherit under the will and which he used or consumed.

[81]Ibid.

[82]Copy letter in S. R. & Co.'s papers.

of Auchinleck and his Brother & Sisters. He is to pay £300 in full for all books and every article which the Executors have claim to in and about the house of Auchinleck, excepting only the Gongs & the diamond Ring."[83]

On 9 December 1805, Forbes gave formal effect to the arbiter's findings by assigning the moveable property to Alexander and the "younger children" in accordance with the final decree. The property assigned was described as:

> All and Sundry Debts and Sums of money heritable and moveable and all articles of moveable property of whatever nature & description, including certain Books, Medals and Pictures at Auchinleck House which belonged to the said deceased James Boswell and are still outstanding and unrecovered or unrealised by me the said Sir William Forbes as his Executor and including all arrears of rent and feuduties and goods and gear of every description. . . . Declaring always however as it is hereby expressly Provided and Declared that this present Disposition and Assignation shall not be held to convey to the said Disponees and Assignees above mentioned the Manuscripts and Letters left by the said deceased James Boswell to the care of Temple and Malone Esquires and of me the said Sir William Forbes with discretionary powers to us to publish more or less of them for behoof of his younger children, which manuscripts and Letters shall be held to remain in the same situation as before granting these presents notwithstanding thereof.[84]

The exclusion of the papers is very curious. However Boswell's will is interpreted, the right of property in the papers must have transmitted to Alexander or to the "younger children" or to the literary executors. If the last, there would have been some point in making the exclusion, but the correspondence between Forbes and Malone, and other dealings, made it obvious that they never regarded themselves as owning the papers.[85] If, on the other hand, Forbes thought that the papers had passed either to Alexander or to the "younger

[83]Copy letter in S. R. & Co.'s papers.

[84]Assignation and Disposition by Sir William Forbes dated 9 and 13 December 1805. Alexander was an assignee only in respect of his one-sixteenth share derived from Veronica's estate.

[85]This is again confirmed by the wording of the assignation quoted above, in which it is only the *care* of the papers which is said to have been left to Forbes, Temple, and Malone, although the will does not in fact use the word "care."

children," he had no right to exclude them from his assignation. The
parties concerned seem simply to have ignored the fact that the papers
must have belonged to someone. They were described as being "in
the same situation as before" and it is unlikely that the draftsman
of the deed had any clear conception of what this meant.

The arrangements for the disposal of the moveable property cul-
minated in December 1805 when Alexander completed his purchase
from the "younger children." In return for the agreed price of £300,
they assigned to him all the books other than the Greek and Latin
ones (which belonged to him anyway), certain other specific articles,
"and in general all and every other article and articles as well not
mentioned in the foresaid enumeration as therein specified in and
about said house of Auchinleck to which we or any of us have right
or any manner of claim whatsoever excepting only two indian gongs
and a diamond ring."[86]

Again there was no specific reference to the papers. The parties
seem to have side-stepped the issue because they regarded the papers
as being in a special category and never really attempted to analyse
the legal rights of ownership. An attitude such as this would explain
the exclusion of the papers from the assignation granted by Forbes.
An alternative explanation was that the general clause in the assignation
by the "younger children," although limited to articles "in and about
the said house of Auchinleck," was wide enough to carry to Alexander
any right they might have had to the papers. The papers, or most
of them, were not at Auchinleck at this date, but they had only been
temporarily removed for perusal by the literary executors and Auchinleck was their proper home.

So far as the litigants in 1938 were concerned, the position was
inconclusive; but if the Court accepted Mrs. Hailey's interpretation
of the will, Isham, as also the Infirmary and Mrs. Vassall's trustees,
could at least argue with some conviction that Alexander acquired
by his purchase from the "younger children" such of the papers as
he did not already own by succession.

WHEN FORBES DIED in 1806,[87] he probably still had in his custody the
papers which Alexander had brought from Auchinleck, and also those
which Malone had sent to him from London. As executor, he had

---

[86]Assignation of moveables & discharge in favour of Alexander Boswell dated 21 and 31
December 1805 (copy in S. R. & Co.'s papers).
[87]On 12 November 1806.

good reason to retain them whilst Alexander and the "younger children" continued to dispute the division of their father's moveable estate; and even after the dispute was settled in 1805, the question of the literary trust still remained to be dealt with. The period of ten years, which he and Malone had agreed should elapse before James examined the papers, expired in the summer of 1806. Forbes's death a few months later brought the matter again to the fore. A large parcel of papers was sent from Scotland to London for consideration by James, who decided that nothing should be published.[88] At least one batch of papers was returned to Auchinleck in 1809, for, on 21 March of that year, Alexander wrote to his brother to say that another trunk had arrived from Sir William Forbes (i.e., the son of the Forbes who was Boswell's executor) containing some of the manuscript of the *Life*.[89] It is interesting that the trunk came from Sir William rather than from James. Possibly James, after perusing the papers sent to him in London, returned them to Forbes, who in due course forwarded them to Auchinleck in two or more consignments.

It may have been the news that her father's papers had been sent back to Auchinleck which prompted Euphemia to write to Malone. Her letter does not survive, but Malone's reply of 4 May 1809, already quoted in full,[90] suggests that she tried to make difficulty over what she believed to be her rights in the papers. This would have been in keeping with her earlier behaviour in the dispute with Alexander in 1805. Malone gave her short shrift. He told her that she was mistaken about the papers and that these were now at Auchinleck where he hoped they would be "suffered to remain in peace."

Malone was of course wrong in thinking that all the papers had gone back to Auchinleck. About two-thirds of them had, but the remainder found their way to Fettercairn. How this came about was of great importance to the success or failure of Lord Clinton's claim. The link between the Forbes family and Fettercairn was explained by Abbott in the introduction to his catalogue.[91] The young Sir William Forbes had married, on 19 January 1797, Wilhelmina Wishart Belsches Stuart, only child of Baron Sir John Stuart of Fettercairn House. After

[88]Letter, Malone to Euphemia Boswell, 4 May 1809, quoted above p. 37.

[89]This letter is now at Yale and came from Malahide. Its existence was not however known in 1938. Alexander wrote: "Another Trunk has arrived from Sir William Forbes it contains some of the Manuscript of the Life, but I was much disappointed at not finding one Letter of Johnsons for it is strange not to have one specimen of his handwriting at Auchinleck."

[90]Above p. 37.

[91]*Fettercairn Catalogue*, Introduction, p. xv., n. 1.

the death of his father in 1806, he presumably undertook the task of returning Boswell's papers to Auchinleck. Unlike his father, he did not know the bulk of papers involved and, although he sent at least two trunkfuls to Alexander, he must have overlooked a large quantity, which was taken with his other belongings to Fettercairn House when this became the family residence. The nature and variety of places in which Abbott found the Fettercairn papers suggest that they were stowed away with little or no appreciation of their importance and that many of them had lain there in oblivion until their discovery over a century later.[92]

There was no clear-cut answer to the problem of the transmission of the papers on Boswell's death. Isham's argument, supported by the Cumberland Infirmary and by Mrs. Vassall's trustees, was that the will carried the papers to Alexander, or alternatively, if they passed to the "younger children," that Alexander subsequently acquired them under his purchase in 1805. As we have seen, the literary executors never claimed ownership for themselves, and Malone thought the papers should be deposited at Auchinleck when the decision as to publication had finally been made.[93] This disposed of one of Lord Clinton's two lines of argument. The other, that he had acquired a good title to the Fettercairn papers by prescription (i.e., lapse of time), was also unsound. As the papers had come to Fettercairn through an oversight and without the knowledge of the Boswell family, and as they had been sent to Forbes in the first place for a fiduciary purpose, there could be no proper foundation for prescription.

Mrs. Hailey's claim to half of a five-sixteenths share by succession from Elizabeth Boswell was less easily disposed of. If the Court were to decide that the younger children inherited the papers and that they were not covered by Alexander's purchase in 1805,[94] Mrs. Hailey would succeed. Isham therefore included a third argument in his claim to show that, even if this were so, at least part of the papers must have belonged to Alexander when he died. James junior, by his will,[95]

[92]Some of the papers were, however, undoubtedly handled between the time of their arrival at Fettercairn and Abbott's visit in 1930. A bundle of letters from SJ found in the wooden box in the courtyard was wrapped in a page of *The Times* of 21 August 1874 (see above p. 124). Some of the contents of Lord Clinton's portfolio, shown to Abbott on his first visit to Fettercairn, must have come from JB's papers—e.g., SJ's letter to JB of 11 July 1784 (see above p. 123).

[93]Malone's letter to Euphemia Boswell of 4 May 1809, quoted above p. 37.

[94]i.e., the transaction effected by the assignation of moveables and discharge cited above p. 200, n. 86.

[95]Cited above p. 168, n. 117.

left everything he had to Alexander. Efforts to trace the wills of Veronica, Elizabeth, and Euphemia were unsuccessful and they were all presumed to have died intestate.[96] On Veronica's death in 1795, her quarter share would have been divided equally among her brothers and sisters. In this way, Alexander would have acquired a one-sixteenth share and the shares of James, Elizabeth, and Euphemia would each have been increased from a quarter to five-sixteenths. On James's death in 1822, Alexander succeeded to his share, and so became the owner of six-sixteenths. This left Elizabeth's share, half of which Mrs. Hailey claimed,[97] and Euphemia's share, which on her death in 1834 would, in so far as not needed to satisfy her creditors, have passed to her heirs.[98]

Alexander always acted as though he were the owner of the papers and, except for their claim in the arbitration proceedings, the "younger children" did not challenge him seriously. It was Alexander who sorted out the papers to bring to Forbes, and they were only out of his hands to enable the literary executors to discharge their trust and to allow James to consider the possibility of their publication. As mentioned, some of the papers later turned up in James's library in London.[99] Whether James was entitled to retain these, or whether he borrowed them with Alexander's permission, is a matter of conjecture. In any event, Alexander was James's sole heir and any papers belonging to James passed to him by legal succession. The remaining papers, other than those taken by mistake to Fettercairn, were eventually returned to Auchinleck, where they remained in Alexander's control until his death in 1822.

THE TRANSMISSION OF THE PAPERS from Boswell to Sir Alexander was only the first step in Isham's claim. The second was to prove that on Sir Alexander's death they passed to his only son, Sir James. In this respect, Isham's argument again coincided with that of the Cumberland Infirmary. The opposing argument came from Mrs. Vassall's trustees, who sought to prove that Sir Alexander's moveable estate

[96]See above pp. 7 and 170. Isham does not seem to have spotted the reference to Euphemia's will in *Boswelliana*, and Buchanan's efforts to trace a will were unsuccessful.

[97]The other half would, on a similarly argued claim, have gone to other descendants of Elizabeth, but none such came forward to claim. See Table III, p. 354.

[98]The heirs would have been those named in her will, if found, or, failing a will, the children of Alexander and Elizabeth as her next-of-kin.

[99]See above p. 19.

(including the papers) passed to his two daughters, Janet Theresa and Margaret Amelia (who became Mrs. Vassall). As Mrs. Vassall's representatives, they therefore claimed a one-half share.[100]

Sir Alexander, it will be remembered, was killed unexpectedly as a result of his duel with James Stuart of Dunearn and was hopelessly insolvent at his death.[101] He had incurred the heavy expense of procuring a seat in Parliament and, during the Napoleonic Wars, he had made large purchases of land at inflated prices with borrowed money. In 1822, prices were depressed and the lands, if sold, would not have realized enough to pay off the bonds, which amounted to more than £40,000. In addition, there were personal debts exceeding £32,000 against assets worth only about £10,000.[102] The children were all under the age of twenty-one and Sir James, who succeeded to the baronetcy and the entailed estate of Auchinleck, was only fifteen. By his will, Sir Alexander left his entire free estate to James, subject to payment of all his debts which his assets were quite inadequate to meet. There was a proviso that if James should repudiate the will or decline to make up title under it, the whole estate should go to his sisters, with the exception of the "Library at Auchinleck" which was still to go to James.[103]

Sir James took legal advice and was strongly recommended not to make up title under his father's will lest he become personally liable to the creditors.[104] He therefore declined the succession and, some years later, even went to the length of executing a formal renunciation.[105] The succession thus opened to Janet and Margaret, but they also wished to avoid personal liability for the debts and took no steps to make up title.

By renouncing the succession, Sir James did not forfeit his right

---

[100]Print of closed record (S. R. & Co.'s papers). At one stage, a claim was lodged by four descendants of Janet Theresa Boswell, but for some reason or other they withdrew their claim and allowed the different claim of the Vassall trustees to be substituted (see above p. 171). Sir Gilbert Eliott, who was also descended from Janet Theresa Boswell, was one of the early claimants, but he withdrew his claim at Lady Talbot's instigation (see above p. 166 and also Table IV, p. 16).

[101]See above p. 355.

[102]Information from "Memorial and Queeries for Sir James Boswell of Auchinleck Baronet [and his guardians]," April 1823 (copy in S. R. & Co.'s papers).

[103]Disposition and deed of settlement by Alexander Boswell dated 11 November 1813 and with codicils dated 24 December 1817 and 25 November 1818 registered in the Books of Council and Session on 7 August 1823 (copy in S. R. & Co.'s papers).

[104]"Memorial and Queeries" cited above and answers thereto by Matthew Ross, dated 7 April 1823.

[105]Renunciation by Sir James Boswell dated 22 October 1831 and registered in the Books of Council and Session on 10 December 1832.

to the "Library at Auchinleck," but he could not claim it until all the debts had been paid. As that was impossible, the creditors were entitled to sell the library, along with any other available assets, to meet their claims. One of the principal creditors was officially confirmed as executor and the administration of the estate was in his hands.[106]

The executor's inventory of the contents of Auchinleck House showed a total of £3,252.9.6d as the value of "sundry Articles of Household furniture, Books, Plate, Bed and table Linen." One of the items in this inventory was "Library of Books" at a figure of £600.[107] This description may have been intended to include the papers and manuscripts in the library, as these were not separately listed. At any rate, it is clear that at this time those of Boswell's private papers which had previously belonged to Sir Alexander were now the legal property of his creditors. Unfortunately, neither the creditors nor Sir Alexander's family knew that a large quantity of these papers still remained in the hands of Forbes's descendants (probably at Fettercairn).

In August 1824, Lady Boswell purchased the "furniture, library and other effects in the house of Auchinleck" from the creditors for £3,000, and then made over her purchase to Sir James as a gift. The evidence of this purchase and gift has only recently been uncovered.[108] It was not available to Isham in 1938, although other

---

[106]Hamilton Douglas Boswell of Garallan was confirmed as executor conform to testament dative *qua* creditor dated 20 February 1824, Commissariot of Ayr (copy in S. R. & Co.'s papers). H. D. Boswell died a few months later and the administration of Sir Alexander's estate was continued by his widow, Mrs. Jane Douglas Boswell of Garallan, who was confirmed as executrix in his place conform to testament testamentary *umquhile* Hamilton Douglas Boswell, 11 August 1824, Commissariot of Ayr (copy in S. R. & Co.'s papers).

[107]The testament dative cited in the preceding note includes as an item "sundry Articles of Household furniture, Books, Plate, Bed and table Linen amounting per Inventory and appraisement by James Morrison Appraiser to the sum of Three thousand two hundred and fifty-two pounds nine shillings and six pence *Summa Inventarii patet*." Amongst the papers now at Yale is the "Inventory and Appraisement of Household Furniture and other Moveable Effects at Auchinleck House, the property of Sir Alexander Boswell Baronet of Auchinleck deceased." This includes "Library of Books" at a figure of £600.

[108]Minute of agreement between the Dowager Lady Boswell and Lady Boswell of Auchinleck (i.e., the widows of Sir Alexander and Sir James), drawn up in 1858 shortly after Sir James's death. This narrates: "Whereas the said first party, after the decease of her husband the said Sir Alexander Boswell, purchased from his Creditors the furniture library and other effects in the house of Auchinleck and paid, in or about the month of August in the year 1824, the price of £3,000 Sterling, all which furniture library and other effects were presented by the first party to her son the said Sir James Boswell and have ever since remained in the house of Auchinleck. . . ." and goes on to confirm that the "furniture library and other effects" are now the exclusive property of Sir James's widow. I found this document quite recently when, by kind permission of Lady Talbot de Malahide, I inspected the contents of 7 massive boxes full of legal papers at the office of Messrs. David W. Shaw & Co., solicitors in Ayr. These papers were held in 1938 by Messrs. Scott Moncrieff & Trail in Edinburgh, but although they were searched then for material relevant to the lawsuit, the minute of agreement must have been missed.

documents were found at that time which referred to Lady Boswell's purchase of the "Library and furniture" at Auchinleck.[109] What these documents did *not* establish was that Lady Boswell's purchase also included the "other effects" at Auchinleck and that she subsequently made a gift of everything to her son. In the absence of such a gift, the items she purchased would have remained her property and would ultimately have passed under her will to her daughter, Mrs. Vassall.[110] It was therefore most important for Isham to prove the gift, but he could only rely on the circumstantial evidence that the contents of Auchinleck apparently remained in Sir James's possession and control until his death in 1857. He knew that this was a weak link in his argument and feared that Mrs. Vassall's trustees might claim the *whole* of the papers on the ground that they were constructively included in Lady Boswell's purchase and then passed to Mrs. Vassall by inheritance. Surprisingly, the trustees overlooked this argument and contented themselves with a claim for only half the papers by direct succession from Sir Alexander.

Although Lady Boswell gave her son the contents of Auchinleck, a letter has very recently come to light which suggests that she still kept the family papers under her strict control.[111] In 1843-1845, William MacKenzie, a teacher of anatomy at Edinburgh University, was engaged in research for I. K. Tefft of the Georgia Historical Society. Tefft was interested in General Oglethorpe, who had played an important

[109]Excerpts from pursuer's print of documents, etc., *in causa* Montgomerie v. Boswell (copy in S. R. & Co.'s papers). This is a compendium of documents relating to a complicated action of multiplepoinding in 1855–56 involving competing claims against Sir Alexander's estate by Sir James and one Matthew Montgomerie in their capacity as creditors. As will be seen below, Sir James bought over all his father's debts except for one of £2,494 due to Sheriff Alexander Boswell (his father's second cousin) and three other trifling debts totalling less than £50. Montgomerie was in turn a substantial creditor of the Sheriff and sought satisfaction of his claim by pressing the Sheriff's claim against Sir Alexander's estate. The parties to the litigation were Mrs. J. D. Boswell, as Sir Alexander's executrix, and Sir James and Montgomerie, as the remaining creditors against the estate. One of the documents in this process is a copy of a proposal by Sir James to his father's creditors of 8 August 1828. This mentions Lady Boswell's purchase of the library and furniture for £3,000 and the carriage for £60 "which afforded a dividend of about 2s. per pound" for the creditors. The purchase is also recorded in an account between the creditors and Messrs. Tod & Romanes included in the same compendium of documents, but nowhere is it said that Lady Boswell purchased the "other effects" at Auchinleck, or gave them to her son.

[110]General disposition and settlement by Dame Grace Cuming or Boswell dated 5 April 1860 (copy in S. R. & Co.'s papers).

[111]Letter, William MacKenzie to I. K. Tefft, 1 February 1844 (in possession of Georgia Historical Society). This important letter was shown to F. A. Pottle late in 1971 and I am grateful to him for drawing my attention to it. I am also grateful to the Georgia Historical Society for permission to quote.

part in the colonial settlement of Georgia. In the *Life,* Boswell had mentioned that Oglethorpe had communicated to him a number of particulars of his life, and that Johnson was concerned that Oglethorpe's life should be written.[112] Mackenzie had been asked to find out about Boswell's papers and in particular whether they contained a life of Oglethorpe. On 1 February 1844, he wrote to Tefft:

> Mr. Miller of Dalswinton and others nearly connected with the Boswells referred me to a gentleman residing in this city who is reported to have *extraordinary* influence with them. He does not wish his name to be mentioned and considers the conversation I held with him as so far confidential. . . . At Sir Alexr.'s decease he was considerably in debt, and his library and MSS were purchased by his wife the Dowager Lady Boswell. They are all at Auchinleck house, in the state in which they were found, at the death of her husband in three boxes carefully sealed up. Dowager Lady Boswell recently writes to her sister the Honble Mrs. Leslie Cumming, in reply to a question from me "that she never heard Sir Alexr. B. allude to any MSS life of General Oglethorpe," and that she does not believe that anything of the kind exists—otherwise she would have heard of it. . . .
>
> Dowager Lady Boswell and her connections dislike greatly any allusion to Dr. Johnson, considering that Mr. James the grandfather degraded himself and his family by acting the toady to the Dr. Sir Walter Scott applied to my informant to get access to Dr. Johnson's letters for Croker's edition of Boswell, but in spite of all his importunities and influence, was met with a firm refusal. It is known that many interesting papers and letters exist in the collection—and all the letters published by Boswell with the suppressed passages. If my friend survives Dowager Lady B., he will then be allowed to examine them all. . . .

The identity of MacKenzie's informant is a mystery. Sir Walter Scott apparently enlisted his aid on behalf of Croker, but does not mention him in his several letters to Croker.[113] The only name which occurs in this correspondence is that of William Boswell, who died in

---

[112]See *Life,* I, p. 127, n. 4, and II, p. 351 and n. 3.

[113]See above pp. 22–23 where this correspondence is quoted from. I am indebted to Alan Bell of the National Library of Scotland who reported on all the letters from Croker to Scott in the National Library, and also to F. A. Pottle for information about the letters from Scott to Croker at Yale. The correspondence on both sides seems to be virtually complete, but we know of at least one stray (see p. 23, n. 102) and there may be others which would shed light on the identity of the mysterious informant.

1841 and whose family was estranged from the Boswells of Auchinleck.[114] Neither he nor his children would have had much influence with Sir James or his mother. Whoever the anonymous informant was, he clearly regarded Lady Boswell as the main obstacle to free inspection of the papers and his confidence that he would be "allowed to examine them all" after her death suggests that he was assured of Sir James's consent.

Lady Boswell survived her son by seven years. It may be that she kept the sealed boxes under her control until her death in 1864 and would not readily have allowed any outsider to inspect them. Sir James may have passed on to her the letters from Croker and Scott to deal with. If so, it was she rather than Sir James who was responsible for Croker's failure.[115] Sir James cannot easily be acquitted of discourtesy, for both letters were addressed to him and neither received any reply; nevertheless, one cannot assume that, if his mother had been out of the way, and especially in his later years, he would have been unwilling to show the papers to a responsible scholar. MacKenzie's letter to Tefft suggests the contrary; and so also does a letter written in 1856 by Hugh Bruce Campbell (Sir James's fourth cousin) to Sir Philip Francis, whose edition of the Boswell-Temple letters had just appeared:

> It remains to be seen whether his Grandson the present Sir James Boswell approve the publication of the letters to Temple, because

---

[114]See above p. 8. In a passage which I have not quoted in my text, MacKenzie wrote: "It unfortunately happens that there is a feud in this family."

[115]In 1962, F. A. Pottle published an article in *Proceedings of the American Philosophical Society* (vol. 106, No. 4) entitled "Notes on the Importance of Private Legal Documents for the Writing of Biography and Literary History." In this article, he speculated on the reason for Sir James's silence in response to Croker's approach. His conclusion was that "Sir James would undoubtedly have referred the request to his lawyers, and they would pretty certainly have told him that *any* reply to it would be risky. Sir James had not listed his grandfather's papers as of any value; if Croker mentioned them, some creditor might demand a further dividend, or might sue to have the settlement set aside altogether on the ground that the assets had not been fully stated." When he reached this conclusion, Pottle did not have the benefit of two vital pieces of information: MacKenzie's letter to Tefft and the minute of agreement which established the circumstances of Lady Boswell's purchase from the creditors. It now seems clear that when Croker's letter arrived, there was no need to worry about the creditors or to take legal advice, as the papers were already the absolute property of Lady Boswell or Sir James. It might also be mentioned that Sir James was not in any event responsible for listing or valuing his grandfather's papers. That was the job of the executor, who may in fact have considered them to be included in his inventory under the item "Library of Books" valued at £600. The point is not material, however, since Lady Boswell's purchase seems to have covered the entire contents of Auchinleck.

if he does, there cannot really be any doubt that "the Archives of Auchinleck" could furnish the materials, or more correctly speaking the means of tracing a great number of Boswells miscellaneous letters.

Of Mr. Crokers reproof (preface to his Edition of the life pa xvii), Sir James has probably with Mr. Crokers readers felt the justice & he might therefore now be induced to respond to a fresh application.

Should you feel a reluctance to apply, & wish Sir James to be previously sounded I would venture to take an opportunity of personally doing it or getting it done when I am in Ayrshire next Summer.[116]

When Sir James came of age in 1828, he made determined efforts to liquidate his father's debts. He offered to buy out the claims of all the personal creditors for a payment of eight shillings in the pound.[117] This was in addition to two shillings in the pound which had previously been distributed in consequence of Lady Boswell's purchase in 1824. Some such proposal seems to have been accepted, for he obtained assignations of all the personal debts except one of £2,494 due to Sheriff Alexander Boswell, W. S. (a grandson of Lord Auchinleck's brother, Dr. John Boswell), and three other small debts totalling less than £50. In this way, Sir James himself became a creditor against the executry for £28,280.2.5d, although the executry funds were of course worth nothing like this figure.[118]

---

[116]A copy of this letter, dated 29 December 1856, has been made available to me by F. A. Pottle. The original is at Yale and came from the late C. B. Tinker's papers. If the papers were still controlled by the Dowager Lady Boswell in 1856, Campbell was apparently unaware of the fact. But he was obviously confident that papers survived at Auchinleck and hopeful that Sir James would be co-operative.

[117]Proposal by Sir James to his father's creditors cited above p. 206, n. 109.

[118]On 10 January 1831, Sir James wrote to William Home, W. S., about the bequest of £2,000 to his mother by the late John Davidson, W. S. Under his parents' marriage contract this was payable to his father's estate, and, as principal creditor, he claimed the major share of it. He explained:

"The personal debt amounted to . . . .  £30,822 15 3
I took assignations of all these debts, excepting Mr. A. Boswell's debt of £2,494, one of £22.4s., one of £12.16.10, and another £13.12s., which together makes £2542.12.10, which deduct from the above sum, ...............  £ 2,542 12 10

£28,280 2 5

Thus I am creditor against the executry funds to the amount of £ 28,280.2.5."
(Copy letter in pursuer's print of documents cited above p. 206, n. 109. See also ibid. as to debt due to "Mr. A. Boswell." Presumably the three other small claims were disposed of.)

At Sir Alexander's death, the papers were split between Auchinleck and Fettercairn.[119] Those at Auchinleck became the property of Sir James through his mother's purchase and subsequent gift to him, but the legal transmission of those at Fettercairn was uncertain. The creditors had first claim on the whole moveable estate, which included the Fettercairn papers. It might be said that these papers were constructively included in Lady Boswell's purchase of the contents of Auchinleck House, since Auchinleck was where they belonged and where they would have been if Forbes had not neglected to return them.

The other view was that the creditors could not have intended the sale to Lady Boswell to include an asset which they did not even know to exist. If this view were accepted, it was still the creditors, or rather their successors, who were entitled to the Fettercairn papers in 1938. This did not matter from Isham's point of view, as Sir James had himself bought out most of the other creditors. Unfortunately, neither Isham nor Buchanan grasped the true situation and both were much concerned by the possibility of a claim by the successors of the Ayrshire Banking Company. They were misled by the fact that in 1833 Sir James had transferred his rights as creditor to this bank. The document of transfer, on the face of it, gave effect to a straightforward sale at a price of £2,855.[120] To complicate matters, the Ayrshire Banking Company had been taken over in 1847 by the Western Bank of Scotland, which later crashed and was liquidated. The successor of the Western Bank was the National Bank of Scotland and a claim from this source was feared. Isham need not have worried. More recent evidence has shown that Sir James did not sell out to the Ayrshire Banking Company as appeared to be the case. He had merely borrowed from them and the document of transfer was granted by way of security for his loan.[121]

---

[119]See above pp. 201–02.

[120]Translation and conveyance by John Douglas Boswell, Esq., and Sir James Boswell, Bart., to the Ayrshire Banking Company, dated 15 and 21 October 1833 (included in pursuer's print of documents cited above). J. D. Boswell was a lawyer in Ayr who acted on Sir James's behalf in acquiring the claims of the various creditors; 79 debts totalling £23,477.18.8d were assigned in consideration of a payment to Sir James of £2,855.

[121]Testament testamentary *umquhile* Sir James Boswell, Bart., 16 March 1858, Commissariot of Ayrshire. Copy obtained by author from Messrs. David W. Shaw & Co., Ayr (see above p. 205, n. 108). This listed Sir James's estate at his death and included a full explanation of this transaction with the Ayrshire Banking Company. Reference is made to "the debt due by Sir James Boswell to the Western Bank of Scotland [successors of the Ayrshire Banking Company], in security of

As it turned out, the rights of Sir Alexander's creditors were ignored by all the claimants in 1938. Isham did not draw attention to the matter, in the belief that to do so might operate to his disadvantage.[122] Instead, he concentrated on rebutting the argument of Mrs. Vassall's trustees that the papers had passed from Sir Alexander to his two daughters. He pointed out that, although Sir James declined the succession, the will provided that he should not thereby forfeit the "Library at Auchinleck"; this phrase might be construed to include the Fettercairn papers on the ground that Sir Alexander meant his son to have *all* the papers whether he renounced the succession or not, and would certainly have included those at Fettercairn if he had known about them; if the Court rejected this, he argued that neither Janet nor Margaret could have acquired any right, as they also declined the succession when they had the chance; if *none* of the three children inherited the papers, they must have gone to Sir James's children, since the bequest in Sir Alexander's will was in favour of "James Boswell my son and the heirs of his body"; when Sir James renounced, he did so for himself only and not also for his children.[123]

A few months before his death in 1857, Sir James made a will leaving his entire property to his wife, Lady Jessie Jane Montgomery Cuninghame or Boswell.[124] As we have seen, Sir James was able to break the entail in 1852,[125] so Lady Boswell inherited not only her husband's personal estate (including such papers as belonged to him), but also the family estate of Auchinleck, now freed from the entail.

Lady Boswell continued to live at Auchinleck until her death in 1884. In her own settlement,[126] she provided that half of Auchinleck

---

which they merely hold the before mentioned assignation of debts against the Estate of Sir Alexander Boswell." Presumably the Western Bank were repaid, as there were ample funds on Sir James's death. Impressed no doubt by his father's premature and violent death, he had insured his life for just under £35,000. If Isham and Buchanan had seen this testament testamentary they would have been saved much worry and needless research.

[122]Had he known the facts as explained above, he would have realized that the opposite was the case.

[123]Whilst Isham's basic argument was that the papers passed from Sir Alexander to Sir James, it suited him equally well if they were found to have passed direct to Sir James's children as this was in any event a subsequent step in his argument.

[124]Disposition and settlement by Sir James Boswell of Auchinleck dated 25 July 1857 and registered in the Books of Council and Session on 8 January 1858.

[125]See above pp. 25–26.

[126]Trust disposition and settlement by Lady Boswell of Auchinleck dated 11 July 1873 and registered in the Books of Council and Session on 17 April 1884.

estate was to go to the trustees acting under the contract of marriage between her younger daughter, Emily, and the Honourable Richard Wogan Talbot (who later became the fifth Lord Talbot de Malahide).[127] The other half, including the mansion-house of Auchinleck, was to be held in trust for the liferent use of her elder daughter, Julia (who became Mrs. Mounsey), and on her death without issue (which happened), it was to be made over absolutely to Emily's marriage contract trustees. The moveable estate was divisible equally between Mrs. Mounsey and Lady Talbot, "excepting always the books and pictures in the Mansion of Auchinleck," which were bequeathed to Mrs. Mounsey.

Emily died in 1898 and, on her death, the one-half share of Auchinleck estate which had been vested in her marriage contract trustees passed to her son, James Boswell Talbot. The other half-share also passed to him in 1905 on the death of Mrs. Mounsey. Mrs. Mounsey left two wills.[128] The first, which was in Scottish form, bequeathed to James Boswell Talbot her nephew, "the books and pictures in Auchinleck House left to me by my late mother." The second will, in English form, confirmed the bequest to her nephew and directed her executor, after satisfying certain legacies, to realize the whole residue of her estate and to make it over to the Cumberland Infirmary.

The vital point at issue between Isham and the Infirmary was what papers, if any, were included in Lady Boswell's bequest to Mrs. Mounsey of "the books and pictures in the Mansion of Auchinleck." Isham's object was to trace all the papers, if possible, into the hands of James Boswell Talbot (who later became the sixth Lord Talbot and as whose assignee he claimed). This meant satisfying the Court that the bequest carried the papers at Fettercairn as well as those at Auchinleck, for Mrs. Mounsey in her will left to her nephew the books and pictures she had herself inherited from her mother. (She seems to have overlooked that she had sold a large part of her inheritance in the Sotheby's sale of 1893 and so could not possibly leave to her nephew what she herself had succeeded to.) Isham's argument was that the phrase "books in the Mansion of Auchinleck" meant the same thing as the "Library at Auchinleck." The library had always been regarded as a sort of family heirloom by Boswell and his descen-

---

[127]Contract of marriage dated 25 June 1873 and registered in the Books of Council and Session on 17 April 1884.

[128]Will dated 25 January 1905, and last will and testament dated 17 June 1905, which together with a codicil dated 24 June 1905 were proved and registered in the District Probate Registry of H. M. High Court of Justice at Carlisle on 24 April 1906.

dants, who, in their wills, tried to ensure that whoever succeeded to Auchinleck House, also succeeded exclusively to the library. Isham stressed that the library should be visualized as a room to which all the books and papers pertained, wherever situated at any given time. Part of the papers were at Fettercairn, but only because of the negligence of the Forbes family. Constructively, they were part of the library at Auchinleck and would have been there if Mrs. Mounsey had known about them. Unfortunately she did not, but, if she had, she would certainly have wished them to remain with the family. She disapproved of Boswell's indiscretions and the last thing she would have wanted was for any of his private papers to go to an institution such as the Infirmary, whose only interest in them would be to obtain cash through public sale.[129]

The justice of Isham's argument was obvious, but Buchanan and Wardlaw Burnet were not optimistic. They thought that the Court would look primarily at the actual wording of the bequests and would not take into account Mrs. Mounsey's probable intention, unless the wording were obscure, which it was not. Strictly interpreted, a bequest of books at Auchinleck could not possibly include papers at Fettercairn. If the Court so held, the Fettercairn papers became the property of Emily Talbot and Mrs. Mounsey in equal shares, either as part of the general moveable estate passing to them under their mother's will, or by direct succession from Sir Alexander when Sir James renounced his inheritance. This, basically, was the argument of the Cumberland Infirmary and it was a formidable one. If it succeeded, Isham would be able to establish right only to Emily Talbot's half-share; the other half would go to the Infirmary as residuary legatee of Mrs. Mounsey.

This suggested the further extremely disturbing possibility that the Cumberland Infirmary might also be entitled to half of the papers which Isham had purchased from Malahide. It all depended on whether Lady Boswell's bequest of "books" could be read to include the papers at Auchinleck, which were subsequently taken to Malahide. If not, a half-share of the Malahide papers, as well as those at Fettercairn,

---

[129]See below p. 230. Isham's arguments as contained in his condescendence and claim printed in the closed record or as later presented verbally in greater detail at the court hearing, were to some extent worked out by Buchanan, Wardlaw Burnet, and Milligan, but to a larger extent they were his own. He co-ordinated and shaped the whole presentation of his case, as to which see the next chapter. Numerous memoranda of consultations in 1938 and notes to counsel survive in S.·R. & Co.'s papers which indicate his dominant role. There are also Wardlaw Burnet's lengthy notes on which he based his speech at the hearing. These notes make it clear how much Wardlaw Burnet depended on Isham's suggestions.

passed to the Infirmary under Mrs. Mounsey's will. In previous cases, the Scottish courts had held that "books" might include manuscripts in certain circumstances, but what they would decide in the case of Lady Boswell's will was doubtful. Isham, who had purchased the papers in good faith from their ostensible owner, was probably protected, but there was an obvious risk that Lord Talbot might have to account for half the price to the Infirmary.

Fortunately Isham, on his visit to Malahide in 1937, discovered evidence which effectively blocked any such claim by the Infirmary. After Mrs. Mounsey's death in 1905, the fifth Lord Talbot purchased from her executor the entire contents of Auchinleck House, apart from the "books and pictures" specifically bequeathed to his son.[130] Thus the papers at Auchinleck passed either to James Boswell Talbot under the bequest of "books" or to his father under the purchase from the executor. In either event they became the exclusive property of James Boswell Talbot when the fifth Lord Talbot died in 1921.

THESE, THEN, WERE THE ARGUMENTS and evidence on which the Court would decide. The final line-up of claimants was Lord Clinton, Isham, the Cumberland Infirmary, Mrs. Vassall's trustees, and Mrs. Hailey. The three really crucial issues were the interpretation of Boswell's will, the transmission on the death of Sir Alexander, and the rights of the Cumberland Infirmary as Mrs. Mounsey's residuary legatee. On the first, Isham was supported by the Cumberland Infirmary and Mrs. Vassall's trustees, but opposed by Lord Clinton and Mrs. Hailey; on the second, he was again supported by the Infirmary, but opposed by Mrs. Vassall's trustees; on the third, he was in direct conflict with the Infirmary alone.

---

[130]Letter, A. N. Bowman (Mrs. Mounsey's executor) to Lord Talbot, 11 April 1906 (TFP). Bowman thanks Lord Talbot for his cheque for £1,140 "for the furniture and effects at Auchinleck purchased by you from myself as Executor of the late Mrs. Mounsey." Bowman refunds 12/6d over-remitted.

# VII

# *The Court Decides*

I SHAM returned to Edinburgh on 13 April 1938 to supervise the final preparations for the court hearing.[1]

His first concern was to put the finishing touches to his claim. The record, containing the written pleadings of the parties, still had to be closed, which gave him the opportunity to suggest final adjustments. He met Buchanan and a period of intense activity ensued. Together they worked, night after night, sifting and analysing the evidence.[2] At the end of the month, he drew up a detailed appraisal of the competing claims and suggested some important improvements to his own pleadings.[3] This was the first of a series of notes and memoranda produced for his counsel.[4] His perception of the facts and the complicated legal issues involved was remarkable. To a large extent, he dictated the presentation of his case in court. Wardlaw Burnet later remarked that the crucial arguments as to the interpretation of Boswell's will could never have been presented without Isham's "great knowledge of the subject and his skill in fastening on the available pieces of evidence."[5]

By 11 May, the last of the claims had been lodged and the record was finally closed.[6] Isham met Buchanan to discuss the soaring costs of the action and the possibility of negotiating an out-of-court set-

---

[1]Letter, Buchanan to Isham, 13 April 1938 (copy in S. R. & Co.'s papers). The date of the hearing (12 July 1938) was not fixed until some weeks later. See above p. 173.

[2]A record of these activities is preserved in the business ledger in S. R. & Co.'s papers (cited below as "S. R. & Co.'s Business Ledger").

[3]Copy in S. R. & Co.'s papers. Sent to counsel on 29 April 1938.

[4]Copies are preserved in S. R. & Co.'s papers.

[5]Opinion by J. R. Wardlaw Burnet for Isham, 21 August 1938 (copy in S. R. & Co.'s papers).

[6]See above p. 173.

tlement.[7] His financial position was grim. The trust funds, on which he depended for a large part of his income, had been mismanaged, and depressed prices on Wall Street made it difficult for him to realize capital. His investment in the Malahide papers was still unproductive, and he owed nearly $3,000 to the Viking Press because the royalties earned by his publication of the *Tour* did not cover the advances paid to him in 1930 and 1936.[8] Charles H. Bennett, co-editor of the *Tour*, wrote to him on 31 May 1938: "May I personally thank you for your assiduity in prosecuting this case? I cannot help feeling that you are doing all the work and spending all the money, while Fred[9] and I and the other American Boswellians will receive all the benefit."[10]

Buchanan and Thackrah were sympathetic. They had both begun to feel an almost personal sense of involvement, and Thackrah was worried lest Isham might decide "perhaps the game is not worth the candle."[11] By way of encouragement, they jointly offered to abate their fees by 20 per cent.[12] Even so, win or lose, Isham's bill was likely to be well beyond what he could afford. By February 1938, legal costs for preliminary work on the case came to over £1,000. This did not include all the work still to be done before the hearing or the fees payable to senior and junior counsel for appearing in court, which Buchanan estimated would total another £500.[13]

Still more worrying was the question of the costs of the Judicial Factor and the other claimants. Buchanan explained that, in an action of multiplepoinding, every claimant with a colourable claim was usually allowed his costs out of the fund *in medio;* and likewise the Judicial Factor's costs would be paid out of the property committed to his charge. The problem was that in this case the fund consisted entirely of literary manuscripts which Isham would wish to retain. This meant that if he were successful and wanted to avoid selling any of the manuscripts, he would have to pay the *entire* expense of the action himself —not only his own costs, but also those of the Judicial Factor and the four other claimants. There were, besides, his own personal expenses. Since 1936, he had been constantly on the move between

[7]Referred to in letter, Buchanan to Thackrah, 14 May 1938 (copy in S. R. & Co.'s papers).
[8]Royalty statement by the Viking Press (IFP).
[9]i.e. Pottle.
[10]Letter in IFP.
[11]Letter, Thackrah to Buchanan, 2 March 1938 (S. R. & Co.'s papers).
[12]Correspondence in S. R. & Co.'s papers.
[13]Letter, S. R. & Co. to Denton Hall & Burgin, 18 February 1938 (copy in S. R. & Co.'s papers).

America and Europe, and had already incurred expenditure of more than £2,000 on hotels and travelling.[14] By May 1938, his total outlay on the case, actual or to be incurred, was at least £4,500 (or $22,500). If the hearing ran into several days, as seemed likely, the final figure would be much higher.

There was much to be said for a general settlement out of court. If Isham could buy out *all* the other claimants on reasonable terms, he would obtain the papers for himself and save the whole costs of the hearing. It might even be worthwhile to settle with an individual claimant because this would eliminate one of the competing arguments and reduce the over-all costs. He had already discussed the possibility of a settlement with his advisers in January 1937 (when Lord Clinton and Sir Gilbert Eliott were the only other claimants).[15] He did not believe that Lord Clinton took his claim very seriously and hoped he might settle for a reasonable figure if allowed to keep the letters to Forbes and any other Forbes papers. No approach was made on either side, however, until 4 May 1938, when N. A. Pattullo, Lord Clinton's lawyer, called to see Buchanan. He asked if Isham were prepared to consider a settlement and, when Isham agreed, he wrote to Lord Clinton for instructions. Pattullo communicated his client's reply on 31 May. It was brief and uncompromising: "Lord Clinton is not prepared to make any proposition at the moment."[16]

This refusal to negotiate was annoying. Although Isham did not fear Lord Clinton's claim, he had to come to terms with him, as with the other claimants, in order to achieve the hoped-for general settlement. He decided that the best move was to get everybody round a table for discussion. Buchanan arranged a joint meeting for 28 June at the office of the Judicial Factor, but, to Isham's chagrin, the other parties refused to attend in person. Instead, they were represented by their solicitors and counsel, which meant that Isham himself could not be present. This was a pity because he, if anyone, had the personality and persuasiveness to win over the meeting. The best he could do was to write out a full statement of his views and leave Wardlaw Burnet to present them for him.[17]

His statement was an eloquent plea for the preservation of the

[14]Extracted from detailed cost statements prepared by W. L. Payne from research in IFP.

[15]See above p. 160.

[16]A record of these negotiations is contained in S. R. & Co.'s Business Ledger for May 1938.

[17]There are many and detailed references to the joint meeting in the files and Business Ledger in S. R. & Co.'s papers, and also a copy of Isham's statement presented to the meeting on his behalf by Wardlaw Burnet.

papers as a single collection which ought, in the interests of scholarship, to be united with his own collection. If the Court were to award the papers in fractions to several claimants, they might then sell their shares to dealers or collectors. In this way the collection would be irretrievably scattered. He stressed the difficulty and expense of valuing the papers for the purpose of a fair division, and warned that the costs to be borne by the successful claimants would leave little financial gain at the end of the day. His own interest derived from his great enterprise of reassembling Boswell's scattered archives and presenting them to the world in the best possible manner. He had already personally paid more than $74,500 for editorial and secretarial work on the Malahide papers, on top of which he had incurred a serious loss on the publication of the private edition. From the point of view of scholarship, public interest, and posterity, he regarded himself as the most. suitable custodian of the papers.

One wonders what would have been the result if Isham had been able to attend the meeting, along with the other claimants, in person. As it was, the chances of coming to terms were slim. The other solicitors present could only refer back to their clients, and the fortnight which remained until the hearing was insufficient to allow agreement to be reached. The meeting did serve the useful purpose, though, of bringing home to everybody the limited financial advantage which would accrue to the successful claimant, and all the solicitors agreed to make immediate estimates of their clients' costs to date.[18] These came to a total of nearly £1,200, excluding Isham's costs and the whole costs of the hearing.[19]

Isham now decided to approach each of the other claimants in turn to try to negotiate individual settlements. Counsel felt that the claim of the Cumberland Infirmary was the most dangerous and strongly advised Isham to buy them out if he could. Lord Clinton's claim had little substance, but the claims of Mrs. Hailey and Mrs. Vassall's trustees were both worth acquiring if the price were reasonable. Between 5 and 7 July, Isham and Buchanan saw the solicitors for all the other claimants. Mrs. Hailey refused to settle and the Cumberland Infirmary were not prepared to negotiate in the absence of an independent valuation which there was insufficient time to obtain. No response at all was received from Lord Clinton, but, on 8 July,

---

[18]Information from S. R. & Co.'s Business Ledger.
[19]Note with reference to expenses, June 1938 (S. R. & Co.'s papers).

Mrs. Vassall's trustees said they were ready to settle.[20] A figure of £200 plus costs was agreed and the claim was formally assigned to Isham on 13 July, the day after the hearing actually commenced.[21]

Isham's efforts to settle did not mean that his final preparations for the hearing were neglected. Between April and July, Buchanan attended more than fifty conferences and meetings, over half of them with Isham present.[22] Buchanan's widow recalls that Isham would summon her husband regularly to his hotel just as he was about to sit down to dinner, and he seldom got home before the early hours of the morning. Isham would sometimes soothe her annoyance by telephoning to invite her to his hotel for a dozen oysters and a glass of champagne.[23]

The last week before the hearing was one of hectic activity. Apart from the negotiations with the other claimants, a huge bulk of papers had to be filed, indexed, and copied for senior and junior counsel. The productions of all the other parties also had to be borrowed, noted, and copied. Numerous meetings were held to discuss the best possible presentation of the case.[24]

The hearing before Lord Stevenson commenced on the morning of Tuesday, 12 July.[25] To avoid expense, the parties agreed to admit certain facts and to accept the authenticity of certain documents without the need for a formal proof.[26] This meant that the hearing took the form of a debate on the legal issues. First to speak was J. F. Strachan, junior counsel for Lord Clinton.[27] His address took up the whole of the first day and most of the Wednesday morning session. He was followed by Milligan, who replied for Isham. Milligan spoke throughout Wednesday afternoon, the whole of Thursday, and most of Friday

[20]Information in this paragraph from entries in S. R. & Co.'s Business Ledger.

[21]Assignation by John Michael Howden, George Moir Byres and John Renshaw Gifford, as Trustees of Mrs. Margaret Amelia Boswell or Vassall in favour of Lieutenant-Colonel R. H. Isham, C. B. E., dated 13 and 14 July 1938 (S. R. & Co.'s papers).

[22]All individually recorded in S. R. & Co.'s Business Ledger.

[23]Information from Mrs. E. P. Buchanan.

[24]Recorded in S. R. & Co.'s Business Ledger.

[25]In S. R. & Co.'s papers is a photo-copy of the official minute of proceedings ("Minute of Proceedings in M. P. and Exon. Ernest Maclagan Wedderburn, D. K. S., Edinburgh (James Boswell's Judicial Factor) against the Right Hon. Charles J. R. H. S. F. Trefusis, Baron Clinton of Maxtock and Saye, and Others"). The principal document is part of the official process (i.e., file of papers) relating to the case now lodged at the Register House in Edinburgh under reference 011/1937. The minute of proceedings contains a summary of the procedure, including timings, at the court hearing.

[26]Joint minute of admissions, signed by counsel for all parties (copy in S. R. & Co.'s papers).

[27]This and the information which follows comes from the minute of proceedings cited above.

morning. Junior counsel for the Cumberland Infirmary and Mrs. Hailes both completed their addresses before the Court adjourned on Friday evening. The time allotted for the hearing had now run out and special extra sittings of the Court were arranged for Monday, 18, and Friday, 22 July, to enable senior counsel to sum up for their respective clients. The proceedings came to an end at lunch-time on the 22nd and it was then a question of waiting for Lord Stevenson to issue his judgement. This might take anything from a few days to several weeks.

If he had wished, Isham could have instructed his counsel to present the Vassall claim alongside his own as an alternative argument. Even though the two claims were inconsistent with each other, Isham stood to benefit if either succeeded. He decided, however, that this would not be to his advantage. The importance of the Vassall claim from his point of view was that it represented the only challenge to his interpretation of the transmission of the papers on the death of Sir Alexander Boswell. To have argued it might have prejudiced his own claim, under which he had at least a chance of being awarded the whole of the papers instead of only a half, as in the Vassall claim. For this reason, the Vassall claim, although never formally abandoned, was not argued at the hearing.

For four weeks, the parties remained in suspense. When Lord Stevenson issued his judgement on 14 August, Isham was staying at Dunvegan Castle on the Isle of Skye as a guest of Flora MacLeod (later Dame Flora). Buchanan cabled the news at once: the papers had been awarded to Isham and the Cumberland Infirmary in equal shares, and there were seven days within which to lodge an appeal.[28] The same day, Buchanan forwarded the full text of Lord Stevenson's opinion from which the following extracts are quoted:[29]

[28]Telegram, S. R. & Co. to Isham, 19 August 1938 (copy in S. R. & Co.'s papers).

[29]The interlocutor (i.e., judgment), dated 19 August 1938, was as follows (certified copy in S. R. & Co.'s papers):

The Lord Ordinary having considered the cause finds that the Claimant Lieut. Col. Ralph Heyward Isham is entitled to one half share of the papers in the cause in so far as these consist of Manuscripts belonging to the deceased James Boswell and the Claimants the Cumberland Infirmary entitled to the other half thereof: Continues the Cause; Grants leave to reclaim.

The cause was continued because it was still necessary to establish which of the papers comprised in the fund had belonged to JB, and which had belonged to others, such as Forbes. Other matters, such as expenses, also remained to be disposed of. "Reclaim" is simply the technical word for appeal. The interlocutor was accompanied by a long explanatory opinion (copy in S. R. & Co.'s papers) from which the quotation which follows is taken.

**LORD STEVENSON**
Judge in the Fettercairn lawsuit.

**THE COURT OF SESSION, EDINBURGH**
The building where the Fettercairn lawsuit was tried.

THE CUMBERLAND INFIRMARY
From the drawing (*c.* 1845) by William H. Nutter.

For the purpose of construing Boswell's Will I shall hold it to be established as a fact that the manuscripts and material for Boswell's publications were at Auchinleck at the date when he signed his Will; that his Journals and certain other papers necessary for the publication of "The Life" were subsequently taken to London for use in connection with these publications; that although they remained there until his death it was his intention to return them to Auchinleck when his publications were completed; and that such papers as were not required for writing "The Life" and in particular letters from his private friends were at Auchinleck at the date of his death.

Professor Pottle in his introduction to his Catalogue of Boswell papers, now in possession of Colonel Isham, states "At the time of Boswell's death they (the papers) were partly in Auchinleck and partly in London. The Journals in particular had been recovered[30] from Scotland because Boswell needed them in writing "The Life," and we have evidence in the letter of Forbes that they had never been returned." This letter is dated 14th August 1795 (No. 41 of Process). As Professor Pottle is a well known student of Boswell and has carefully perused the whole of the papers in Colonel Isham's collection I accept the above statement as an accurate account of the location of Boswell's papers at the date of his death. The only other point I think material in assisting me to interpret the Will is the fact that the last surviving literary Executor understood that all the Boswell papers were ultimately returned to Auchinleck after the death of Sir William Forbes. I assume that all Boswell's younger children were also aware of this fact. There is no evidence that they put forward any claim to the papers. . . .

Of the alternative interpretations of the Will I prefer that submitted on behalf of Colonel Isham. The expression "all manuscripts of whatever kind" is wide enough to include manuscripts of Boswell's "own composition and all letters by whomsoever they were written lying in the house of Auchinleck." It correctly describes the location of the papers at the date when the Will was signed and points to the subject matter of the gift. Was this gift recalled by the removal of the papers from Auchinleck? I do not think so. The correspondence and letters to which I have referred show that Boswell looked upon Auchinleck as the home of his archives and that he was collecting letters and papers to be placed there. Auchinleck remained his permanent home. Any

---

[30]Pottle is misquoted. The word should have been "removed," not "recovered."

documents taken to London were taken there to enable him to publish the "Life," but their permanent resting place was, I think, Auchinleck. I am therefore of opinion that the clause in the Settlement to which I have referred is habile to carry all manuscript writings left by Boswell. (Theobald on Wills, pp. 179-180).

A further difficulty arises in ascertaining what Boswell intended by the words "I leave to Sir William Forbes" and others . . . my "manuscripts to be published for the benefit of my younger children as they think fit." Did he mean in the event of there being no publication that Forbes and his co-legatees Malone and Temple were to get these documents as their own property? I do not think so. I think that these gentlemen got no beneficial gift under this clause, that they had imposed upon them a duty, namely, to publish if they thought fit. Temple died shortly after Boswell and his executors made no claim to any share of the documents. Forbes refers to receiving the papers from Alexander as "a part of that collection with the charge of examining which our late worthy friend honoured Temple you and me" (14th August 1795), and Malone uses a similar expression in his letter to Euphemia (No. 43 of process). These expressions show how these gentlemen construed the directions during their lifetime. I think they were correct in interpreting them. In particular Malone, the last survivor of the literary Executors in the letter above referred to clearly indicates that he had abandoned any right he might have had in favour of Alexander. Boswell in his Codicil leaves to Malone "the care of" his papers for writing the life of Johnson. I find no direction in the Will or Codicil which detracts from the gift of all manuscripts of whatever kind to Alexander other than a direction that the gentlemen named should publish such as they thought fit and pay the proceeds of such publication to the younger children. I certainly do not think the clause can be read as a gift of the papers to the younger children. All that is given to the younger children is the proceeds of the publication. This is made very clear from the terms of Boswell's Codicil to which I have already referred. I therefore determine that Alexander Boswell as the testator's eldest son was entitled to demand delivery of these papers from Forbes. I think it clear that Forbes received these papers or some of them from Alexander for the sole purpose of determining which of them the Literary Trustees should publish—in other words that he received them for a trust purpose. This being so in my opinion the plea of prescription[31] is not applicable.

---

[31]This disposed of Lord Clinton's alternative claim based on prescription.

If Alexander had a right to demand delivery of the papers, this right transmitted to the widow of his son James in terms of the documents to which I have already referred. In my opinion, however, it did not transmit to Mrs. Mounsey under the gift of "books in Auchinleck." It is, I think, doubtful whether "manuscripts" will pass under a gift of "books," but the manuscripts which are claimed in this case were not in Auchinleck at the date of the Settlement of James's widow or at the date of her death. The right to demand the manuscripts therefore passed equally to her two daughters as part of the residue of her estate. Lady Talbot and Mrs. Mounsey shared this right between them. Lady Talbot's share passed under her Marriage Contract to her son the present Lord Talbot, who has assigned his right thereto to Lieut. Col. Isham. Mrs. Mounsey's share passed under the residue clause of her Will. I shall therefore rank Lieut. Col. Isham and the Cumberland Infirmary equally to the fund *in medio* and meantime shall continue the case to ascertain which of the documents in dispute fall within the description "manuscripts of whatever kind lying in the house of Auchinleck."

Wardlaw Burnet advised against an appeal.[32] He feared it would expose the favourable part of Lord Stevenson's judgement to challenge without producing any better result. It would also greatly increase the costs. Isham accepted his advice and no appeal was lodged by any of the other parties.

As soon as he heard the Court's decision, Isham cabled the news to Pottle who wrote back: "My heartiest congratulations. It has been a gallant fight, and (though I never expected to say it) the judgement seems to have been fair and not too long protracted."[33] Later, when Isham was able to give him a personal account, he commented: "What an evening! I think I had better drop Boswell and begin to write *your* Biography against the day when it will be needed. In 2039 they will be publishing Pottle's *Life of Isham*, revised and enlarged by Doctor Boswell."[34]

Despite Pottle's congratulations, Isham's troubles were far from over. Lord Stevenson did not settle how the expenses of the action were to be borne; nor how the papers should be allocated as between Boswell items (awarded to Isham and the Infirmary in equal shares)

[32]Opinion for Lieut.-Col. Isham by J. R. Wardlaw Burnet, 21 August 1938 (copy in S. R. & Co.'s papers).
[33]Letter, Pottle to Isham, 22 August 1938 (IFP).
[34]Letter, Pottle to Isham, 2 January 1939 (IFP).

and Forbes items (which belonged to Lord Clinton).[35] Sooner or later, a further hearing would have to be held to deal with these matters and, until then, the papers had to remain in the custody of the Judicial Factor. The chances were that the expenses of all parties would be awarded out of the fund. This meant that Isham and the Infirmary would have to pay the entire bill between them or sell sufficient of the papers to realize the required sum. Pottle suggested that Isham should offer the Johnson letters to the Infirmary in return for the journal material and other Boswell items.[36] This did not appeal to Isham; nor did the Infirmary favour a settlement which would involve a physical division of the papers.[37] What Isham feared was that the Infirmary might insist on putting the whole collection up for sale and splitting the proceeds after settling the expenses.

It was clear that Isham would have to buy out the Infirmary. His chief problem, as always, was an acute shortage of money. He dreaded the hearing on expenses because he knew it would result in his having to produce money which he did not have. If he did succeed in making a deal with the Infirmary, it would presumably be on the basis of his relieving them of all liability for expenses; he would then have to pay the total bill of costs within a very short time or the Judicial Factor would take matters into his own hands and auction the papers.

A possible solution was to interest a university or other institution in purchasing all the papers (from both Malahide and Fettercairn) at a price which would cover the cost of buying out the Infirmary, repayment of Van Alen's loan,[38] and still leave something to set against

---

[35]Towards the end of October 1938, Buchanan arranged with Lord Clinton's solicitors that they would get Abbott to compile a list of items comprised in the fund claimed by Lord Clinton (as being Forbes rather than Boswell items). The list was received and approved by the Infirmary and by Isham before his return to America in November. It was as follows:

1. All letters from JB to Forbes. *Fettercairn Catalogue*, Nos. 1320 to 1360.
2. *Fettercairn Catalogue*, Nos. 365, 366, 373, and 381, being drafts of letters in Forbes's handwriting.
3. *Fettercairn Catalogue*, Nos. 1411 and 1414, being letters to Forbes.
4. *Fettercairn Catalogue*, No. 1430, being a copy of a letter by the Bishop of Killaloe in Forbes's handwriting.
5. *Fettercairn Catalogue*, No. 1604, being Forbes's copy of the Round Robin.

A fresh allocation was made subsequently, as to which see below p. 266.

[36]Letter, Pottle to Isham, 22 August 1938 (IFP).

[37]Intimated to Buchanan by telephone by J. & J. Galletly (the Infirmary's solicitors) on 26 October 1938 (recorded in S. R. & Co.'s Business Ledger). Some years later Isham changed his mind about parting with the SJ letters, as to which, see below p. 270.

[38]This still stood at $142,836 plus interest. See above pp. 93 and 98.

his own outlay.[39] Soon after his return to America in late November 1938, he made overtures to Bernard Knollenberg of Yale and Wm. A. Jackson of Harvard. Jackson wrote in January 1939[40] to say that Harvard was "sincerely interested" in the collection. Knollenberg was also enthusiastic—so much so that Pottle was reluctant to negotiate with any other librarian. In February 1939, he wrote to Isham, who had suggested he might approach Meikle of the National Library of Scotland: "I have not written to Meikle because Knollenberg took up the matter so vigorously that I thought it would hardly seem decent if I were trying to sell the Papers to another Librarian. . . . Knollenberg will do what can be done . . . he is a man of great address and resourcefulness."[41] Serious negotiations were therefore confined to Yale. Knollenberg confirmed Yale's definite interest, but said he would be unable to interest any donor until Isham had secured clear title to the Fettercairn papers.[42]

Meanwhile, in Scotland, a serious new difficulty was created by the unexpected intervention of Abbott into the proceedings. Abbott was in the unhappy position of having discovered the papers in the first place, spent a vast amount of time working on them in anticipation of editing them for publication, and having received no payment for his labours. Lord Clinton did contribute £225 to cover the wages of one copyist, but Abbott himself was paid nothing.[43] In the early 1930s, he had forged ahead with his work, content to leave the questions of title and copyright to Chapman and Lord Clinton. Now, he found himself without the papers and without any remuneration.

Lord Clinton decided to ask the Court for reimbursement of his outlay of £225 in addition to his ordinary costs as a claimant in the action.[44] Much more serious for Isham, in his financial predicament, was Abbott's decision to claim a very substantial sum as personal

[39]£39,235 on his purchases from Lord Talbot (see above p. 97, n. 37), not to speak of publishing and editorial costs and other expenditure besides.

[40]Letter, W. A. Jackson to Isham, 13 January 1939 (IFP).

[41]Letter, Pottle to Isham, 22 February 1939 (IFP). Isham did however speak to Meikle by telephone a week or two later and on 10 March 1939 he met James Maclehose, Chairman of the Trustees of the National Library of Scotland, for lunch in London (letter, Maclehose to Isham, 9 March 1939 [IFP]). Their meeting did not lead to any serious negotiations.

[42]Reported in letter, Pottle to Isham, 18 December 1939 (IFP).

[43]Memorial for Judicial Factor for opinion of counsel, 1939 (copy in S. R. & Co.'s papers).

[44]At a meeting between Buchanan and Pattullo (Lord Clinton's lawyer) on 31 January 1939, the latter said Lord Clinton would be claiming reimbursement of the £225 as well as his expenses as a claimant (S. R. & Co.'s Business Ledger). In fact, Lord Clinton did not press this when the costs were finally dealt with. See below p. 273.

remuneration for his work. In February 1939, his lawyer, Mr. J. C. Scott, called on Buchanan and presented him with a "Note of Expenses" according to which Abbott had spent not less than 4,000 hours working on the papers between November 1930 and March 1936.[45] £1,000 was proposed as a fee plus £80 for out-of-pocket expenses. This was quite unexpected because in the agreement between the Judicial Factor, Abbott, and the Oxford University Press, Abbott had agreed to publication of his catalogue "without any payment to him in virtue of royalties or otherwise," and the Press had agreed to bear the whole cost of publication.[46] On 8 February, Buchanan cabled the news to Isham who was sufficiently worried to set sail for Europe four days later, although this meant leaving his personal affairs in America at a most awkward time.

One may sympathize with Abbott's point of view, but his action undoubtedly caused great difficulty for Isham. Isham saw no reason why he should pay anything for work he had never commissioned. He had his own expert in Pottle, whom he would obviously have employed in preference to Abbott if he had had any say in the matter. Abbott after all was not a Boswellian specialist. Isham consulted Pottle, who wrote back: "Any man who embarks on a long piece of work without an assurance from someone that he will be paid must be working for something besides money."[47] Isham therefore firmly refused to contribute anything towards a fee for Abbott.

Abbott's reaction was to threaten suit for his remuneration against the Judicial Factor, and also against Isham and the Cumberland Infirmary for their interest as successful claimants.[48] His solicitors warned that they would oppose any attempt to wind up the multiplepoinding proceedings until the question of his fee had been settled. A summons was actually prepared and sent in draft to Wedderburn, who persuaded Abbott to delay service until he had had an opportunity to discuss the matter with the Accountant of Court and to obtain counsel's opinion.[49] Wedderburn took the advice of R. P. Morison, K.C., one of the foremost Scottish advocates. Morison could find no legal basis

[45]Recorded in S. R. & Co.'s Business Ledger. The "Note of Expenses" is in S. R. & Co.'s papers.

[46]"Minute of Agreement between Ernest Maclagan Wedderburn and Others re compiling, editing and publishing Catalogue of papers", 30 October and 4 and 6 November 1936 (copy in S. R. & Co.'s papers).

[47]Letter, Pottle to Isham, 26 May 1939 (IFP).

[48]Information in letter from Mackenzie & Kermack to Steedman Ramage & Co., 6 May 1939 (S. R. & Co.'s papers).

[49]Ibid. A copy of the condescendence relative to the summons is in S. R. & Co.'s papers.

for Abbott's claim against Wedderburn and doubted whether he could succeed against Isham or the Infirmary either. Morison advised that further procedure in the multiplepoinding should be stayed until Abbott's claim was disposed of and, if he *did* sue, Wedderburn should insist on Isham and the Infirmary granting an indemnity against the costs of defending the action.[50]

There matters rested for some time. Weeks and then months passed by without Abbott serving his summons, but the threat remained. Neither Isham nor the Infirmary dared agree to a hearing on expenses in case this should provoke Abbott into action; Wedderburn could not wind up the Judicial Factory until Abbott had been dealt with; and negotiations between Isham and the Infirmary were impeded because neither side knew how much it might cost to settle with Abbott nor how the Court would award expenses at the end of the day. In March 1939, Buchanan's latest estimate of the legal costs of all parties, plus the full amount of Abbott's claim, was £5,700.[51] This stood to be considerably reduced if Abbott's claim failed or was withdrawn, or if Lord Stevenson could be persuaded to make the unsuccessful parties to the action responsible for their own costs. The Infirmary were reluctant to come to terms with Isham until they knew how these things would work out. Everyone, therefore, waited to see what Abbott would do, and Abbott did nothing, except to leave his threat dangling. The legal merits of his claim may have been negligible, but its nuisance value could hardly have been greater.

In the meantime, Isham made use of his presence in Britain to tackle the problem of acquiring the share of the papers awarded to the Infirmary. He had good reason to hope that they would be sympathetic. He had told them of their possible claim in the first place. He had given them free access to all his evidence and, but for his researches, their claim could never have been properly stated. To a large extent, they had simply adopted his arguments. Lord Stevenson's decision, though doubtless sound from a legal point of view, was grotesquely at variance with Mrs. Mounsey's probable wishes. The Infirmary had no moral right to any share of the papers: they were simply benefitting from the carelessness of the Forbes family a hundred years earlier and Mrs. Mounsey's ignorance when she made her will.

[50]Memorial for Judicial Factor for opinion of counsel with opinion of R. P. Morison, dated 27 June 1939, attached (copy in S. R. & Co.'s papers).
[51]Copy estimate in S. R. & Co.'s papers.

It is interesting to note the following comment from a contemporary periodical:

> The literal carrying-out of the judgement might involve difficulties reminiscent of the Court of King Solomon, but that may be a matter of arrangement. What strikes the literary observer is the irony of the situation: here are the private papers of James Boswell going to benefit an institution in a town associated with the most painful and humiliating incidents of his life, and that by the will of one who not only was unconscious of their existence, but who, during her lifetime, did everything she could to prevent access to the repositories of one who, far from being regarded as a literary genius, was considered simply to be a blot on the Boswell family escutcheon.[52]

The Infirmary also had Isham to thank for enhancing the pecuniary value of the Fettercairn papers. To a large extent, he had created the market for Boswelliana by the way in which he had dealt with the Malahide collection. But despite this enhanced value, if the Infirmary were to retain their share, they might find themselves with very little profit after paying their own costs and half the costs of all the other parties. They might also be expected to pay regard to public interest, which made it highly desirable that the Fettercairn papers and those from Malahide should be reunited. All these considerations led Isham to hope that the Infirmary would be friendly and would agree to sell their share to him for a modest sum, provided he undertook to keep them clear of expenses.

Their reaction to his approach could not have been more daunting. His request for a meeting with the Infirmary's governing body was met with a refusal to see him or to enter into any direct discussions. All negotiations, he was told, must be conducted through the medium of solicitors. The following correspondence[53] is worth quoting because it shows the efforts which Isham made and the manner in which he was treated. On 6 March 1939, he wrote to Mr. J. Rippier, the Secretary of the Infirmary:

Dear Mr. Rippier,
     In September of last year I happened to express to Mrs.

---

[52]*The National Review*, vol. III, No. 669, November 1938, p. 659, from "Scottish Notes," by "Theages." The writer correctly points out the irony of the situation, although his characterization of Mrs. Mounsey rests mainly on inference.

[53]Copies of the correspondence are in S. R. & Co.'s papers.

A. Thomson of Carlisle my view that, the Court having found your Institution and myself equally entitled to the Papers of James Boswell found in Fettercairn House, a meeting should be held between the Governing body of your Institution and myself to discuss, and, so far as possible, resolve generally matters relating to the fund *in medio* in which we found ourselves in the position of having a mutual and equal interest.

Mrs. Thomson kindly undertook to convey my expression to you and this led to one or two telephone conversations between us, in which I expressed, not only my willingness to go to Carlisle to confer with any or all the Members of your Governing Body, but also my hope that they would be pleased to receive me. Particularly did I express myself as believing that both speed and economy would be served by a meeting of the Principals to discuss the purely extra-judicial problems: but in the end I was advised that all matters were in the hands of your Solicitors.

The news that such a meeting could not be arranged I received with both disappointment and chagrin. Disappointment because I felt that such a meeting was necessary and desirable in our joint interests; chagrin because I had allowed myself to believe that, in as much as it was I who in the first instance instructed my Solicitors to advise you of the possibility of your having a claim, and as also it was I upon whose shoulders your Case rested down to the Will of Mrs. Mounsey, your Governing Body would have been pleased, not to say anxious, to meet me at any time.

I returned to America in November, having some weeks before notified your Solicitors of my necessity to do so. On the 8th of February of this year I received a cable from my Solicitors here to the effect that the Solicitors of Professor Abbott had advised them that he was about to lodge a large claim against the Papers. Although I was much involved in my American matters at that time, I felt it necessary to come here immediately with a view to examining this serious matter. Since my arrival here I find that my Solicitors have been notified (as well as the Judicial Factor), that Professor Abbott's claim is for "recompense" and that it is to be for £1,000. In this connection I would point out that Lord Clinton has already paid Professor Abbott £225, which he has naturally put in as part claim against the fund *in medio*.

In view of this turn of events I asked my Solicitors to prepare for me an approximate estimate of the total legal expenses incurred to date in this matter. It amounts to £4,445. To this they add as possible future expenses, Professor Abbott's claim, £1,000; expenses of litigating such claim, should that be necessary,

£250—making a total of £5,695. On top of this, they point out that there will be additional costs and expenses connected with the final settlement.

Another thing; as regards the sale of the Papers, either by Auction or in any other way, it would first be necessary to have an appraisal made of them. To appraise Manuscripts it is necessary for an expert to read through each one, for the reason that the value of a Manuscript depends, to the greatest degree, upon its contents. It is also necessary that a possible purchaser should be provided with sufficient quotations of the most important parts of each Manuscript to enable him to judge and bid its sound value. For example, should a letter be described in a Catalogue as follows:— "Edmund Burke. An interesting letter touching on American affairs." How, by such an inadequate description could a purchaser form any idea of the letter's value, or decide how much to bid? Is the letter worth five shillings, or five pounds? He cannot know, and I think that in these days he would be conservative in his bid.

Such an appraisal, which is, I assure you, absolutely necessary, would be—if made by any of the few men capable of doing it—a very expensive affair. As I say, pre-requisite to his appraisal would be his reading of every and all of the Manuscripts. A study of the Fettercairn House Catalogue convinces me that this could not be done by anyone in less than four months full time. I believe that no man with the requisite knowledge of Eighteenth Century writings and their present-day values could be persuaded to go to Aberdeen and complete this job for less than £1,000. For my part, I think the Court—and Scholars generally—will agree that I am as knowledgeable as anyone in matters concerning the value of Eighteenth Century writings, since I have devoted over twenty years of my life to their study and acquisition. I would not therefore expect to be required to shoulder any of the expenses of an Appraiser whom your lack of knowledge of these things might make it necessary for you to employ.

From the above, the enormous expense already entailed in this matter, as well as that which appears on the horizon, may be seen. I see also, all too clearly, the unfortunate situation into which you and I are falling, for I have perceived with alarm the incredible collapse of prices fetched by Manuscripts of this kind, both in London and New York, during the past number of years.

During the past six months particularly have prices gone to pieces. I should like to give you an example that I heard from the famous dealer, Dr. Rosenbach, a few weeks ago. A rare book with much annotation in the handwriting of Dr. Benjamin Franklin, came up for sale some years ago. Dr. Rosenbach was the under-bidder at $6,800: the book sold for $6,900. About two months ago this book again came up for auction at the Hearst Sale. Dr. Rosenbach was commissioned to bid for it up to $6,000. The book was knocked down to him for $800.

I very seriously doubt that if the Fettercairn House Papers were sold by auction to-day, they would bring, after deducting selling charges, a sum equal to that already involved in their acquisition. It is for this reason that I make bold to write you this letter, which I presume neither your generous-mindedness nor my previous actions in this case in your interest, nor my reputation as a patron of Scholarship, can permit you to misinterpret.

If I do not dare use the words of Mr. Chamberlain and say "I intend to come to see you," at least I may say that I could *wish* to do so, for it seems to me that we have arrived at such a point of expenses that if we continue with Lawyers and Hearings we shall find, in the end, that our victory is very hollow indeed. In fact, if the expenses already incurred should appreciably increase, I may find myself unable to meet my share of them and would, in that case, be forced to decline to take up the interest in the Papers which the Court has awarded me.

I cannot see that a meeting between your Executive Body and myself would involve us in the least. On the other hand, there must be many questions which they would like to put to me, to which my replies might be helpful. If I had indefinite time at my disposal, I should perhaps be inclined to let matters drag on, take they ever so long, but as my home is in America, and the matters which urgently claim me are there, I find it necessary to depart from this Country in, at most, ten days' time.

As I do not see a prospect of my being able to return before some long time (perhaps a year) I presume therefore to suggest that you convey copies of this letter to the authoritative Member or Members of your Governing Body immediately, with a view to ascertaining if it will be agreeable for them to meet me.

I plan to stop in Carlisle on Wednesday of this week on my way to London, and could be located there at the house of Mr. and Mrs. Thomson.

Rippier passed on Isham's letter to Mr. C. H. Allan Hodgson, Chairman of the Infirmary, who wrote back on 9 March:

Dear Sir,
      Your letter of the 6th instant, addressed to the Secretary of the Cumberland Infirmary, has been passed to me, as Chair-

man, for consideration and I have given the same careful perusal.

Before, however, going any further in the matter I, of course, naturally feel that the correct procedure would be that you, through your agents, should communicate with our agents and they would then deal with the matter in the ordinary way.

I cannot ascertain from your letter exactly what is the purpose of your request for a meeting with my Board without the intervention of the usual agents, nor do I gather from your letter what are the specific matters which you propose should be discussed at that meeting. It may probably be my inability to grasp the situation accurately, because of course you know far more about this matter than I do, but if you would be good enough to write me and give me some information as to the particular matters which would form the subject of discussion, I have no doubt my Board would give it careful consideration.

Isham's reply to Hodgson, dated 15 March, brought the correspondence to an end:

Dear Sir,

Your letter of the 9th March has reached me here and I note that you have carefully perused my letter of the 6th instant, addressed to the Secretary of your Institution.

You state that you "naturally feel that the correct procedure would be that you, through your Agents, should communicate with our Agents and they would then deal with the matter in the ordinary way." You also say that you cannot ascertain from my letter "exactly what is the purpose of your request for a meeting with my Board," and you ask me to inform you, "as to the particular matters which would form the subject of discussion."

The matters which I had deemed desirable for discussion between us are not legal and are, I venture to suggest, sufficiently indicated in my letter. And, surely, looking to the great expense which has already been involved in the legal costs, it is not only natural but desirable in the interests of the Infirmary and myself alike, that these matters should be discussed between us without incurring the, to my mind, unnecessary expense and delay occasioned by the intervention of solicitors.

If I attempted to achieve some progress in this matter in a direct manner and not in what you call "the ordinary way," I did it for reasons already indicated, and for the further reason that I did not see how such an extraordinary matter could be dealt with satisfactorily in "the ordinary way"; for it seems to me that our problem is, as was Solomon's, to divide the baby.

I am sure that in a case of this nature concerning, as it does, not only your Institution and myself, but also the World of

Scholarship, you would not have failed to have had copies of my letter, or at least the contents thereof, conveyed to your Board, and I presume, therefore, that the terms of your letter are an expression of their feelings; in which case I have no more to say.

Although upset by what he thought to be the Infirmary's inconsiderate attitude, Isham realized that sooner or later he would have to come to terms with them. He travelled to Edinburgh to see Buchanan and asked him to negotiate with the Infirmary's Scottish solicitors, Messrs. J. & J. Galletly. This firm thought that the Infirmary would favour a settlement and asked Isham to make a proposition. Isham instructed Buchanan to offer £800, plus all expenses. On 22 March, J. & J. Galletly telephoned Buchanan with the Infirmary's counter-proposition. They wanted for their share of the papers a sum equal to half the difference between the ascertained costs of all parties and £10,000. On the basis of Buchanan's latest estimate of costs, this meant a price of between £2,000 and £3,000; and in addition Isham was to pay the costs of all parties, including the Infirmary, and to relieve the Infirmary of all liability to any of the other parties. The Infirmary's figure of £10,000 was presumably a completely arbitrary one as they had had no chance to make a proper appraisal of the papers. On Isham's instructions, Buchanan informed J. & J. Galletly that the Infirmary's terms were so much in excess of Isham's proposal, or indeed any proposal he could make, that they did not offer a basis for further discussion.[54]

A hearing of the Court to deal with the question of expenses would normally have been held soon after Lord Stevenson issued his judgement; but, for some reason, the other parties did not press the matter until early in 1939. Isham was happy enough to postpone the hearing as long as possible, or at any rate until he could raise some money. It also suited him that the Infirmary should be apprehensive of having to pay half the costs of the Judicial Factor and the unsuccessful claimants. At the beginning of February 1939,[55] Buchanan reported that he could not obtain any further postponement, and Isham cabled back from America:

Please strongly represent to Court the injustice of Boswell's heirs being put to great expense at this time to obtain what has always

---

[54]Information in this paragraph from fully recorded details in S. R. & Co.'s Business Ledger.
[55]Cable, Buchanan to Isham, 1 February 1939 (copy in S. R. & Co.'s papers).

been theirs by right and what they have been for generations deprived of by the negligence of Forbes. . . . Clinton should be denied costs of his unjustified claim and should be made to pay costs entailed by heirs to obtain that portion of their inheritance which Forbes as executor and trustee failed to deliver.[56]

The date fixed for the hearing was 9 February,[57] but, with only three days to go, Abbott intimated his claim.[58] His unexpected intervention enabled Buchanan, with the support of the Infirmary's solicitors, to postpone the hearing until 17 February.[59] It was again postponed until 22 March to allow Wedderburn time to consider the situation;[60] for Abbott, as mentioned, had warned that he would try to delay the final decree until his claim had been settled.[61] On 22 March, Lord Stevenson was ill and the hearing had to be put off yet again.[62] He was still unfit at the start of the Court's summer session and unlikely to return to his duties before the autumn. Buchanan thought that the hearing should wait until then because it would be unwise to ask another judge to deal with the matter who was not familiar with the intricacies of the case.[63]

Isham returned to America in May 1939, having achieved little or nothing by his visit.[64] During the summer months, Buchanan, along with the solicitors for the Infirmary and the Judicial Factor, gave much anxious thought to the problem of Abbott's claim.[65] At the beginning of August, Abbott intimated, through his solicitors, that unless a satisfactory proposal for settlement of his remuneration was made before the end of September, he would sue not only the Judicial Factor but also Isham and the Infirmary for their interests as successful claimants.[66] Counsel advised that Abbott had little chance of winning his

[56]Cable, Isham to Buchanan, 8 February 1939 (S. R. & Co.'s papers).

[57]Cable, Buchanan to Isham, 31 January 1939 (copy in S. R. & Co.'s papers).

[58]He intimated it for the first time on 6 February 1939. (See above p. 228.) Ironically, his intervention meant a temporary reprieve for Isham on the embarrassing question of expenses.

[59]Letter, Buchanan to Thackrah, 13 February 1939 (copy in S. R. & Co.'s papers).

[60]Letter, Buchanan to Isham, 9 March 1939 (copy in S. R. & Co.'s papers).

[61]See above p. 228.

[62]Letter, Buchanan to Isham, 10 April 1939 (copy in S. R. & Co.'s papers).

[63]Letter, Buchanan to Isham, 15 May 1939 (copy in S. R. & Co.'s papers).

[64]From 8 May 1939, Buchanan's letters are addressed to him in New York (correspondence in S. R. & Co.'s papers).

[65]Many meetings recorded in S. R. & Co.'s Business Ledger and much correspondence on their files.

[66]Reported in letter, Buchanan to Isham, 22 August 1939 (copy in S. R. & Co.'s papers).

case, but Wedderburn said that he would only defend the action if Isham and the Infirmary agreed to bear his whole costs.[67] Buchanan sent Isham a full report on 22 August and recommended that Isham should join with the Infirmary in meeting the costs of the defence.[68]

Only a few days later, the outbreak of war between Britain and Germany diverted everybody's attention to much more serious problems. It gave Isham an excuse for not replying to Buchanan's letter. By mid-October, Abbott had still not served his threatened summons and Buchanan cabled Isham to say that Lord Stevenson was at last fit to deal with the question of expenses.[69] Isham replied with a long letter which carefully avoided giving Buchanan any positive instructions.[70] It is worth quoting from this at length because it helps to explain Isham's withdrawal during the war years and why so little progress was made during this period to bring the Fettercairn case to a conclusion:

Dear Eric:
As you know I always felt that war was inevitable—yet now that it has come I can scarcely believe it. I feel as though the foundations had been knocked from under life and from under me. Quite frankly, I find myself without much interest in anything and with little ability to concentrate. I want so much to be doing something to help, but there seems to be nothing I can do at the moment.

The regulations made since the war by our Secretary of State have invalidated all American passports, and it is impossible to get a passport to go to any belligerent country unless one can prove an almost vital necessity for so doing. The regulations also impose severe penalties on any American joining a belligerent army so it is no longer just a question of losing one's citizenship, as one did in the last war. So I am stuck and I don't like it.

I have recently been down to Washington to offer my services to the Government here. I do think that my experience would be valuable to them here, particularly in the direction of *contra espionage*. I am praying that they will see fit to use me.

Regarding the Boswell business—of course the war makes the final solution seem much farther away and much more difficult

[67]Ibid. Counsel was R. P. Morison, K. C., whose opinion is cited above p. 229, n. 50.
[68]Ibid.
[69]Cable, Buchanan to Isham, 12 October 1939 (copy in S. R. & Co.'s papers).
[70]Letter, Isham to Buchanan, 24 October 1939 (S. R. & Co.'s papers).

than ever. Even if I gained my share of them physically, it is questionable if I should risk them on the seas to get here, what with submarines and mines drifting about. In the meantime, the publication of my own papers continues to be held up, which deprives my publisher and myself of the returns that would come to us therefrom. . . .

Upon my return from Washington, I received your cable about proceeding with the expense hearing. It seems to me that the Abbott matter ought to be disposed of prior to this, for the cost of the manuscripts cannot be established until we are through with Abbott and know the expenses incurred by dealing with him.

If the trustees of the infirmary knew of my willingness to deal with them I think they would be much annoyed that the brusque non-co-operative attitude of their Chairman had prevented this, for they must know that the war has greatly decreased people's interest in Mr. Boswell and his circle, and I think it will be a long time before the world will be sufficiently peaceful and calm to regain an active interest in Eighteenth Century literature. These considerations, of course, enormously affect the value of the manuscripts themselves. I hate to think what they would bring today if sold by auction. . . .

Business here has improved in some lines, such as steel, but generally speaking, it is about the same as it was, which is to say rotten.

God bless you, and when you write, give me some news of yourself and your family. I think of you with great affection.

Yours, ever

Ralph H. Isham

# VIII

# *"Headaches and Heartaches"* 1

T HE war years were sad and difficult ones for Isham. In June 1937, he had married for the third time. This marriage, to Christine Viscountess Churchill,[2] had failed almost at once and had ended in divorce at Reno in 1938. Isham now lived a lonely existence in a New York hotel,[3] frustrated by his inability to play an active part in the war (as he had done with such distinction in 1914–18). He offered his services to the American government, but was refused. His sons by his second marriage, Heyward and Jonathan, were away from him most of the time at school and college. His much-loved daughter, Samantha, child of his first marriage,[4] died tragically in the summer of 1941, leaving two children. For the time being, his characteristic energy and resilience deserted him.

Buchanan and Burgin[5] made repeated efforts to get his instructions so that progress could be made towards completing the Fettercairn case, but, for the most part, he did not reply to their cables or letters. He was probably deterred by Buchanan's warning that any resumption of activity would precipitate the date on which he would have to provide further substantial funds.

In March 1940, he reopened the negotiations with Knollenberg

---

[1]Quotation from Isham letter cited below p. 262, n. 100.
[2]Widow of the first Viscount Churchill.
[3]The Hotel Gladstone, 114 East Fifty-Second Street, New York.
[4]To Miss Marion Gaynor, daughter of Mayor William J. Gaynor.
[5]Dr. E. Leslie Burgin, of Messrs. Denton Hall & Burgin, Isham's London solicitors. Thackrah was called up for military service with the Durham Light Infantry and Burgin took over the handling of Isham's affairs.

for the sale of the papers to Yale. He estimated that £5,000 would be sufficient to enable him to buy out the Infirmary and clear all the costs. Pottle advised Knollenberg that this figure was reasonable, and Knollenberg invited Isham to make a definite offer; he would then see if the necessary money could be raised. Isham cabled Buchanan asking him to find out unofficially what the Infirmary would accept for their share of the papers if they were relieved of all liability for costs, Abbott's claim, and war risks.[6] Buchanan had difficulty in getting a definite figure. The Infirmary's solicitors indicated that their clients would not consider anything less than £1,000, but they would not commit themselves to this amount.[7] Unfortunately the possibility of a deal with the Infirmary at such a favourable price was not followed up and the negotiations with Yale came to nothing.

Meanwhile, Isham's financial position continued to deteriorate. His suit against his family trustees dragged on and his trust income was reduced by $500 a month from August 1940.[8] He had little hope of finding outside financial backing because of the uncertain economic climate and because of the massive $142,836 already invested in the papers by Van Alen.[9] Van Alen was still patiently waiting for a return on his investment. In December 1940, Isham wrote to Flora MacLeod in Skye: "I have not let this at all affect the boys. My own belt I have tightened gladly. Now Yale have expressed a desire to buy the papers, but of course I am hamstrung because the Fettercairn House papers are still in Aberdeen and undivided. It does seem as though fate were being pretty rough on me, but I try to remember that fate is being pretty rough on a large part of the world these days."[10]

Fate was soon to deal with him even more roughly. On 10 January 1941, a cable arrived from Burgin:

Long and curious letter received Joyce Talbot reporting existence many further originals your claims to which this lady seems to ignore. . . .[11]

[6]Cable, Isham to Buchanan, 1 May 1940 (S. R. & Co.'s papers).
[7]Letter, Buchanan to Isham, 15 July 1940 (copy in S. R. & Co.'s papers).
[8]Letter, Isham to Flora MacLeod, 17 December 1940 (copy in IFP).
[9]See above pp. 93 and 98.
[10]Letter of 17 December 1940, cited above.
[11]Cable, Burgin to Isham, 10 January 1941 (IFP).

There was a horrid similarity to the cable from Chapman which had announced the Fettercairn discovery in 1936, and an equally maddening lack of information. What could Lady Talbot possibly have found? In 1937, Isham had personally scoured Malahide from cellar to attic, and he was confident that the papers which he then found were the last remnants of Boswell's archives there.[12] He had specially mentioned to Lady Talbot certain items which Boswell was known to have preserved and which had never come to light, notably the letters from Garrick. He had asked if there were no places, however unlikely, where these might be found, and he referred to the odd corners where Abbott had made some of his most important finds at Fettercairn; but she had assured him that there was nowhere else to search.[13]

Isham cabled back to Burgin at once for more information, and Burgin replied:

> Her Ladyship announces discovery six letters from Garrick correspondence with Temple with Biographer's children with John Johnston and complete manuscript of Life except pages already transferred to you. She suggests sale of your portion and hers for benefit air raid victims in Ayrshire but does not refer your claim under Agreement 21st August 1927. . . .[14]

A few days later, Burgin despatched a copy of Lady Talbot's letter.[15] She explained that, in December 1939, Malahide Parish Council had requested that a loft in one of the farmyard buildings should be cleared for use as an emergency grain store. The loft was tightly packed with old furniture which had never been disturbed during her time at Malahide. A new staircase had to be erected down which the furniture could be carried and the job was not tackled until October 1940. After several men had spent a full day clearing the lumber, two large packing cases[16] were discovered in the corner furthest from the door. Both

[12]See above p. 162.
[13]Letter, Isham to Lady Talbot, 5 March 1942 (IFP).
[14]Isham's cable is dated 10 January 1941 and Burgin's reply cable 12 January 1941 (IFP).
[15]Lady Talbot's letter (copy in TFP) is dated 17 October 1940, but Burgin did not forward it to Isham until 15 January 1941 (date of his covering letter in IFP). Burgin had delayed because Thackrah was serving in the army and Burgin wanted to discuss the matter with him on his next leave.
[16]The reference to "two large packing cases" is interesting. It will be remembered that when Tinker visited Malahide in 1925, Lady Talbot told him there were two cases of papers from Auchinleck which had never been opened since their arrival in Ireland (see above p. 53). Could

THE GRAIN LOFT AT MALAHIDE

were inaccessible until the loft had been cleared. One case was stuffed full of Boswell papers and the other contained papers of Sir Alexander Boswell's time. The boxes were labelled in the handwriting of the late Isabel Lady Talbot (the fifth Lord Talbot's second wife) and some of the manuscripts were wrapped in newspapers of 1917. Lady Talbot thought it likely that the papers had been packed by the late Lady Talbot when the last of the effects were moved from Auchinleck and that the boxes had been pushed out of the way at Malahide without anyone bothering to unpack them or even being aware of their contents.

Lady Talbot said she was keeping the discovery completely secret and was going through the newly found manuscripts as time permitted. She assured Isham that she would give him any portions of the journals, but so far only one small bundle had turned up. She confessed her embarrassment at the discovery of the rest of the manuscript of the *Life* and suggested that Isham might restore his pages and join with her in presenting the whole manuscript to be sold for the benefit of air-raid victims in Ayrshire.[17]

Isham was stunned by the news. He still had to find the money needed to obtain possession of the Fettercairn papers, and now he was faced with having to acquire a further mass of papers essential for the completeness of his collection. It was a cruel situation and unfortunately, in his agitation and dismay, he reacted in a way which made friendly negotiations with Lady Talbot impossible. He cabled back to Burgin:

Reference cable take immediately any necessary steps to take possession of papers my name under 1927 agreement plus written representations on occasion of 1930 discovery and verbally to us 1936 that no additional papers could remain in castle. Price paid for pages Life and Hebrides Tour based on 1930 assurance which free delivery of items personally discovered 1936 confirmed. . . . If necessary put Talbot on notice I will contest any

---

these be the same two cases? Lady Talbot assures me that she has no recollection of mentioning two unopened cases to Tinker. Since he reported the fact in a letter written so soon after the event, she supposes she must have said something. She can only assume that she was prompted at the time by the butler or some other member of the staff who knew of the arrival of the cases at Malahide. At any event, by the time Isham appeared on the scene, she had completely forgotten about the two unopened cases, if she ever knew of their existence. The 1940 grain loft discovery came as a complete surprise to her.

[17]She did not of course know that this was impossible because of his sales to Rosenbach. (See below p. 252, n. 64.)

sale or other disposition. Have letters photostated sending copies several mails. Send originals air mail small lots. Glad contribute 1,000 guineas maximum joint name Ayrshire victims. . . .[18]

Meanwhile Burgin had acted on his own initiative. Without writing for Isham's instructions, he had served notice on Messrs. A. J. & A. Robinson, Lady Talbot's Dublin solicitors, formally reserving any rights which Isham might have in the new papers.[19]

Isham and Burgin both made serious tactical errors in dealing with the situation. Lady Talbot, in her letter was friendly and sympathetic to Isham's difficulties. The new discovery was not her fault even if her suggested sale of the manuscript of the *Life* could hardly be expected to appeal to Isham. True, she might have thought of searching the outbuildings in 1937, but so for that matter might Isham.[20] The legal effect of the 1927 agreement had already been scrutinized and it was extremely doubtful whether it covered future finds; otherwise Isham would not have had to pay for the croquet box papers in 1930. The papers which he discovered in 1937 were handed to him by the Talbots as a *gift* and not because they recognized he had any legal right to them. Isham had to come to terms with Lady Talbot over the 1940 find, and the way was open for him to do so on a friendly basis. The worst possible approach was to antagonize her by intimating to her solicitors a claim which was probably without foundation and threatening court action to enforce it. Messrs. Robinson replied to Burgin repudiating all claims by Isham to the new papers, other than journal material. They referred to Isham's own breach of faith in failing to respect his undertaking as to censorship and added that the Talbots resented the suggestion that they had in any way overlooked his claims.[21]

On receiving Isham's cable, Burgin sent a copy to Buchanan and asked him to proceed at once with "the necessary action."[22] Buchanan was more cautious. He advised that the legal basis of Isham's claim would have to be established and that in any event the Talbots were

---

[18]Cable, Isham to Burgin, 22 January 1941. Copy in S. R. & Co.'s papers sent with letter, Denton Hall & Burgin to Steedman Ramage & Co., same date.

[19]By cable dated 14 January 1941 and letter dated 15 January 1941 (copies in TFP).

[20]The previous discovery at Malahide had of course been in 1937, not 1936 as stated by Isham in his cable. See above pp. 161–62.

[21]Letter, A. J. & A. Robinson to Denton Hall & Burgin, 30 January 1941 (copy in S. R. & Co.'s papers).

[22]Letter dated 29 January 1941 (S. R. & Co.'s papers).

not subject to the jurisdiction of the Scottish Courts. This meant that any proceedings would have to be raised in Eire.[23] Burgin travelled to Edinburgh for a conference with Buchanan and Wardlaw Burnet on 8 February 1941. The whole matter was considered in detail and the conclusion was that Isham had no enforceable claim on the new papers unless he could produce additional evidence.[24]

The Fettercairn case was also discussed. Early in January, Isham had again asked Buchanan to ascertain a definite figure which the Infirmary would accept for their share of the papers[25] and the Infirmary's solicitors had confirmed their earlier tentative figure of £1,000 plus legal costs estimated at about £400.[26] It was now decided, however, that it would be unwise to continue negotiations with the Infirmary as the news of the new finds at Malahide might leak out and the Infirmary might try to claim half of these papers also. This was an extraordinary and an unfortunate decision. Any possible claim by the Infirmary to a share of the papers at Malahide was effectively blocked either by the terms of Mrs. Mounsey's will or by the fifth Lord Talbot's purchase of the contents of Auchinleck from Mrs. Mounsey's executor.[27] Buchanan, Wardlaw Burnet, and Burgin all seem to have forgotten this point and, as a result, Isham was dissuaded from negotiating a deal with the Infirmary on what would have been very favourable terms.

So far as the now dormant court proceedings were concerned, it was agreed that there should be no resumption of activity unless one of the other parties forced the issue. Isham was glad to postpone the question of expenses, and there was always the risk that if a hearing were arranged, Abbott might be provoked into serving his summons. Buchanan and Burgin worked out the terms of a joint cable to Isham which was despatched the same day:

Have had advantage consultation Edinburgh to-day senior counsel. All feel we must have full details your dealings written and verbal with Talbots since 1926. Your first difficulty is make 1927 agreement extend these important later discoveries and then pro-

---

[23]Letter dated 5 February 1941 (copy in S. R. & Co.'s papers).

[24]Memorandum of this conference in S. R. & Co.'s papers. Wardlaw Burnet died unexpectedly a few days after the conference.

[25]Cable, Isham to Buchanan, 7 January 1941 (S. R. & Co.'s papers).

[26]Confirmed in letter from J. & J. Galletly to Steedman Ramage & Co., received 17 January 1941 (details recorded in S. R. & Co.'s Business Ledger).

[27]See above p. 214.

cedural difficulty arises all claims must be made Irish Courts. Will put Talbot on suitable notice. Inclined consider moment inappropriate proceed with purchase from Cumberland their share Fettercairn papers as in view Scots judgement they may be interested new discovery. Have you considered visiting this country?[28]

Isham did not reply to this cable nor to subsequent communications from Burgin. Irish solicitors and counsel were retained as a precautionary measure, but it was impossible to make any move without Isham's authority.[29] In April, the Judicial Factor's solicitors asked Buchanan how matters stood, as they were being pressed by Abbott.[30] In June, Abbott's agents wrote requesting permission for him to proceed with the task of editing the Fettercairn papers[31]—an astonishing request from someone who was still threatening suit for a large sum of money. In June 1943, the Judicial Factor's solicitors again wrote to Buchanan pressing for some progress and they mentioned, disturbingly, that the Infirmary now wanted all the papers put up for sale in view of the high prices being obtained for manuscripts at Christie's in London.[32]

On all these matters, Buchanan tried, through Burgin, to get instructions from Isham, but Burgin found that Isham simply did not reply. His only communication in more than two and a half years was a cable in June 1941 agreeing to the Judicial Factor's suggestion that the papers should be deposited for the duration of the war with the British Linen Bank at Newtonmore (a village in the Scottish Highlands), and that war risk insurance should be dispensed with as he could not afford the expense.[33] Buchanan was compelled to tell the Judicial Factor that he was unable to get instructions and would not therefore be initiating any action himself. It was, of course, possible for any of the other parties to reopen the case and ask the Court to deal with costs or any other relevant matters. Buchanan would have been powerless to object and it is surprising that no such step was

---

[28]Copy in S. R. & Co.'s papers.

[29]Letter, Burgin to Buchanan, 13 March 1941 (S. R. & Co.'s papers).

[30]Reported in letter, Buchanan to Burgin, 5 April 1941 (copy in S. R. & Co.'s papers).

[31]Reported in letter, Steedman Ramage & Co. to Denton Hall & Burgin, 4 June 1941 (copy in S. R. & Co.'s papers).

[32]Letter, Mackenzie & Kermack to Steedman Ramage & Co., 23 June 1943 (S. R. & Co.'s papers).

[33]Reported in letter, Denton Hall & Burgin to Steedman Ramage & Co., 4 June 1941 (S. R. & Co.'s papers).

taken as all the solicitors involved in the case were still lying out their fees. As to Abbott, Buchanan politely refused his request, explaining that as proceedings were still in Court, the papers remained in the control of the Judicial Factor and, in view of the risk of war damage, it was necessary that they should be kept meantime in a safe place.[34]

In December 1943, Burgin was sent on a Government mission to America and arranged to meet Isham in New York.[35] Buchanan supplied him with a long list of points to put to Isham.[36] The most pressing was the question of costs, but Buchanan warned against any action if Isham were unable to pay. Burgin returned in May 1944 to report that Isham would not take any major decisions concerning the Boswell papers until after the war. There matters had to rest. Buchanan was again pressed by the Judicial Factor's solicitors in October 1944 and again he had to reply that he had no authority to make any move.[37]

Meanwhile, unknown to Buchanan or Burgin, Isham had communicated with Lady Talbot direct. On 5 March 1942, he sent her a long and recriminatory letter which was bound to cause offence.[38] He was under severe pressure at the time. He still felt deeply the death of his daughter Samantha and was worried about his son Jonathan, who had spent a month in hospital with concussion. The burden of rising land taxes was so heavy that he had been forced to forfeit certain tracts in default.[39] The Boswell situation was, in his own words "a damnable mess."[40] His outburst to Lady Talbot may have been deplorable, but it was understandable.

On receiving Isham's letter, Lady Talbot decided she could no longer cope with the situation by herself. She sent him a sharp reply and instructed Mr. A. B. Spingarn, a New York attorney, to deal with the whole matter on her behalf.[41] In writing to Spingarn, she stressed

[34]Reported in letter, Steedman Ramage & Co. to Denton Hall & Burgin, 4 June 1941 (copy in S. R. & Co.'s papers).

[35]Letter, Denton Hall & Burgin to Steedman Ramage & Co., 11 November 1943 (S. R. & Co.'s papers).

[36]"Notes for meeting with Dr. Leslie Burgin—13 December 1943" (copy in S. R. & Co.'s papers).

[37]Correspondence in S. R. & Co.'s papers.

[38]Letter in TFP.

[39]Letter, Isham to Flora MacLeod, 22 May 1942 (copy in IFP).

[40]Letter, Isham to Flora MacLeod, 19 October 1941 (copy in IFP).

[41]The reply to Isham is dated 21 March 1942 (copy in TFP). Lady Talbot's instructions to Spingarn were contained in a very long letter dated 24 April 1942 (copy in TFP), which included a detailed account of the Malahide story and her dealings with Isham since 1926. This important

that, despite the offence given by Isham, she was sympathetic to his difficulties, and would still prefer all the manuscripts to be in a single collection if possible. She was also anxious to avoid a public clash in court, although she was well aware that Isham had little grounds for claiming the new papers. She told Spingarn: "I imagine his lawyers tell him he has no legal case. . . . The 1927 receipt—however it could have been interpreted at the time—is in legal opinions here counterbalanced by Colonel Isham having purchased papers since—up to 1931. What solution there is to the present impasse I do not know."[42]

Chastened by Lady Talbot's response, Isham wrote to her again on 7 May in a much more conciliatory tone.[43] He explained how disastrous for him had been the lack of completeness for so many years and how it had hindered his publication plans. These facts, coupled with the huge expense of editorial work and pursuing the Fettercairn case, would probably have prevented him from ever becoming involved with the Boswell papers had he been able to foresee what was in store for him. Owing to his straitened circumstances, he was unable to make any proposal for his acquisition of the new papers. He could only leave it to Lady Talbot to state her own ideas.

It is greatly to Lady Talbot's credit that she did not bear resentment. She cabled Spingarn to say no further action was needed as Isham had changed his attitude and made a satisfactory apology.[44] To Isham she sent the following letter:

Dear Colonel Isham,
    Thank you for your letter of May 7th. Lord Talbot asks me to say that he does not think the time opportune to make any suggestions. We both sympathise with your anxiety over the situation, and Lord Talbot will take no step regarding the papers without first acquainting you. In the meanwhile I will give what time I can to studying them.
    It seems to me that the letters on account of their very quantity

---

letter is elsewhere cited as "Spingarn Letter." Spingarn was an excellent choice: a good lawyer with strong literary interests, a member of The Bibliographical Society (London) and the Oxford Bibliographical Society. He understood Isham's difficulties and, in the years which followed, handled negotiations with just the right blend of sympathy and firmness. Isham developed a high regard for him, to the extent of presenting him with a manuscript letter from his collection some years later (see below p. 344). Spingarn was best known for his leading role in the struggle for equal rights for American Negroes. He died on 1 December 1971 at the age of ninety-three.

[42]Spingarn Letter.
[43]Letter in TFP..
[44]Cable acknowledged in letter, Spingarn to Lady Talbot, 3 June 1942 (TFP).

are of no great market value. I found only a few standing out as individually of value—so far as I can judge. The bulk consists of domestic letters, notes for law cases, etc. There is one interesting bundle about John Reid, including a very pathetic letter from Reid himself.

I am under the impression these papers may have been in the box collected by Sir Alexander from the Trustees. I am right, am I not, in thinking there was such a box? You will remember that we found two similar boxes of papers—one all MSS. of Sir Alexander and the other box in which these Boswell papers were found.

They seem to be in some sort of order, but I am sure the late Lord Talbot never saw them, although 1915[45] newspapers were amongst them. I think these must have been put in just as packing for the journey here, and the label was in the writing of the late Lady Talbot. She may have found this box of papers in the attics at Auchinleck and overlooked their non-appearance at this end. Lady Talbot might not have attached the same importance to them which the late Lord Talbot would have done, and she would have been concentrating on many other details of the move and she was also very busy indeed with war work all through the war. After the war you will remember Ireland went through a period of great anxiety, lasting until the late Lord Talbot's illness and death. It seems to me quite possible that all recollection of this box can have passed from the late Lady Talbot's mind from the moment she labelled it.

I am explaining this to you as although I know it does not help matters, I would at least like you to believe that no-one has been as much to blame as you were first inclined to think. We must all face the matter with goodwill, and at the end of the war see what suggestion can be made.

Yours sincerely,<br>Joyce Talbot de Malahide[46]

Lady Talbot's considerate attitude speaks for itself. Without her forbearance, and her genuine anxiety not to disperse the archives, the history of the Boswell papers would have been very different.

As THE END OF THE WAR approached, Isham's thoughts turned once more to the Boswell papers. By 1945, Pottle had almost completed

---

[45]In her letter of 17 October 1940 (see above p. 243), Lady Talbot wrote of 1917 newspapers.
[46]Letter dated 4 June 1942 (copy in TFP).

his notes for the long-delayed trade edition of the journals, but the
lack of the London journal 1762-63, and other important material
included in the Fettercairn find was so serious that he preferred not
to publish without it.[47] Isham agreed, but it meant that there was
no prospect of an early return from a trade publication. His precarious
financial position made a sale of his whole collection to Yale or some
other suitable institution a matter of urgency. In 1942, he had told
Van Alen that the "manuscripts just must be sold in the immediate
future."[48] Van Alen readily offered generous terms for the release
of his interest, commenting: "I understand fully the hardships you
have undergone to attempt to preserve these valuable sources of
scholarship and I will be gratified in this day of war and uncertainty
if anything can be salvaged for us from this venture."[49] In fact, Van
Alen had virtually written off the value of his investment in the papers.
To his friend and lawyer, G. Campbell Becket, he wrote (with extraordinary good humour considering the extent of his loss): "The papers
would keep me awake nights if I hadn't resigned myself to the worst,
which, in this case, is worse than death. I wish all Guggenheims, &
appendages would die in a body & leave us in peace—for good measure
I'll include the Colonel & the Papers & Formaldahide Castle in this
wish."[50]

Unfortunately, the existence of the Fettercairn papers in Scotland
and the new find at Malahide presented a serious obstacle to any
sale. A tentative approach to the Wrenn Library of the University
of Texas in 1943 came to nothing,[51] and Knollenberg of Yale had

---

[47]Letter, Pottle to Isham, 24 November 1945 (IFP).

[48]Letter, Van Alen to Isham, 25 February 1942 (IFP).

[49]Letter, Van Alen to Isham, 7 October 1942 (IFP). Van Alen's investment in the Boswell
papers was confined to Isham's purchases from Malahide up to 1931. This presented problems of
apportionment if Isham obtained the Fettercairn papers and the new papers from Malahide, and
then sold the entire collection. Van Alen agreed in this event to accept a percentage of the net
proceeds of sale after deducting all expenses, including legal fees and costs in connection with the
Fettercairn law-suit, and the cost of buying out the Cumberland Infirmary. The agreed percentage was to be 25 percent of the net up to $150,000, plus 50 percent of the amount between
$150,000 and $200,000 and 30 percent of any excess over $200,000. (Letter Alfred P. Walker
[Isham's attorney] to G. Campbell Becket [Van Alen's attorney], 12 May 1942. Copy supplied
to me by Mr. Becket with consent and approval of Van Alen.)

[50]Letter, Van Alen to Becket, undated, but its content and position in Becket's file show it was
contemporaneous with the correspondence cited in the last note (copy provided by Becket).

[51]Copy letter (undated), Brune & Gordon, Attorneys at Law, to Miss Fannie Ratchford,
Librarian of the Wrenn Library. Reference to Isham's negotiation with Texas is also made in a
letter from G. Campbell Becket to Van Alen dated 13 October 1943 (copy supplied to me by Mr.
Becket).

no further proposals to make. In 1945, Isham asked his friend President Herbert Hoover if he could help. Hoover approached several institutions in the eastern United States, but got no response.[52] He then tried the Huntington Library in California, which expressed an immediate interest and arranged for Dr. Louis B. Wright, a member of its research staff, to travel to New York to meet Isham and see the papers.[53] Despite an enthusiastic report from Wright, the Library trustees reluctantly decided that their limited resources did not permit them to finance so costly an acquisition. Wright wrote to Isham on 11 August 1945, communicating the trustees' decision and adding:

> Let me express the personal hope that some angel of Yale University may decide to purchase your documents for the Yale library. That is where they logically ought to go, for Pottle is there and he is the ideal man to make the best use of them.[54]

Before he could interest Yale, Isham had to obtain the new papers from Malahide and also the whole of the Fettercairn papers, which meant buying out the Cumberland Infirmary and paying the entire legal costs of the case. A large sum of money was needed which he did not have and which he had no immediate prospect of raising.

In March 1945, he wrote to Buchanan explaining how difficult things had been for him during the war. His suit against his family trustees still had to be decided, but, when it was, his first thought would be to obtain the Fettercairn papers and to have a showdown with Abbott. He asked Buchanan to find out whether the Infirmary were still willing to sell out for £1,000 and said that he would himself negotiate with the Talbots for the latest find at Malahide when the war was over.[55]

Isham was shocked to hear in reply that Buchanan was seriously ill—so ill that there were doubts as to his recovery. There was certainly no prospect of his early return to business.[56] Wardlaw Burnet and Burgin had both died and Thackrah was in the army. Bereft of his advisers, for six months Isham did nothing. Then, on 19 October

---

[52]Letter, Hoover to Isham, 6 May 1945 (IFP).

[53]Letter, W. B. Munro of the Huntington Library to Hoover, 1 May 1945 (IFP).

[54]Letter in IFP. In referring to an "angel of Yale University," Wright was probably punning deliberately. James Rowland Angell had been president of Yale 1921–1937.

[55]Letter, Isham to Buchanan, 7 March 1945 (S. R. & Co.'s papers).

[56]Letter, Steedman Ramage & Co. to Isham, 11 April 1945 (copy in S. R. & Co.'s papers).

1945, he took the initiative into his own hands and sent off letters to Lady Talbot and to the trustees of the Infirmary.[57]

He reminded Lady Talbot of her promise to reconsider what was to be done with the new papers after the war and asked her to send him the journal material which she had conceded to him. Lady Talbot sympathized with Isham's problems, but, after their previous differences, she was determined that the business side of any dealings should be handled by Spingarn, her New York attorney.[58] She suggested to Spingarn that Isham might exchange the pages of the manuscript of the *Life* which he had previously acquired from Malahide in return for all the newly found papers, apart from the *Life* manuscript.[59] She still did not know that this was impossible as Isham had already sold his portion of the manuscript to Rosenbach, apart from a few leaves.[60] She also wrote direct to Isham asking if Pottle could come to Malahide to verify that what had turned up was indeed the final manuscript of the *Life* and to go through the other papers.[61] These "other papers" had never been properly identified. Illness, bad eyesight, and the demands of war work had prevented her from devoting any time to the work of sorting and listing, a task which in any event she did not feel qualified to undertake. At the time of the discovery, she had reported six letters from Garrick and a large correspondence with Temple, John Johnston, and with Boswell's children.[62] There was clearly much else besides, for what was found in the grain loft was "two packing cases full of papers."[63] The possibilities were intriguing and exciting.

In February 1946, Isham and Spingarn met in New York to discuss terms. Isham was forced to admit that he had sold most of his portion of the manuscript of the *Life* at a price[64] which placed a very high value indeed on the much larger portion still in Lady Talbot's hands.

[57]Letter, Isham to Lady Talbot, 19 October 1945 (TFP) and letter, Isham to trustees of Cumberland Infirmary, 19 October 1945 (copy in S. R. & Co.'s papers). As to Isham's letter to the Infirmary and the negotiations which followed, see below p. 261 *et seq.*

[58]Letter, Lady Talbot to Isham, 24 October 1945 (copy in TFP). Lady Talbot also wrote direct to Pottle inviting him to come to Malahide to sort and identify the new papers. Pottle's reply dated 25 March 1946 is in TFP. He declined her invitation because of prior commitments. For reasons explained below Isham preferred *not* to have the new papers expertly appraised.

[59]Letter, Lady Talbot to Spingarn, 25 October 1945 (copy in TFP).

[60]See below n. 64.

[61]Letter, Lady Talbot to Isham, 24 October 1945 (copy in TFP). See also n. 58 above.

[62]Letter, Lady Talbot to Isham, 17 October 1940 (copy in TFP).

[63]Ibid.

[64]The sales were to Rosenbach in 1928 and 1935 for $17,500 and $35,000 respectively. See above pp. 80 and 108 and below Appendix III, pp. 331–32.

He wanted more information from Lady Talbot about the other new papers, but was afraid to have them expertly examined in case this should result in a higher valuation than the price he intended to offer. He told Springarn that it would be impracticable for Pottle to examine the papers at Malahide without the help of assistants and the necessary facilities for reference. He offered a "token payment" of £2,000 for the new papers (except the *Life* manuscript) and insisted that he had to have them to complete his project of the scholarly publication of all of Boswell's private papers. He pointed out that he would never have embarked on the enterprise in the first place had he known how much additional material would come to light.[65]

Lady Talbot authorized Spingarn to accept Isham's offer.[66] The terms of the deal were agreed upon at a further meeting in New York, following which Spingarn wrote to Lady Talbot asking for full details of the manuscripts to be sold.[67] He explained that Isham wanted to know exactly what he was getting for his £2,000. Lady Talbot replied that the whole collection would fill a cabin trunk one foot, by one and a half feet, by three feet[68]—thus making a price of approximately £450 per cubic foot! She had not been able to do more than sort the papers roughly into bundles, without noting details of what each bundle contained. She sent Spingarn the following list of bundles, which, as the basis of a major literary purchase, must surely be unique for its lack of informative detail and its tantalizing promise of undiscovered treasures:

| | | |
|---|---|---|
| Bundle A. | | 57 misc. letters to J. Boswell. |
| " | B. | 49 misc. letters to J. Boswell. |
| " | C. | 56 misc. letters to J. Boswell. |
| " | D. | 68 misc. letters to J. Boswell. |
| " | E. | Odd Poems by J. Boswell and some misc. |
| " | F. | Pieces of Opera and misc. literature. |
| Large Bundle G. | | Letters to and from W. Temple. |
| " " | H. | Misc. literature by J. Boswell. |
| " " | I. | Misc. literature by Boswell, including notes for "The Life." |

[65]Information in this paragraph comes from a letter (in TFP) from Spingarn to Lady Talbot dated 28 February 1946 reporting on his meeting with Isham in New York.
[66]Letter, Lady Talbot to Spingarn, 5 March 1946 (copy in TFP).
[67]Letter, Spingarn to Lady Talbot, 21 March 1946 (TFP).
[68]Letter, Lady Talbot to Spingarn, undated (copy in TFP).

| Small Bundle J. | Garrick's letters, and Warren Hasting's letter. |
| " " K. | 33 letters to J. Boswell. |
| " " L. | 72 letters to and from J. Boswell. |
| " " M. | Letters from Boswell to J. Johnston. |
| Large Bundle N. | Small packets of letters. |
| Small Bundle O. | "A letter to the People of Scotland" by J. Boswell.[69] |
| " " P. | Correspondence with Henry Dundas. |
| Large Bundle Q. | Notes of J. Boswell's. |
| Small " R. | Sale of first edition of "The Life" and papers connected with it. |
| Large Bundle S. | 89 Misc. letters by J. Boswell. |
| Small Bundle T. | Letters to Lord Hailes. |
| " " U. | 47 Misc. letters by J. Boswell. |
| Large Bundle V. | 134 letters written to J. Boswell. |
| Small Bundle W. | 49 letters to J. Boswell. |
| " " X. | 46 letters by J. Boswell. |
| " " Y. | 34 letters by J. Boswell. |
| " " Z. | Personal accounts and receipts and notes of the sale of "The Life." |

Bundle Notes.
Bundle Misc. literature.
50—Small packets of letters.[70]

Both Isham and Spingarn were nonplussed. Isham insisted on more information and Spingarn wrote to Lady Talbot asking for it.[71] She replied that the preparation of an accurate catalogue was quite beyond her and suggested that Isham should complete the purchase on the basis of her general description.[72] Isham's long experience of successive discoveries of Boswell papers left him in little doubt that the 4.5 cubic feet of papers as listed by Lady Talbot would be worth much more than £2,000. His financial position was so bad, however, that he had to make the best deal he could. He therefore offered to buy the new papers (inclusive of publication rights), uncatalogued and sight-unseen, for the reduced price of £1,750. This was to include all papers found at Malahide since 1940, other than the manuscript

[69]This was later discovered to be the manuscript or printer's copy of JB's *A Letter to the People of Scotland*, 1785 (see *Literary Career*, p. 108). The manuscript is now in the Hyde Collection.

[70]Copies of this list are in IFP and TFP.

[71]Letter, Spingarn to Lady Talbot, 23 May 1946 (TFP).

[72]Letter, Lady Talbot to Spingarn, 31 May 1946 (copy in TFP).

of the *Life,* to which he made no claim.[73] Lady Talbot accepted and
a sale agreement was drawn up which provided for delivery of the
documents at Malahide or in Dublin not later than 1 September 1946.[74]

Isham still had to find the money to pay for his purchase. There
had been no improvement in his financial affairs. In April 1946, he
had sold the entire remaining stock of volumes of the private edition
to Guinzburg for $8,600, but this merely cancelled a debt of the same
amount which he had owed Guinzburg since January 1945.[75] Outside
help was essential and fortunately it came in the person of the late
Donald F. Hyde.

Hyde was a lawyer by profession, but his consuming interest was
books and book-collecting. He and his wife, Mary Crapo Hyde, began
their collection soon after their marriage in 1939. The result of their
efforts today is the Four Oaks Library, one of the finest private
eighteenth-century libraries in the world, containing, amongst other
treasures, the greatest collection of Johnsonian books and manuscripts
in existence. Hyde met Isham through their common interests and
became his friend and his lawyer. From 1946 onwards, he championed
Isham's cause in America for purely nominal fees, just as Buchanan
did in Scotland. He was motivated by an intense personal regard for
Isham's courage and achievement, and the knowledge that Isham's
interests and the interests of Boswellian scholarship were one and
the same. A quiet and kindly man, he was nevertheless completely
and uncompromisingly a supporter of Isham's cause. His single-
mindedness of purpose may have given offence to some, but his role
was of vital importance in achieving the ultimate goal. Boswellians
owe him a debt which deserves to be acknowledged.

Hyde provided practical help at once in the form of an unsecured,
interest-free loan of $5,000. This supplied Isham with the funds he
needed. As a token of his appreciation, he promised that when he

---

[73]Letter, Spingarn to Lady Talbot, 7 June 1946 (TFP).

[74]Agreement dated 1 August 1946 between James Baron Talbot de Malahide and Ralph H.
Isham (TFP).

[75]Details of this transaction in April 1946 are in IFP. Guinzburg bought:

| | |
|---|---:|
| 25 complete sets @ $15 per volume | $6,750 |
| 23 miscellaneous numbered volumes @ $10 per volume | 230 |
| 189 unnumbered volumes @ $7 each | 1,323 |
| 22 unbound volumes @ $1 each | 22 |
| 11 leather-bound volumes from set 208 @ $25 per volume | 275 |
| | $8,600 |

Guinzburg paid Isham by returning the latter's note to him for $8,600, dated 10 January 1945.

had the papers he would give Hyde the opportunity to purchase, at half its appraised valuation, the manuscript of *A Letter to the People of Scotland,* one of the few items specifically mentioned by Lady Talbot in her list.[76]

The papers were delivered in bulk in a large trunk weighing some 200 pounds to Isham's agent in Dublin. Isham promised Lady Talbot to keep the whole transaction as confidential as possible and not to make any press release until it had been approved by her. For this reason, he arranged that the papers would not be handled by any agent with an expert knowledge of the book or antiquarian trades. It was also vital that the papers should not enter the United Kingdom, as, once in, it might be difficult to get them out again owing to the stringent British customs and exchange control regulations. It was decided to ship the papers direct from an Irish port to the United States and Lady Talbot obtained the necessary Irish customs clearance. The original plan to put the trunk aboard the S.S. *Washington,* sailing from Cobh on 1 September 1946, was thwarted by a strike in the port of New York; instead, the papers were shipped from Dublin on board the S.S. *American Forwarder,* which arrived in Boston on 14 September.[77]

Four days later, Isham attended and spoke at the first American Birthday Party for Dr. Johnson, given by the Hydes at Four Oaks Farm.[78] Mrs. Alfred Kay, who was present, has given this amusing account of the occasion and its aftermath:

> The last speaker was Ralph Isham, who had finally arrived from Boston. Rising from his place, in stately fashion, he walked slowly to the great chair where he seated himself as though by right. His theme was the defense of the individual known as the "book collector." He gave good proof of his claim as he depicted his battle to obtain his latest treasure, still marooned in Boston Harbor on the strike-bound freighter, *American Forwarder.* Ralph pictured himself pacing the dock for the past three days trying to rescue the precious locker trunk in between calls to the S.P.C.A. about the plight of a shipment of thirsty horses also immured

---

[76]Letter, Isham to Hyde, 20 August 1946 (copy supplied to me by Mrs. D. F. Hyde). It was not known at this stage whether the manuscript was JB's *A Letter to the People of Scotland* of 1783 or 1785. It turned out to be the latter.

[77]Elaborate care was taken over the arrangements for shipment of the papers and there is a lengthy correspondence on the subject in IFP and TFP from which the information for this paragraph has been taken. .

[78]18 September 1946.

on board the ship. He had remained until that afternoon gazing in fury at the rusting steel plates of the ship until he finally forced himself to accept defeat and set forth, *sans* treasure, reaching Four Oaks Farm at the last possible moment. . . .

As a postscript, we should recount the rescue of the old Malahide leather-bound trunk from the freighter. (Ralph had specified that the shipment should appear to be normal luggage.) Immediately after the dinner, Ralph returned to Boston post-haste and nothing was heard from him until 1:30 Sunday morning, when he awakened the Kays with a phone call to ask if Alfred could get the trunk insured. It was now in Ralph's room at the Ritz Hotel in Boston, still unopened. Ralph was in a state of paralysis, afraid either to transport it to New York, or to open it alone in Boston. Alfred, not in the best possible humor at that hour, told Ralph he would wire his insurance company requesting coverage and that Ralph should get on a train before noon and bring the trunk to New York. This he did, traveling in a drawing room on the *Congressional.* He spent the trip showing the papers to a young lady named Boswell who happened to be aboard the train.

The next scene in the drama occurred the following night in Ralph's apartment. In the presence of Mary, Don, and the Kays, the little trunk was opened and a collector's orgy ensued. Packets of papers were strewn over floor and furniture. All evening (and long into the night) there were excited cries from every corner of the living room. "Oh! Listen to this!" But, of course, no one did listen. Each of us was too excited about the document in his own hand. It was a unique experience.[79]

Isham soon realized that his latest acquisition formed a collection which, in its richness and variety, nearly matched the material from Fettercairn. Like the Fettercairn papers, the main bulk consisted of correspondence. There were 160 letters from Temple to Boswell, which, when added to an identical number of Temple letters previously discovered at Fettercairn and 4 Temple letters included in Isham's original purchase from Malahide, virtually completed Temple's side of the Boswell-Temple correspondence. Most unexpectedly the trunk also contained 24 long and interesting letters from Boswell *to* Temple,

---

[79]*Four Oaks Farm,* ed. Gabriel Austin, privately printed, Somerville, New Jersey, 1967. The quotation comes from the chapter contributed by Elizabeth Kay, "The First American Birthday Party for Dr. Johnson," pp. 96–98.

written during Boswell's Continental tour of 1763–66. Nobody then supposed that Boswell had retrieved any of his own letters to Temple; as we now know, he obtained some of them when he visited Temple in the autumn of 1792, so that he might make extracts for an intended account of his travels. He died without ever returning them.[80] Thus, just over one hundred years after the sensational discovery of Boswell's letters to Temple in Boulogne, it became possible to plan publication of both sides of the correspondence.[81]

There were also 139 letters to Boswell's close friend John Johnston of Grange and a mass of correspondence between Boswell and his children as well as other family letters. The total number of letters was well over 1,300 and, amongst the most important, were letters to and from Wilkes and Garrick, two letters from Rousseau to his mistress, Thérèse Le Vasseur, a fine letter from Fanny Burney to Johnson, and another letter from Boswell to Voltaire. Other correspondents included Baretti, Beauclerk, Edmund Burke, Dr. Burney, George Dance, Henry Dundas, the Earl of Eglinton, Lord Hailes, Warren Hastings, the Bishop of Killaloe, Bennet Langton, Malone, Sir Joshua Reynolds, and Mrs. Thrale.

Apart from letters, there were many other exciting items: part of Boswell's sketch of his life written for Rousseau;[82] an important group of Johnsonian autographs including the nearly complete manuscript of *The Vanity of Human Wishes* and a manuscript draft of *London*;[83] the manuscript of Boswell's *A Letter to the People of Scotland* (1785);[84] two more pages of Boswell's account of his conversation with Rousseau; about 85 more pages of journal material (some of it filling gaps in the journal material previously acquired by Isham); a number of wholly unexpected Reynolds autographs, including an interesting biographical memoir of Goldsmith not previously known to exist; and a large pile of letters, detached journal leaves, and other documents which Boswell had sent to the printer as copy for inclusion in the text of the *Life*, as well as a considerable quantity of preliminary notes, outlines, and

[80]See Temple's letter to Sir William Forbes of 27 April 1796 quoted above p. 187.

[81]Although nearly all of Temple's letters to JB seem to have survived, more than half of JB's letters to Temple must be missing. On JB's side of the correspondence, we have only some 128 letters as against more than 300 on Temple's.

[82]The missing portion of this sketch turned up later with the Grand Tour papers which accompanied the *Life* manuscript acquired by Yale in 1950 (see below, p. 298). The whole sketch is published in Pottle's *James Boswell—The Earlier Years 1740–1769* (1966).

[83]Now in the Hyde Collection.

[84]Now in the Hyde Collection.

drafts relating to the *Life* and the *Tour*. Over and above all this, there was a mass of memoranda, jottings, newspaper clippings, invitations, and other documents of all kinds.

The *Life* manuscript stayed at Malahide, apart from two pages which must have slipped into the trunk unnoticed.[85] Lady Talbot showed the remaining leaves of the manuscript to Geoffrey D. Hobson of Sotheby's, who wanted to catalogue them for her;[86] she also considered offering them to Arthur A. Houghton, Jr.,[87] who had bought from Rosenbach and now owned the 110 pages from the croquet box.[88] In the end, however, she decided to postpone any action regarding her portion of the manuscript whilst there was any hope of reuniting the whole.[89]

Pottle, after a visit to Isham's New York apartment,[90] described the new papers as "richer in possibilities for scholarly research and publication than one would have any right to expect. . . . They are an almost inexhaustible mine for articles, small papers, and notes."[91] Taking a wider view, he envisaged publication of three extensive related works as soon as the Fettercairn papers could be united with the rest: a complete edition of the journals in say ten volumes; a new edition of Boswell's correspondence in twelve or more volumes; and a new edition of Boswelliana in one volume.[92]

Another visitor to Isham's apartment, shortly afterwards, was David Nichol Smith, Emeritus Professor of English Literature in the University of Oxford. Nichol Smith was attending an eighteenth-century seminar organized at Smith College in his and C. B. Tinker's honour. There, he met Isham who invited him to see the new papers from Malahide.[93] Nichol Smith has left his own vivid account of what must have been a memorable evening:

[85]See below Appendix III, p. 332.
[86]Letter, Hobson to Lady Talbot, 19 June 1946 (TFP).
[87]Letter, Lady Talbot to Spingarn (copy in TFP). The letter is undated but acknowledges Spingarn's letter to her of 21 March 1946. She expresses interest in what Houghton would be prepared to offer for her portion of the manuscript.
[88]See below Appendix III, p. 332.
[89]Letter, Lady Talbot to Hobson, 5 July 1946 (copy in TFP).
[90]116 East Fifty-third Street.
[91]"The Isham Collection," an 8-page typewritten document by Pottle (in IFP), containing a detailed survey of the new papers.
[92]Ibid.
[93]As narrated by Herbert Davis in "David Nichol Smith" from *Studies in the Eighteenth Century*, papers presented at the David Nichol Smith Memorial Seminar, Canberra, 1966. Edited by R. F. Brissenden, 1968, Australian National University Press, Canberra. (See p. 14.)

And now I venture to interpose a brief reference to my own contact with the Boswell papers. In January, 1947, Colonel Isham asked me to dine with him in his flat in New York. Bundles of the papers were lying on tables still unassorted, though one or two treasures had been singled out. He showed me a character sketch of Goldsmith all in the handwriting of Sir Joshua Reynolds, which proved that the great painter who always conveyed on his canvases the characters of the men and women whom he painted had skill with his pen as well as with his brush. When Isham read it out to me, I thought it the best character sketch of Goldsmith that I could hope to know. He showed me part of the manuscript of Johnson's *London*, the only part of the manuscript of *The Vanity of Human Wishes*, and it is of particular interest in view of a remark that Johnson made to Boswell about his method of composing verses. "I have generally had them in my mind," he said, "perhaps fifty at a time, walking up and down in my room, and then I have written them down, and often from laziness have written only half lines." Here was corroboration of this remark: the second half of many of the lines was in a darker ink than the first half. You will believe that the hours passed quickly in this unforgettable evening and early morning, for I did not get away to my hotel till long after midnight. No less memorable was my last visit to him a day or two before returning to England. He had no sooner greeted me than he said, "I have something to show you." It was a slip of paper on which Boswell had written two lines of *The Vanity of Human Wishes,* and one word of it was corrected in Johnson's handwriting. The lines are in the passage which mentions the Bodleian Library:

O'er Bodley's dome his future labours spread.

Boswell pointed out to Johnson that the word "spread" occurred in two adjacent lines, and Johnson at once substituted another word in one of them. This he did in talk, but it was an authentic emendation that had to be put on record. "For perfect authenticity," he says, "I now had it done with my own hand," and he adds in a footnote that he deposited the slip of paper in the Bodleian. As we had sought for it there in vain, we had concluded that it was lost; but it had never been there; Boswell had forgotten to carry out his intention. The slip of paper had come to light in New York. When I pointed this out to Isham he sat quiet for a moment, and then he said, firmly, "take it back with you." A collector such as Isham cannot escape criticism. I have called him a determined collector, but I would add that in my relations with him he has been an eminently just collector. I took the slip back with me by plane, and I have often wondered what the observations of Johnson and Boswell would have been had they known of its flight over the Atlantic. My first duty when I got back to Oxford was to do what Boswell had intended. I deposited the slip in the Bodleian.[94]

Nichol Smith might also have mentioned another gift by Isham to the Bodleian Library in 1947—a copy of Johnson's D.C.L. diploma at Oxford. Although not in Boswell's hand, it was endorsed by him in such a way as to show that it was part of the printer's copy for the *Life*. The original diploma, as already mentioned, was found at Malahide in 1937, given by the Talbots to Isham, and presented by him in turn to the Bodleian in 1938.[95]

ISHAM NOW CONCENTRATED his energies on the one major problem which still confronted him—the acquisition of the Fettercairn papers. Editing on the scale contemplated by Pottle could only be adequately undertaken by a university. Yale was the obvious choice, with its tradition of Boswellian studies and its team of expert scholars led by Pottle; but no deal with Yale, or any other university for that matter, was possible until Isham had the Fettercairn papers. To obtain physical possession of these along with clear legal title became his most urgent consideration.

As we have seen, he wrote direct to the trustees of the Cumberland Infirmary on 19 October 1945.[96] He asked whether their offer to sell

[94]For this quotation, I have followed the text published under the title "A Boswell Fragment" in *Meanjin*, vol. XI, No. 3, Spring 1952, pp. 292–93, being an extract from an address "Samuel Johnson and the New Boswell Papers" delivered by Nichol Smith in 1951 at the University of Melbourne. Nichol Smith's account is also published in *Studies in the Eighteenth Century*, cited above, pp. 15–16, but there are textual variations. It will be remembered that 143 years earlier Malone tried to carry out JB's intentions when he wrote (on 3 March 1804) to Sir William Forbes requesting him to search for the slip so that it might be deposited in the Bodleian. See above p. 190 and relative footnotes. See also *Life*, III, p. 358. Forbes's inability to find the slip did not deter Malone from making further enquiry. On 28 September 1808, we find him writing to James Boswell junior at Auchinleck again asking for "a slip of paper on which Johnson made the correction of the word *spreads*, substituting *burns* in its place, in the poem of *London*. This was promised to the Bodl. Liby." (Letter at Yale.) Malone's reference to *London* is a mistake. It should have been *The Vanity of Human Wishes*.

[95]For fuller details, see above p. 162, n. 89.

[96]See above pp. 251–52.

for £1,000 still stood, pointing out that the costs which the successful claimant would have to bear now came to nearly £3,000; and there was still the risk of a claim from Abbott.

Three months later, a reply came from the Infirmary's solicitor, Mr. T. D. Harston.[97] He explained that the trustees had a duty to get the best possible price. They had taken expert advice and, as a result, were prepared to accept £2,250, provided Isham gave a full indemnity against all claims, costs, and expenses. If Isham did not agree to these terms, they would have no option but to ask the Judicial Factor to put the whole collection up for sale.

A few days before Harston's letter arrived, Isham received word that Buchanan had recovered and was back at business.[98] He told Harston that Buchanan would now deal with all future negotiations for him,[99] and wrote to Buchanan putting him fully in the picture. He explained his financial difficulties and his anxiety over the delay in his publication plans: "If I can't get on with my publications soon, I will lose my editor as well as my publisher. What a lot of headaches and heartaches Mr. Boswell has given us!"[100]

At this stage, the turn of political events in Britain made the completion of a satisfactory deal with the Infirmary a matter of even greater urgency. On 23 May, Thackrah (who had recently returned to legal practice from war service) wrote to Isham to warn him of the Government's proposed Bill to nationalize the British hospitals.[101] When the Bill was enacted, the trustees of the Infirmary would be superseded by a Government body under the Ministry of Health. The prospect of fresh negotiations with Government officials was daunting: they might even refuse to sell altogether on the grounds that the papers were of national importance and should be kept in Britain. It was imperative to come to terms with the Infirmary as soon as possible.

Unfortunately, at a time when speed was so important, Isham was held up for six months by another unforeseen difficulty. In arranging the shipment of the new papers from Malahide, he became aware of possible Government restrictions on the export of rare manuscripts from Britain. The last thing he wanted was to buy out the Infirmary and pay all the costs, only to find that the papers had to remain in

---

[97]Letter, Harston to Isham, 11 January 1946 (copy in S. R. & Co.'s papers).
[98]Letter, Buchanan to Isham, 4 January 1946 (copy in S. R. & Co.'s papers).
[99]Letter, Isham to Harston, 14 February 1946 (copy in S. R. & Co.'s papers).
[100]Letter, Isham to Buchanan, 6 February 1946 (S. R. & Co.'s papers).
[101]Letter, Thackrah to Isham, 23 May 1946 (copy in S. R. & Co.'s papers).

Britain. He wrote to Buchanan for information and Buchanan replied that an export licence would be essential before the papers could be taken out of the country.[102]

It was left to Thackrah to try to obtain export clearance from the Board of Trade in London. Almost at once he became entangled in red tape. How, he was asked, could Isham apply for a licence to export papers which he did not own and without having any idea of the date of their shipment? A formal licence at this stage was quite impossible. Instead, Thackrah asked for a letter confirming that, if and when Isham obtained the papers, he would be permitted to export them to America. The officials concerned were reluctant to commit themselves in a hypothetical situation. Lord Hinchingbrooke had recently been asking some awkward questions about the loss of Britain's antiquarian treasures, and they feared possible repercussions if the Fettercairn papers were allowed out of the country. Thackrah refused to give up: he took the officials through all the complexities of the Fettercairn case, he went through Abbott's catalogue with them, item by item, and he explained the effect of Lord Stevenson's judgement. Eventually, after six months of persistent effort, he succeeded in extracting the necessary letter.[103]

Thackrah reported his success to Buchanan on 9 October 1946.[104] On 10 October, Abbott intimated through his solicitors that his claim for remuneration still subsisted.[105]

Buchanan, as ever, was cautious, but Isham had had enough. He was not prepared to delay matters any longer because of a threatened claim which (in his own picturesque phrase) "has no more chance of succeeding than the Duke of Windsor."[106] He told Buchanan to make a firm deal with the Infirmary immediately and promised, if necessary, to indemnify the Judicial Factor and the Infirmary against any expense arising out of a claim by Abbott.[107] He asked Buchanan to try to get the price down to £2,000 because of Abbott's activity,

[102]Letter, Isham to Buchanan, 12 April 1946 (S. R. & Co.'s papers) and letter, Buchanan to Isham, 24 April 1946 (copy in S. R. & Co.'s papers).

[103]Information in this paragraph based on correspondence with Thackrah in S. R. & Co.'s papers.

[104]Letter in S. R. & Co.'s papers.

[105]Letter, J. & R. A. Robertson to Steedman Ramage & Co., 10 October 1946 (S. R. & Co.'s papers).

[106]Letter, Isham to Thackrah, 15 November 1946 (copy in S. R. & Co.'s papers).

[107]Letter, Isham to Buchanan, 26 November 1946 and cable, Isham to Buchanan, 9 December 1946 (S. R. & Co.'s papers).

but delay was to be avoided at all costs. He was afraid that publicity about his latest acquisition from Malahide might tempt the Infirmary to raise its price.[108]

The Infirmary refused to budge on the question of price. Buchanan reported that to settle the deal, he would need £2,250 plus £450 to cover the Infirmary's costs.[109] Isham cabled back to go ahead.[110] He promised to remit £2,700 any time after the New Year, although at the time he still did not know where he would find the money. Only a few weeks before, he had written to Thackrah: "I suppose I am a fool to keep penalizing myself financially in the pursuit and acquisition of Mr. Boswell's archives, but I can't seem to help it. Where in God's name I will find the money to clear up the Fettercairn situation I haven't any idea, but I go on hoping."[111]

Isham explained his predicament to Hyde, who tried, unsuccessfully, to raise funds from various sources. In the end, Hyde suggested that the only solution was to sell some of the new papers from Malahide.[112] This did not appeal to Isham, who had sacrificed so much to acquire them. In desperation, he went round various banks to try for a loan.[113] Refusal followed refusal until at last, on 21 February 1947, he persuaded the Continental Bank and Trust Company of New York to advance $12,000, repayable after three months, on security of a few selected manuscripts from his collection. When the three months were up, he was able to obtain a series of renewals which kept the loan alive until March 1948, although reduced in principal by then to $8,500.[114] A cheque for $1,000 from *Life* magazine for the use of his materials for an article on the Boswell papers, received in July 1947, provided some small but welcome relief.[115]

The bank loan did not solve Isham's problems, but at least it enabled him to send the money to settle with the Infirmary when

[108]Ibid.

[109]Letter, Buchanan to Isham, 10 December 1946 (copy in S. R. & Co.'s papers).

[110]Cable, Isham to Buchanan, 13 December 1946 (S. R. & Co.'s papers).

[111]Letter, Isham to Thackrah, 17 October 1946 (copy in S. R. & Co.'s papers).

[112]Letter, Hyde to Isham, 7 January 1947 (IFP). Hyde wrote: "My conclusion is that you should immediately liquidate sufficient of the material in the trunk [i .e., from Malahide] to meet the expenses of procuring the 'Fettercairn Papers.' "

[113]Correspondence in IFP, e. g., letter to Union County Trust Co., 14 February 1947, requesting a loan of $30,000. The request was refused.

[114]The promissory notes relative to this series of loans are in the IFP.

[115]Letter, *Life* magazine to Isham, 30 July 1947 (IFP). The article did not appear until the issue of December 4, 1950 (vol. 29, No. 23) under the title of "The Boswell Detective Story," by Hamilton Basso.

needed. Buchanan in the meantime had despatched a formal offer which, after elaborate revision and adjustment, was finally accepted by the Infirmary's solicitors on 23 January 1947.[116] As the papers were still in the hands of the Judicial Factor, the Infirmary refused to warrant either their condition or their delivery.[117] This meant that before settlement of the deal, Buchanan had to arrange for every item to be checked and verified against Abbott's catalogue.

The seven boxes containing the papers were now in the vault of the head office of the British Linen Bank in Edinburgh, where they had been brought after the war.[118] In September 1945, Chapman had asked both Isham and the Infirmary for permission to use the Fettercairn material for his planned edition of Johnson's letters.[119] Isham, with Pottle's approval, allowed Chapman not only to use, but even to publish any of the Johnson letters found at Fettercairn, and also to quote from Boswell's letter books from 1769 to 1782—a remarkably generous gesture in view of Chapman's role in "Operation Hush." Armed with permission from Isham and the Infirmary, Chapman spent a week in Edinburgh in May 1946 during which he was allowed free access to all the papers.[120] Later on, some thirty letters by Johnson were sent temporarily to the Bodleian Library in Oxford so that he could examine them there.[121]

[116]The original offer was despatched by Steedman Ramage & Co. to Messrs. J. & J. Galletly (acting for the Infirmary) on 15 December 1946. The revised and adjusted offer is dated 21 January 1947. J. & J. Galletly's formal acceptance is dated 27 January 1947. (Correspondence in S. R. & Co.'s papers.)

[117]This was a condition of the revised offer.

[118]Confirmed in letter, Mackenzie & Kermack to Steedman Ramage & Co., 20 December 1946 (S. R. & Co.'s papers).

[119]Letter, Chapman to Isham, 25 September 1945 (IFP).

[120]Letter, Chapman to Isham, 21 November 1945. Chapman wrote: "I had hardly ventured to hope for the unpublished letters." A subsequent letter (21 March 1946) shows that Isham permitted Chapman to use and publish any portion or all of the Johnson letters from Fettercairn (*Fettercairn Catalogue*, Nos. 1472 to 1590). A letter from Chapman to Isham of 28 May 1946 reports his having spent a week in Edinburgh where he was courteously received by the Judicial Factor and given access to the seven boxes of papers in the vaults of the British Linen Bank. A request for permission to quote also from Boswell's letter books, 1769–82 (*Fettercairn Catalogue*, Nos. 1364 and 1365), was also granted by Isham (letter dated 22 June 1946). (All correspondence from IFP.)

[121]Letter, Mackenzie & Kermack to Steedman Ramage & Co., 20 December 1946 (S. R. & Co.'s papers). The Johnson letters handed by the Judicial Factor to Dr. Malcolm of the Signet Library on 12 November for onward transmission to the Bodleian were:

Johnson to Brocklesby (*Fettercairn Catalogue*, Nos. 1476–95)
Johnson to Cruikshank (*Fettercairn Catalogue*, Nos. 1497–1503)
Johnson to Dr. Mudge (*Fettercairn Catalogue*, Nos. 1545–47)

The Judicial Factor now confirmed that all the papers should be complete except for the Johnson letters sent to Oxford.[122] At Buchanan's suggestion, Isham asked the late Dr. C. A. Malcolm, Librarian of the Signet Library in Edinburgh, to make a detailed check against the catalogue. Malcolm was also asked to distinguish "manuscripts belonging to the deceased James Boswell" (awarded by the Court to Isham and the Infirmary), and Forbes family papers (which belonged to Lord Clinton).[123] As mentioned,[124] in November 1938 Abbott had already listed the items which he considered to be Lord Clinton's property, and his list was approved both by Isham and the Infirmary. Why Malcolm should have been asked to prepare a fresh allocation is not clear.

Malcolm presented his report on 28 February 1947.[125] He confirmed that, with the exception of five items[126] (which he subsequently traced), he had found all the documents listed in the catalogue and they were in good condition. He decided that Forbes's representatives were entitled to all of Boswell's letters to Forbes[127] (which included five unsigned drafts[128]), and also Forbes's copy of the Round Robin.[129] Everything else he awarded to Boswell's representatives, apart from a copy, in Forbes's hand, of a letter to Boswell from the Bishop of Killaloe[130] which he omitted from his allocation altogether. Abbott had listed this item in 1938[131] as Lord Clinton's property, along with four draft letters in Forbes's hand[132] and letters to Forbes from Alexander Boswell[133] and Mrs. Margaret Boswell.[134] These were certainly Forbes's papers and it seems that Malcolm's allocation was neither as complete nor as careful as it should have been.

Malcolm also found amongst the papers a number of items of

---

[122]Ibid.

[123]Letter, Steedman Ramage & Co. to Dr. Malcolm, 28 January 1947 (copy in S. R. & Co.'s papers).

[124]See above p. 226, n. 35.

[125]Copy in S. R. & Co.'s papers.

[126]*Fettercairn Catalogue*, Nos. 1047, 1054, 1057, 1093, and 1465.

[127]*Fettercairn Catalogue,* Nos. 1320–60.

[128]*Fettercairn Catalogue*, Nos. 1324, 1339, 1340, 1345, and 1346.

[129]*Fettercairn Catalogue*, No. 1604.

[130]*Fettercairn Catalogue*, No. 1430.

[131]See above p. 226, n. 35.

[132]*Fettercairn Catalogue*, Nos. 365, 366, 373, and 381.

[133]*Fettercairn Catalogue*, No. 1411.

[134]*Fettercairn Catalogue*, No. 1414.

varying importance which had not been noted by Abbott in his catalogue. Of these he allocated to the Boswell family:

1. A letter of Sir Joshua Reynolds to Sir William Chambers dated 22 February 1790, complaining of misrepresentation over his resignation of the Royal Academy presidentship.
2. A copy of a letter of Reynolds, unsigned, relating to his resignation of the Royal Academy presidentship.
3. A letter from Temple to Boswell (with Truro postmark) with a separate sheet containing a postscript written in different handwriting from that of the letter, dated 18 July—no year.
4. Two news-cuttings from a newspaper of 1780 showing "Letters to the Antigallicans."

The remaining uncatalogued items he considered to be Forbes property. These comprised:

1. Seven drafts of letters from Forbes to Boswell (corresponding with the letters Numbers 363, 364, 371, 374, 375, 378, and 382 of the catalogue).
2. A bundle of letters by various members of the Boswell family to Forbes.
3. A box containing the Beattie papers (the quest for which had led Abbott to Fettercairn in the first place).
4. A miscellaneous assortment of letters, envelopes, and family papers having no connection with Boswell or his archives.

Whilst Malcolm was busy working on his report, Abbott's solicitors again approached Buchanan about their client's claim.[135] This time, Buchanan made it quite clear that in no circumstances would Isham entertain such a claim.[136] Buchanan's main concern was not so much that a suit by Abbott might succeed as that it might impede closure of the deal with the Infirmary. For this reason, he made no mention of the transaction to Abbott's solicitors, and did everything possible to hurry matters along.

Settlement with the Infirmary was to have taken place on 28 February 1947,[137] but it was delayed by a series of snags. Malcolm did

[135]Letter, J. & R. A. Robertson to Steedman Ramage & Co., 31 January 1947 (S. R. & Co.'s papers).

[136]Letter, Steedman Ramage & Co. to J. & R. A. Robertson, 4 February 1947 (copy in S. R. & Co.'s papers).

[137]In terms of the offer of 21 January 1947 (copy in S. R. & Co.'s papers).

not find all of the five missing papers until 21 March.[138] Buchanan discovered that the trustees who had formed the governing body of the Infirmary in 1938 had been superseded in 1945 by a new corporate body whose title had to be checked. This meant bringing in Denton Hall & Burgin, as the Infirmary was an English body and questions of English law were involved. Unfortunately, Thackrah, who had collaborated with Buchanan since 1936, was no longer available. In mid-February, Buchanan received word that he had given up the law to enter a Carthusian monastery.[139]

By the end of March, Buchanan was in funds and all the necessary documents had been drafted and approved. By the end of April, the documents were completed and signed, and, on 2 May 1947, settlement finally took place. The assignation was intimated to the Judicial Factor and, at long last, all the Boswell papers found at Fettercairn were Isham's, subject only to completion of the court proceedings. From Abbott, there was still no positive move.[140]

Before Isham could obtain delivery, the question of expenses had to be disposed of. The Judicial Factor's costs and, most probably, those of all the other parties would be awarded by the Court as a charge against the fund *in medio* (i.e., the papers). Buchanan advised that it would be a waste of time and money to oppose such an award of expenses in court. Instead, he suggested that a figure should be agreed with each of the other parties informally, and that in return for payment, they should be asked to sign a joint minute asking the Court to find no expenses due to or by any party (except the Judicial Factor), and to rank and prefer Isham to the whole of the papers. The Court's decree in these terms would then entitle Isham to delivery of the papers on settlement of the Judicial Factor's costs.[141]

Once more, Isham's problem was to find the money. He had still not obtained judgment against his family trustees and his general financial position was worse than ever. Buchanan told him that he would need approximately £2,500 to settle the expenses and could do nothing until he had the money.[142] Isham did not have it to send and his efforts to raise a further bank loan proved futile. The months slipped

[138]Letter, Steedman Ramage & Co. to J. & J. Galletly, 21 March 1947 (copy in S. R. & Co's papers).
[139]Letter, E. G. M. Fletcher (of Denton Hall & Burgin) to Buchanan, 14 February 1947 (S. R. & Co.'s papers). Fletcher looked after Isham's affairs in London from now on.
[140]Information in this paragraph from correspondence in S. R. & Co.'s papers.
[141]Letter, Buchanan to Isham, 11 August 1947 (copy in S. R. & Co.'s papers).
[142]Ibid. and separate "Estimate of approximate costs" in S. R. & Co.'s papers.

by and no progress could be made. The papers remained in Malcolm's care in the Signet Library, where Isham's son, Heyward, on a brief visit to Edinburgh in the summer of 1947, was permitted to have a glimpse of them. Heyward was interested to find that Mr. Robertson, an assistant librarian, was working for Lord Clinton on a pile of the non-Boswellian papers from Fettercairn. These included a bundle of correspondence between certain Loyalists in the American War of Independence.[143]

Later that summer, the Hydes also visited Edinburgh. Hyde met Buchanan who explained the steps to be taken before the papers could be shipped to America. He repeated that until he had the money to settle the costs, he could make no progress.[144] Isham had asked Hyde to get photostats of the London journal 1762–63 whilst in Edinburgh, but this proved impracticable in the short time available. Hyde was, however, able to see the Fettercairn papers in the Signet Library and to list the other papers belonging to Lord Clinton, including the American ones. These were of considerable interest and, at Isham's request, Buchanan tried unsuccessfully on several occasions to persuade Lord Clinton to sell them, along with the remaining items in the *Fettercairn Catalogue* which Malcolm had allocated to Lord Clinton.[145]

By February 1948, Isham had still not been able to raise the necessary funds and was being harassed for repayment of his loan from the Continental Bank, raised a year earlier to cover the settlement with the Infirmary.[146] His position was becoming desperate, when Hyde stepped in to propose a solution. In a letter of 4 February 1948, he wrote:

Dear Ralph,
I have given considerable thought to the matter of your bank loan and the financing of the Fettercairn Papers. I wish we were in a position to be able to underwrite the whole project, but as you know that is not the case.
I have one solution which may or may not appeal to you.

[143]Information contained in letter from Mackenzie & Kermack to Steedman Ramage & Co., 25 July 1947 (S. R. & Co.'s papers).

[144]Letter, Buchanan to Isham, 18 September, 1947 (copy in S. R. & Co.'s papers).

[145]Information about the Hydes' visit from correspondence in S. R. & Co.'s papers. The Hydes were in Edinburgh in September 1947. On 22 October, Buchanan wrote to Lord Clinton's solicitors (Mackenzie & Kermack) on Isham's instructions offering £250 for the remaining papers belonging to Lord Clinton (copy letter in S. R. & Co.'s papers). Mackenzie & Kermack declined to negotiate until everything had been cleared up and the Judicial Factor given his discharge.

[146]See above p. 264.

I have delayed suggesting it until you have tried other sources of help. I know how hard it is to raise money when one needs it for everyone is inclined to place restrictions beyond the equities and discount the value of material because you cannot make immediate delivery. In the suggestion that I am now making I have tried to balance the equities to be fair to both of us.

My thought is that I pay you now the sum of $12,500 for the Johnson Diary and the 119 Johnson Letters in the Fettercairn Papers. The delivery of the Diary would be made at the present time and the delivery of the Letters would be deferred until they are received from Scotland. . . .[147]

Hyde also promised to arrange a fresh loan of $8,500 from the Chemical Bank and Trust Company which would enable Isham to clear his existing loan from the Continental Bank. The new loan would be guaranteed by Hyde on terms which would allow it to remain outstanding for some time without the bank insisting on any repayments of principal.[148]

Hyde later increased his offer to $14,000, which Isham accepted gratefully.[149] A few months before, Isham had spoken to R. J. Barry of C. A. Stonehill, Inc., about the possibility of selling the 119 Johnson letters from Fettercairn. Barry valued them at about $10,000 and offered to try to find a purchaser.[150] The problem was, of course, to find a purchaser who would pay the full market price weeks, or even months, before getting delivery. This was just what Hyde now offered to do, and in addition he was prepared to pay a fair sum for the little Johnson Diary found at Malahide in 1937 and given to Isham by the Talbots.

On 9 March 1948, Isham at last cabled to Buchanan: "After infinite difficulty have arranged to cable you within fortnight requisite funds complete transaction."[151] No sooner had the money been sent, than Isham became impatient to have the papers. After only four weeks,

[147]Letter in IFP.

[148]Ibid.

[149]The terms of the transaction were recorded in an interchange of formal letters between Isham and Mr. and Mrs. Hyde dated 12 March 1947 (IFP); $10,000 was allocated to the 119 Johnson letters from Fettercairn (equivalent to C. A. Stonehill's valuation) and $4,000 on the little Johnson diary. It was a condition that Isham would remit £2,500 to Buchanan to enable him to deal with the costs of the Fettercairn case and procure delivery of the papers.

[150]Letter, R. J. Barry of C. A. Stonehill, Inc., New Haven, to Isham, 10 November 1947 (IFP).

[151]Cable in S. R. & Co.'s papers.

he cabled Buchanan to ask why the papers had not been shipped.[152] Buchanan cabled back: "Whilst lines final procedure were to extent possible considered in advance this does not shorten time required to carry same through."[153]

There was in fact still much to do: the amount of the Judicial Factor's and the other parties' expenses had to be negotiated and agreed upon; a joint minute had to be prepared and approved by all the solicitors concerned; an indemnity in favour of the Judicial Factor had to be adjusted and signed; and a court hearing had to be arranged so that the final decree could be pronounced.

There was also one other essential requirement. Before property forming the fund in any action of multiplepoinding can be made over to the successful claimant, it is necessary to obtain clearance from the Inland Revenue that there is no outstanding claim for death duties. Inexplicably, this point had not previously been considered by Buchanan nor by anyone else. The Judicial Factor now raised the matter because he was obliged to obtain Revenue clearance before he could hand over the papers.[154]

The Judicial Factor's solicitors opened negotiations with the Inland Revenue, but soon got bogged down in a mass of complicated detail. They agreed that Buchanan, who was more familiar with the background of the case, should handle the negotiations instead. The Revenue claimed duty on the value of the whole of the papers passing on the deaths of Sir Alexander Boswell, Sir James Boswell, and Sir James's widow, and on the value of the half shares of the papers which passed on the deaths of Sir James's two daughters, Emily Lady Talbot and Mrs. Mounsey. Buchanan argued that any duty should be nominal as, until recently, little or no value had been attached to the papers. The Revenue official agreed so far as earlier transmissions were concerned, but pointed out that as Isham had just paid the Infirmary £2,250 for a half share, the present value was considerable. In view of the special circumstances, however, he was prepared to accept £600 in full settlement. Strictly speaking, it was the heirs (i.e., the Talbot family and the Infirmary) who were accountable for the duty, but to have asked them to pay would certainly have caused further difficulty and delay. The only alternative was for Isham to

[152]Cable, Isham to Buchanan, 14 May 1948 (S. R. & Co.'s papers).
[153]Cable, Buchanan to Isham, 15 May 1948 (copy in S. R. & Co.'s papers).
[154]Letter, Buchanan to Isham, 22 May 1948 (copy in S. R. & Co.'s papers).

pay the duty himself and, on 25 June, Buchanan wrote to tell him so.[155]

For Isham this was very nearly the last straw. Angry and dismayed, he drafted the following cable to Buchanan:

> Paid editorial work and printing costs 21 volumes Boswell Papers has resulted in loss to me of about $90,000 irrespective of my 21 years work on same. This has resulted in establishing and enhancing value of Boswell Papers. As no Boswell heir from Alexander to present Lord Talbot knew of existence Fettercairn Papers and had they done so in early days they would be inventoried as valueless, and as no generation until Talbot and Cumberland had any knowledge or enjoyment thereof and as whatever present value exists I have created by work and expenditure, the Crown can justly claim but little. I am willing to pay £125 nuisance value. If this is not acceptable will arrange with my Congressman to present question in Congress. Immediate reply necessary.[156]

The cable was never in fact sent. Instead he put in a high temperature transatlantic telephone call which reached Buchanan at 1.30 A.M. at a remote farm-house in Dumfries-shire where he was staying with clients. Everybody had gone to bed and neither Buchanan nor the farmer's wife was too pleased at being disturbed in the middle of the night.[157] So deep was Isham's chagrin, however, that he very nearly abandoned his fight for the Fettercairn papers altogether. On 29 June he cabled Buchanan:

> Cannot suffer further red tape and nonsense. Kindly return monies cable. Let Judicial Factor sell manuscripts auction. Arrange unlimited bid for me Johnson letters.[158]

The same day he reconsidered and sent a second cable cancelling his first:

> Government adviser requests cancellation earlier cablegram

---

[155]Information in this paragraph as reported to Isham by Buchanan in his letter of 25 June 1948 (copy in S. R. & Co.'s papers). Details of the various persons on whose death the Inland Revenue claimed duty are from a letter by the Estate Duty Office to Mackenzie & Kermack of 28 May 1948 (copy in S. R. & Co.'s papers).

[156]Draft in IFP.

[157]As described by Buchanan later in a letter to Hyde, 7 July 1948 (copy in S. R. & Co.'s papers).

[158]In S. R. & Co.'s papers.

otherwise his activity and interest possible. Kindly confirm cancellation by cable.[159]

Buchanan cabled his reply on 1 July:

Note earlier cable cancelled. Long meeting today with head official who eventually offered without prejudice to accept £275 complete settlement all claims which I consider very favourable. Strongly recommend you authorise me pay immediately said amount towards which as genuine friendly gesture willing on final accounting with you deduct £100 from our legal costs beyond abatement I already contemplate. Please cable.[160]

The crisis was over. Isham cabled his approval[161] and Buchanan paid the duty.[162] The Inland Revenue gave clearance on 5 July and the way was now open to obtain delivery of the papers. The Hydes were then in London and Heyward Isham was in Paris, and they all planned to sail to America together on board the *Queen Mary* on 23 July.[163] The aim was to have the Fettercairn papers on board also, but time was short. Within the next few days, the Judicial Factor's indemnity was adjusted, the bills of the solicitors for the Judicial Factor, Lord Clinton, and Mrs. Hailey were paid, and application was made for the necessary export licence. Malcolm arranged to pack the papers to be delivered to Isham in five large boxes, securely roped and sealed.[164]

The court proceedings, after years of inactivity, had, in the picturesque phraseology of Scots Law, "fallen asleep." Before any further step could be taken, it was necessary to "awaken the cause" by means of a "minute of wakening." This was duly lodged,[165] and the Judicial Factor enrolled a motion asking the Court to give effect to the minute, to endorse Malcolm's report and allocate the papers accordingly, and to dispose of the question of expenses.[166]

---

[159]Ibid.
[160]Copy in S. R. & Co.'s papers.
[161]Cable dated 3 July 1948 (S. R. & Co.'s papers).
[162]Cable, Buchanan to Isham, 5 July 1948 (copy in S. R. & Co.'s papers).
[163]Information from Mrs. Hyde confirmed by her private journal for 1948.
[164]A detailed record of all these activities in S. R. & Co.'s papers.
[165]Joint minute of wakening, No. 67 of process.
[166]Motion enrolled on 14 July 1948 (copy in S. R. & Co.'s papers).

On 16 July, Lord Sorn pronounced the necessary interlocutor[167] and Buchanan cabled Isham with the news:

Delivery obtained today. Court's order pronounced by your friend McIntyre now Lord Sorn. No word yet from Heyward but endeavouring have papers available London by Tuesday. . . .[168]

Isham cabled back:

Am naturally delighted and relieved. How very nice that it was given to our friend McIntyre to pronounce order marking the successful end of our twelve years of struggle and anxiety. Cannot possibly express extent of my appreciation and gratitude for your devotion wisdom and friendship. . . .[169]

Buchanan now collected the five sealed boxes from the Signet Library, along with a certificate by Malcolm that they contained exclusively the papers allocated by him to Boswell's representatives in his report of 28 February 1947.[170] Malcolm's certificate, like his report, was inaccurate.[171] The papers which he withheld from the boxes (as belonging to Lord Clinton) followed the more logical listing suggested

---

[167]The interlocutor was in the following terms:
  The Lord Ordinary in respect of the Joint Minute of Wakening No. 67 of process holds the cause as wakened; on the unopposed motion of the pursuer and real raiser finds that the documents enumerated in the Report by Dr. C. A. Malcolm dated 28th February, 1947, No. 68 of process, form the fund *in medio;* holds the said Report as being the Condescendence of the Fund *in medio,* and approves thereof; ranks and prefers the claimants Lt.-Col. Ralph Heyward Isham, C. B. E., and the Cumberland Infirmary equally between them to that part of the Fund *in medio* designated in the said Report as belonging to Boswell's Representatives and being the documents falling within the description "manuscripts of whatever kind lying in the house of Auchinleck," and ranks and prefers the Claimant Lord Clinton to all other papers comprised in the Fund *in medio* and decerns; ordains the pursuer and real raiser to deliver the documents contained in the Fund *in medio* to the Claimants hereby found entitled thereto; finds the said Lt.-Col. Ralph Heyward Isham liable to the pursuer and real raiser and to all the claimants in expenses taxed as between solicitor and client and remits the accounts thereof when lodged, to the Auditor of Court to tax and to report.

[168]Cable, Buchanan to Isham, 16 July 1948 (copy in S. R. & Co.'s papers).

[169]Cable, Isham to Buchanan, 19 July 1948 (S. R. & Co.'s papers).

[170]Buchanan uplifted the boxes on 16 July, immediately after the interlocutor of the Court was pronounced. They were deposited for temporary safe custody in the head office of the Bank of Scotland (letter, Steedman Ramage & Co. to Denton Hall & Burgin, 16 July 1948, copy in S. R. & Co.'s papers). A copy of Malcolm's certificate, dated 16 July 1948, is in S. R. & Co.'s papers.

[171]See above p. 266.

by Abbott in 1938, and *not* the listing in his own report.[172] This discrepancy is surprising in view of the explicit terms of his certificate and the Court's direction that the report should be followed. Isham was nevertheless sufficiently appreciative of Malcolm's services to send him an important Boswell manuscript for presentation to the Signet Library. Unhappily, this manuscript, although received by Malcolm and catalogued, now seems to have gone amissing. A copy of the text has been preserved, however, and, as it is otherwise unavailable, it is printed in an Appendix along with Malcolm's own historical note.[173]

The Fettercairn papers now made their progress from Scotland to America.[174] Buchanan met the Hydes for dinner at the Mayfair Hotel in London on Monday, 19 July, and, later that evening, they went to the station to collect the papers, which had arrived from Edinburgh, escorted by a member of Buchanan's firm. The Hydes had made arrangements for the papers to be kept in the safe at Claridge's, but a look at the five huge boxes made it clear that the hotel safe could not contain even one of them. Instead, they were put into room 215, where the hotel placed a guard until the Hydes' departure.

Two days before sailing date, the export licence was issued and, on Friday the 23rd, the Hydes met Heyward Isham for the drive to Southampton. The five crates were strapped on top of a Rolls-Royce. Despite a flat tyre in the middle of the journey, the party arrived at Southampton in good time and export and customs clearance proceeded without a hitch. On the dot of 1 P.M., the *Queen Mary* set sail with the Fettercairn papers aboard. Once again there was no safe large enough to hold them and they were given a private cabin to themselves, near the Hydes. Their presence on board created considerable interest and various persons, including the ship's captain, asked if they might come to view the boxes. One night Isham telephoned excitedly from New York to enquire after the health of the "Quintuplets." He was pleased to hear they were well and laid plans to

[172]For Abbott's listing, which was actually followed, see above p. 226, n. 35. For example, Abbott claimed for Lord Clinton (correctly it would seem) *Fettercairn Catalogue*, Nos. 1411 and 1414 (letters to Forbes from Alexander Boswell and Mrs. Margaret Boswell), but Malcolm in his report awarded them to Isham. If he had followed his own report, as the Court directed he should, and his certificate stated he had done, Nos. 1411 and 1414 would have been packed in the boxes for delivery to Isham. But they were not. They and the other items listed by Abbott were retained for Lord Clinton and now form part of the Fettercairn Papers deposited in the National Library of Scotland.

[173]See below Appendix VI, pp. 350–51.

[174]The narrative which follows is based on information supplied by Mrs. Hyde and contained in her private journal for 1948.

meet the boat and celebrate with a "coming out" party on the night of arrival.

Sadly, he was suddenly stricken with mononucleosis. When the *Queen Mary* berthed in New York on 28 July 1948, he was unable to witness the triumphant arrival of the papers, but his friends Halsted B. VanderPoel and Herman W. Liebert were on the quay and shouted greetings to the Hydes and Heyward at the deck rail. They rejoiced in Isham's success and, from his bed in hospital, Isham rejoiced too at victory after twelve long years of struggle.

# IX

## *Fulfilment of Hopes*

ON the evening of the *Queen Mary*'s arrival in New York, John Kieran broadcast on CBS News:

> Today, on the British liner *Queen Mary*, there arrived in New York two shades out of the past, two ghosts from the eighteenth century ... Dr. Samuel Johnson and James Boswell, Esquire. Surely they must have been aboard. . . .[1]

Kieran reported that America had now come into possession of "the last great store of Boswell-Johnson manuscripts" which had arrived in five large steel cases—now to be opened and examined in New York. He speculated excitedly on the contents.

A short paragraph appeared two days later in *The New York Times*, but it was several months before further details were released. Isham was seriously ill and wanted to wait until he was fit again to enjoy his moment of triumph. His collection of Boswell papers was at last virtually complete, and the time was ripe to reopen negotiations with Yale or to look for some other suitable buyer. There had still been no public announcement of his big purchase from Malahide in 1946 and the news of this, along with the full story of the Fettercairn papers, was bound to create a literary sensation. As a potential seller, he had to obtain maximum publicity of the right sort and at the right time. He knew better than anyone how to stage-manage the affair, and it was essential for him to be on the scene.

[1] 28 July 1948 (typed copy in IFP).

By October, he had recovered from his illness and, to a privileged circle of friends, he sent the following irresistible invitation:

*The Boswell Papers discovered at Fettercairn House in 1931 and for twelve years in the custody of the Court of Session are now released and have reached these shores.*

*The cases in which the MSS. are contained will be opened at eight-thirty on Saturday evening, twenty-third October, 1948, at One Hundred Sixteen East Fifty-third Street, New York City.*

*May I hope that you will be present to share with me this long-delayed experience?*

*R. H. Isham.*

Edward C. Aswell, vice president of McGraw-Hill Book Company, wrote afterwards to Isham:

> It still causes my spine to tingle when I recall that I sat in your apartment and actually held in my hands the long-lost and now newly-discovered journal for the years 1762 and 1763, part of the original manuscript of the *Life of Johnson,* as well as some of the letters both to and from Boswell's great contemporaries. I think I shall never forget the excitement of the occasion. . . . Your collection is, I am sure, without parallel in literary history.[2]

A few days later, on Friday 5 November, Isham arranged a special exhibition at the Grolier Club which was attended by scholars and eighteenth-century experts, including representatives from Yale, Columbia, and Princeton universities. A list of manuscripts was prepared for the occasion and the cases were opened so that those present might see and handle the papers for themselves. One bemused scholar is reported to have said: "There is enough here to keep fifty scholars busy fifty years."[3]

Over the week-end, an official release was made to the press and, on Monday 8 November, the story was featured prominently in all the leading newspapers. The publicity was everything Isham could have wished. His photograph appeared on the front page of *The New York Times* over the caption: "Priceless Literary Treasure of Thousands of Items Puts Biographer of Johnson and His Times in a New Light." Inside, an entire page was devoted to the story. Apart from the *Times* reporter's own account, there were photographs of some of the manuscripts, a leading article on Isham's achievement, and a long article by Herman W. Liebert,[4] whose scholarly reputation gave it special authority. Liebert spoke of "an event of the first importance to literary and historical scholarship," and described the papers as "the greatest collection of manuscript material that has ever been assembled about a single man or a single period." "The new-found documents are not," he wrote, "a parcel of old letters and papers, but the potentiality of growing wise beyond the dreams of scholarship about one of the greatest periods in human history."[5]

---

[2]Letter, Aswell to Isham, 15 November 1948 (IFP).
[3]See reports in *The New York Times* and *The New York Herald Tribune* of 8 November 1948.
[4]Then a research assistant in the Yale Library.
[5]Liebert was paraphrasing SJ. See *Life,* IV, p. 87.

The leading article paid tribute to Isham's achievement in reassembling documents "which a wanton fate scattered, as it seemed, beyond hope of recall":

> To Colonel Isham, by whose perseverance this great historical record has once more been made one, the world of scholarship, and the wider world which loves Boswell and his hero, the good Doctor, owe a great debt. His accomplishment is another evidence, if any is needed, of the function performed by the collector, that strange but invaluable being who preserves the past for the benefit of the future.

Similar if slightly less extensive publicity was given in *The New York Herald Tribune, The Washington Post,* and other leading newspapers, as well as *Time* magazine.[6] The story was also featured in broadcasts by Edward R. Murrow and Lowell Thomas.[7]

Most of the reports contained one confusing piece of information which should be explained here. This was that Isham had acquired some 1,300 pages of the original manuscript of the *Life.* The manuscript which Boswell sent to the printer as copy consisted of a "master manuscript" of more than 1,000 consecutively numbered quarto leaves in his own hand, together with a mass of "papers apart." These papers apart were letters, journal leaves, and other papers, some in his own hand and some in the hands of others, which he had not bothered to write out again, but had sent to the printer, suitably adapted, for inclusion in the text. The 16 pages included in Isham's original purchase from Malahide in 1927 and the 110 pages from the croquet box, purchased in 1930, were all part of the master manuscript. The residue of the master manuscript, running to more than 900 pages, found at Malahide in 1940, remained at this time the property of the Talbots (apart from two leaves which had slipped unnoticed into the 1946 shipment[8]). The "1,300 pages of the original manuscript" referred to in the 1948 press reports did not include any of the master manuscript. They consisted of papers apart as described above, accompanied by a large quantity of notes, outlines, and drafts prior to the printer's copy.[9]

[6]See *Time,* 29 November 1948, p. 102.

[7]Both broadcasts were made on 8 November 1948 (typed copies in IFP).

[8]See above p. 259.

[9]For fuller details and references relative to the MS. of the *Life,* see below Appendix III, pp. 330–33.

After the excitement had subsided, Isham's first consideration was to find a suitable buyer. Only when the papers were placed where they would be protected from dispersal and where resources would be available for scholarly editing and publication, could he regard his work as complete. The dismal state of his finances added further impetus. He had to raise money quickly to pay off his debts and he wanted, if he could, to restore to some extent the wreck of his personal fortune.

At almost any time, he could have sold selected manuscripts at a large profit, but this would have been a negation of all he had striven for. To Dr. Frederick M. Hanes of Duke University he had written in 1942, when his spirits and his finances were at their lowest: "I do not at present contemplate selling any Boswell manuscripts separately. It has always been my belief that the world of scholars and of readers would suffer an irreparable loss by their dispersal."[10] Before 1948, the only major items sold from the collection were the portion of the manuscript of the *Life* purchased by Rosenbach, and the Johnson letters and diary purchased by Hyde.[11]

His chief hope always had been, and still was, that the papers would go to Yale, his *alma mater*, but negotiations were constantly bedevilled by the successive discoveries of new papers. This had been the nub of his problem: to sell his collection as a whole, it had to be complete; to make it so, he had to have money; and to raise money, he had to sell. Over the years, as we know, he approached or was approached by a number of institutions other than Yale,[12] but his lack of enthusiasm in these dealings shows where his true preference lay. It was a preference which found practical expression in his will, by which he left his whole collection to Yale, should both his sons predecease him.[13]

Yale was the logical choice: it had a great library rich in the field of eighteenth-century literature, and, above all, it was incomparably strong in Boswellian scholarship. Pottle, the doyen of Boswellian scholars, had worked intimately on the papers for some twenty years

[10]Letter, Isham to Hanes, 9 June 1942 (copy in IFP).

[11]The only other sales I can trace *before* 1948 are the 2 letters from JB to his wife included in Rosenbach's first purchase (see above p. 80). In or after 1948, he sold quite a large number of items to Mr. and Mrs. Hyde which are now in the Hyde Collection. For details, see below Appendix V, pp. 346–48.

[12]Princeton in 1927, Harvard in 1929 and 1939, the Wrenn Library of Texas in 1943, and the Huntington Library in 1945. (See above pp. 92–93, 227, and 250–51.)

[13]The terms of the bequest are mentioned in a letter from Isham to Hyde of 17 November 1948 (copy in IFP).

and was the ideal man to lead and co-ordinate the task of editing and publishing them. He took the view that by acquiring the whole collection "Yale would provide itself with a larger, more coherent, and more important project in research and publication than can usually be based on any manuscript collection, no matter how extensive or valuable."[14]

As we have seen, Isham had made at least three previous attempts to sell to Yale. The first had been in 1932[15] when he was suffering from the financial pressure caused by an expensive settlement with Geoffrey Scott's executors, the aftermath of the Wall Street crash, the cost of acquiring the croquet box find from Malahide, and the decision to expand the private edition. Because of the slump, money was short and the market value of manuscripts was depressed. Isham had found it difficult to state a price and Yale had not known whom to approach for funds. Then, in 1939, with the Fettercairn case decided, Isham had reopened negotiations.[16] Knollenberg, on behalf of Yale, had been enthusiastic, but with the outbreak of war the chance of early delivery of the papers had receded, and the negotiations had petered out.

In 1947, Isham had let it be known that he was disappointed by Yale's reluctance to offer financial support and their apparent lack of interest compared with that of other institutions.[17] In fact, James T. Babb, the Yale Librarian, was desperately anxious to acquire the collection, but, until Isham had clear title to the Fettercairn papers, it was difficult to raise funds. The previous year, Babb had met Van Alen's lawyer, G. Campbell Becket, who reported afterwards: "Jim, who is the Yale Librarian, is dying to have Yale buy the collection which really does belong in New Haven. I gather if he finds any doddering millionaire who is anxious to improve his federal estate tax status Jim will be right there with a fountain pen."[18] In September 1947, Babb had written to assure Isham that Yale was still tremendously interested. "Our position is, however, that until the papers are completely assembled, the title completely cleared, and some sort of firm and reasonable price set on them, we can do nothing definite."[19] Isham

---

[14]"The Isham Collection," 8-page typed document by Pottle (copy in IFP).
[15]See above p. 102.
[16]See above p. 227.
[17]Letter, J. T. Babb to Isham, 8 September 1947 (IFP). The "other institutions" were presumably Columbia and Harvard, as to which see below.
[18]Letter, Becket to Van Alen, 27 August 1946 (copy provided by Becket).
[19]Letter, Babb to Isham, 8 September 1947 (IFP).

had retorted that he needed money at once to obtain delivery of the Fettercairn papers and that, as these and his earlier acquisition from Malahide had been fully catalogued, he saw no reason why they could not negotiate, provided that the 1946 acquisition from Malahide was adequately listed.[20] Babb had agreed that with a proper listing of what was to be sold and with a firm price set, they might be able to proceed and had suggested that work on the listing should begin;[21] but nothing definite had been arranged by the time the Fettercairn papers arrived in America in July 1948.

Isham was now due to deliver to Hyde the 119 Johnson letters from Fettercairn (previously sold to him along with the little Johnson diary from Malahide).[22] He also agreed to let Hyde purchase certain other manuscripts—some from Fettercairn and some from Malahide. These were mainly Johnsonian items, although a few important Boswell manuscripts were included.[23] All the items were ones which Isham felt could be detached without affecting the saleability of his collection or seriously prejudicing its completeness. It nevertheless indicates his affection for and gratitude to Hyde that he was prepared to depart from his usual rule of never separating any significant papers from his main collection, unless under financial compulsion.

Serious negotiations with Yale were resumed in November 1948. They were protracted and complicated, and Isham thankfully left Hyde to handle everything for him.[24] Yale was the only serious contender, although in 1946 Hyde had sounded out James L. Clifford of Columbia,[25] and Jackson of Harvard,[26] and in January 1949 the papers were shown to Miss Fannie Ratchford, Rare Book Librarian of the University of Texas.[27] Isham no doubt felt that a little competition would put Yale on its mettle.

The money for Yale's purchase was raised more quickly and more easily than anyone could have expected. This was largely due to the efforts of Liebert, who, before joining the Yale Library staff, had been a newspaper man. It was he who had organized the extensive press

---

[20]Letter, Isham to Babb, 5 December 1947 (copy in IFP).

[21]Letter, Babb to Isham, 31 December 1947 (IFP).

[22]See above p. 270.

[23]As a result of Hyde's purchases from Isham, the Hyde Collection now contains the most important group of papers, originally forming part of JB's archives from Malahide and Fettercairn, outside Yale. This group of papers is listed below in Appendix V, pp. 346–48.

[24]Information from Hyde's legal papers.

[25]On 11 December 1946 (Hyde's legal papers).

[26]On 18 December 1946 (Hyde's legal papers).

[27]Hyde's legal papers.

publicity about the Isham collection in November 1948. He was carpeted for it afterwards by his superiors at Yale; but official strictures turned to congratulations when, almost immediately after and as a direct result of the publicity in *The New York Times*, The Old Dominion Foundation of Washington, established by Paul W. Mellon, a graduate of the Yale class of 1929, offered an unsolicited gift of $300,000 towards acquiring the papers. This sum, though substantial, did not represent a price which would enable Isham to discharge his financial obligations and still leave him with adequate reimbursement of his personal expenditure over the years. Yale's chief hope of raising the extra money lay in finding a commercial publisher prepared to risk a very large sum that trade publication of the journals would be profitable. This hope was realized when the McGraw-Hill Book Company, whose vice president, Aswell, had been so impressed by his glimpse of the papers in Isham's apartment, offered $150,000 for the commercial publishing rights.[28] Yale accepted the offer, subject to clearance of title, and sufficient funds for a purchase from Isham were thus assured. Aswell's efforts, inspired by his own enthusiastic interest in the Boswell papers, did much to bring about the successful outcome of these negotiations. He and McGraw-Hill deserve great credit for their willingness to embark on a massive but commercially uncertain venture which was, and still remains, unique in publishing annals.

Hyde meanwhile still had a great many difficulties to resolve. Yale required clear title to all the papers along with full publication rights. This meant disentangling all the contractual commitments affecting the papers made by Isham over a period of some twenty years. There were the publishing agreements with the Viking Press and William Heinemann, the private financial agreements with Guinzburg and Van Alen, an agency agreement with Brandt & Brandt, and Pottle's editorial contract.[29] Pottle's contract dated back to 1929, but circumstances had changed so radically since then that there was no hope of applying it literally. Hyde felt that it was inappropriate for Pottle to do any more work or even to have access to the papers until their disposition was finally settled.[30] In June 1947, he had written to Pottle to say

[28]Official press release by Yale University News Bureau, released for morning papers of Monday, August 1, 1949. The actual amounts were not stated in the release, but the sale agreement cited below p. 289, n. 47, refers to $150,000 contributed by McGraw-Hill and $300,000 by "an anonymous donor," now known to be The Old Dominion Foundation. It is a fact that the interest of both donors was aroused by the report in *The New York Times* on 8 November 1948—a powerful vindication of the effectiveness of the publicity arrangements.

[29]See above pp. 79, 90, 94–95, 98, and 144.

[30]Letter, Hyde to Isham, 21 May 1947 (IFP).

the contract was broken and that Pottle should make no further use of the papers meantime.[31] Pottle, with considerable tact, had in fact refrained from visiting Isham to study the new papers in detail, knowing that if he did so, he would be bound to make use of what he saw, and this might prejudice the possibility of a sale to an institution other than Yale.[32] Hyde also denied Pottle's claim to a balance of $5,000 of remuneration under his contract on the ground that its strict terms had not been implemented.

After so long a collaboration with Isham, Pottle must have felt hurt that the question of his contract was not dealt with on a more friendly basis. It was not his fault that events had rendered his contract incapable of fulfilment; and, so far as his claim for remuneration was concerned, he had made it clear that he did not wish to press for payment immediately. The truth of the matter was that Isham was weary after years of stress and pressure. Hyde offered the support he needed and he thankfully left it to Hyde to resolve all the difficulties which he no longer felt able to cope with himself. Hyde regarded Isham not just as a collector, but as one who had pursued, fought, and spent far beyond his means.[33] It was Hyde's responsibility, as Isham's lawyer and friend, to pave the way for a quick sale, and this necessitated the removal of any commitment to Pottle or others. It is much to Pottle's credit that he agreed to relinquish all rights and claims under his contract without payment of any consideration.[34]

Guinzburg was harder to deal with.[35] Isham was grateful for his help in the past and tried, when he could, to favour him beyond the consideration of any contractual agreement. In 1947, he had shown him the contents of the trunk from Malahide and given him a typescript of the Reynolds Memoir of Goldsmith, which he offered to the Viking Press for publication. Guinzburg had kept him waiting for months without an answer while publication offers from other firms had to be turned down. When serious negotiations with Yale began, Isham met Guinzburg to try to pin him down to what he considered to be his rights under their agreements. The meeting was not a success. Isham considered that Guinzburg was entitled to publication in sets of the private edition, derivative volumes, and publication of

[31]Letter, Hyde to Pottle, 23 June 1947 (copy in IFP).
[32]Letter, Pottle to Hyde, 24 May 1947 (copy in IFP).
[33]Draft letter, Isham to Pottle, undated (IFP).
[34]Mutual release, Isham and Pottle, dated 29 June 1949 (IFP).
[35]The information and quotations which follow in this paragraph come from a long letter, Isham to Hyde, 17 November 1948 (draft in IFP).

a half share of the Fettercairn papers (which was all Isham had acquired through the legal process referred to in their contract). He did not think that Guinzburg had any magazine or newspaper publication rights or any claim on the papers acquired from Malahide in 1946. Guinzburg, in Isham's words, "gave an example of soft and gentle dodging that was elegant." He thought that by modern standards the royalties had been set too high in the first agreement (with which Isham was prepared to agree); he hedged on the question of magazine and newspaper publication and generally avoided committing himself on anything. Isham wrote afterwards to Hyde: "This business with Guinzburg, which in my conception was simple, has astonishingly developed into a dismal fog from which I long to emerge."

Hyde took over the negotiations and, in February 1949, Guinzburg offered to release all rights under the existing Viking contracts, provided that any material which the new institutional owner of the papers decided to issue through a commercial publisher should be offered in the first place to Viking.[36] This was of course unacceptable to Yale because of the proposed sale of publishing rights to McGraw-Hill. Hyde wrote back to tell Guinzburg that unless he changed his mind he might frustrate the whole deal.[37] A rather prickly correspondence ensued until Babb of Yale interceded in the negotiations. Through his efforts, Guinzburg agreed on behalf of Viking, in May 1949, to release all rights in the Boswell papers, other than the copyright of *The Portable Johnson and Boswell,* for payment of $25,000, provided the sale to Yale was consummated within ninety days.[38] This was accepted and Guinzburg was duly paid out.[39]

With the help of Aswell, agreement was reached over a release from the Heinemann contracts. McGraw-Hill were prepared to offer Heinemann the British Empire publication rights (exclusive of Canada) for the entire Boswell collection, provided they would relinquish all rights under their existing contracts. It was risky to disclose this to Heinemann until agreement had been reached with Guinzburg, but immediately this was achieved, Aswell telephoned to A. S. Frere in London to put his proposition.[40] Frere agreed and Heinemann granted the necessary release subject to Isham settling his debit balance of

---

[36]Letter, Guinzburg to Hyde, 24 February 1949. (This letter is now missing from Hyde's legal papers where it belongs, but its contents can be inferred from subsequent correspondence.)

[37]Letters, Hyde to Guinzburg, 1 April and 22 April 1949 (Hyde's legal papers).

[38]Letter, Guinzburg to Hyde, 31 May 1949 (Hyde's legal papers).

[39]Copies of release documents dated 30 June 1949 are in Hyde's legal papers.

[40]Aswell confirmed his telephone call by letter the same day, 1 June 1949 (copy in IFP).

$5,189.41 in respect of royalties advanced but not earned.[41] Brandt & Brandt were also co-operative and agreed to release Isham from his agency agreement on repayment of the commission of $875 still due to them.[42]

There remained the problem of an accounting with Van Alen, who, between January 1930 and February 1931, had invested $142,836 in the Boswell papers. His interest was confined to Isham's original purchase from Malahide and the contents of the croquet box; but under his agreements he was entitled to insist that whatever sum was received from Yale for this portion of the papers should, after meeting all costs and expenses, be applied in the first place in repaying his outlay of $142,836 with interest at six per cent to date.[43] To have enforced this strictly would have left Isham with very little at the end of the day, after clearing all his other commitments. (Apart from the payments due to Brandt & Brandt, Heinemann, and Viking, he still had to redeem his loan of $8,500 from the Chemical Bank and Trust Company to release the batch of manuscripts which they were holding as collateral security.)

Van Alen was in Paris in the summer of 1949, but he agreed through his lawyer, Becket, to release all his rights for a payment of only $100,000.[44] This meant a loss on his original capital investment of nearly $43,000 and the unpaid interest over a period of nineteen years came to approximately $163,000 (uncompounded). His total personal loss on the Boswell papers may therefore be set at over $200,000. Becket certainly felt that his client had taken a "financial licking," and wrote to Isham: "Whether the $100,000 figure is fair both to you and to James depends entirely on the final sale price and I must say, Ralph, your old friend Joshua Reynolds couldn't have painted a drearier canvas than the one you sketched out to me on the telephone the other day."[45] At the same time Becket could not restrain his admiration for Isham's achievement: "If Donald [i.e. Hyde] has worked like a Trojan this past year or two, you have been Hector himself for a much longer siege and no matter how rosy or grey the financial picture, may I say that I cannot commit my Isham–Van Alen folders

[41]Letter, William Heinemann, Ltd., to Hyde, 4 August 1949, acknowledging the payment of $5,189.41 and enclosing the release document dated 5 August 1949 (Hyde's legal papers).

[42]Assignment to Yale University and release of Isham by Brandt and Brandt, dated 13 July 1949 (Hyde's legal papers).

[43]See above p. 94.

[44]Letter, Becket to Hyde, 11 May 1948 (copy supplied by Becket). Release document dated 28 June 1949 (Hyde's legal papers).

[45]Letter, Becket to Isham, 18 June 1948 (IFP).

JAMES H. VAN ALEN

DONALD F. HYDE
In the library at Four Oaks Farm.

to the 'Dead Files' category without congratulating you on your whole spectacular achievement and the imagination and persistence required for its successful accomplishment."[46]

Becket might have added that without Van Alen's backing and continuing forbearance, Isham could never have completed his private edition, let alone tackled the acquisition of the Fettercairn papers and the later finds at Malahide; that without Van Alen, the scattered archives of James Boswell would probably never have been fully reassembled. The financial contributions of McGraw-Hill and The Old Dominion Foundation have been frequently publicized; that of Van Alen, over $200,000, deserves similar acknowledgement.

On 28 June 1949, Isham signed an agreement with Yale for the sale of his collection for a price of $450,000 (the exact total contributed by McGraw-Hill and The Old Dominion Foundation).[47] The agreement covered his entire collection with the exception of a few items which he was allowed to retain as personal mementoes or for presentation as gifts.[48] These included a manuscript page of the *Life*, being one of the two pages found in the 1946 purchase from Malahide. The closing date, when the papers were to be delivered and the price paid, was set for 2 P.M. on 28 July 1949, in the Yale University Library.[49] A few weeks earlier, Liebert had written to Isham: "Perhaps alone I know how good a friend you have been to Yale in all this, and to me. That the papers are coming to Yale is largely your doing. . . ."[50]

Meanwhile Hyde was kept very busy trying to satisfy the minutely detailed requirements of Yale's lawyer, Frank E. Callahan. He was asked to produce virtually every scrap of paper ever granted to or by Isham since 1926 which might conceivably affect the Boswell papers, along with all the necessary assignments and releases, and a sworn affidavit covering the papers found at Malahide in 1930 and 1937, for which there was no document of title. Isham had to produce a list of all his places of residence since 1926, full details of every item lost, sold, or given away, a note of all copies and typescripts ever

---

[46]Ibid. It is only fair to say that Van Alen himself was surprised and delighted to receive $100,000 for an investment he had long since regarded as worthless. He wrote to Becket from Paris on 27 July 1949: "Will surprises never cease? It's that tough Canadian Becket blood that eventually wrenched 100 G.s from the jaws of death" (copy letter supplied by Becket).

[47]Agreement in Hyde's legal papers.

[48]For full details see below Appendix V, p. 342 *et seq.*

[49]In terms of the sale agreement.

[50]Letter, Liebert to Isham, 19 May 1949 (IFP).

made, and a statement of all persons, besides Yale, who would have any publication or other rights after closure of the deal.[51]

Buchanan had to be contacted in Scotland to send a certified copy of the decree of the Court of Session, and other papers to prove title to the Fettercairn papers.[52] Further documents were needed to deal with the assignment of statutory copyright and all the publication rights, and the plates for the Viking-Heinemann edition of the *Tour* had to be retrieved.[53] Isham wrote to Buchanan: "The Yale lawyers drove us almost to distraction. . . ."[54]

Miraculously, Hyde had everything ready for the closing to take place on 20 July, a week ahead of schedule. The portion of the manuscripts which for years had lain in the New York Public Library was withdrawn and, on 14 July, two cars laden with eight trunklike cases, accompanied by armed guards, transported the whole collection to New Haven, arriving safely at the Yale University Library at 5.30 P.M.[55] All was now set for the closing—the climax and culmination of Isham's labours. Mrs. Hyde, who accompanied Isham and her husband to New Haven, recorded the trip in her diary:[56]

Tuesday, 19 July
. . . Hydes and Bob Metzdorf on the train early. No Ralph. Anxious period of waiting. Still no Ralph. Train departs for New Haven. There is a telephone on the train, one of the first the travellers have seen, and Don makes a call to Fritz Liebert,[57] host for the evening, to report Ralph's absence. Fritz appalled. Don, considering all possibilities, makes a tour of the train—and finds Ralph in the last car—telling a new acquaintance the story of the Boswell papers. "Donsky, old boy, I couldn't make that car of yours and this is altogether agreeable."

[51]Details in Hyde's legal papers.

[52]Letter, Hyde to Buchanan, 6 June 1949 and subsequent correspondence (S. R. & Co.'s papers).

[53]Details in Hyde's legal papers.

[54]Letter, Isham to Buchanan, 30 August 1949 (S. R. & Co.'s papers).

[55]Letter, Babb to Isham, 14 July 1949 (IFP). Babb's receipt, dated 15 July 1949, refers to "81 slip cases and boxes, 5 New York Public Library Manuscript Division boxes, 5 items in folders and envelopes all picked up at the New York Public Library; 2 tin boxes, 1 folio letter file picked up at the Bank of the City of New York; and 1 trunk picked up at Col. Isham's apartment." In token of his appreciation to the New York Public Library for storing his papers for so long, Isham presented them with a letter of JB. See below Appendix V, p. 344, for details.

[56]Kindly made available to me for the following quotation by Mrs. Hyde.

[57]i.e., H. W. Liebert, known to his friends as "Fritz".

THE BOSWELL PAPERS ARRIVE AT YALE UNIVERSITY, 1949
Left to right: Edmund Malone (campus police), H. W. Liebert (then research
assistant in the library), Paul W. Winkler (senior cataloguer), James T. Babb
(librarian), and James McNulty (campus police).

COMPLETION OF THE SALE OF THE PAPERS TO YALE, 1949
Left to right: Babb, Isham, Liebert, and Edward C. Aswell (vice president of
McGraw-Hill). Isham, surrounded by the Boswell papers, signs the documents of
transfer.

Delighted and relieved, Fritz greets Ralph in New Haven. Drives him with Hydes and Bob to 210 St. Ronan Street and there the Lieberts, very great hosts, always sensitive to the particular occasion, provide a perfect evening. Just a few people including Professor Tinker and Ted Hilles. All are told to go home "after one drink" so that Ralph, who has a propensity to stay up until 4.30 A.M., will have no excuse to do so. Utter silence by 11 P.M. at 210 St. Ronan Street.

Wednesday, 20 July. *Closing Day*
    Ralph is called an hour before the Hydes.
    Breakfast at 8 in the garden (closing is to be at 10). Fritz Liebert reports on Ralph's progress—he is shaving now—hear running water. Time passes, Fritz and Don become increasingly nervous for the closing is to be on the dot, precise and official. Press and photographers. Breakfast of a sort is finally taken up to Ralph's room. Car is waiting, motor running. Fritz and Don in great discomfort. 9.45 A.M. Ralph comes down the stairs—walks into the garden. Every detail of his appearance and costume perfect. He says (shielding his eyes) "God! I have never seen such a beautiful sunrise."

When it was all over, Isham collapsed. He wrote to Buchanan some weeks later:

> One way or another the business kept me under a great strain for a very long time, as no one will understand better than your good self. When it was over I collapsed completely and was in bed with a nurse for three weeks—with a nurse in attendance I mean! But it seems the Devil wouldn't have me, so I am still on this side of the Styx and feeling stronger every day.[58]

The news of Yale's acquisition was released officially at the end of the month, and, on 1 August, the Boswell papers again made front page news in *The New York Times*. "Yale Gets Boswell Papers; All Will Be Published Soon," proclaimed the headline. Isham was quoted as saying:

> I have long held two major hopes. First, that Boswell's vast collection of manuscripts, having survived incredible vicissitudes for upward of 150 years, and consisting mainly of unpublished material, would be lodged permanently in an institution where scholars

---

[58]Letter, Isham to Buchanan, 30 August 1949 (S. R. & Co.'s papers).

could devote themselves to its editing: second, that it would, with all proper speed, be made available to the public. The present transfer fulfills the one and inaugurates the other.

It was announced that the editing and publishing plans would be in the hands of an editorial committee headed by Pottle and including amongst its members Liebert, Aswell, and Professor Frederick W. Hilles, chairman of the Yale Department of English.[59] Some forty or fifty volumes were envisaged to include the entire journals, an edition of the correspondence, a new edition of the *Life* with the suppressed passages restored, a definitive biography of Boswell, and the hitherto unknown works of Johnson, Reynolds, and others. Twenty-four distinguished scholars, twelve of them British, eleven American, and one Dutch, were invited to form an advisory committee. The immense task of preparing a definitive catalogue was entrusted to Pottle's wife, Marion S. Pottle, who had previously worked with her husband on the Malahide *Catalogue*. Quarters were assigned in the Yale University Library to "the Boswell Factory," as it came to be called, immediately adjoining "the Walpole Factory." W. S. Lewis, in charge of the editing and publication of Horace Walpole's papers, offered complete cooperation. "It will be a wonderful thing," wrote Liebert, "to have these two great projects going on next door to each other. . . . There will be little about the second half of the [eighteenth] century that can't be discovered in JB's papers or HW's."[60]

Isham's task was still not quite complete, for there remained in Ireland more than 900 pages of the "master" manuscript of the *Life*. "This exception," as his friend Hyde explained, "became the thing that kept Ralph awake at night, assisted the solvency of the telephone company, and prevented his friends from a good night's sleep."[61]

Yale was equally anxious to make good the gap in its collection and asked Isham to negotiate on its behalf. He was authorized to offer up to £10,000 for the manuscript on the understanding that he would try to buy it at the lowest possible price.[62] The only considera-

[59]Official press release by Yale University News Bureau.

[60]Letter, Liebert to Isham, 22 September 1949 (IFP).

[61]From remarks made by Donald F. Hyde during the fifth annual Johnson dinner held at the Grolier Club, New York, 18 September 1950 (cited below as "Hyde Remarks"). Typescript kindly supplied to me by James L. Clifford.

[62]Confirmed in a formal letter from F. W. Hilles and H. W. Liebert of Yale to Isham, 6 March 1950 (copy in Hyde's legal papers). The terms had evidently been agreed upon verbally some months earlier, for Isham opened his negotiations with Spingarn in December 1949.

tion he was to receive was to be allowed to retain the other page of the *Life* manuscript included in the 1946 purchase from Malahide.[63]

The sixth Lord Talbot had died on 22 August 1948 and the title and property had passed to his first cousin, Milo Talbot.[64] The new Lord Talbot was a bachelor and a member of the British Foreign Service. Apart from periods of leave, he did not take up residence at Malahide until 1956. Meanwhile, Lady Talbot had left Malahide, taking with her the *Life* manuscript which had been given to her by her husband some years before his death.[65] It was therefore with Lady Talbot, or rather her New York attorney, that Isham had to open negotiations.

On 15 December 1949, he wrote to Spingarn offering, on Yale's behalf, to buy the residue of the *Life* manuscript for the sum of £8,000.[66] This was much below the full market value but, as always, Lady Talbot was ready to be generous in the interests of scholarship and the completeness of the collection. She told Spingarn that, although she would not normally have considered such a low offer, she would accept on the strict understanding that the manuscript would go to Yale without anybody making a profit or commission on the deal.[67]

The negotiations were concluded successfully early in May 1950.[68] Mr. and Mrs. Hyde, accompanied by their friend Frederick B. Adams, Jr., director of the Pierpont Morgan Library, were then *en route* for Europe, and Isham wanted Hyde to go to Ireland to collect the manuscript. He explained his plan to Spingarn[69] and telephoned to Hyde on board ship. Let Hyde now take up the story for himself:

> In mid-Atlantic, while the three of us were dining comfortably, a steward came to the table and advised that Mr. A. Sham of New York was on the line. Mr. A. Sham conveyed the news that he had completed the negotiations for the purchase of the manuscript of the *Life*—would we go and have a look at it and confirm its authenticity or call it all off on the basis of inaccuracy? As

[63]Letter, Liebert to Isham, 21 July 1950 (IFP). See also below Appendix III, p. 332, n. 10.

[64]The seventh Lord Talbot de Malahide died April 1973. He was the son of Colonel Milo Talbot, who, it will be remembered, read JB's journal at Malahide whilst looking after the castle in the winter of 1907–08 and later persuaded his brother, the fifth Lord Talbot, to submit it to Sir John Murray for publication.

[65]The gift also included any other Boswell papers which might remain.

[66]Copy letter in IFP.

[67]So Spingarn informed Isham at a conference in New York. Reported in letter, Spingarn to Lady Talbot, 17 January 1950 (TFP).

[68]Letter, Spingarn to Lady Talbot, 11 May 1950 (TFP).

[69]Ibid.

Ralph said, Lady Talbot wanted an American scholar to look at it, but I told her you knew Boswell's handwriting and that was all one needed to know. I must confess that our pleasure over the completion of the negotiations was immeasurably increased by the realization that we had an easy introduction to Lady Talbot. We prepared a letter to her with some care which Fred posted in Southampton—as we were continuing to Paris. Upon our arrival in London four days later we found an envelope from Ireland marked on the outside and twice underlined, "Very Urgent." [70]

The letter contained an invitation to the Hydes from Lady Talbot to spend a night at her country house in the West of Ireland. [71] She explained:

I would like to meet you as I have here a suit case full of the final residue of Boswell papers, the present Lord Talbot having combed the papers at the Castle very thoroughly. I think Colonel Isham has seen these few oddments but I would prefer you to judge of whether or not they go to him. I do not think they are important, except for one printed first proof of the *Tour*, not quite complete, which I would be willing to sell. Any mss. in Boswell's hand (except *the* mss. of the *Life* of course) I would consider as Colonel Isham's. But I think they are only copies of letters he already has, legal papers, etc.

Neither Isham nor the Hydes had supposed that Lady Talbot had anything to deliver besides the manuscript of the *Life;* but now she spoke of proof sheets of the *Tour* as well as the best part of a suitcase full of other material. There was a distinct possibility of further discoveries and, a week later, the Hydes were "flying across the Irish Sea in a state of high expectation." [72] On 1 June, they arrived at Mount Shannon, Lady Talbot's attractive fishing lodge in County Clare. After luncheon, they adjourned to the sitting-room, where the suitcase awaited them. According to Hyde's own narration: [73]

The top was thrown open and we saw that it was filled with manuscript material—the triumph of experience over hope. Our dilemma was that the other guests had been promised a long

---

[70]Hyde Remarks. See above p. 294, n. 61.
[71]Letter, Lady Talbot to Hyde, 18 May 1950 (copy in IFP).
[72]Hyde Remarks. See above p. 294, n. 61.
[73]Ibid.

drive for tea on the coast. What could we do in an hour? The manuscript of the *Life* came out first—1,046 pages written on both sides for the most part and weighing 8.5 pounds. It consisted of the text of the *Life* from the beginning to the end.[74] Lady Talbot had listed the missing pages; we checked notes we had made on those pages owned by Arthur Houghton and found that with a few exceptions they made up the whole. It was needless to spend more time on that; we would confirm the bargain. How could we gain any concept of the remainder in the time allotted to us? We drew out pencils and paper and asked for permission to make notes. "Do you really think anyone would be interested?" queried Lady Talbot. As she rushed in and out of the room, for reasons I do not know, the two of us grabbed bundle after bundle looking and listing as rapidly as manuscripts have ever been gone over. Never did we state an opinion or draw a short breath, obeying an agreement we had made in advance. This was not the time for scholarship; it was the moment for the shrewd eye. . . .

After only an hour, the Hydes had to tear themselves away to join Lady Talbot and her other guests on the planned picnic excursion to the coast; but they had seen enough to know that here was yet another large and important collection of Boswell papers. That night Hyde telephoned excitedly to New York to tell Isham the news.[75] The authenticity of the *Life* manuscript was confirmed. The proof-sheets of the *Tour* were apparently complete and their interest was enhanced by heavy annotations in the hands of Boswell and Malone. There were also a few proof-sheets of the *Life*, similarly annotated. The manuscript of the Hebridean Journal,[76] found in the croquet box at Malahide in 1930, was now augmented by 126 pages of copy which Boswell prepared in 1785 to preface and conclude his journal when he edited it for the printer; and also 161 pages of inserts and

[74]This statement needs qualification. Although the last numbered page was 1,046, there were not 1,046 pages in the suitcase. Isham had already acquired 16 pages (plus a 4-page paper apart) in 1927 and a further 110 pages in 1931. The suitcase did, however, contain more than 900 pages, representing almost the entire residue of the manuscript. Only some half dozen numbered pages have never been recovered. See below Appendix III, p. 330–33. It should also be mentioned that the leaves of the "master" manuscript are numbered on only one side, the *versos* being left blank for additions and substitutions. Probably the majority of the leaves do show *some* writing on the *versos*, but a good many are blank, and many have only a few words or a few lines of writing on the *versos*.

[75]Hyde Remarks. See p. 294, n. 61.

[76]i.e., JB's original journal forming the basis of the published *Tour*.

some 50 pages of other related items. Journal material included 80 pages, fully written in French from the Italian Tour, and 20 pages written in Dutch. Amongst the large number of letters to Boswell were 10 from Lord Auchinleck, and 11 from Temple, and more than 150 from other correspondents, including David Hume and Voltaire. There were also many copies of Boswell's letters to other persons, including Rousseau, Voltaire, Temple, Hume, and Wilkes. Of special interest was a large dossier (containing about 125 items) on John Reid, the sheep-stealer, to whose trial and execution most of volume IX of Isham's private edition had been devoted. Other notable pieces were: the manuscript of Boswell's "Parliament, an Epistle to Dempster," "No Abolition of Slavery," and a rough draft of "William Pitt the Grocer of London"; the manuscript of Johnson's advertisement to the second edition of his *Journey to the Western Islands;* a letter from Johnson to Sir Joshua Reynolds telling of the death of Henry Thrale; a long account of the escape of Prince Charles Edward after the battle of Culloden by John MacLeod of Raasay; the missing portion of Boswell's autobiographical sketch written for Rousseau in 1764;[77] his roster of letters sent and received, 1765–67; expense accounts of his French and Italian Tours; legal notebooks; a notebook of memorabilia; loose pages of Boswelliana; and many more miscellaneous papers, including a few rare printed items.[78]

Where had they come from—these "new new Boswell papers" as Hyde christened them? Lady Talbot had referred in her letter to "the present Lord Talbot having combed the papers in the Castle very thoroughly," and she believed that Isham had already seen what, with superb understatement, she described as "these few oddments." In fact, Isham had never seen them before, nor is it conceivable that he would have passed them over if he had. Hyde thought he knew the answer. On the way to see Lady Talbot, he and Mrs. Hyde had paid a brief visit to Malahide:

> We lunched at Malahide with the new Lord Talbot, unrelated to James Boswell, but nevertheless intrigued by him. He was friendly, comparatively young, blonde and handsome—a bachelor and a member of the British Foreign Service. He told us of the

[77]The remainder of the sketch was included in Isham's 1946 purchase from Malahide. See above p. 258.

[78]Information in this paragraph about the contents of the suitcase comes from "Handlist of the Boswell Papers, 1950 Malahide Find" (3-page typescript in IFP), and the official Yale press release, 18 September 1950.

finding of the new Papers during a weekend house party when his guests were helping him sort through the family papers in the Castle.[79]

Hyde's account, through no fault of his own, was inaccurate and misleading. There was no house party and no discovery of any new papers at Malahide. Unfortunately, an official press release issued shortly afterwards by Yale was equally misleading: "Malahide Castle having passed, on the death of Lord Talbot, to the next heir, a thorough search of the rambling structure was made, and the additional cache of more than 500 items amounting to several thousand pages was found in a storeroom believed to contain nothing of that period."[80]

The truth of the matter is that the so-called new new Boswell papers were part of the 1940 grain loft find, and this explains why Isham did not see them when he searched Malahide in 1937. During the war years, Lady Talbot had made little or no progress in going through the papers from the grain loft, which had remained in boxes in the strong-room of the castle until Isham reopened negotiations at the end of the war.[81] They were then fetched out, but Lady Talbot, daunted by their bulk, did not feel up to making a proper list. As we have seen, she made a very brief and rough inventory which served as the basis of her sale to Isham.[82] When he took delivery in 1946, he believed that nothing remained at Malahide except the portion of the *Life* manuscript excluded from the sale. Unfortunately, Lady Talbot had omitted from the consignment a quantity of other papers, originally from the grain loft, which thus remained in the strong-room. When she left the castle in 1948, she took with her such remaining papers as she could find. Any that she missed and that the new Lord Talbot came across, he passed on to her. These were the papers which now filled the suitcase produced for Hyde's inspection. She thought they represented an unimportant residue that had already been seen and passed over by Isham. She did not realize that they were of major importance and that Isham was entitled to their delivery as forming part of his 1946 purchase.

[79]Hyde Remarks. See p. 294, n. 61.

[80]Press release dated 18 September 1950. The inaccuracies have been frequently repeated in other published accounts. See for example Christopher Morley's preface to the McGraw-Hill printing of JB 's *London Journal* and Hamilton Basso's story published in *Life* magazine on 4 December 1950.

[81]Lady Talbot has told me that ill-health, bad eyesight, and pressure of other commitments made systematic work on the papers during the war impossible.

[82]See above pp. 253–54.

The stories about the seventh Lord Talbot having discovered fresh Boswell papers are, in his own words, "based on moonshine."[83] He has pointed out the ambiguity of Lady Talbot's letter to Hyde: "What she meant was not that the suitcase full of papers was the result of my combing the castle, but that it contained what was in her opinion positively the final residue of the Boswell papers, as I had (she thought) combed the castle and found nothing."[84] He has also explained Hyde's story about the finding of new papers at a week-end house-party: "Any papers I may have told a story about finding during a house-party had been previously discovered in my predecessor's lifetime. I was no doubt being facetious, as I sometimes am."[85]

Lady Talbot agreed that all the additional papers except the proof sheets of the *Tour* should go to Isham without charge as having been omitted from his previous purchase. The proof sheets she considered to be still her property. She had not mentioned them before because they were printed and she thought Isham's interest lay in manuscript material. Hyde now pointed out that they ought to be joined with the rest of the collection at Yale and she agreed to his proposal that she should sell them to Isham for £2,500 on condition that he transfer them to Yale for the same sum.[86] Lady Talbot herself arranged the necessary export licence. Care was taken to ship the papers direct from the Irish Republic, for the loss of the Fettercairn papers to America had caused much adverse press comment and difficulties would certainly have been encountered if the papers had entered the United Kingdom. When they reached America, the *Life* manuscript and the proof sheets of the *Tour* were transferred to Yale at cost, as arranged. The other papers from the suitcase were Isham's personal property, so Yale agreed to buy them for a further $22,250. The total purchase money of $51,650 was provided by The Old Dominion Foundation and the McGraw-Hill Book Company in the same proportions as for the original purchase.

Isham's work was finally accomplished; but his success had its sad counterpart. For twenty-five years, the Boswell papers had been his consuming passion. Now that they were no longer his and there

---

[83]Letter, Lord Talbot to Pottle, 7 June 1960 (from Lord Talbot's copy).

[84]Ibid. The contents of the suitcase were in fact far from being "positively the final residue of the Boswell papers" as to which see Appendix I, p. 305 *et seq.* There were also the few "mementoes" listed in the Yale sale contract of 1949 as retained by Lady Talbot, some of which she has now parted with. See below Appendix I, pp. 313 and 317.

[85]Letter, Lord Talbot to R. F. Metzdorf, 24 June 1960 (from Lord Talbot's copy).

[86]Letter, Hyde to Isham, 2 June 1950 (IFP).

THE BEINECKE RARE BOOKS LIBRARY, YALE UNIVERSITY
Present home of the Boswell papers.

was no goal to strive for, he seemed to lose his interest in life. He was sixty years of age, and afflicted with emphysema. He paid little attention to his health, which became progressively worse. Ironically, the protracted legal battle with his family trustees ended at last with a settlement of nearly $150,000[87]—too late by several years for his time of dire financial need. Money had ceased to be a problem since the sale of his collection to Yale. What he felt most acutely now was a sense of isolation and neglect. He believed, not altogether fairly, that he had been deserted by friends and scholars. In fact, he still had many loyal friends, but his habit of sleeping throughout the day and staying up most of the night discouraged social contact. As his health continued to deteriorate, his attitude to others became increasingly demanding and his nocturnal life turned into an invalid's life. During these years, he found his chief consolation in the success of his two sons and, above all, in the devoted love and care of his fourth wife, Sarah McAdoo.[88] On 13 June 1955, at the age of sixty-four, he died at his home in New York.

His achievement is without parallel in literary history. He rescued from oblivion or dispersal perhaps the greatest collection of eighteenth-century literary manuscripts ever formed, at a financial risk which came close to ruining him; he made them available to scholars and to the world; and he ensured their preservation in the hands of the university best equipped to edit and publish them. Shortly before his death, his friend W. L. Payne told him: "I saw what others must have seen, the years of indomitable perseverance, the patience, the infinite letters, cables, conferences; the despairing hopelessness of it all—of ever getting it all together. . . . The job is at last done and scholars everywhere are your eternal debtors."[89]

He would have been the first to admit that he was a collector rather than a scholar; but his enormous enthusiasm for Boswell, his human understanding of the man, and his ability to communicate these things vividly to others did more than anything else to establish his collection as one of the great treasures of English literature. After hearing him speak to the English Graduate Union of Columbia University in 1949, Edward C. Aswell, vice president of McGraw-Hill, remarked:

[87]The attorneys acting for Isham were Messrs. Carey, Schenk & Jardine of Newark, New Jersey, from whose files this information comes.

[88]Sarah Lummus McAdoo, who survived Isham, and now lives in Sicily.

[89]Letter, W. L. Payne to Isham, (undated), (IFP).

You, to a degree that seems to me most extraordinary, have always known, as few do, that the proper study of mankind is man. Last night I could not help noting the vast distance which set you apart from the academic people who surrounded you as you read passages from your precious archives and brought instantly to life, there in the room, the great man long since dead who wrote the words you uttered. . . . The scholarly group who listened to you last night could spend years poring over your archives till they got them by heart without getting for themselves the sense of the living man whose record they are as you gave it to them in a single hour.[90]

The end of Isham's story is not the end of the story of the Boswell papers. The most recent events are described in the Appendix which follows. But still there are mysteries to be solved and missing papers to be found. What was the fate of Boswell's Dutch journal which he lost in his own lifetime?[91] What happened to the many letters from Boswell to Temple which were *not* retrieved from Madame Noël's shop in Boulogne?[92] And why have Boswell's letters to and from Johnson never been found?[93] The answers to these and other questions may one day be known, and then it will be possible to write another (it would be rash to say the last) chapter in the Boswell story.

[90]Letter, Aswell to Isham, 10 March 1949 (IFP).

[91]A large quarto manuscript of over 500 pages. For the circumstances of its loss, see *Boswell in Holland 1763–1764*, 1952, p. x (Heinemann edition).

[92]See above p. 26 and also p. 258, n. 81.

[93]See below Appendix II, p. 319 *et seq.*

# APPENDIX I

# *Still More Boswell Papers*

"My God! Is there no end to the Boswell saga?"[1]

This was Isham's understandable reaction when, in the summer of 1951, his friend Selwyn Cregeen reported a rumour that Lady Talbot had just received an old deed-box from her Edinburgh solicitors' office, containing more Boswell manuscripts.[2] Cregeen's information turned out to be inexact. The discovery was nothing more than a single notebook containing a treatise on the election law of Scotland, written out in Boswell's hand to his father's dictation. Lady Talbot had reported the find to Isham several months before and, as an export permit had been refused, it had been agreed that the notebook should be presented to the National Library of Scotland.[3]

The events of the last twenty years suggest, however, that there is indeed "no end to the Boswell saga." The great collection at Yale has been steadily enlarged by a stream of further acquisitions. Some of these have been items truly forming part of Boswell's own archives; others have been items of Boswellian interest from the archives of other persons. Into the latter category come letters sent by Boswell to various correspondents, many of which are still scattered or untraced. The purpose of this Appendix is to give an account of some of the more important discoveries and acquisitions during the period from 1950 to 1971.[4] In the years to come there are bound to be others.

BETWEEN 1950 AND 1953, only minor additions were made to the Yale collection. Some of these were purchases and others were gifts, the

---

[1]Letter, Isham to Selwyn Cregeen, 3 July 1951 (copy in IFP).
[2]Letter, Cregeen to Isham, 12 May 1951 (IFP).
[3]The notebook is now in the National Library of Scotland.
[4]The information for this Appendix comes chiefly from the following sources: detailed notes

donors being D. F. Hyde, C. B. Tinker, Arthur Lovell, H. W. Liebert, W. S. Lewis, H. B. VanderPoel, Thurston P. Blodgett, Mrs. Roy Arthur Hunt, and Isham himself. Most of the new material comprised letters to and from Boswell or members of his family or other letters of Boswellian interest. Isham's contributions included a manuscript of Boswell containing a memorandum of his visit to Voltaire in December 1764, another manuscript of Boswell containing an article for foreign newspapers on the French translation of the *Account of Corsica*, a 12-page manuscript, partly in Boswell's hand, with comments on Fielding's *Tom Jones*, and an amusing "mock brief" for the Lancaster Assizes, sent to Boswell as a practical joke and endorsed by him "a circuit joke by which I was for some time deceived."[5]

In 1954, Yale acquired an important group of papers which had originally formed part of the archives of Boswell's cousin and man of law, Robert Boswell, W.S. They were purchased from Mrs. Roxburgh of Locks Heath, Southampton, a descendant of Robert Boswell. They comprised fifty-three letters from Boswell to Robert Boswell, nine other letters to Robert Boswell, a few letters to Boswell from various correspondents, and some fragments.[6] The purchase was negotiated through the well-known book-dealer R. J. Barry of C. A. Stonehill, Inc. From the same source, the Boswell Papers Editing Fund at Yale also purchased, with the aid of a gift from H. W. Liebert, a number of old charters and other documents from Robert Boswell's papers.[7] A few other items (all letters) were also added to the Yale collection this year by purchase and by gift from Liebert.[8]

---

given to me by Marion S. Pottle on the various acquisitions by Yale after 1950 and copies of inventories of major purchases lent to me by the Boswell Office at Yale; notes, correspondence, and lists made available by Mrs. D. F. Hyde, R. F. Metzdorf, Lady Talbot de Malahide, and the late seventh Lord Talbot de Malahide, supplemented by their personal recollection of events; and my own knowledge of events in which I was directly involved.

[5]It should be noted that from time to time, Isham sent in to Yale items which should have been included in the 1949 delivery, but which had been mislaid at that time. These included papers apart and notes for the *Life*, JB's note of "presents given of my second edition of Doctor Johnson's Life," JB's Italian Journal of his jaunt with Lord Mountstuart, a note from Macqueen to JB, a small slip written in Sir William Forbes's hand, and JB's Epithalamium, Dr. Johnson to Mrs. Thrale, and other verses.

[6]For a description of these letters, see S. C. Roberts's article, "More Boswell Letters," in *The Times Literary Supplement*, 1 January 1954.

[7]Amongst these was a Register House Extract (c. 1800) of a *Diploma Edwardi Comitis de Kincardine*, 1647, which Yale presented to the Earl of Elgin in February 1956.

[8]Letters from JB to Andrew Gibb and Isaac Reed and 5 letters from various members of the Boswell family (none of them to JB). Another purchase by Yale this year was the manuscript of one of Sir Alexander Boswell's songs: "We'll come out yet."

In 1955, another important group of letters came to Yale. These were twenty-four letters from Boswell to his friend Andrew Erskine. Erskine's sister, Janet, married Sir Robert Anstruther of Balcaskie in Fife and she was the only one of Andrew's five brothers and sisters to leave issue. Presumably her children inherited Boswell's letters to Andrew, which thus came to be at Balcaskie. When Pottle visited Scotland in 1953, the Earl of Crawford took him to visit Balcaskie, where he was shown the letters. Sir Ralph Anstruther, the owner, was not at home, but Pottle wrote to him after his return to America and arranged terms for purchase. These letters were the originals of Boswell's side of the correspondence which he published in 1763 as *Letters between The Honourable Andrew Erskine and James Boswell, Esq.* The originals of Erskine's letters have never turned up.

In the summer of the following year, 1956, R. F. Metzdorf, Secretary to the Boswell Editorial Committee, visited Britain, where he communicated with Mrs. Elizabeth M. Hailey. This was the same Mrs. Hailey, descended from Boswell's daughter Elizabeth, who had entered as a last-minute claimant into the Fettercairn lawsuit.[9] From her, Metzdorf purchased the seal ring given by Boswell to his brother T. D. Boswell, and he arranged for Yale to acquire a few letters. The correspondents were various members of the Boswell family, none of them Boswell himself.[10]

In 1957 and 1958, the only additions to the Yale collection were two letters presented by Liebert and Tinker,[11] and a letter from Boswell to Bennet Langton purchased at Sotheby's jointly by Yale University Library, the Elizabeth W. Mainwaring Fund and the Boswell Papers Editing Fund. In January 1959, J. M. Osborn of Yale, an enthusiastic collector as well as a distinguished scholar, placed a number of items from his own collection on permanent deposit with Yale so that they should be available for research. These consisted of letters from Boswell and his children to various correspondents, a letter from Malone to Euphemia Boswell, and a manuscript of James Boswell junior. The same month, Liebert likewise made two items from his collection available for research at Yale although still retaining

---

[9]See above pp. 171–72.

[10]Three letters from Sir Alexander Boswell to William Boswell, two letters from T. D. Boswell to Elizabeth Boswell and two more from him to William Boswell, and two letters from William Boswell to Montgomery Boswell.

[11]From Liebert, a letter from JB (in Ross's hand) to Andrew Gibb; and from Tinker, a transcript of a letter from JB to Bruce Campbell.

ownership: a letter from Boswell to Henry Dundas and a circular letter to the Bishop of Carlisle by the committee on the monument to Johnson in Westminster Abbey, signed by Boswell, Reynolds, Burke, and Malone. Later that year, some small gifts of letters were received from Liebert and H. B. VanderPoel.[12]

In the summer of 1960, Charles McVicker, a member of the Yale faculty, stayed at Malahide as a guest of the seventh Lord Talbot. He brought back with him to America a package containing about 170 leaves of Boswell material. There were some folded sheets of Boswell's notes of the voting at the Carlisle election in December 1786, a journal of Boswell's brother, Lieutenant John Boswell, a water-colour sketch painted by Veronica Boswell at the age of nine, an incomplete 4-page manuscript of Boswell's "Hints for Observations on the United Provinces," and a quantity of material found wrapped in *The Morning Post* of 12 February 1907 (probably the result of a sorting by the fifth Lord Talbot). This last material was badly rotted and flaking and required expert handling and restoration. The bulk of it remains fragmentary. Amongst the Boswell manuscript items were notebooks, slips, journal notes, a short list of books, and part of a composition in French. The nature of the material suggested that it had originally been part of the contents of the croquet box. Presumably Lady Talbot had ignored it as being too fragmentary to be of any value. Recognizing its importance, Lord Talbot presented it to Yale.

The year 1961 was a very important one for the acquisition of new material, largely due to the efforts of R. F. Metzdorf. In the early summer, he crossed the Atlantic and, whilst in Europe, visited Lady Talbot at Abbeylea, her home near Dublin, John P. D. Boswell at Auchinleck, and the seventh Lord Talbot at Malahide. At Abbeylea, he was allowed to go through the papers which Lady Talbot had brought with her when she left Malahide after her husband's death. He sorted out a collection of some 500 pieces of Boswellian interest. These included Boswell's commonplace book and two sets of the *Hypochondriack* papers (printed) with Boswell's correspondence relating to them. In the same bundle was found a letter from Boswell to Temple of 6 July 1784. There were also Boswell's correspondence connected with choosing a successor to Mr. Dun as minister of Auchinleck, a collection of Carlisle election broadsides, some more volumes of Lieu-

---

[12]From H. B. VanderPoel, a letter from JB to Gibb; and from Liebert, a copy of a letter from JB (not in his hand) to Lord Dreghorn, a letter of Sir James Boswell, a naval document signed by T. D. Boswell, and a document witnessed by James Boswell of Balbarton. In January 1960, Liebert also presented a letter from James Boswell junior to Henry Ellis.

tenant John Boswell's journals, and a large number of Boswell's newspaper essays (especially "Rampagers," occasional essays contributed to *The Public Advertiser*) and clippings.

Lady Talbot also permitted Metzdorf to inspect the family legal papers held at the office of her Scottish solicitors, Messrs. David Shaw & Co. of Ayr. Some seven boxes of these papers had recently been delivered from the Edinburgh solicitors who had formerly acted for the family for over a century. Metzdorf set aside about a hundred pieces as of interest. Most related to Sir James Boswell's case to break the entail in 1852, but there were also a list of wines at Auchinleck in Boswell's hand, a copy of a letter from Boswell to the Prussian Boswells of 10 June 1791, and a copy of Boswell's diploma for the Prussian Boswells.

Lady Talbot agreed to terms for the purchase of all these papers by Yale and funds were provided by The Old Dominion Foundation and McGraw-Hill. With typical generosity, Lady Talbot turned over the price received (which was substantial) to be used towards restoring the roof of Auchinleck House.

Metzdorf also found at Abbeylea a number of valuable printed items, some of which were annotated or docketed by Boswell or Johnson. Lady Talbot sold three of the most important to Mr. and Mrs. Hyde in June 1961. These were proof sheets of *Taxation no Tyranny*, corrected by Johnson and docketed by Boswell, a printed legal document relating to the case of Thomas Robertson, docketed by Boswell that Johnson wrote the last four paragraphs, and Boswell's proposals for Charlotte Lennox's *Shakespeare Illustrated*, 1793, also docketed by Boswell.[13] The other printed pieces were sent for sale at Parke-Bernet on 3 October 1961 (lots 276–80, 282–84, 332, 355, 356, 434, and 466). All of these lots except 276 and 282 were bought for the Hyde Collection.

On his visit to Auchinleck, Metzdorf found that there still remained a large mass of papers relating to the management of the estate *c.*1722–1836, comprising several hundred pieces. It was difficult to be sure who owned these and Metzdorf saw J. P. D. Boswell's lawyer in Edinburgh to discuss the matter. Fortunately, any problems which might have arisen were avoided when Lady Talbot waived all claims. A letter was despatched to Yale offering them the papers and terms for purchase were agreed upon.

At Malahide, Metzdorf was astonished to be shown a further mass

---

[13]Lady Talbot must have had two copies of the proposals because another copy, also docketed by JB, was included in the papers from Abbeylea sold to Yale.

of family papers, more than enough to fill five large suitcases. Much of the material consisted of the "chartulary" of the Boswells of Auchinleck, a legal record of titles, charters, and the like dating back to the first Laird, Thomas, killed at Flodden in 1513. There were also earlier charters and other documents of the Boswells before they owned Auchinleck, several genealogical accounts of the family, and numerous titles relating to various lands acquired over the centuries. Boswell had apparently sent some of his chartulary material to Robert Boswell, who had never returned it, and it was some of this which Yale had purchased in 1954 from R. J. Barry of C. A. Stonehill, Inc. But the main bulk had remained at Auchinleck from whence it had gone to Malahide.

Metzdorf was also shown a welter of all sorts of papers and letters pertaining to the families of the several lairds or families connected by marriage with them, especially those of the second Earl of Kincardine and his Countess, Veronica van Sommelsdyck, and her Dutch relations. There were relatively few papers of or contemporary with Boswell himself: a few manuscripts in his hand of minor importance, some correspondence between him and his overseer Bruce, and other papers relating to the management of Auchinleck estate, a few letters to him from various persons, a burgess ticket for Inverkeithing, 1774, an 8-page fragment of a manuscript in his hand about the storage of the records of Scotland, papers relating to minor financial transactions, receipted school bills, legal documents, and printed and peripheral material. There were also some early playbills, a list of Greek and Latin books at Auchinleck in Mrs. Boswell's hand, and two desirable collectors' pieces: Johnson's diploma from Trinity College, Dublin, 1765, and his father's (Michael Johnson's) parchment burgess ticket from the City of Lichfield, 1710. Later generations of the Boswells were well represented. There were many letters to Sir Alexander from prominent people, papers relating to his business affairs and estate matters, correspondence about his literary pursuits and manuscript copies of some of his poems; also papers of James Boswell junior, related to his work on Malone's Shakespeare, and letters of the time of Sir James Boswell.

Lord Talbot agreed that the whole collection as seen by Metzdorf should be sent to Yale to be listed and appraised. Metzdorf could not cope with such a bulk of material in his luggage, but two suitcases were taken over to America in the autumn of 1961 in the care of

Herbert T. F. Cahoon, Curator of Autograph Manuscripts at the Pierpont Morgan Library, New York. Three more suitcases and a carton followed in the summer of 1962.

Whilst at Malahide, Metzdorf also saw a small manuscript notebook of Johnson's containing the last two leaves of *The Vanity of Human Wishes*, a partial draft of Act V of *Irene,* and an account with Mr. Stuart, 1746, relating to the *Dictionary.* This and other interesting items had originally been seen lying in one of the many drawers of the ebony cabinet by the Hydes on a visit to Malahide in 1956. It was of the greatest possible interest to them as Isham had already sold them the manuscript of *The Vanity of Human Wishes,* lacking only the last two leaves. Metzdorf pointed out to Lord Talbot the importance of reuniting the whole manuscript. Lord Talbot wrote to Lady Talbot at Abbeylea and both agreed that the notebook should go to the Hydes.[14] It was handed over to them in October 1961 and a facsimile of the whole manuscript was privately printed by them for distribution at the annual dinner of the Johnsonians in New York, on 21 September 1962.

Lord Talbot still retained at Malahide at this time a few display items. Of these, the only one which now remains is Boswell's grant of £500 to his daughter Veronica in recognition of her fondness for Johnson.[15]

In 1962, Metzdorf was again active in Britain and Ireland. On 4 June, he arrived at Crawley Grange, near Bedford, home of Mr. and Mrs. Ian Boswell. There, he found pictures of Lord Auchinleck and T. D. Boswell and was told that there were papers in the attic. More recent enquiries, however, indicate that Crawley Grange contains little of Boswellian interest.

Three days later, Metzdorf was in Peebles, Scotland, visiting Dr. Philip Boswell, a retired dentist, descended from Robert Boswell, W.S., and heir male of the Boswells of Auchinleck.[16] Dr. Boswell had a few inscribed books, some manuscripts relating to family history and genealogy, some student notes of Dr. John Boswell taken at Leyden (including one of Boerhaave's lectures), and two letters by Boswell, one to Robert Boswell and the other, dated January 1763, to Dr. John

[14]Letter, Lord Talbot to Lady Talbot, 26 May 1961 (TFP).

[15]I do not know whether this manuscript will remain at Malahide following the death of Lord Talbot in April 1973.

[16]i.e., he would have succeeded to Auchinleck as heir of entail if Sir James Boswell had not broken the entail in 1852. See Table V, p. 356.

Boswell. The latter was of some importance, being contemporary with the London journal. All this material remained in Dr. Philip Boswell's ownership, but Metzdorf served the useful function of establishing its existence and whereabouts.[17]

The following day, 8 June, Metzdorf reached Auchinleck, where he worked on four boxes of papers from the house of the late Miss Margaret Boswell of Sandgate, Ayr. Miss Boswell was J. P. D. Boswell's aunt and the papers were really Auchinleck papers taken to her house when Auchinleck had been requisitioned during the war. Metzdorf listed some 134 items as of interest—mainly Auchinleck estate papers and business letters *c.* 1787–1833, and papers by or relating to Sir Alexander Boswell. There were a few Boswell items, including a couple of letters to him from T. D. Boswell and a printed legal paper, but by and large there was not much of special interest. The collection was offered to and purchased by Yale.

Metzdorf's final stop in 1962 was at Malahide, where he picked up the remainder of the papers which he had sorted out a year earlier. They reached Yale on his return to America later in the summer.

The next four years were relatively uneventful. A letter from J. C. Lettsom to Boswell and a draft of this letter were purchased by the Yale Library Associates in 1963. In 1964, Lord Talbot sent over another package of material to be added to the five suitcases already at Yale. In December 1966, a number of Boswellian items from Tinker's library were added to the Yale collection. These had in fact passed to Yale by bequest after Tinker's death in 1963, but it was not until December 1966 that they were placed with the other Boswell papers. They comprised seven letters to Boswell from various correspondents, a draft letter from Melchiore Cesarotti to Boswell, three letters from Sir Alexander Boswell to various correspondents, letters from Euphemia Boswell, T. D. Boswell, and Sarah, Duchess of Marlborough, to various correspondents, an engraving of Dance's drawing of Boswell, Boswell's manuscript "Uxoriana Or My dear Wife's excellent Sayings," and (added a few months later) a draft letter from Thomas Percy to Boswell.[18]

[17]Dr. Philip Boswell died recently and his books and papers have presumably passed to his heirs.

[18]See *The Tinker Library*, The Yale University Library, 1959. The items transferred are catalogue numbers 293–95, 297, 298, 300–07, 347, 367, and 1660. The engraving of the Dance drawing is uncatalogued. Two of these items had been included in the papers sold at Sotheby's by Mrs. Laurence Eliott in June 1932 (as to which, see above pp. 102–04). They were the manuscript of "Uxoriana" (lot 271) and the letter from the Duchess of Marlborough to Mr. Rudd endorsed by JB (lot 279).

In 1967, further papers from the Talbot family were added to the Hyde Collection. It is beyond the scope of this book to present a comprehensive survey of Boswell papers *not* at Yale, but it must be mentioned that, after Yale, the largest and finest Boswellian collection in the world is to be found in the Hyde Library at Four Oaks Farm in New Jersey. The foundations of this collection were laid in a series of purchases from Isham between 1946 and 1949 (noted in detail in Appendix V) and the purchase in 1948 of the great Johnsonian and Boswellian collection of R. B. Adam of Buffalo.[19]

It will be remembered that in 1956 the Hydes had found at Malahide the little Johnson notebook containing the end of the manuscript of *The Vanity of Human Wishes;* and that in 1961 this was reunited with the remainder of the manuscript already in their possession. But the notebook was not the only thing they had found. In one of the many compartments of the ebony cabinet were a number of other papers of considerable interest. These remained at Malahide until April 1967 when Lord Talbot agreed to let Mrs. Hyde have them. They consisted of letters to Alexander Boswell from his father, and from his sisters, Veronica and Elizabeth, a letter to Sir James Boswell from his maternal grandmother about Sir Alexander's duel, Boswell's journal notes for fifteen days (probably September 1790), a transcript of "The Ballad of Chevy Chase" in Boswell's youthful hand, a legal document noted by Boswell, some manuscripts of Lord Auchinleck, miscellaneous family papers, and a few rare printed pieces.

At this time, Lady Talbot still retained in her possession a few mementoes from the Boswell papers. The existence of such mementoes was known to Yale, for Isham had mentioned them when selling his collection in 1949, and the sale contract listed six specific items. In October 1967, Lady Talbot sold two of these items to Mrs. Hyde: a letter from Johnson to Mr. Cave, and a small leather-bound notebook containing Boswell's manuscript notes on a legal case heard by him as Recorder of Carlisle in 1789. Lady Talbot also produced another interesting piece not previously known to exist, for it was not amongst the six items listed in the Yale contract. This was a packet docketed by Boswell "Specimen of Otaheite Cloth given to me by Sir Joseph Banks when he was in Edinburgh," and containing eight samples of

---

[19]For more information about the Hyde Collection see the article written by Mr. and Mrs. Hyde for *The Book Collector,* Autumn 1955 (vol. 4, No. 3, p. 208 *et seq.*); and also *Four Oaks Library* (ed. Gabriel Austin), privately printed, Somerville, New Jersey, 1967, and especially the articles on Samuel Johnson by R. F. Metzdorf and on James Boswell by Charles Ryskamp.

cloth, with a list in pencil on the inside of the packet describing the samples. Presumably Banks brought these back with him after sailing round the world with Captain Cook on the *Endeavour,* 1768–1771. Mrs. Hyde purchased this item from Lady Talbot, along with a bundle of printed proof sheets of publications from Sir Alexander Boswell's Auchinleck Press.

It was not until 1967 that Yale finally decided to acquire the large mass of papers sent over from Malahide by Lord Talbot in 1961 and 1962. Since then, little of importance has been added to the Yale collection: a single letter to Boswell from Henry Hutton, purchased in 1968 with money provided by Mrs. Hyde, a letter from Boswell to Richard Rudd, purchased in 1971 with the help of the Tinker Fund and the Library Associates, and a further purchase from Lady Talbot in 1972, details of which are given below.

SINCE BEGINNING my research for this book, I have been personally involved on several occasions in dealing with papers of Boswellian interest. In May 1963, I was walking along York Place in Edinburgh when I passed a door bearing the plate of "Howden & Molleson, C.A." It struck me that the name was familiar in some recent context. I then remembered that this was the firm of chartered accountants which had attended to various Auchinleck estate matters in the early part of this century. On the spur of the moment, I went inside and asked to speak to somebody who knew about Auchinleck estate. The receptionist looked blank and passed me on to a more senior assistant who also had never heard of Auchinleck. I then saw one of the junior partners to whom I explained my interest. He said that the only person who might be able to help me was their elderly senior partner, Mr. G. M. Byres. Soon, I found myself speaking to Mr. Byres. He vaguely remembered hearing Auchinleck estate mentioned many years ago and promised to have his firm's archives searched for any records which might relate to my work. Several weeks later, he telephoned to say that all the old papers had been sent for salvage during the war, but in the bottom of an otherwise empty deed box he had found a small scrap which might be of interest. He promised to send it on for my perusal. When it arrived, I was amazed to discover that it was a fragment of Boswell's journal. It was a single sheet folded to make four pages, beginning halfway through the entry for 28 August 1780, continuing with the whole of the entries for 29 and 30 August, and ending halfway through the entry for 31 August.

How the manuscript came to be in the hands of Howden & Molleson is a mystery. Perhaps when Auchinleck was let to Mr. McCrone in 1918 he came across it and passed it on to Howden & Molleson as estate factors. Whatever the explanation, I was able to convince Mr. Byres that Yale was now the legal owner.[20] Mr. Byres turned the manuscript over to me and I delivered it to Yale when I visited America in October 1963. I was pleased to learn that it precisely filled a gap in the journal manuscript already at Yale.

In 1968, I visited Fettercairn for the first time. That summer, I had the pleasure of accompanying Mrs. Hyde and L. F. Powell on a tour through Scotland following the footsteps of Boswell and Johnson in 1773. When we received an invitation to lunch from Mrs. Somervell, grand-daughter of Lord Clinton and present owner of Fettercairn, we were glad to make a detour to visit the scene of Abbott's dramatic discoveries. We were taken to the library, where a large wooden box awaited us. We were told that it had only just arrived from Durham. It was said to contain all the material of Boswellian interest[21] removed years before by Abbott, with Lord Clinton's permission, for study at Durham.

Time was limited and we could do no more than sift quickly through the contents of the box. Nothing could have been more tantalizing. Besides a thick wad of letters in Boswell's hand, we saw letters of Johnson, Malone, Reynolds, and others, and hundreds of letters of Boswell's children. Sensing my frustration, Mrs. Somervell invited me to spend a week-end at Fettercairn in the autumn when I would be allowed to examine the contents of the box in detail.

I returned to Fettercairn in September 1968 and set to work. To my surprise, I began to find a number of Boswell items nowhere mentioned by Abbott in his catalogue, including letters to Boswell from Joseph Warton and Reynolds, and a copy in Mrs. Boswell's hand of an important letter from Boswell to Reynolds referring to Johnson's death and requesting the return of his (Boswell's) letters to Johnson. I was also delighted to find a previously unrecorded letter from the Rev. W. J. Temple to Forbes which proved Temple's concern for his responsibilities as one of Boswell's literary executors.[22]

None of these papers had I expected to find; but I did hope

[20]Isham having purchased the entire journals from Lord Talbot (including any subsequently discovered portions) and Yale having acquired Isham's title.

[21]It will be remembered that the Court of Session did not award everything listed in the *Fettercairn Catalogue* to Isham and the Cumberland Infirmary. Certain items, including JB's letters to Forbes, were excluded as belonging to Forbes's descendants rather than to JB's; and there was also a good deal else of interest, such as the correspondence of Malone and JB's children with Forbes, not listed in the *Catalogue*.

[22]Quoted above p. 187.

and expect to locate the three Johnson manuscripts mentioned by
Abbott in the introduction to his catalogue (though not listed in the
catalogue itself). These were a letter from Johnson to Forbes,[23] a copy
made by Johnson for Reynolds of his famous letter to Macpherson,
and Johnson's letter to Boswell of 11 July 1784.[24] Lack of information
about the first of these manuscripts had already created problems
for at least one Johnsonian scholar.[25] Abbott had described finding
in the library cupboard at Fettercairn what he "had long been looking
for and knew must be somewhere—Johnson's letter to Sir William,"
but without indicating its date or contents or why he should have
expected to find it. It was unlisted in the catalogue since it was a
Forbes rather than a Boswell item. But the two other Johnson manuscripts had clearly come from Boswell's archives and their omission
from the catalogue is inexplicable; nor can I understand why none
of the litigants in the Fettercairn lawsuit tried to claim them. The
letter from Johnson to Boswell was, after all, the *only* such letter of
substance to have survived.[26] To my great pleasure, all three manuscripts soon emerged from the box and I spent the rest of that afternoon absorbed in my first attempt to master Johnson's baffling
handwriting.

The total contents of the box ran to several hundred items which
I have already described in some detail in an earlier footnote.[27] None
of the material had hitherto been generally available to scholars and
less than a sixth was represented by items listed in Abbott's catalogue. Even Yale had been unable to print the texts of such of the
material as was known to exist. Now that Abbott had at last relin-
quished it, there was a chance that it might be made accessible to
all. I explained the position to Mrs. Somervell, who responded just
as I hoped she would. She wanted the papers to remain in Scotland,
but was determined that no scholar should be deprived of their use.
When I left Fettercairn, the box of papers was in the back of my
car and, the next day, I delivered it, on her instructions, to the National
Library of Scotland. The papers remain there, freely available to any
scholar who wishes to refer to them.

I was still anxious to establish positively what papers, if any,
remained in the hands of Lady Talbot. I knew that two of the six

[23]See *Fettercairn Catalogue*, p. xxii.
[24]Ibid., p. xvii.
[25]For Mary Hyde when writing her article "Not in Chapman" published in *Johnson, Boswell and their Circle*, Oxford, 1965.
[26]See below Appendix II, pp. 323–24.
[27]See above p. 125, n. 28.

items listed in the 1949 Yale contract as retained by her had been sold in 1967 to Mrs. Hyde. I was curious to know if she still had the other four and whether she owned any other unlisted items. The chance to find out came in the summer of 1971 when I was due to visit America. I arranged to break my journey in Dublin and Lady Talbot kindly allowed me to call to inspect all the papers in her possession. A number of "display items" were produced for my perusal which included the four I expected to find. But there were others too which neither Yale nor I had known about. I was then invited to rummage in the bottom drawer of a large metal filing cabinet, filled with a jumble of papers. A quick look told me that all of these papers must at one time have belonged at Auchinleck. I set to work, listing everything methodically. Five folded slips, inscribed by Boswell, each held some intensely personal keepsake: his wife's purse, a lock of her hair, her wedding ring, some fragments of the velvet coffin coverings of certain members of the Royal Family, removed by young James Boswell as a schoolboy when the vault was opened for the funeral of the Duke of Cumberland in 1790, and a piece of bark cut by Boswell from the stump of King Charles's oak tree at Boscobel, which, according to Boswell's inscription, he had "viewed with veneration in Autumn 1792." There were also an invitation from the Thrales to Boswell, docketed by him, and a slip in his hand referring to the ebony cabinet.[28] The most touching item was a folded paper from which the contents were missing. On it Boswell had written: "Two stalks of Lilly of the Vally which my dear wife had in her hand the day before she died."

A few other items of interest emerged from the filing cabinet: a notebook of Lord Auchinleck, a small etching by Alexander, a racecard marked by Sir James Boswell, and some printed material. Lady Talbot also showed me a fine Goldsmith mourning ring, Boswell's own inscribed copy of Thomas à Kempis's *De Imitatione Christi* (Antwerp, 1664), and a Bible inscribed by Boswell to the effect that it had been given to him by Lord Mountstuart in Italy in 1765.

Lady Talbot decided that Mrs. Hyde should be given the first chance to acquire all of these things, with the exception only of the five folded slips and the keepsakes which went with them, and the Goldsmith mourning ring. These she wished to retain as mementoes. When I reached America, I reported the details to Mrs. Hyde, who has now purchased the items on offer for her collection.

I also took with me to America an offering for Yale. Shortly before

---

[28]The invitation is reproduced as an illustration in *The Impossible Friendship*, by Mary Hyde, Harvard University Press, 1972 (facing p. 16).

leaving Lady Talbot's house, I noticed in her sitting room a small bookcase containing mostly modern volumes; but what caught my eye were twelve quarto volumes splendidly bound in red morocco. I pulled one out and found it was a chartulary volume with a fine eighteenth-century binding, containing various Auchinleck charters and deeds copied by hand in impeccable copperplate. The other eleven volumes were the same. Lady Talbot agreed that these volumes should be offered to Yale, along with some old title deeds and an Auchinleck estate cash-book for 1790–91 which I found in the bottom drawer of the filing cabinet. Yale accepted, and the purchase has now been concluded.

The residue of the contents of the drawer consisted of a miscellany of old manuscripts and historical documents (some of them copied by Lord Auchinleck or annotated by him), and a few printed pieces, but nothing of interest either to Mrs. Hyde or to Yale. A few have gone to the National Library of Scotland and the rest are being disposed of privately. They cannot be said to be Boswell papers except in so far as they must at one time have belonged at Auchinleck.

This cannot be the end of the story. Anyone who has attempted a systematic search of a large rambling house, such as Malahide or Fettercairn, will realize that one can never be sure that nothing has been missed. Lady Talbot now has no papers other than the few mementoes I have mentioned; and none can remain at Auchinleck, which has been gutted internally for the eradication of dry rot. But who can doubt that somewhere at this moment still more Boswell papers are lying hidden and that one day they will be found?

# APPENDIX II

# *Boswell's Correspondence with Johnson*

Boswell's correspondence with Johnson, counting both sides, ran to more than 225 letters.[1] These must have been amongst his most treasured possessions, but only a handful are known to survive—four letters, a fragment, and a draft of Boswell's; and two letters (one incomplete), and a brief note of Johnson's. What happened to the remainder is the chief unsolved puzzle of the Boswell papers.

R. W. Chapman, in his edition of Johnson's letters, points out that nowhere in Boswell's journals or registers of letters is a letter from Johnson recorded which is not also recorded in the *Life*.[2] He lists 103 letters from Johnson to Boswell, of which there are only two not printed or quoted from in the *Life*.[3] One of these is a mere scrap (an invitation running to nine words); the other is a short letter of introduction which probably never reached Boswell. Chapman is almost certainly correct in his conclusion that Boswell kept all of Johnson's letters and printed them all in whole or in part in the *Life*, except for a number of "cards or notes" in the third person.

Boswell's side of the correspondence, according to Chapman, comprised at least 125 letters. He printed about fifty in the *Life* and described or mentioned as many again. The existence of the rest can only be established from references in the journals and registers of letters. As these are themselves incomplete, one cannot preclude the possibility that other letters may exist.

A definitive text of the entire correspondence will not be established until the missing documents have been traced. At the moment,

[1]See SJ *Letters*, III, pp. 276–96.
[2]Ibid., III, p. 276.
[3]Ibid., Nos. 355 and 550.1.

319

we have no text at all for more than half of Boswell's letters nor, with a single exception, for the many passages from Johnson's letters omitted in the *Life*. Chapman also points out that we cannot rely entirely on the textual accuracy of what Boswell printed.[4] Johnson's hand is notoriously difficult and, as the actual manuscripts were usually sent to the printer as copy,[5] misreadings must have occurred. Boswell no doubt respected Johnson's texts, but would have had to face the problem of correcting minor errors, supplying inadvertent omissions, and so forth. In the case of his own letters, he may have indulged in editing of a more extensive nature.[6] Only the recovery of the manuscripts will solve these problems and supply the many texts which are lacking.

When Boswell died in London in 1795, he was working on a third edition of the *Life*. It is reasonable to suppose that he had the materials for his book beside him at his house in Great Portland Street. These materials included not only the letters from Johnson to himself, but also his own side of the correspondence, which he had retrieved from Johnson in 1784. He tells us in the *Life:* "I generally kept copies of my letters to him [i.e., Johnson], that I might have a full view of our correspondence, and never be at a loss to understand any reference in his letters. He kept the greater part of mine very carefully; and a short time before his death was attentive enough to seal them up in bundles, and order them to be delivered to me, which was accordingly done."[7]

Malone, as we have seen, took charge of the papers in London immediately after Boswell's death.[8] He "carefully examined" them and then sent them to Sir William Forbes in Scotland.[9] I do not believe his examination revealed the letters from Johnson to Boswell. He did not mention any when writing to Forbes in 1796, although he did remark on other correspondence concerning Voltaire and Rousseau.[10] In 1804, when he asked Forbes to hunt out the originals of several

[4]SJ *Letters*, III, p. 308.

[5]JB, however, occasionally made copies to send to the printer. Chapman mentions copies of 7 letters from SJ to JB made by or for JB, all of which were found at Malahide. (See SJ *Letters*, III, pp. 277–78. The letters are Nos. 163, 181, 185, 222, 435, 475, and 575.) Only in one letter (185) is there to be found the text of a sentence not printed in the *Life*. Chapman suggests that JB may have made such copies because of a reluctance to submit suppressed passages to the printer's eye.

[6]Some evidence of this is presented below p. 328.

[7]*Life*, II, p. 2.

[8]See above p. 6.

[9]See above p. 186.

[10]See above p. 186.

Johnson letters, he wrote:

> I had conceived . . . that Mr. Boswell had kept Dr. Johnson's Letters addressed to himself in a distinct parcel; but if this is not the case, & they are blended with the other materials of his work, wd it not be adviseable to take them *all out,* and arrange them in chronological order, to be preserved as an honourable testimony to the Author, in the Library at Auchinleck?[11]

If the letters had passed through Malone's hands in London, he would have known for certain whether they were in a separate bundle or not and could have told Sir William that the papers he sought were amongst those he had previously sent from London. I conclude, therefore, that although the letters are likely to have been in London when Boswell died, somehow or other they eluded Malone.

I am nevertheless puzzled by the fact that Malone apparently did not know that Forbes had in his possession a large number of original letters from Johnson to correspondents other than Boswell. In his letter to Forbes of 3 March 1804, he wrote: "I suppose amongst Mr. B's papers he cd not have had many *original* letters from Johnson, not addressed to himself."[12] One hundred and nineteen such letters were found at Fettercairn[13] and presumably they were in Forbes's custody in 1804. If Malone was unaware of this, they cannot have been with the papers which he sent from London to Forbes, nor with those which Forbes sent to him for perusal in London. They must therefore have come to Forbes from Auchinleck, which seems to refute my suggestion that the materials for the *Life* were in London when Boswell died. I can only conjecture that Boswell, after completing his book, detached these letters in order to return them to the various persons to whom they belonged; but that he was reluctant to part with them unless pressed to do so, and in this manner a large number of them remained at Auchinleck. I still feel that most of his other materials for the *Life*, including his correspondence with Johnson, was probably in London at his death.

Malone, I think, was correct in his belief that Boswell kept Johnson's letters to himself in a separate bundle. He had collaborated closely with Boswell in working on the *Life* and was in a position to know how Boswell handled his materials. Most of these materials have now been recovered, but *both* sides of the correspondence with Johnson

---

[11]Letter, Malone to Forbes, 4 May 1804 (Fettercairn Papers). Already quoted above p. 191.

[12]Letter, Malone to Forbes, 3 March 1804 (Fettercairn Papers). Referred to above p. 189.

[13]*Fettercairn Catalogue*, Nos. 1472 to 1590.

are still missing, with the few exceptions already mentioned. This suggests that Boswell also detached and kept separate his own letters to Johnson. The riddle is: where did he keep the precious bundles and what happened to them when he died?

When Malone wrote to Forbes in 1804, he thought they must be either in Sir William's possession or at Auchinleck. Unfortunately, Forbes's letter reporting on the result of his search has never been traced, but Malone's editing of the fourth edition of the *Life* suggests that it was unsuccessful.[14] This does not prove conclusively that Forbes did not have the letters. The materials through which he had to search were, in Malone's words, "an immense mass." He may not have had the time or inclination to sift through them all in detail. Indeed, one of the items Malone asked him to find, a letter from Johnson to Lucy Porter, was very probably in his hands at this time for it subsequently turned up at Fettercairn.[15]

If the letters ever were at Auchinleck after Boswell's death, they cannot be there now. The house is empty of furniture and most of the plaster has been stripped from the walls. There is no place left for a bundle of manuscripts to hide. Young Alexander, it will be remembered, delivered to Forbes soon after his father's death "all letters that can possibly concern literary subjects." The correspondence with Johnson certainly came into this category and, if Forbes had received it, he ought to have been able to deal with Malone's request. Alexander may have missed the bundles of letters, but I am inclined to believe they were not there. If Boswell had elevated them to the status of family heirlooms and placed them in the ebony cabinet (as he did a few other letters), they had been removed by the time the contents of the cabinet were inventoried in 1805.[16] Most of the papers at Auchinleck, including those returned after perusal by the literary executors, were subsequently found at Malahide. The absence of the letters suggests that they were not at Auchinleck. They may of course have been destroyed or removed before the family papers were taken to Ireland about 1905, but this seems to me unlikely in view of the fact that the great bulk of the papers was neither removed nor destroyed.

There *may* still be papers at Fettercairn, but I doubt it. Abbott's search of the house in 1931 was systematic and thorough. Since 1968, I have visited Fettercairn several times and Mrs. Somervell has kindly allowed me to search wherever I wished. I found a vast quantity of

---

[14]See above p. 191, n. 55.
[15]*Fettercairn Catalogue*, No. 1562. See also above p. 191, n. 56.
[16]See above p. 12.

family papers in cupboards, attics, disused bedrooms, and storage rooms, some of it in trunks and boxes, some of it crammed into pieces of furniture, and all of it in considerable confusion. A van-load of this material has been sent to the National Library of Scotland, but whilst it contains much of interest, there are no fresh Boswell papers. I cannot pretend, however, that my own searches have been exhaustive. It is still just possible, though unlikely, that Fettercairn has not yet yielded up the last of its treasures.

When Forbes died in 1806, the papers entrusted to his care were probably at his house in Edinburgh. His elder son (who married the Fettercairn heiress) returned at least two boxes of papers to Auchinleck,[17] and it is generally assumed that what he inadvertently failed to return he took to Fettercairn with the rest of his father's papers. But Forbes's younger son (Lord Medwyn, a Scottish judge) may also have taken some of the family papers. He certainly had one major manuscript—Sir William's journal of his Continental tour, 1792–93, in seven volumes running to a total of well over 2,000 pages. If he took this, he may have taken other papers in which Boswell material could have been intermingled. The seven volumes were presented to the National Library of Scotland in 1935 by his great-granddaughter, Miss Forbes of Medwyn, but I have made no serious attempt to establish contact with this branch of the family.

The very small portion of the Boswell-Johnson correspondence which has been traced offers no clue as to the disappearance of the remainder. Only one complete letter from Johnson to Boswell is known to survive. That is the letter of 11 July 1784 contained in the portfolio of documents which Lord Clinton produced for Abbott's inspection at Fettercairn.[18] Only the second paragraph of this letter is to be found in the *Life*. In the complete text which follows, I have noted any discrepancies between what Boswell printed and what Johnson wrote:

> To James Boswel Esq
>   Edinburgh
> Dear Sir
>     Why you should desire to hear your own reasons for your own actions I cannot find.
>     I remember, and entreat you to remember that virtus est

---

[17]See above p. 201.
[18]See *Fettercairn Catalogue*, p. xvii. Chapman lists the letter as No. 973 in SJ *Letters*, but gives no text. The manuscript is in the Fettercairn Papers.

vitium fugere, the first approach to riches is security from poverty. The condition upon which you have my consent to settle in London, is that your expence never exceeds your annual income. Fixing this basis of security, you cannot be hurt, and you may be very much advanced,— The loss of your Scottish business which is all that you can lose, is not to be reckoned as any equivalent to the hopes and possibilities that open here upon you. If you succeed, all question of prudence is at an end, every body will [think]¹⁹ that done rightly²⁰ which ends happily, and though your expectations, of which I would not advise you to talk too much, should not be wholly²¹ answered, you can hardly [fail]²² to get friends who will do for you all that your present situation allows you to hope; and if after a few years, you should return to Scotland, you will return with a mind supplied by various conversation, and many opportunities of enquiry, with much knowledge and materials for reflexion and instruction.

I am setting out to morrow for Lichfield and Ashbourne; my health has not mended since you left me, but I am yet in hopes of benefit from the country. Of your kind negotiation I have yet found no consequence, but I shall leave it in the hands of Sir Joshua, and try to go down with hope and tranquillity. The Asthma is very oppressive, but the water does not much rise above the leg. I take squills in powder often three grains a day, or at least forty drops of vinegar of squills. I have observed a phænomenon which I did not expect. Forty drops of vinegar of squills (I suppose of any vinegar) fills not more than half the space occupied by forty drops of water, so much greater is the cohesion or mutual attraction of water than of vinegar. Let me know how much of the vinegar your Physitians generally consider as a powerful dose.

If you direct to me hither, the letters will be sent to me, but when I come to Ashbourne if I find myself disposed to stay, I will write to you there. Convey my respects to Mrs Boswel.

I am Dear Sir &c

Sam: Johnson

London July. 11. 1784

Boswell, in accordance with his usual practice, left it to the printer to regularize spelling, capitalization, and punctuation. I have not noted

---

¹⁹The insertion is in JB's own hand, but the *Life* does not indicate he has supplied a word.

²⁰The *Life* incorrectly gives "right."

²¹The *Life* incorrectly gives "totally."

²²The insertion is in JB's own hand, but the *Life* does not indicate he has supplied a word.

individual variations of this sort, but comparison of the printed text with the original will disclose nine changes of punctuation and two of spelling. The more important conclusions, however, are to be drawn from the substantive variations. They show that Boswell was ready to supply missing words without indicating the fact to his readers, and that his collation of proof and manuscript was not careful enough to eliminate misreadings by the printer.

We can also discover the type of passage which Boswell omitted—a rather blunt opening paragraph and a passage dealing with Johnson's illness and its treatment. I cannot help feeling that it is the omitted parts of this letter which the modern reader would find the most vivid, the most spontaneous, and the most interesting. I should also think that to be true of many of the unpublished passages in the one hundred other letters still untraced. By that, I do not intend any criticism of Boswell's biographical method. For publication of the *Life,* there were good artistic and practical reasons for the suppression of such passages.

I cannot fully explain the survival of this one letter at Fettercairn, but I can suggest a possible link. Less than a month after writing to Boswell about the latter's plan of taking his family to London, Johnson wrote on the same subject to Forbes. This is the letter which Abbott found on a shelf in the library at Fettercairn. As it is unpublished and its contents may have some relevance, I give here a complete text.[23]

To Sir William Forbes. Bart
    in Edinburgh
Sir
    When Mr Boswel first communicated to me his design of removing his family to London, I thought of it like all the rest of his Friends; for a while it seemed possible that his desire might evaporate in talk, or that the trouble and difficulty of such a migration might overpower his inclination. I was therefore content to say little, but what I said, he will tell you, was all discouragement. By degrees however I found his ardour for English Honour, and English Pleasure, so strong that, he would have considered all open and declared opposition, as envy or malignity, or distrust of his abilities. I therefore withdrew my prohibition on these terms.
    That he should not come to London till he had money saved

---

[23]See *Fettercairn Catalogue,* p. xxii. This letter is not listed in SJ *Letters.* The manuscript is in the Fettercairn Papers.

by himself, and unborrowed, sufficient for the removal and estab-
lishment of his Family.

That while he resides in London, he shall live on what he
receives from his estate, and gets by his practice, without anticipation, or contraction of debts.

To these conditions, he will own, that he has agreed, and
if [he]²⁴ keep his own stipulation, you see, Sir, that no great
mischief can be incurred. He can lose nothing but his Scottish
business in the Scottish courts, which the appeals, and other inci-
dental employment may easily recompense.

The danger is, and that danger is very great, lest he should
be driven by his passions beyond the bounds which he has con-
sented to fix. The mischief then may be such as both you and
I sincerely wish him to escape. I have told him, with as much
energy as I could call to my assistance, that He is too rich for
an Adventurer, and by a game so hazardous and daring, he stakes
more than he can win.

Since I began this letter, I have received from him a gloomy
account of his perplexity and irresolution; and his present intention is to delay his removal. To gain time is a great advantage.
Reason and the advice of his Friends will probably prevail. Every
reason against his removal will be stronger another year

I am Sir, with great respect
your most humble servant
Sam: Johnson

[The date and place are obscured by a worn fold of the paper,
but Forbes's docket reads:
"Saml Johnston Ashbourne 7 Augt. 1784."]

Boswell obtained the original of this letter when he was collecting
materials for the *Life*. On 7 November 1787, he wrote to Forbes: "Dr.
Johnson's letter to you is a very good one, but from its subject cannot
appear for some time."²⁵ But although he did not print the letter
in the *Life,* he did not return it immediately to Forbes. In a letter
of 12 December 1788, he assured Forbes: "You may depend on your
... letter from him being carefully preserved for you."²⁶ I do not
know when Forbes finally retrieved his letter, but it seems to me possible
that when Boswell returned it, he also sent Forbes his own letter from

²⁴The insertion is in JB's own hand.
²⁵*Fettercairn Catalogue*, No. 1336. The manuscript is now in the Fettercairn Papers.
²⁶*Fettercairn Catalogue*, No. 1339. The manuscript is now in the Fettercairn Papers.

Johnson. It cannot surely be a coincidence that the only complete surviving letter from Johnson to Boswell was discovered in the same place as a letter from Johnson to Forbes written about the same time and dealing with the same topic. The letter to Boswell has survived at Fettercairn, I think, not because *all* the missing letters were there, but because it complemented the letter to Forbes and was therefore singled out as being of special interest to him.

At the beginning of this Appendix, I mentioned that out of 103 letters from Johnson to Boswell listed by Chapman, there are only two not printed or quoted from in the *Life*.[27] These two are the only other items from Johnson's side of the correspondence which have been traced. One of them is a brief note which reads: "Mr. Boswel's company is desired at the Blackmore's head." The blank space on this note is filled with Boswell's journal entries covering 24 September 1777 to 28 January 1778. It was found at Malahide and has obviously survived because Boswell kept it with his journal material rather than with his letters from Johnson.[28] The other item is a short letter of introduction (incomplete) written by Johnson for an unidentified lady who wanted to make use of Boswell's professional skills as an advocate in the Scottish courts.[29] Johnson wrote a *second* letter of introduction for the same lady which Boswell received and printed in the *Life*.[30] Chapman plausibly suggests that Boswell never received the other letter for there would have been no point in giving him both. It is probable therefore that the document which has survived, although intended originally for Boswell, never formed part of the Boswell papers. G. B. Hill printed it in his edition of Johnson's letters in 1892 when it was in the possession of Mr. G. J. Campbell of Inverness.

On Boswell's side of the correspondence, only six items have been located. Two complete letters and a fragment of another were amongst the papers acquired by Isham in his original purchase from Malahide. The earlier letter, dated 20 September 1779, is not printed in the *Life*, but Boswell refers to it and quotes a brief addendum which must have been on a separate sheet, for it has not survived with the manu-

---

[27]In stating the figure of two, I have not included a card in SJ's hand conveying a dinner invitation from Mr. Thrale to JB. SJ wrote the card for Thrale at the latter's bidding. The card is in the Hyde Collection. See Mary Hyde's *The Impossible Friendship*, Harvard University Press, 1972, p. 61, for the text, and p. 61, n. 103, for an explanation of how it may have been detached from JB's papers.

[28]See SJ *Letters*, No. 550.1; also *Malahide Catalogue*, Nos. 53 and 466. The manuscript is now at Yale.

[29]SJ *Letters*, No. 355.

[30]SJ *Letters*, No. 354, printed in the *Life*, II, p. 277.

script of the letter itself.[31] The other letter, dated 1 October 1782, is neither printed nor referred to in the *Life*.[32] The fragment is a single leaf containing an omitted portion from Boswell's letter to Johnson of 14 February 1777, partially printed in the *Life*.[33] The explanation for the survival of these manuscripts may be connected with the fact that Boswell did not print any part of them in the *Life*. This cannot be the whole answer for, if it were, one would have expected to find at Malahide *all* the other letters which Boswell did not print.

The croquet box, discovered at Malahide in 1930, yielded a further item—a rough draft or copy of the letter of 29 April 1779, partially printed in the *Life*.[34] Boswell used the paper on which this was written to jot down a journal entry and presumably kept it with his journal materials rather than with his letters.

The two other surviving letters from Boswell to Johnson came neither from Malahide nor Fettercairn. One of them, dated 22 November 1779, was sent by Johnson to Lucy Porter, who never returned it.[35] It eventually passed into the Tinker Collection and is now owned by Yale. It is not known through whose hands it passed before it came to Tinker. The other letter, dated 3 March 1772 (printed with alterations in the *Life*), is now in the Hyde Collection (being formerly in the R. B. Adam Collection).[36] Its previous history is not known. Tinker printed it in his edition of Boswell's letters and suggested that it was Boswell's copy rather than the actual letter sent to Johnson. Pottle, on the other hand, is convinced that the letter is the original, and I accept this view. In either event, it is impossible to explain how the letter became detached from the Boswell family papers and so escaped oblivion. A comparison of the actual with the printed text reveals Boswell's willingness to subject his own letters to extensive alteration and stresses the importance of recovering all the original texts.

With the few exceptions I have mentioned, the fate of the letters on both sides of the correspondence remains a mystery. I have already

[31]The letter is *Malahide Catalogue*, No. 175. It is printed in private edition, XIII, p. 312. See also the *Life*, III, p. 399. The manuscript is now at Yale.

[32]The letter is *Malahide Catalogue*, No. 184. It is printed in private edition, XV, p. 248. The manuscript is now at Yale.

[33]The fragment is *Malahide Catalogue*, No. 174. It is printed in private edition, XII, p. 241. The manuscript is now at Yale.

[34]This item is *Malahide Catalogue*, No. 174 b. It is also catalogued for its journal entry under No. 64a. *Malahide Catalogue* gives the date incorrectly as 20 April 1779. It is printed in private edition, XIII, p. 270. The manuscript is now at Yale.

[35]The letter is *Tinker Catalogue*, No. 301. It is printed in JB *Letters*, No. 199a, pp. 296–97.

[36]JB *Letters*, No. 111, pp. 185–87. Compare the version printed in the *Life*, II, p. 144.

explained why I do not think that they now are, or ever were after Boswell's death, at Auchinleck or Fettercairn. Malahide has been searched so often that I cannot believe it holds any more surprises. Inevitably, I return to the conclusion that the letters were in London when Boswell died. He is likely to have taken special pains to select a really safe repository for the precious bundles. Perhaps he chose too cunning a hiding place so that Malone missed it when clearing the house; or perhaps for greater security he deposited the letters with his publisher or his banker in London or some other outside custodian.[37] Whatever the true explanation, my own belief, a purely intuitive one, is that one day the missing letters will reappear.

---

[37]It will be remembered that in 1785 he had temporarily stored the materials for the *Life* with his publisher, Mr. Dilly. His bankers were Coutts & Co. in the Strand, who of course still exist. I have spoken to the archivist there who tells me that the vaults are crammed with old documents, many of them unindexed.

# APPENDIX III

# *The Manuscript of the "Life of Johnson"*

Boswell spent many years gathering together his materials for writing the *Life*. For detailed information as to what these materials were and how they were collected reference must be made to Marshall Waingrow's book *The Correspondence and Other Papers of James Boswell relating to the Making of the Life of Johnson*.[1]

It has been explained that Boswell, when preparing his manuscript for the printer, did not bother to copy out again many letters, sheets torn from his journals, memoranda, and other materials intended to be included in his text. These were sent, suitably revised, to the printer for use as copy. They were keyed to a new and original manuscript, running to more than 1,000 consecutively numbered quarto leaves, which I have previously described as the "master manuscript."[2] It is the "master manuscript" with which this Appendix deals.

Isham's purchase from Malahide in 1927[3] included sixteen pages of the manuscript with a paper apart on four leaves (five pages). The pages were:

503–513  
529–530  
533  
538  
553  

[1] Heinemann, London, and McGraw-Hill, New York, 1969, elsewhere cited as *Correspondence, etc. re Life*.

[2] See above p. 280.

[3] See above p. 69.

The 4-leaf paper apart is headed "to be taken in on p. 494." It corresponds to vol. 1, pp. 501–12, of the first edition text, beginning "It is to be regretted . . ." and ending ". . . astonishment at Johnson's Latin conversation."[4]

In 1927, it was thought that this was the only portion of the manuscript which had survived. Isham sold pages 513, 529, 530, 533, 538, and 553, and the paper apart to Rosenbach soon after his return from Malahide. The price was $17,000, which included also two letters from Boswell to his wife.[5]

Rosenbach retained page 553 and the paper apart, which are now in the Rosenbach Foundation, Philadelphia.[6] He seems to have sold the other five pages individually, each laid inside a first edition of the *Life*—at any rate, three of them were so dealt with:

p. 513     Sold to Paul Hyde Bonner. Later resold (still laid in its first edition) at American Art Association, Anderson Galleries, Sale 4086, 15 February 1934, Lot 21. The present owner is Mrs. Palmer Dixon of New York.

p. 533     Sold to Mr. and Mrs. Donald F. Hyde and now in the Hyde Collection.

p. 538     Sold to Mrs. Sherburne Prescott of Greenwich, Connecticut, and still in her possession.

The present whereabouts of pages 529 and 530 is unfortunately unknown. The Rosenbach Foundation has no information and John F. Fleming, Rosenbach's business successor, has been unable to trace the names of the purchasers. It seems very likely that these two pages were sold, like the others, laid inside first editions of the *Life*. They may have been sold to a single purchaser, as they are consecutive pages. They are now the only pages of the master manuscript which are untraced[7] and it is to be hoped that the present owners will make themselves known.

[4]Information supplied by John F. Fleming to Mrs. Donald F. Hyde (letter dated 10 January 1968).
[5]See above p. 80.
[6]Inventory No. 415/29.
[7]Apart from the following pages which have never recovered: pp. 496, 608–12 and most of 614.

Isham retained pages 503–12 and they remained in his ownership until his whole collection was sold to Yale in 1949.

The next batch of manuscript to come to light was found in the croquet box at Malahide in 1930.[8] It was purchased by Isham and yielded a further 110 pages:

| | | |
|---|---|---|
| 497–502 | 6 | pages |
| 514–528 | 15 | " |
| 531–532 | 2 | " |
| 534–537 | 4 | " |
| 539–552 | 14 | " |
| 554–607 | 54 | " |
| 613 | 1 | " |
| 615–628 | 14 | " |
| | 110 | pages |

There was also a scrap cut from the bottom of page 620. Isham sold all this material to Rosenbach in February 1935 for $35,000.[9] Rosenbach resold to Arthur A. Houghton, Jr., the present owner.

The remainder of the manuscript, more than 900 pages, was found at Malahide in 1940 amongst the papers in the grain loft. When Isham bought these papers in 1946, the *Life* manuscript was excluded, but a few leaves did find their way into the large trunk which Lady Talbot despatched to him from Ireland. The contract for the sale of Isham's collection to Yale in 1949 lists as coming from the trunk: "MS. of Life, 10 pp. of, all but 2 in other hands." This suggests that there were only two pages of the master manuscript, and these were probably pages 384 and 385, which remained in Isham's ownership until his death in 1955. The sale contract permitted him to retain for himself one page of manuscript out of the trunk and a year later it was agreed that he might retain another in return for his help in negotiating on Yale's behalf for the purchase of the remainder of the manuscript from Lady Talbot.[10] This purchase was successfully concluded in the summer of 1950 at the price of $22,400.[11] Page 384 is now owned by Isham's son Jonathan, and page 385 by his son Heyward.

[8]See above p. 95.

[9]See above p. 108.

[10]Schedule C of the 1949 sale contract allowed Isham to retain for himself "one page of the MS. of the *Life of Johnson* of his own selection." This must have been one of the two pages from the trunk because the only other pages then in his collection were pp. 503–12, all of which went to Yale. On 21 July 1950, H. W. Liebert on behalf of Yale wrote to Isham that in consideration of the sale of the remainder of the MS. and other papers acquired by him from Lady Talbot in that year, he was to receive "one page of the manuscript of the *Life of Johnson* selected by you from among the pages included in the Malahide 1946 acquisition, this to be in addition to the one page specified as your property in the original agreement." Since the two pages of the MS. owned by Isham at his death were pp. 384 and 385, it is clear that these were the two pages which came over in the trunk.

[11]See above p. 300. Yale paid Isham $51,650 for the manuscript *and* other items which he acquired in 1950 from Lady Talbot.

The present ownership of the master manuscript may therefore be stated as follows:

| | | |
|---|---|---|
| Dedication | pp. 1–6 | Yale |
| Advertisement | pp. 1–6 | " |
| Introduction | pp. 1–13 | " |
| Text | pp. 1–383 | Yale |
| " | p. 384 | Jonathan T. Isham |
| " | p. 385 | Heyward Isham |
| " | pp. 386–494 | Yale |
| "    Paper Apart 4 shs. | p. 494 | Rosenbach Foundation |
| " | p. 495 | Yale |
| " | p. 496 | Never recovered |
| " | pp. 497–502 | A. A. Houghton, Jr. |
| " | pp. 503–512 | Yale |
| " | p. 513 | Mrs. Palmer Dixon |
| " | pp. 514–528 | A. A. Houghton, Jr. |
| " | p. 529 | Purchased by Rosenbach in 1927. Present whereabouts unknown. |
| " | p. 530 | " |
| " | pp. 531–532 | A. A. Houghton, Jr. |
| " | p. 533 | Hyde Collection |
| " | pp. 534–537 | A. A. Houghton, Jr. |
| " | p. 538 | Mrs. Sherburne Prescott |
| " | pp. 539–552 | A. A. Houghton, Jr. |
| " | p. 553 | Rosenbach Foundation |
| " | pp. 554–607 | A. A. Houghton, Jr. |
| " | pp. 608–612 | Never recovered |
| " | p. 613 | A. A. Houghton, Jr. |
| " | p. 614 | Never recovered (except for a scrap at Yale) |
| " | pp. 615–628 | A. A. Houghton, Jr. |
| " | pp. 629–1046 | Yale |

The following numbers have been used twice (i.e., there are two separate sheets each bearing the same number):

12, 356, 681, 833, and 839 (all at Yale)

The papers apart which make up the remainder of Boswell's manuscript number more than 1,000. Most of them have survived and are now at Yale.

# APPENDIX IV

# *Boswell and Thérèse Le Vasseur— The Missing Journal Leaves*

Boswell's journal for the period 12 January to 23 February 1766 consists of a bundle of loose leaves from which the entries for 1 to 11 February are missing.[1] In the same bundle is a slip of paper with the words "Reprehensible Passage" in Sir William Forbes's handwriting and initialled by him—presumably referring to the content of the missing pages.

According to Isham, these leaves (some six in number) were burnt by Lady Talbot during his visit to Malahide in 1927. His story was that he and Lady Talbot had been working hard on the papers all day and, when it was time to go to bed, he was allowed to take the journal leaves to look at in his room. There, he was thrilled to find a racy and detailed account of Boswell's amour with Rousseau's mistress, Thérèse Le Vasseur, during a journey from Paris to London. He came down the next morning, highly excited, and showed the passage to Lady Talbot. She is said to have been shocked by the frankness of Boswell's account and to have thrust the offending leaves into the fire.

Isham frequently related this story and eventually it was published in *The New Yorker*[2] through his telling it at a dinner party.[3] The *New Yorker* version differs from Isham's account in some details and wrongly refers to a letter being burnt rather than a portion of the journal:

[1]*Malahide Catalogue*, No. 11.
[2]*The New Yorker*, 19 October 1929, by Alexander Woollcott.
[3]Letter, F. A. Pottle to L. F. Powell, 2 May 1930 (copy in IFP): "The story of Boswell's affair with Thérèse no doubt got abroad from the Colonel's own relation. He has told it on many occasions and it got into "The New Yorker" through his telling it at a dinner party."

Here I am merely telling of the scene before the fireplace at Malehyde [*sic*] Castle where Lady Talbot de Malehyde (she is our Geoffrey Kerr's sister, by the way) was pawing in the sacks for something wherewith to convince Colonel Isham that the family really could not part with such painful intimacies. Finally, she fished out a Boswell letter recounting his return from Paris, whence he had affably agreed to pilot the *chère amie* of the exigent Rousseau, who, in exile in London, was clamoring for her. Boswell tried to exact his fee as escort at every inn on the way, seeking to demonstrate to the incredulous French girl that Scotsmen had their good points too.

"You see," said the chatelaine of the castle, "we couldn't very well let things like that be published."

And while the agonized but impassive Colonel Isham looked on, her pretty hand crumpled up the priceless letter and threw it into the fire.

Isham gave an account of the contents of the missing leaves to his editor, Geoffrey Scott, who noted it down as follows:

Contents of some 12 pp. of Boswell's Diary burnt by Lady Talbot de Malahide before selling the MSS.

All these pages were concerned with B's intrigue with Thérèse le Vasseur. He describes how, when it came to the point, he felt no desire & became alarmed that he wouldn't be able to do himself credit. How he made an excuse to leave the room & in going took a bottle of wine from the table & concealed it from Thérèse. How, outside the door he drank the whole bottle of wine to fortify himself. How in spite of this he made a failure of it. Disappointment of Thérèse. When he brought it off she was not satisfied & said he was a very imperfect lover. How she trained him. She asked him as a man who had travelled much had he not noticed how many things were achieved by mens' hands & how she instructed him. He tried to talk about Rousseau, to pump her for *dicta philosophi* & this bored her. How she took his education in hand. "I felt like a child in her hands, not a lover." Good progress. Technical details. She rode him "agitated like a bad rider galloping down hill." How he was bored with technical love making. He reflected "it is a mistake to run away with an old man's mistress." She hurt his feelings by saying, "Don't imagine that you are a better lover than Rousseau."

Scott's note, which is preserved at Yale, is undated. Pottle recollects Isham saying that he gave his account to Scott soon after his return from Malahide in 1927, because Scott was anxious to record it and, in particular, to preserve all *ipsissima verba* which Isham could recall.

The first published version of the story appeared in 1930 in volume VII of the private edition.[4] Scott had died the year before and the account was compiled by Pottle in consultation with Isham:

> No intention of laying siege to Thérèse seems to have occurred to Boswell before he started for London in her company. But the intimacy of travel and the proximity in which they found themselves at the inns each night soon precipitated an intrigue. The complications which ensued were so comic that it would have been a pity had they been utterly lost to the world. In the simplicity of his conceit Boswell had thought to win the gratitude of Thérèse by allowing her to experience the superiority of his own vigorous youth over the senile fondness of Rousseau. But Thérèse stunned and humiliated him by flatly denying any superiority; she granted him youth and vigour, but maintained that he lacked art, and of the two she preferred art. Then, seeing him crestfallen, she begged him not to be hurt; there was still time, and she would take it upon herself to give him a thorough course of instruction *in arte amoris*. Boswell approached the first lesson not with eagerness, but with trepidation. The apartment in which they were lodged that night was a private dining room with the bed in an alcove at the end. Thérèse retired early, urging him to follow. Boswell, overcome with terror, devised a pretext for going back to the main room, where he seized a full bottle of wine which, by his direction, had been left in a corner, and drained it on the spot to bolster his flagging spirits.
>
> He confessed that he felt like a child in her hands, not a lover. Her lectures bored him, and after a little he brought up the subject of Rousseau, hoping at least to gather a few *dicta philosophi* for his Journal. Thérèse in her turn found that extremely dull. It was a mistake, he finally reflected, to run away with an old man's mistress.

It is noticeable that this published account omits some of the more explicit details contained in Scott's notes. After so many years, Pottle cannot be sure of the reason for this, but points out that in 1930 one still had to be careful about what one published, even in a private edition. Isham, too, probably thought it wise to be discreet, for he was already in trouble with Lady Talbot over the censorship issue.

[4] pp. 65–66.

In 1955, these considerations no longer applied, and a revised version of the story was prepared by Frank Brady, with Pottle's assistance, for *Boswell on the Grand Tour: Italy, Corsica, and France 1765–1766*.[5] A preliminary draft was submitted to Isham who supplied a good many new details, some of them inconsistent with the earlier versions. This was Brady's account as published:

It does not appear that before leaving Paris Boswell had formed any scheme of seducing Thérèse, and the day of his departure found him tense and harassed by difficulties in getting started, and deeply unhappy over his mother's death. But the intimacy of travel and the proximity in which the pair found themselves at inns at night precipitated an intrigue almost immediately. On the second night out they shared the same bed; Boswell's first attempt, as often with him, was a fiasco. He was deeply humiliated, the grief he was trying to repress came back upon him, and he wept. Thérèse, with a Frenchwoman's tenderness and sympathy, put her arm around him to console him and laid his hand on her shoulder. His grief and embarrassment waned; as he recorded on another occasion, his powers were excited and he felt himself vigorous. Next day he was very proud of himself, and in the coach he congratulated Thérèse (who was almost twenty years his senior) on her good fortune in having at last experienced the ardours of a Scotch lover. Thérèse stunned him by denying that she had great cause for gratitude: "I allow," she said, "that you are a hardy and vigorous lover, but you have no art." Then, with quick perception seeing him cast down, she went on, "I did not mean to hurt you. You are young, you can learn. I myself will give you your first lesson in the art of love."

Since Boswell's success as a lover depended on his maintaining a feeling of superiority, this announcement filled him with terror. The apartment in which they were lodged that night was in the shape of an L: a private dining-room with the bed in an alcove at one end. As bedtime approached, he grew more frightened. In the earlier period of his life, as the journal printed in the present volume shows, he drank little, but on this occasion he secured from the servant a full bottle of wine and concealed it in the dining-room. Thérèse retired; Boswell remained reading. Thérèse called him; he went in clutching the wine, but instead of joining her, he paced up and down asking questions about Rousseau. At last, when no further diversion would avail, he drained the bottle and reluctantly slipped into bed.

[5]McGraw-Hill edition pp. 277–79, Heinemann edition pp. 293–94.

He gave some details of her instruction. He must be gentle though ardent; he must not hurry. She asked him, as a man who had travelled much, if he had not noticed how many things were achieved by men's hands. He made good technical progress, though he was not wholly persuaded of her right to set up for a teacher; he said she rode him "agitated, like a bad rider galloping downhill." After a while her lectures bored him, and he brought up the subject of Rousseau, hoping at least to gather a few *dicta philosophi* for his journal. Thérèse in her turn found that dull. It was a mistake, he finally reflected, to get involved with an old man's mistress.

The first entry of the journal on the other side of the hiatus not only furnishes unequivocal evidence of the liaison, but also vindicates Boswell's claim to vigour.[6]

The authenticity of these various accounts has been thrown into doubt by Lady Talbot's consistent and emphatic denial that she burnt the missing leaves. As early as 1930, when events should still have been fresh in her mind, she wrote to Isham: "We have been told that some newspaper had an article in it saying I had burnt some of Boswell's letters. This was a deliberate untruth. I have never burnt a letter by James Boswell in my life."[7] If it had been otherwise, there would have been little point in Lady Talbot denying it in a private letter to the only other person concerned. The fact that she confused the nature of the charge against her and spoke of letters rather than journal leaves makes her denial, if anything, more convincing.[8] And in his letter of reply, Isham made no attempt to contradict her denial.[9]

Lady Talbot has maintained the same position to this day. In a B.B.C. broadcast of 12 August 1951, she said: "That I burnt and destroyed papers is absolutely untrue"; and in a letter to Pottle of 17 May 1958, she wrote: "I cannot tell you what happened to 'the many leaves which were removed.' I did not remove them and I did not burn them. I most emphatically deny that I burnt any papers."[10]

[6]The entry for Wednesday 12 February 1766 begins: "Yesterday morning had gone to bed very early, and had done it once: thirteen in all. Was really affectionate to her."
[7]Letter dated 15 April 1930 (copy in TFP).
[8]Possibly she saw or was told about *The New Yorker* article, quoted above, in which Woollcott wrote of the burning of a letter, not journal leaves.
[9]Isham replied on 6 May 1930 (letter in TFP). He dealt with other matters raised in Lady Talbot's letter, but avoided any mention of the alleged burning.
[10]Copy in TFP.

Certainly there was no need for Lady Talbot to burn manuscripts containing indecent material, especially as she was very conscious of the pecuniary value of the journals.[11] Isham had undertaken to respect her censorship and she had no reason in 1927 to suppose he would not comply with this undertaking. She did not remove or destroy other manuscripts containing equally indecent material, her method being to delete the offending passages with Indian ink or black paint, but not to withhold physical delivery of the manuscripts themselves.

Scott, of course, had no reason to disbelieve the story of the burning when he heard it in 1927, and he apparently accepted the basic authenticity of Isham's account of the contents of the missing leaves. So also did Pottle until comparatively recently; but he now suspects that Isham's account is a "brilliant historical fiction by a highly imaginative man who knew Boswell's journal forward and backward."[12]

Pottle's arguments are compelling. He points out that Isham made no mention of certain outstanding events which ought to have figured prominently in the missing manuscript. The mail packet from Calais was delayed for several days by a terrible storm, so bad that the Channel coasts were littered with wrecked ships. Pottle thinks that Boswell would certainly have mentioned this and, had Isham read the actual journal leaves, he would not have forgotten such a detail or suppressed it in the retelling. Pottle also doubts Isham's account of Boswell's sexual incapacity with Thérèse, pointing out that Boswell did not normally find himself impotent with a female of inferior social status such as Thérèse.

In a private note to me, Pottle has enlarged on the grounds for his disbelief. For many years, he broadly accepted Isham's original account as recorded by Scott. The surviving manuscript on either side of the hiatus guaranteed that the intrigue occurred and there was little doubt that leaves were removed because of the nature of their contents. He believed implicitly in Isham's account of the burning, which implied that Scott's notes were substantially correct. Pottle was nevertheless uneasy about some of the details and most of the language said to be *ipsissima verba:* "They are not Boswellian, and they are very much in Isham's vein. Boswell reports many acts of sexual intercourse, but if he gives any detail (which he very rarely does), it is almost

---

[11]In a letter (in Hyde Collection) of 9 November 1925 to R. B. Adam, Tinker wrote, reporting on his visit to Malahide: "I do not mean that they [i. e., the Talbots] are unaware of the value of the Boswellian documents—they rather overestimate their market value, I think . . . ."

[12]F. A. Pottle: *James Boswell: The Earlier Years 1740–1769*, McGraw-Hill, New York, 1966, p. 277.

invariably in elegant periphrasis." Pottle's uneasiness grew when, in 1955, Isham added many precise details which he had not given to Scott in 1927, nor to Pottle himself for the 1930 published version. For example, in Scott's report the wine was drunk before the first encounter, whereas, in the 1955 account, it was drunk a night later before the course of instruction. Also, more *ipsissima verba* were given and some of the original ones dropped, which was unlike Isham, who usually recalled Boswell's words with great precision. Pottle, however, still "continued to hope that there was *some* truth in the account" because he "still believed without question that Lady Talbot burned the missing leaves." But later she convinced him that she was telling the unqualified truth in saying that she had not done so. "That," writes Pottle, "took the underpinning completely out from under my belief in Isham's story, and my belief collapsed."

It has to be admitted that Isham was an exceptionally gifted raconteur with a very fertile imagination. According to his friend A. E. Newton, he could never resist embellishing the truth for the sake of a good story.[13] The prevailing inaccuracy of popular accounts of the story of the Boswell papers stems to a considerable extent from Isham's own colourful narration. This is especially noticeable in the historical preface to the trade edition of the *London Journal* by his friend Christopher Morley.[14] Lady Talbot has also told me that Isham was given to inventing dramatic details with which to embellish accounts of various discoveries of papers at Malahide, and he tried to persuade her to agree to their inclusion in press releases.

Like Pottle, I accept that Lady Talbot genuinely has no recollection of throwing any papers on the fire. If she had wilfully burned six leaves of the manuscript journal because she was scandalized by their contents, she is not likely to have forgotten (though she might have done so if she had burned them inadvertently). I also agree with Pottle that the details which Isham added to his story over the years are suspect. But I find it hard to believe that there is not at least an element of truth in his original account, that he could have deliberately misled Geoffrey Scott, his chosen editor, and allowed the scholarly distinction of his private edition, which cost him so many sacrifices, to be compromised by a hoax of his own perpetration. If Pottle is right and Isham did indeed fabricate the whole story, I can only assume he was manoeuvred into a false position from which he was unable to retreat.

---

[13]Letter, A. E. Newton to R. B. Adam, 9 November 1927 (Hyde Collection).
[14]McGraw-Hill, 1950.

This could have happened if he had intended the story only for private telling and matters had got out of hand by the article appearing in *The New Yorker.* At any rate, Isham stuck to his guns. On 7 October 1940, he wrote in a letter to his friend M. Lincoln Schuster: "Next, Boswell's description of his *affaire* with Rousseau's mistress was given in his loose-leaf Journal of the period—not in a letter. Lady Talbot tossed into the fire most of the leaves covering this episode. Fortunately, enough remains, at either end, to give the show away."[15] And in a letter of 12 August 1949 to Frederick L. Allen, editor of *Harper's Magazine,* he declined the latter's invitation to write the story of the Boswell papers because it might hurt living people: "You see, the person who consigned certain of the manuscript to the flames . . . is still very much alive."[16]

[15]Copy in IFP.
[16]Copy in IFP.

APPENDIX V

# Boswell Papers from the Isham Collection Not at Yale

The collection of Boswell papers sold by Isham to Yale in 1949 represented, with certain exceptions, all the papers from Malahide and Fettercairn which he acquired over the years and a few from other sources. The exceptions were as follows:

1. *Papers retained by Isham for his own collection*

After Isham's death in 1955, these passed to his sons, Heyward and Jonathan.

*Heyward Isham* now owns:
Visiting Card: Mr. Boswell, Great Portland Street/47.
Visiting Card: Mrs. Lennox, No. 2 Crown Street, Westminster.
Business Card: Daniel Rosier, Wine and Brandy Vaults.
A small card in Boswell's hand: Mr. Matthew Collet who shaved Dr. Johnson for 24 years lives in Plumbtree Court, Shoelane No. 14 wishes to be made a Porter in the India House, Francis Fowke Esq. Resident at Benares.
A social note from Miss Monckton to Boswell. "Saturday the 4th."
Folio 385 of the manuscript of the *Life.*
Proof pages of the *Life.* 1 sheet folded to form 4 pages, numbered 301, 300, 301, 302 (*sic*).
Boswelliana: 1 leaf in Boswell's hand folded to form 4 pages, beginning: "When the mixed administration. . . ."
A small card, in a hand similar to Boswell's, but not his, reading: "Memento Brogues. from the Isle of Sky.—such as described by Dr. Johnston (*sic*) in his account of The Hebrides."
Letter, James Boswell junior to Boswell, from Westminster School, 22 February 1792, with notation by Boswell.

A scrap with manuscript notes by Boswell about the index for the second edition of the *Life*.

Printed Broadside: Boswell's verses on Alderman Curtis's election.[1]

Printed Pamphlet: A Conversation between His Most Sacred Majesty George III. and Samuel Johnson, LL.D. Illustrated with Observations by James Boswell, Esq., 1790.[2]

One piece cut from a length of ribbon inscribed to Paoli.

*Jonathan Isham* now owns:

Visiting Card: Dr. Gibb at Home—Fridays Lent Term.

Visiting Card: Le Cte. Luce de Gaspari Chambellan du Roi de Pologne.

Ticket to the Shakespeare Jubilee.

A small card in Boswell's hand: Mr. Boswell presents his compliments to Mr. Henry Winyard. Gt. Portland St. 25 Febry.

"Macdonalds genealogical cards." 6 cards.

Wrapper, endorsed by Boswell: Premiums given to James Boswell at Westr. School 1791 (and containing a silver crown of 1786).

Card of Admission to Luton House: Admit Jas Boswell & Company to see Luton when family are absent. Bute. May '81.

Folio 384 of the manuscript of the *Life*.

Proof pages of the *Life*. 1 sheet folded to form 4 pages, numbered 267, 268, 269, 270.

A scrap in Boswell's hand detailing his dream of Dr. Johnson. 6 February 1785.

Eton College Ticket, printed:
Pro more et monte
1790
Vivant Rex et Regina.

A scrap in Boswell's hand, beginning: "A gentleman in Ireland to whose seat the Bishop of Killaloe and a good party went. . . ." An anecdote about an Irish bull.

A small sheet, containing a printed paragraph about George III's comment to Boswell after Johnson's death: "There will be many lives of Dr. Johnson; do you give the best."[3]

Printed Broadside: William Pitt, the Grocer of London.[4]

---

[1]Not listed in *Literary Career.*

[2]See *Literary Career,* p. 137.

[3]The paragraph was intended for inclusion in the Advertisement to the second edition of the *Life,* but withdrawn before printing because of Malone's strong protest. JB presumably had several copies run off by the printer. Isham had two copies: this one which he retained and another which went to Yale.

[4]See *Literary Career,* p. 141.

Printed: The Principal Corrections and Additions to the first Edition of Mr. Boswell's Life of Dr. Johnson, 1793. Uncut and unopened with manuscript corrections in ink.[5]

2. *Papers given away by Isham prior to 1949*

*The Bodleian Library, Oxford*
Johnson's D.C.L. Diploma, 1775.[6]

A slip of paper in Johnson's hand recording a change of reading in *The Vanity of Human Wishes*.[7]

A copy of the wording of Johnson's D.C.L. Diploma, not in Boswell's hand, but endorsed by him.[8]

*The Signet Library, Edinburgh*
A 2-page manuscript in Boswell's hand of an Address to the King on the defeat of Fox's East India Bill, which he hoped the Dean and Faculty of Advocates would adopt as their own at their Anniversary meeting, 20 December 1783.[9]

*New York Public Library*
A 3-page letter from Boswell addressed to Mr. Spottiswoode, written in the third person, 23 February [1788?].[10]

*Arthur B. Spingarn* (Lady Talbot's New York lawyer)
A letter from Francis Barber to Boswell, 19 February 1779.[11]

*Van Cartmell* (a friend of Isham's)
One leaf of manuscript in Boswell's hand from Isham's 1927 purchase from Malahide. No further details are known. The leaf passed to Van Cartmell's daughter, now Mrs. Robertson F. Alford, who lives in Japan. Mrs. Alford sold the leaf and the present owner is unknown.

*Paul Hyde Bonner*
Pottle recollects a slip of paper (two or three lines of writing) being a receipt for two gun-barrels. It was among the Isham papers when he took over as editor of the private edition. Later, when he could not find it, Isham told him he had given it away to his Long Island friend and neighbour, Paul Hyde Bonner. The Bonner Library was sold by the American Art Association and

[5]See *Literary Career*, p. 212. This was not an exclusion from the sale to Yale 1949. It came into Isham's possession in 1951 as a gift from Lady Talbot.
[6]See above p. 162, n. 89.
[7]See above p. 261.
[8]See above p. 261.
[9]See Appendix VI, p. 349. See also private edition, XVI, p. 16.
[10]See above p. 290, n. 55.
[11]See *Correspondence etc. re Life*, p. 15.

Anderson Galleries, 15 February 1934. The receipt remembered by Pottle was not in the sale, but Lot 20 was a manuscript memorandum of JB referring to the gun-barrels. F. W. Hilles bought this memorandum in 1953 from a dealer and it is now placed with the Boswell papers at Yale. What happened to the receipt is uncertain, nor do we know whether Bonner got the memorandum from Isham or from another source.

*Mr. and Mrs. D. F. Hyde* (for the Hyde Collection)
  A torn page of Johnson's *Dictionary* annotated by Boswell, from the Malahide grain loft discovery.

*Frederick W. Hilles*
  Three pages of reading notes in the hand of Sir Joshua Reynolds copied out of the first volume of Johnson's *Lives of the Poets*. [12]

Isham's contract with Yale in 1949 listed as exclusions a few items described as gifts by him to the sixth Lord Talbot. These were not in fact gifts, but items which the Talbots had specifically retained from what was sold to Isham. They were thus never part of Isham's collection. After 1950, there still remained in the hands of Lady Talbot and the seventh Lord Talbot a great deal more Boswellian material than the mere half-dozen items mentioned in the Yale contract of 1949. For details of this material and its present location, see Appendix I.

3.  *Papers lost whilst in Isham's ownership*

  Eighteen or more letters from Margaret Montgomerie to Boswell. [13]

  A number of letters from James Bruce to Boswell with minutes of Boswell's replies endorsed on them. [14]

4.  *Papers sold by Isham prior to the main sale to Yale*

*Sales to Rosenbach*
  Two letters from Boswell to his wife (1927). [15]

  6 pages of the manuscript of the *Life* and a paper apart on 4 leaves (1927). [16]

  110 pages of the manuscript of the *Life* (1935). [17]

[12]Isham presented these notes to Hilles in 1946 because Hilles possessed the very volume from which these notes had been made by Reynolds as well as the letter SJ wrote to Reynolds when presenting the 1783 edition to him.
[13]See above p. 85.
[14]See above p. 85.
[15]See above p. 80.
[16]See above p. 80 and Appendix III, p. 331.
[17]See above p. 108 and Appendix III, pp. 331–32.

*Sales to Mr. and Mrs. D. F. Hyde for the Hyde Collection*

These sales were completed at various times between 1945 and 1949, and included the following items:

Johnson's diary, 1765–84. (Found at Malahide in 1937.)

119 letters by Johnson to various correspondents. (*Fettercairn Catalogue,* Nos. 1472–1590.)

Johnson manuscript: A list of books for Astle. (*Fettercairn Catalogue,* No. 1594.)

Letter: Mrs. Thrale to Johnson, 28 April 1780. (*Fettercairn Catalogue,* No. 1451.)

Letter: Mrs. Thrale to Johnson, 30 June 1784. (*Fettercairn Catalogue,* No. 1452.)

Boswell manuscript: A transcript from Johnson's diary. (*Fettercairn Catalogue,* No. 1595.)

Boswell manuscript: Another transcript from Johnson's diary. (*Fettercairn Catalogue,* No. 1596.)

Letter: Francis Barber to Boswell, 7 January 1786. (*Fettercairn Catalogue,* No. 17.)

Letter: Rev. J. B. Pearson to Boswell, 2 April 1784. (*Fettercairn Catalogue,* No. 668.)

Boswell manuscript: Book of Company at Auchinleck. (Found at Malahide in 1937.)

Johnson manuscript: *The Vanity of Human Wishes* (except the last 2 leaves, now also in the Hyde Collection by separate purchase from Lord Talbot in 1961). (Malahide grain loft discovery.)

Johnson manuscript: A fragment of *London.* (Malahide grain loft discovery.)

Johnson manuscript: "Annales"—diary entries recorded 10 November 1734. (Malahide grain loft discovery.)

Johnson manuscript: Early diary notes, 1729–34. (Malahide grain loft discovery.)

Johnson manuscript: Translation of Sallust's *Catiline.* (Malahide grain loft discovery.)

Johnson manuscript: Case of Collier v. Flint. (Malahide grain loft discovery.)

Boswell manuscript: *A Letter to the People of Scotland,* 1785. (Malahide grain loft discovery.)

Proof sheets (2 pages) of Boswell's *A Letter to the People of Scotland,* 1785, annotated by Boswell. (Malahide grain loft discovery.)

10 miscellaneous letters and sheets pertaining to the above viz.:

    1. Boswell's draft of presentation paragraphs to the Lord High Chancellor, the Earl of Lonsdale, and Mr. Justice Willes. 1 quarto sheet. From General Paoli's house, 25 May 1785.

2. Boswell's presentation drafts to John Wilkes and William Bosville. A scrap of paper.

3. Cancelled pages 20, 21, and 67, with manuscript annotations by Boswell.

4. Letter: J. W. Craufurd to Boswell, 31 December 1785 and draft of Boswell's reply, 10 January 1786, written thereon.

5. Letter: J. W. Craufurd to Boswell, 20 April 1786.

6. Letter: J. W. Craufurd to Boswell, 29 April 1786.

7. Draft of presentation paragraph to Lord Binning, London 1790, in hand of an amanuensis, docketed by Boswell.

8. Note of thanks in the third person to Boswell from Lord Binning, 3 March 1791.

9. Note from Sir George Howard to Sir John Dick, thanking him for perusal of Boswell's *Letter,* 29 May 1785.

10. Folder labelled: "Concerning / Court of Session / being diminished / Materials / for an Appendix / together with the / Resolutions of the / Counties and some observation[s]."

Boswell manuscript: Draft letter to Mrs. Thrale, 23 March 1776. (Malahide grain loft discovery.)

Boswell manuscript: Draft letter to Mrs. Thrale, 19 March 1782. (Malahide grain loft discovery.)

Copy (in Lawrie's hand) of Boswell's letter to Mrs. Thrale, 25 May 1782. (Malahide grain loft discovery.)

Copy (in Lawrie's hand) of Boswell's letter to Mrs. Thrale, 9 July 1782. (Malahide grain loft discovery.)

Copy letter: Boswell to Mrs. Thrale, 20 December 1782. (Malahide grain loft discovery.)

Boswell manuscript: "Boswell of Auchinleck"—family genealogy. (Malahide 1937 discovery.)

Boswell manuscript: One page starting: "Wednesday, go to execution." (Malahide grain loft discovery.)

Boswell manuscript: One page starting: "1782, Dr. Johnson said of Mrs. Thrale. . . ." (Malahide grain loft discovery.)

Boswell manuscript: Four pages starting: "Having read a Postscript (dated *Naples*) to *Signora Piozzi's* Anecdotes. . . ." (Enclosed with the next item.) (Malahide grain loft discovery.)

Letter: Boswell to Malone, 3 April 1786, about Mrs. Piozzi and enclosing the above 4-page manuscript. (Malahide grain loft discovery.)

Letter: Mrs. Thrale to Boswell, 15 August 1777, enclosing the next item. (Malahide grain loft discovery.)

A copy in Mrs. Thrale's hand of Johnson's Ode to her "from

Skie," annotated by Boswell, enclosed with the above letter. (Malahide grain loft discovery.) The original manuscript of this piece in SJ's hand is also in the Hyde Collection, but it did not come from Malahide or Fettercairn. It was sold at Sotheby's in 1891 and came into the Hyde Collection via the R. B. Adam Collection.

Letter: Mrs. Thrale to Boswell, 13 May 1782. (Malahide grain loft discovery.)

Letter: Mrs. Thrale to Boswell, 3 June 1782. (Malahide grain loft discovery.)

Letter: Mrs. Thrale to Boswell, 4 July 1782. (Malahide grain loft discovery.)

# APPENDIX VI

# *A Missing Boswell Manuscript*

In his journal for 20 December 1783, Boswell wrote:

> News had come by express that the House of Lords had made a noble stand against Fox's East India Bill, which would have overwhelmed the Crown. This rejoiced my Tory Soul; and in the forenoon I went down to the Library and drew up an Address to his Majesty from the Dean and Faculty of Advocates to congratulate him on it, and I moved for our addressing at our Anniversary meeting this day. The dastardly fellows, affraid to take an open part, were all against it. I despised them, and felt myself an ancient Constitutionalist.[1]

Isham presented the 2-page manuscript containing Boswell's Address to the Signet Library, Edinburgh, in September 1949 in recognition of the help received from Dr. C. A. Malcolm, the Librarian, in checking the Fettercairn papers. Dr. Malcolm acknowledged the gift gratefully, indicating that it would be placed in a glass case in the Upper Hall of the Library.[2] Several years ago, the Upper Hall was redecorated and the glass cases with their contents were removed. As a result, the manuscript is now missing. Although it is catalogued, neither Dr. Malcolm's successor, Mr. Christie, nor Mr. Ballantyne, the present Librarian, has been able to find it. Its existence is not generally known to Boswellian scholars and it is not mentioned in Frank Brady's book *Boswell's Political Career* (1965)[3] to which it is relevant.

Fortunately, the full text of the manuscript and an explanatory historical note by Dr. Malcolm were printed in the Annual Report

[1] Private edition, XVI, p. 16.
[2] Letter, Malcolm to Buchanan, 16 September 1949 (S. R. & Co.'s papers).
[3] Frank Brady: *Boswell's Political Career*, New Haven and London, Yale University Press, 1965.

by the Library Committee of the Signet Library, November 1949. As these are not otherwise available, they are reprinted here by kind permission of the Society of Writers to H.M. Signet:

> "The Humble Address of the Dean and Faculty of Advocates in that part of Great Britain called Scotland
> Most Gracious Sovereign
> We your Majesty's most dutiful Subjects the Dean and Faculty of Advocates in that part of Great Britain called Scotland assembled this day at our anniversary meeting beg leave with sincere and fervent hearts to congratulate Your Majesty on the noble stand made by Your Majesty's Hereditary Counsellors the House of Lords against a Bill pending in Parliament for vesting the affairs of the East India Company in certain commissioners which carried in its bosom a new and formidable establishment of power independent of Your Most Sacred Majesty, the effect of which might have proved destructive to our excellent Constitution the Monarchy of these Kingdoms.
> It is the glory of our Profession to have the title of *Antistites*[4] *Justitiae* and one of our first maxims *Suum cuique tribuere*. We should therefore think ourselves unfaithful and unworthy were we to be forgetful of what is due to the King as Supreme, or indifferent when any encroachment is threatened upon the rights of the Crown.
> Permit us Sir upon this important occasion to approach Your Majesty's Throne to assure Your Majesty of our steady attachment to your Royal Person and that we shall at all times be ready to support Your Majesty with our lives and fortunes against every factious attempt to diminish your Royal Prerogative."

As postscript Boswell has written at the head of the paper: "It was carried not to address. But this was a good Sketch. . . . I am not certain that I moved for it."

The Bill to which Boswell referred had occasioned considerable public excitement. Fox, who had introduced the Bill, was accused of trying to transfer the powers of the East India Company to seven commissioners of his own party, holding office for four years and controlling as trustees the property of the Company.

---

[4]"Antistites," i.e., Overseers.

Though violently opposed by Pitt, Dundas and Grenville, and its authors abused and caricatured, Professor Grant Robertson, historian of the period, regards the Bill as a "sincere and statesman-like effort to deal with a great problem on comprehensive lines"; but, he adds, "George III., Pitt, Thurlow and the East India Company did not consider nor apparently wish to consider it on its merits. Every effort to inflame popular feeling and the prejudices of the vested interests was employed. Fox, not the imperial problem, was made the issue. . . . Foiled in the Commons, where the Bill was carried by a large majority, the King stooped and stooped low to conquer. He authorised Lord Temple to influence votes in the Lords by informing waverers (truly enough) that anyone voting for the Bill would be considered as a personal enemy to the Crown.

"On Dec. 17 the Bill was thrown out in the Upper House by 19 votes. The next day the King, with graceless haste, dismissed . . . the Secretaries of State; and at the age of 24 Pitt accepted the invitation to form a Ministry."

Hunt, also, in the 'Political History of England,' said the Bill was a "genuine attempt to benefit the natives of India and would not probably have had any really serious consequences in England though the control of the Indian patronage for four years would have strengthened Fox's party, and, if it had afterwards been vested in the Crown, would have given some opportunity for the exercise of corrupt influence by Ministers.

"When the Commons learned that Lord Temple had been informed of the King's message, they voted by 153 to 80 that it was now necessary to declare that to report the King's opinion on any question pending in Parliament with a view to influence votes is a high crime and misdemeanour."

The Faculty Minutes have no mention of any motion to send an Address to the King, probably because the decision not to do so might be misinterpreted as a sign of disloyalty. Had the motion been carried, Boswell, it may be surmised, would have read his "good Sketch" in the hope that it would be sent.

TABLE I

*Transmission of the Boswell papers from James Boswell to Yale University*

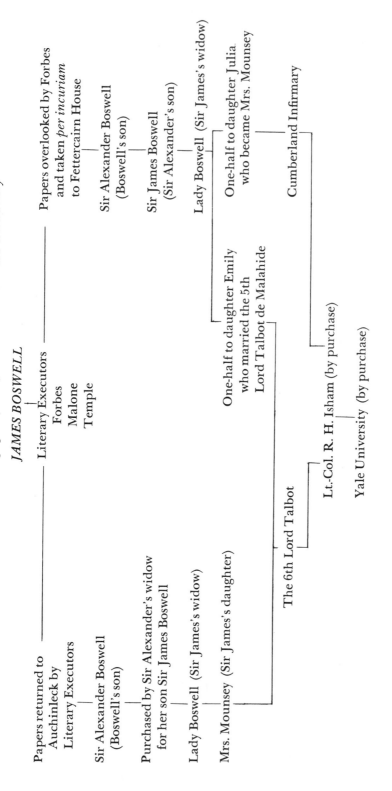

**JAMES BOSWELL**

Literary Executors
Forbes
Malone
Temple

Papers returned to Auchinleck by Literary Executors

Sir Alexander Boswell (Boswell's son)

Purchased by Sir Alexander's widow for her son Sir James Boswell

Lady Boswell (Sir James's widow)

Mrs. Mounsey (Sir James's daughter)

The 6th Lord Talbot

Lt.-Col. R. H. Isham (by purchase)

Yale University (by purchase)

One-half to daughter Emily who married the 5th Lord Talbot de Malahide

Papers overlooked by Forbes and taken *per incuriam* to Fettercairn House

Sir Alexander Boswell (Boswell's son)

Sir James Boswell (Sir Alexander's son)

Lady Boswell (Sir James's widow)

One-half to daughter Julia who became Mrs. Mounsey

Cumberland Infirmary

NOTE: A number of steps in the transmission of the papers, as indicated above, are open to argument owing to the ambiguous wording of wills and other factors. In the case of the papers taken to Fettercairn House, the Table follows the findings of the Court of Session in 1938 (see Chapter VII). Elsewhere, the most probable explanation has been adopted.

**TABLE II**

JAMES BOSWELL (the Biographer)  m.  *Margaret Montgomerie*
(d. 1795)

Children:

- *Sir Alexander Boswell* (d. 1822)  m.  *Grace Cuming*
- *James Boswell junior* (d. 1822, unmarried)
- *Veronica Boswell* (d. 1795, unmarried)
- *Euphemia Boswell* (d. 1837, unmarried)
- *Elizabeth Boswell* (d. 1814)  m.  *William Boswell* (d. 1841) — SEE TABLE III

*Sir Alexander Boswell* m. *Grace Cuming* — children:

- *Sir James Boswell* (d. 1854)  m.  *Jessie Jane Montgomerie Cuninghame* (d. 1884)
- *Janet Theresa Boswell* (d. 1836)  m.  *Sir William Francis Eliott* (d. 1864) — SEE TABLE IV
- *Margaret Amelia Boswell*  m.  *Maj.-Gen. Vassall of Balhary* (Mrs. Vassall survived her husband and died in 1890 without issue)

*Sir James Boswell* m. *Jessie Jane Montgomerie Cuninghame* — children:

- *Julia Grace Jessie Jane Boswell*  m.  *George Mounsey* (Mrs. Mounsey survived her husband and died in 1905 without issue)
- *Emily Harriet Boswell* (d. 1898)  m.  *The Hon. Richard Wogan Talbot* afterwards the 5th Lord Talbot de Malahide (d. 1921, having remarried. His second wife was Isobel Gurney.)

*Emily Harriet Boswell* m. *The Hon. Richard Wogan Talbot* — child:

- *The Hon. James Boswell Talbot* afterwards the 6th Lord Talbot de Malahide (d. 1948 without issue)  m.  *Joyce Gunning Kerr*

The 7th Lord Talbot de Malahide, Milo John Reginald Talbot, a cousin of the 6th Lord Talbot and unrelated to James Boswell, died in 1973. He was succeeded by his cousin, Reginald Stanislaus Victor Talbot.

NOTE: Colonel Isham's claim in the Fettercairn lawsuit (see Chapter V) was based on the descent from James Boswell of the Sixth Lord Talbot, whose assignee Isham was. The Cumberland Infirmary claimed as residuary legatee under the will of Mrs. Mounsey. Mrs. Vassall's testamentary trustees also claimed. For details of other claimants, see Tables III and IV.

TABLE III

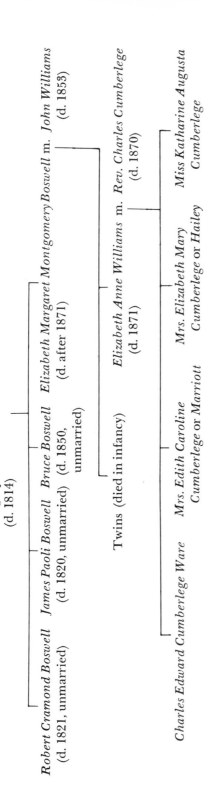

NOTE: Mrs. Hailey was a claimant in the Fettercairn lawsuit and C. E. Cumberlege Ware contemplated making a claim although he did not in fact do so (see Chapter V). Elizabeth and William Boswell are both thought to have died intestate. If Elizabeth succeeded to any share of her father's papers, the likelihood is that this share passed to her last surviving child, Mrs. Williams. Mrs. Williams survived her daughter, Elizabeth Anne, and by her will bequeathed the residue of her estate to her granddaughters, Mrs. Hailey and Miss K. A. Cumberlege. The latter died on 21 February 1936 leaving a will by which Mrs. Hailey succeeded to the residue of her estate. This excluded any tenable claim by C. E. Cumberlege Ware or Mrs. Marriott. For details of other claimants in the lawsuit, see Tables II and IV.

TABLE IV

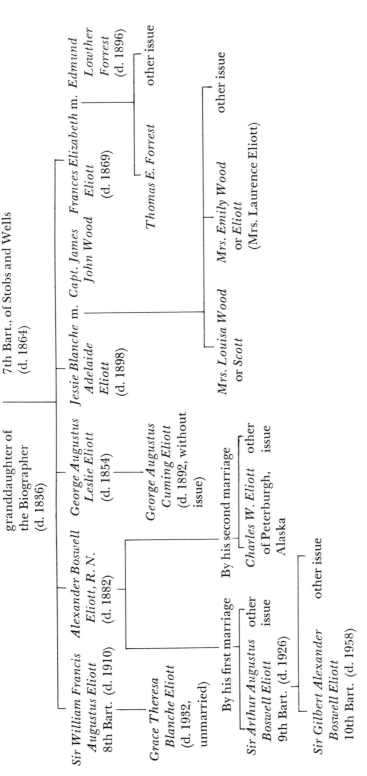

NOTES: Sir Gilbert Eliott intimated a claim in the Fettercairn lawsuit, but withdrew it at Lady Talbot's suggestion before the case came to court. Charles W. Eliott, Mrs. Louisa Scott, Mrs. Emily Eliott, and Thomas E. Forrest lodged a joint claim which they withdrew shortly before the court hearing and the claim of Mrs. Vassall's trustees was substituted in its place (see Chapter V). For details of other claimants, see Tables II and III.

It was Mrs. Emily Eliott (otherwise referred to as "Mrs. Laurence Eliott") who sent a batch of Boswell papers for sale, anonymously, at Sotheby's in 1932 (see Chapter III, pp. 102–104).

TABLE V

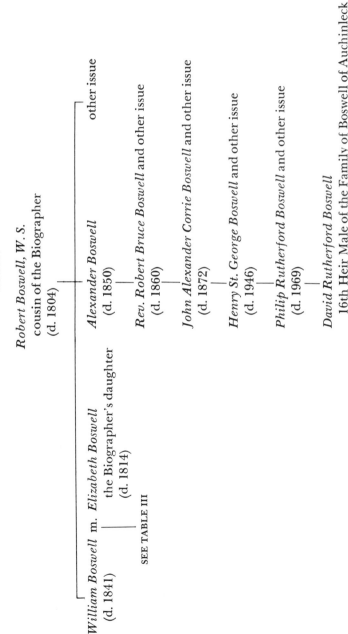

Robert Boswell, W. S.
cousin of the Biographer
(d. 1804)

other issue

Alexander Boswell
(d. 1850)

Rev. Robert Bruce Boswell and other issue
(d. 1860)

John Alexander Corrie Boswell and other issue
(d. 1872)

Henry St. George Boswell and other issue
(d. 1946)

Philip Rutherford Boswell and other issue
(d. 1969)

David Rutherford Boswell
16th Heir Male of the Family of Boswell of Auchinleck

William Boswell   m.   Elizabeth Boswell
(d. 1841)                  the Biographer's daughter
                                 (d. 1814)

SEE TABLE III

NOTE: This table is deliberately simplified to show the lineage of the present heir male of the family of Boswell of Auchinleck. At the time of the Fettercairn lawsuit, Henry St. George Boswell was the heir male, i.e., he would have succeeded to the entailed estate of Auchinleck if Sir James Boswell had not broken the entail in 1852 (see Chapter I, pp. 25–26). At one time, it seemed possible that Henry St. George Boswell might claim in the lawsuit (see Chapter V, p. 154).

**TABLE VI**

*Sir William Forbes* (the 6th Bart.) — Boswell's Executor
(d. 1806) His eldest son was:

*Sir William Forbes* (the 7th Bart.) m. *Wilhelmina Wishart Belsches Stuart*
(d. 1828) His heir was:       She was the only child of Baron
      Sir John Stuart of Fettercairn
      House. In this way, Fettercairn
      House passed into the Forbes
      family.

*Sir John Stuart Hepburn Forbes* (the 8th Bart.)
(d. 1866) leaving the residue of his estate
to his only daughter:

*Harriet Williamina Stuart Forbes* m. *Charles Henry Rolle Trefusis*
(d. 1869)       He later became 20th Baron
      Clinton and Saye. His heir was:

*Charles John Robert Hepburn Stuart Forbes Trefusis*
21st Baron Clinton and Saye and owner of
Fettercairn House when Professor Abbott
called in 1930.

NOTE: The purpose of this table is to explain how papers entrusted to
Boswell's executor could have found their way to Fettercairn House to
be discovered there in 1930 by Professor Abbott (see Chapter IV).

357

# *Index*

NOTE: The abbreviations JB and SJ refer to James Boswell and Samuel Johnson. Under most personal names, references to letters are grouped at the end of other subentries, followed by titles of works.